THE WOMAN

WHO COULDN'T BE STOPPED

Delphine Wedmore, S.C.C.

ACKNOWLEDGEMENTS

Sincere and warm thanks to Sister Angelica Hengesbach, who commissioned and constantly encouraged this work; to Sister Andre Blanchard, who supported and evaluated it; to Sister Lawrentia Daleiden, who patiently typed the manuscript; to Sister Virgina Seabert and Sister Teresilda Daleiden, who edited it; to Sister Mary Gerard Neuhaus and Sister Mary Gondeberta Remmert, who translated valuable resource documents from German; to Sister Patrice Noterman, teachers and seventh and eighth graders of St. Theresa School, Palatine, Illinois, and to Sister Carol Herlofsky and the girls of Josephinum High School, Chicago, Illinois, all of whom read and evaluated early chapters; to the Sisters of St. Joseph Convent, Wilmette, Illinois, who gave me special room and equipment; to Sister Mary Thecla Malawey, who taught me to use the word processor. Finally, thanks to all the Sisters who read, commented on and prayed for this endeavor.

AUTHOR'S NOTE:
All the incidents in this book are based on fact with the exception of two or three which are legendary or inferred. I have attempted to present the life of Mother Pauline and its events in their sequential order. In some instances, I have reconstructed the dialogue. In others I have used exact words taken from her autobiography, notes, letters, or other reliable sources as listed in the back. My one aim has been to portray this remarkable woman of God as the unique and invincible person she was.

To
Sisters of Christian Charity
the world over
I lovingly
dedicate this book.

Chapter I

Gently the doctor uncurled the tiny fingers that had twined around his thumb as he bent listening to the baby's chest. Slowly he raised himself. So did the pretty woman in the bed close to the crib, boosting herself on her elbow and looking at him with dark eyes that seemed bent on piercing his mind. He shook his head and turned to the tall, impressive man in uniform who stood near him by the crib. The father's face was strong and serious, and his blue eyes showed deep concern.

"I must confess I really don't know what has happened since I delivered this little girl four days ago," said the doctor, "On June third I handed your wife a perfectly healthy baby, and today, June seventh—" He broke off and tapped his glasses on his palm.

Bernardine's usual composure broke. "Doctor, please! What is wrong?" She reached toward the crib and began to breathe fast and heavily.

1

The doctor and her husband both moved quickly toward her.

"Frau Mallinckrodt, please," said the doctor, pressing her down gently.

"For the baby's sake, you must try to be calm. You cannot soothe the little one if you yourself are upset."

The words were like magic. She lay back quietly. Only her wide, wide eyes messaged her worry, her fear. Then she caught her breath. Cautiously, she reached out her hand to her husband.

"Detmar—" she said, hesitatingly.

"Yes, my dear?" he answered, taking her hand.

She has not been baptized yet," and she looked at the flushed little face in the crib in a way that made him feel weak.

For a moment Detmar Mallinckrodt closed his eyes while two images flashed before his mind—the pleading face of his wife and the words of the law of 1803. To her he had promised that their children would be raised as Catholics. By the law he was bound at the risk of losing his government position to raise the children in his religion—Lutheran. He needed desperately to keep that government job. But he could not bear to think of breaking his promise to Bernardine in the one thing that mattered so much to her. Between his love for her and his fear of official dismissal he felt as if he were being crushed from back and front at the same time.

"Detmar?" The anxiety in her voice broke his conflict.

"I know, Dina!" He was searching for a reason to give her. "But we have to wait for her godmother, Aunt Sophia."

The doctor looked from one to the other. "Surely

you're not thinking of taking that child to church! It cannot be done. She is much too weak. You may not take that risk."

"Then we must call the priest at the cathedral, Detmar. He can baptize her here, and Mama can take Aunt Sophia's place. Please, Detmar."

"Yes, yes, of course," he said and patted her hand. "Let me see the doctor out, and then I shall send word to the cathedral."

The doctor bowed. "I shall return this evening to see the little one. In the meantime, Frau Mallinckrodt, do get some rest."

The full, filmy white curtains were lustrous with the strong sun-rays of spring, and shadows of baby leaves on the lovely linden trees outside were moving on the baby's face as the curtains fluttered in the late afternoon breeze. Bernardine lay tense, watching the child anxiously.

Several hours passed. Surely Detmar had found the priest. Her eyes moved over the porcelain basin, the crucifix, the towel, the candle ready and waiting on the table in the center of the room.

The door opened softly, her mother entered, and came over to her. "They are here, dear," she said and stooped to carefully pick up the baby.

Detmar came in quickly, followed by the priest. Both stepped to the bedside.

"Father, my wife, Frau Mallinckrodt; Dina, this is Father Ildephonse Buse from the cathedral," said Detmar, slightly out of breath.

The priest looked at her keenly and lightly took her hand. "Frau Mallinckrodt, my pleasure. Your little girl will have God's life very, very soon."

It all went very quickly. At last with a thrill Ber-

3

Bernardine von Mallinckrodt, Pauline's mother

Detmar von Mallinckrodt, Pauline's father

nardine saw the special water flow down the baby's hair and heard it plink musically into the basin as the priest said slowly and solemnly:

"I baptize you, Maria Bernardine Sophia Pauline, in the name of the Father and of the Son and of the Holy Spirit."

With a few more quick movements and prayers, Father Buse completed the anointing and looked at the child. He motioned the grandmother to carry her to her mother.

As Bernardine tenderly took the child, she seemed electrified with joy. Her dark hair, her black eyes, her lips, her smile—all were shining.

"Thank you, thank you," she said to her husband and the priest and then turned her whole attention to the bundle in her arms. She heard the door close, and she was alone with her newly-baptized daughter.

"Pauline," she whispered. "My little Pauline! Nothing could stop you, could it?" Not even her kiss wakened the little one, sleeping soundly with remarkable peace.

That evening the doctor came once more, and once more he bent over the crib. For a long while he listened to the tiny chest, fending off with one hand the little legs that were kicking with the joy of life. Once more he gently uncurled the tiny fingers from around his thumb and stood looking at the cooing baby with amazement.

"What is it with this child?" he asked. "What did you do to her? This morning she was too weak to move and scarcely able to breathe. This evening she is strong and lively, and her breathing is regular and sound." He eyed the parents questioningly.

Detmar smiled but stood silent, like a stalwart

4

guard between the crib and his wife's bed. Bernardine laughed softly.

"Doctor," she said, "the only thing we did to Pauline was to have her baptized here, right here."

The doctor shrugged. "I've always considered myself a normally religious man, but I didn't know that baptism cures illness. Anyway, your daughter is perfectly healthy now, and that's the most important thing. Good night, Frau Mallinckrodt." He turned to leave, accompanied by Detmar.

It was June 7, 1817 in Minden, Germany, and four-day-old Pauline had, with the grace of God, overcome her first obstacle.

After some time, the Mallinckrodts moved at the invitation of the priest there to another house which was part of cathedral property. Naturally the cathedral was close by. Bernardine was delighted at the prospect and could hardly wait for the repairs and re-decorating to be completed. The house was larger and had a lovely garden surrounded by an ivy-covered wall with a door that led directly to the city hall where Detmar worked. The Weser River, too, was nearby and would refresh them with its breezes. All in all, it was ideal for each of them: the cathedral for Bernardine, the city hall for Detmar, the garden for Pauline.

But for her father, trouble was not yet over. As the months rolled by, he was determined, as vice-president of Minden, his first official position, to perform with excellence, befitting a Mallinckrodt and his own character. Love for his country and loyalty were key qualities of that character. But there was something even deeper and stronger in Mallinckrodt: love for what is right and true, for personal freedom and honor. Nothing could stir those in him more than the ones he loved with all the intensity of his deep, powerful personality.

But as he stood once again at the crib beside his wife and two-year-old Pauline, his promise to Bernardine and his own conviction of religious freedom threw him in a mental tug-of-war with the law of 1803. He began to pace the floor, his face stern and frowning. Bernardine, understanding, prayed silently.

Had he not served his country well, even before his marriage? Had he not spoken fearlessly against the seizure of Prussia by Napoleon and been sentenced to death by him, saved later only by the Frenchman's downfall? His following record, too, was good. Pauline's baptism had been an emergency and had been private. Besides, the law of 1803 was not really being greatly spread or enforced. But—that very fact was dangerous. That made it so much easier to catch unwanted or suspected officials off guard and dismiss them. For his family his dismissal would mean a life of poverty. He could not subject them to that. He could not take the risk again. The family of Minden's vice-president was too visible and would be watched.

He stopped abruptly, picked up the toddling Pauline and turned to his wife. "I'll have the maid put her to bed for her nap. George must be baptized at the Lutheran church. I'll make arrangements." He left without waiting for an answer.

Bernardine firmly took hold of herself. She knew why Detmar had decided as he did, to have George baptized in the Lutheran church. She knew he desperately wanted to keep his promise to her and surmised the agony he experienced in that decision. She

6

loved him too much to add to it by begging or arguing. But how could she raise a Catholic daughter and a Lutheran son? She knew Detmar would have no hand in the religious training of their children. There was but one thing to do: pray and wait.

By the time Hermann was born, there was a silent understanding, an unspoken agreement that he too would be baptized in the Lutheran church. Pauline was now four years old, and Bernardine had begun to teach her her prayers. Pauline, in turn, was determined that her first little brother, George, should learn them too and spent plenty of time and energy playing teacher. Detmar had seen and heard it all and had said nothing. Bernardine knew without doubt that her husband had obeyed the law out of sheer necessity, but that beyond that, the religious education of the children was totally in her hands. He would not interfere. With that she was and had to be content.

Besides, caring for her household and three small, happy, healthy children engrossed her completely. She loved to hear their laughter and see them run to their tall father as he returned from his office through the gate of the stone wall. After dinner and recounting the day's events, the family found favorite spots in the living room and settled down. Mallinckrodt would smoke his pipe, read the paper, watch with pleasure as the children played and Bernardine glanced up occasionaly from her needlework. The little ones' good-night was usually punctual and prompt and loving, and Bernardine always gave the final pat and tuck. Then she would come down to spend precious hours of sharing experiences, troubles, hopes, and dreams, both his and

7

hers.

One evening, as she came from upstairs, he waved a paper toward her.

"I finally did it," he said.

"What is it?" she said, taking the paper.

"It's the deed for the estate at Boedekken." She looked at him quizzically.

"It's really an old, old monastery with farm lands and buildings dating back to 800 A.D. at the time of St. Meinolphus who founded it for the education of women. After that it was the home of Augustinian monks for several centuries; later it fell into the hands of Jerome Bonaparte, and then our government took it. It is up for sale, and it's beautiful, Dina. The buildings are sturdy, and the countryside and air are delightful. It will be excellent for sheep-raising while we are living elsewhere. Best of all, it's near your mother in Borchen, and someday, Dina, when I re-tire, we can all go there and enjoy both places."

Dina put her hand on his shoulder. "That will be lovely, Detmar," she murmured, "but I don't think we shall be going there for quite a while."

If it were left to her, they would be moving, yes, but to another very old city with splendid buildings and natural health baths. They would be going to Aachen or Aix-la-Chapelle (as it was pronounced in French) because Mallinckrodt would have received a new appointment.

More and more, as the weeks passed, she heard conversation at the parties in her home turn to the almost inevitable changes to be made among high-ranking officers. There would be a vacancy in the office of President von Reimann of Aachen, and there were predictions as to who would fill it. She knew von Reimann personally and hoped, hoped, hoped that he would recognize her husband for the fine governmental officer he was.

The appointment came before Christmas, and everyone was excited. It was to be effective February, 1824, when Detmar would assume his duties as Vice-President of Aix-la-Chapelle, in charge of finance and forestry. As soon as the Christmas season had passed, many boxes were packed and closets emptied. The carriage made many trips.

Late in January the Mallinckrodts themselves arrived at their home in Aix-la-Chapelle, the former imperial city and the headquarters of Charlemagne. The city hall, where Detmar worked was part of the complex, massive buildings the great emperor had erected for himself, his court, and his soldiers a thousand years before. Most impressive, perhaps was the cathedral or Dom, as it was called. Pauline was awed even by the distant sight of it as she walked to the school on Seilgraben Street, which was conducted for Catholic girls by two ladies, Fräulein Ludger and Fräulein Renard, both from France. Her mother had been very happy over this opportunity to send her to a Catholic school since there had been only one school in Minden which was public.

Pauline was seven years old now and tall for her age. She was extremely alert and lively, with a boyish force and drive in all her movements. She was a natural leader, and once she had a goal, would stop at nothing. Often she had succeeded in capturing single-handedly her brothers' fort when they all played soldier at home. She would make the two boys march behind her as she triumphantly carried their flag and hers in a victory parade around the garden. George and little Hermann were never quite sure just what that big sister of theirs would do. But they did know that she had a loving heart and that when she bossed them, she was being like a little mother.

One morning as Pauline skipped to school, her foot suddenly slid and scraped on something. She stopped to look and stooped. It was glass—small pieces of glass strewn far apart! She was alarmed and looked back over her shoulder as if she expected someone to walk to that very spot. She must not let *them* walk on this! She winced as she pictured bare feet cut, bleeding, and imbedded with the glass.

Quickly, she set to work, brushing the pieces together, ignoring the dirt and the little pricks in her fingers. But now what? Then she seized her school-bag and opened it. Somewhere the bells of a church began to chime the time. She would have to hurry! She would be late for school, and Fräulein Ludger was very strict about punctuality. Well, so was her father. But *this* had to be done. There was no other way. No matter what it was, she would have to take the punishment Fräulein Ludger would give. She closed the bag over the glass and began to run.

Pauline arrived just as the students were being seated, and the teacher looked at her in surprise but merely motioned for her to take her place. It was unusual for her to be late, but then, she did have a long way to walk.

One morning when Pauline had appeared only when the class was almost over, Fräulein Ludger's patience broke. "Pauline!" she said angrily. "Come here! Where on earth have you been? And why are you late again? This is the third or fourth time you have come late, and I am sure your mother sends you out soon enough. And look at your knees and your hands."

She broke off as she stared at Pauline's schoolbag. Pauline's eyes followed hers and saw the queer sharp little bulges at the sides. The class began to snicker.

"Child, bring that schoolbag to me," ordered Fräulein Ludger as she sat down at her desk. Without a word, Pauline carefully laid it on her desk and waited, turning her grimy hands inward toward her sides. Fräulein Ludger opened the bag, and out slid books and many bits of glass.

She gasped and threw up her hands. Then she stood up.

"Pauline! Where on earth did you get this glass? And *why* is it in your bag?" She began to wonder about this child.

Pauline raised her head and met the teacher's eyes. "I'm sorry, Fräulein," she said softly. "I'm sorry for coming late, really—but—I had to stop to pick up that glass. I just *had* to."

The child's clear blue eyes reflected so much honesty and a pain that the teacher knew intuitively was not self-pity, that her indignation turned to total curiosity.

"Why, Pauline?" she said more kindly. *"Why* did you *have* to stop and pick up glass when you knew you would be late for school?"

"Because—" and her voice sounded close to tears, "because they would cut their feet on the glass—and I just couldn't let that happen, Fräulein Ludger."

"*Who* would cut their feet on the glass, Pauline? Who are *they*?"

She was bending down to Pauline now, holding her gently by the shoulders and looking trustingly into her face. The class was quiet, waiting.

"The blind children, the poor children who are blind," she burst out. "They have no shoes, and they can't see the glass! They cut their feet! I've seen blind children in the streets, but I didn't think of their feet until I found the glass in the street on the way to school a few weeks ago."

"So that's why you have been coming late," said Fräulein Ludger. "Pauline, what you did was a very loving thing. Don't worry about being late—nor about the blind children. I think something can be done. I shall speak to the authorities about the glass. Go empty your bag, dear, and wash your hands. It's time for class."

Fräulein Ludger kept her word, and after her trip to the city hall, the glass began to disappear from the streets. Pauline was jubilant.

Her favorite subject was religion, and the teacher was a priest, Father Trost. Lately, though, Pauline had felt quite uncomfortable and even embarrassed in that class. The other girls knew so much more than she. Father Trost asked questions about things she had never heard, and her classmates all seemed to know the answers. She was puzzled. She had listened carefully, eagerly to everything her mother had told her. She had mastered it all too, forgetting nothing. Why couldn't she answer the questions? Her mother told her and her brothers the Bible stories. With a child's unerring sense for genuineness, she knew her mother was a devout Catholic. Then why did these girls know so much more than she about her faith?

"You've been very quiet the last few days, Pauline," remarked her mother some days later as Pauline went to kiss her goodnight. "Is something wrong?"

Pauline was standing against the chair within the circle of her mother's arm, smoothing down the end of a lace doily that kept curling up on the chair. The boys had already gone upstairs to bed. She glanced sideways at her father. Just then he looked up from his reading and took his pipe from his lips.

"Yes," he teased. "What shall we do without the noise? I'll have to hire someone to outshout the boys, I guess."

Pauline smiled but said nothing. After a moment, she turned to her mother.

"Mother, may I ask you and Father some questions about religion? So many times at school I don't know the answers to what the priest asks. When the other girls answer, it just makes me want to know more and more."

Her father coughed and put his pipe back in his mouth. He frowned and looked intently at his paper. Her mother tucked an imaginary stray lock of hair into place a bit nervously and wet her lips. She seemed to want to speak, but nothing came. She sat there, silent, looking down.

Pauline was almost stunned by the tension she was sensing. For the first time in her life she began to understand something of the unspoken suffering caused by difference in religion in the hearts of two strong-minded people who love each other deeply. Somehow, too, without any telling, she knew her mother had been handling the matter of religion with great delicacy and prudence, hiding many anxieties in her heart with silence and patience for her hus-

13

band's sake. Pauline was sorry she had asked the question.

"Good night, Father," she said, kissing his cheek gingerly. Then she ran quickly upstairs.

Next day after class, Pauline waited till the room had emptied. She walked slowly to her teacher's desk.

"Fräulein Ludger," she said.

"Yes, Pauline. You haven't found more glass, I hope."

"No. There is something I must ask you. What—what can—what should I do when there are things about religion I need to talk about at home, and my parents—well, my parents don't agree about them or don't want to hear about them and it gets—"

"Very unpleasant?" finished Fräulein Ludger.

"Yes," said Pauline, looking at her almost hopelessly.

Her teacher put her arm around the child's shoulders. "Go to God, Pauline, and tell Him about it. And not only that. Take everything to Him, every tiny, little thing—especially things that people wouldn't bother about. You can always go to Him, and He will always understand and care. The answers to your questions will come, too, in time. Just trust Him and wait."

She looked down into the clear blue eyes and patted the blond-brown head, glinting like wheat in the slanting rays of sun that streamed through the window.

There was no answer. Pauline stood there, speechless, like one who has suddenly grasped a marvel, a treasure. Fräulein Ludger had just given Pauline a key to the Power that would carry her,

14

tireless and invincible, for years to come.

Chapter II

"Ohhh, Bertha, Bertha!" called Pauline, stretching out her arms and stooping to scoop up her year-old baby sister as the little one waddled energetically to her. "I haven't seen you for a long time. Did you miss me?"

For answer, Bertha clasped her arms around Pauline's neck in an almost strangle-hold that her big sister broke by tickling her. Frau Mallinckrodt watched, pleased and amused. It had been a long time. The spring of 1827 was finally here after what had seemed an endless winter. Pauline had started classes at St. Leonard's School in October and had boarded there during the winter. She was home now for the holidays and would return to St. Leonard's after Easter vacation as a day student.

Her mother studied her oldest child carefully. Pauline had certainly grown. Even though only ten, she was tall and strong—and a tomboy. Bernardine sighed. They had hoped that sending her to St.

Leonard's would change that. Perhaps it did and would. After all, the school had a long and good tradition. It was founded in 1626 by nuns called Ladies of the Holy Sepulcher, whose lives were devoted to loving and meditating on the Passion of Jesus and His Resurrection. They had conducted a fine school for girls until 1802 when, like all religious, they were driven out. Not long after, the school was re-opened by Catholic women. At present, Frau Nikolay was at the head of a staff of excellent ladies, especially the well-known teacher and poetess, Luise Hensel.

Pauline was not yet in Fräulein Hensel's class, but her schedule and program of studies was basically like the other girls' even though some were on different levels. Classes were held from Monday through Friday from nine till noon and from two till five, and from nine till noon on Saturday. The curriculum included Bible History, Religion, Reading, Mathematics, Crafts, Singing, French, and German. Introduction to Philosophy, Earth Science, World Literature, Nature Study and Calligraphy were also taught.

Although Pauline, George, and Hermann studied hard as their parents expected, they had time for fun too. The children especially enjoyed the parties given at their home for the family, the von Hartmanns from their mother's side and the Mallinckrodts from their father's side. In those parties they were always included. Because of their father's position, though, it was necessary that he and his wife frequently entertain high officials and wealthy people. Then the children were briefly seen and sent to their playroom with the maid. But by special concession, they were allowed to listen to the music and watch the dancing after dinner from a well-hidden spot upstairs until tea was served at ten o'clock.

During vacation and holidays a special teacher came to the house to teach them dancing, especially the French Quadrille. George became the leader. Bernardine was pleased to see that Pauline was learning to dance well and gracefully and enjoyed it. Perhaps she would become a lady, after all.

To help with that, no doubt, Mathilde von Hartmann, one of Pauline's cousins close to her in age, was invited by the Mallinckrodts to stay with them and go to school with Pauline. She came in June of 1828 and was treated like a daughter of the family. Pauline was glad to have a girl her age as a companion, but she often domineered all the others, Mathilde, George, Hermann, and little Bertha, with her ideas and energy.

Soon, however, there came into the house several times each week someone whose very presence brought peace and commanded respect. He was Father Anton Claessen, a member of the school board of Aix and dean of the group of priests connected with the cathedral. He held the delicate position of head of Catholic schools at a time when the government was becoming increasingly hostile to church freedom. He was well liked and admired by his priests and people for his unwavering allegiance to the Church and for his widespread love and concern for all. This was the priest who had accepted from Frau Mallinckrodt the task of instructing in their religion the two girls and two boys of the Mallinckrodt house.

Pauline was excited and eager for the lessons. "Did you know," she said to Mathilde and the boys

18

while they were waiting for their first lesson, "did you know that Father Claessen speaks so well about God every Friday during Lent that *thousands* of people go to the cathedral at five o'clock in the morning to hear him? They go right to work from there."

"*Thousands* of people, Pauline?" objected Hermann.

"Yes. I heard Mother and Father talking about it, and they said *thousands*."

"That's an awful lot of people to get up for five o'clock," said George.

"He must be very, very good," said Mathilde.

"And *we're* going to have him!" cried Pauline, pointing with a sweep of her hand to all four of them. They looked at each other with big eyes and raised eyebrows. They were awed.

But soon all four felt comfortable with their new religion teacher and looked forward to his coming. They were not the only ones. Mallinckrodt himself enjoyed Father Claessen's company and was impressed by his honesty and learning, as well as by his tact in never interfering in matters outside of religious instruction. Frau Mallinckrodt, in turn, received wise advice from him, and as she saw him prepare each child individually for confession and Holy Communion, was so happy that she almost purred.

As weeks merged into months, Pauline was the first to be ready for her First Communion. God had heard her prayers and sent someone to answer her questions. Hungrily she had absorbed everything the priest taught her. It was showing in her behavior. She had received the Sacrament of Reconciliation very seriously—very joyously. That was becoming typical of Pauline: she was a remarkable combination

19

of seriousness and happiness. Now at twelve she would receive the Holy Eucharist.

St. Foillan's was the church where the children and Bernardine attended Mass. It stood literally in the shadow of the great cathedral, right behind it, at the narrowing curve of the street that suddenly opened into a wide plaza at the right. Compared to the cathedral, St. Foillan's was small but had something of the same medieval structure and stone, the chapel to our Lady, and that atmosphere of worshipful solemnity. It was here that the wonderful event took place, and Pauline truly received God Himself.

She was kneeling there on this first most unforgettable day, trying hard to make a fervent thanksgiving and at the same time to control her excitement. She found herself stopping completely in the middle of the prayers while her mind and imagination were engrossed with the image of Jesus and the absolute wonder of taking Him totally into herself. So she was startled when Father Claessen came down to her pew after Mass and gently tapped her on the shoulder.

"Come, Pauline," he whispered. She rose and walked with him, the rest of the family following. They turned into the side chapel of Mary. There, enshrined on the altar was *"die schone Madonna,"* the lovely Lady, gazing down on them. The statue was indeed beautiful and very precious. Faithful children of Mary had venerated her through this image for over four hundred years. It dated from the year 1420, and its proportion alone was a work of art.

Father Claessen placed Pauline before the Madonna and stood behind her with his hand on her shoulder. Both were looking up to our Lady.

20

"O holy Mary, Mother of God," prayed Father Claessen. Pauline could feel the devotion in his deep, resonant voice. "Today I place under your special protection, this child, Pauline. From now and forever be a mother to her. Teach her your virtues. Give her your humility, and above all, teach her your oneness with God's will. Amen."

The words recorded themselves deeply on Pauline's memory. So did the unusual feeling that accompanied them, almost the same feeling she had experienced after Communion of being received and of being loved so very—she couldn't find the word. It was hard for her to leave there when the family finally turned to go.

The children's education at home continued, especially as they grew and developed. For everyone there were lessons in horseback riding and dancing; also quoits and target shooting for the boys. Frau Mallinckrodt taught them all to put aside coins for the poor and took Pauline and Mathilde with her frequently on visits to needy families. The girls would help her distribute gifts, listen as she gave the poor kindly advice, and join warmly in the prayers she said with the mothers and children before they said goodbye.

These visits to the poor were different from those Pauline experienced with her favorite teacher, Luise Hensel. She had finally advanced to Luise's class and found that this lady had a tremendous charisma with students, positively sparking their goodness and generosity. The girl in her class who achieved the highest grade in lessons and conduct for the week was allowed to accompany her on her visits to the poor on Saturdays. That made them really try, espe-

Bishop Claessen, Pauline's teacher, friend and confessor

Luise Hensel, Pauline's favorite teacher

cially Pauline.

When she was lucky enough to go along, she found that Luise not only gave to a poor sick mother the coins that she and her students had saved but also cleaned up the children, the room, and the bed of the ailing mother herself. To be able to help with that service was Pauline's delight although she knew that her parents would hardly approve of her cleaning the homes of the poor.

But that was, by far, not all that she learned from Fräulein Hensel, who was a convert as well as a poetess. Frequently, Luise poured her intense faith and love for God into lovely lines of verse. But she rarely showed them to anyone. More frequently she did share with the girls who followed her after school all that she found beautiful in Catholicism, expressing it in fresh inspiring ideas that a poet would use. Pauline always tried to be the first one to Luise's room in the former old convent, running quickly up the stairs with Anna, Clara, and Frances and trying to sit the closest to her. There they talked about God and religion and asked question after question. At times Luise spoke so movingly of loving God and of trying to atone for sinners that it made them want to be martyrs.

"I really don't think it's very likely that you will be martyrs," said Luise, smiling gently at the seriousness in the girls' young, eager faces. "But there is something you could do instead that—"

"What?" they interrupted in a chorus.

"Well, there is an old Way of the Cross that the nuns here long ago used to follow and venerate in the convent garden. It leads to a replica of the Holy Sepulcher of our Lord. You could make the Way of the Cross here often and offer the Passion of Jesus to make up for sin and save sinners. Outside of Holy Mass, nothing, absolutely nothing pleases our Lord more than prayerfully re-living what He suffered for us." She folded her sewing and carefully put her needle away.

The girls stopped too. One had been molding wax figures for next year's Christmas crib; two had been making clothes for them from scraps of satin and brocade. They were all suddenly quiet. A challenge had been issued. Who would take it?

Anna soon found out. One morning she saw Pauline making the Way of the Cross before class and was not surprised when she noticed her at the Stations frequently from then on.

Lent came, and finally, Good Friday. It was a schoolday at St. Leonard's, and all the students were to make the Way of the Cross together. Pauline was looking forward to it. She was gathering her books and bag when her mother came to her room.

"You must stay home today, Pauline dear," she said a little breathlessly and sat down on a chair. "It's Good Friday."

Pauline was more than surprised. She was puzzled. "Yes, Mother, because it is Good Friday, everyone at St. Leonard's will be making the Way of the Cross together. I don't want to miss it." She paused and then blurted: "I didn't think you would want me to miss it, either."

For an instant Bernardine looked away as if restraining herself. Then she took her daughter's hand and looked into the girl's eyes, now even with her own.

"Pauline," she said in a low voice, "Good Friday

is the most sacred day of the year for your father, and he does *not* want you or any of the children to spend it at school. We simply must honor his feelings in this matter. You understand that, don't you? He makes very few demands of us in regard to religion."

Once more Pauline felt the tension in her normally serene mother and sensed that she could relieve it by simply obeying, without making Bernardine feel guilty.

"Yes, Mother, I understand," she said and squeezed the gentle hand. Her mother smiled and walked away.

Pauline sat down thoughtfully. She could not get her mind off those Stations. The booklet had described so vividly what Jesus had gone through, and the prayers said so well many of the things she felt and wanted to say. Most of all, the whole world would be honoring the Passion today, Good Friday, the day it happened. She knew the prayers almost by heart—and the Stations too. Perhaps—Oh! she knew what she would do! She walked happily out the door.

It was three o'clock, and Bernardine was going from room to room, looking for Pauline. Where was that girl? She had been to Pauline's room and then through the rest of the house without success. It was not like her. There was only one place left, which, of course, would be fruitless. But she had to try every place. She came to the door leading to the attic stairs and opened it.

"Pauline!" she exclaimed in surprise. There, kneeling on the top step, hands folded, eyes closed, Pauline was softly saying aloud the prayers for the last Station. The attic stairs were perfect for the Way of the Cross, Pauline had thought. There were just fourteen, and she could go up on her knees. Good for a little penance.

As she finished her prayer, Pauline turned around and said brightly, "Yes, Mother?"

Bernardine shook her head and laughed a little to herself. Secretly she was proud of this daughter of hers. "I was looking all over for you. Nothing could stop you, could it?"

After Easter vacation, Pauline returned to school, rising early each morning for the walk to St. Leonard's. She especially liked her German classes because Fräulein Hensel asked them to write essays or letters on any topic they chose. Pauline could let her imagination go free, and she wrote eagerly, drawing on her love for things in nature, her trips, days spent at Borchen with her grandmother, the stories she had heard. Her creativity was appreciated by Luise who always wrote little notes on each paper. Pauline could hardly wait to get them back. Often the notes were rewarding: "Your hard work really pleases me," or "The principles expressed in this letter are truly praiseworthy." Pauline treasured those. But her quick mind often forced her hand to race across the paper so that her writing was unclear and her words badly formed. At times like that, the note said: "Definitely well thought out, but definitely badly written." Such words from such a teacher only made Pauline determined to control her pen and her energy. She *would* have a better handwriting! At last, after days of effort and patience, it finally came: the note she had worked so long and hard to get. "Your work really pleased me, my little Pauline, and your improved handwriting makes me happy."

Now that she had made her confession and First Communion, Pauline was no longer instructed by Father Claessen. He became her regular confessor. A gentleman named Vonderbank was now her religion teacher at St. Leonard's, and his marks on her examination papers matched those of Luise Hensel. If George and Hermann had gotten hold of those, they would have counted a total of "Very good" eight times, "Good" forty-five times and "Faulty, incorrect" only three times. His remarks on her longer compositions ranged from "Done correctly with much care" to "All questions very well done." She had reason to be proud of her work.

The months flew by, and Pauline became more and more busy. Besides her classes, there were many hours of study at home. Then there were regular instructions by her mother for her and Mathilde in housekeeping and working well with the servants. The two girls also took turns in accompanying Frau Mallinckrodt on her afternoon walks and going to the theater, which Pauline loved. They continued their riding and dancing lessons too. Meanwhile Pauline was growing, growing, so that at thirteen she was unusually tall.

One afternoon she was walking home from school with Anna, her school bag on her back as usual. Because she was so tall, the heavy bag made her bend forward. It looked clumsy, but Pauline, disregarding it, went on chattering happily with Anna until they passed a group of ladies who stared at her. They shook their heads and among themselves said something muffled. What was wrong with that Mallinckrodt girl? Was she mentally retarded that she must still be going to school at sixteen when she should have entered society? Or had she been been kept back in school because of slowness? Both Anna and Pauline caught the meaning of their look and Anna sensed the hurt that Pauline felt. She was trying to think of something to say when Pauline suddenly stopped and swung the bag off her back. They had come to a church.

"I'd like to throw this bag away," she said. "I'm going in here, Anna."

"And I'll go with you," Anna said. The semi-darkness of the church seemed to blot out the unpleasant things of life. They knelt in silence near the steady sanctuary light. Pauline looked intently at the tabernacle and frankly told the Lord her feelings. Finally, she prayed: "Lord, give me humility. Mother Mary, help me to be humble like you."

After a while she stood, took her bag in hand, and genuflected. Then she walked to the door, erect and straight and at peace. She had used the trauma of growing too fast physically, to grow strong spiritually.

Chapter III

Pauline unlatched the window and pushed it wide open. She threw back her head and drew in the fresh fragrant air of May. Down below was their garden, and on the other side of its stone wall was the part that surrounded the hotel for health-seekers. For centuries, from as far back as Pliny the Elder before Christ, people had been coming to Aix to use its natural thermal baths. The Mallinckrodts had moved to this house some time before, and Pauline was glad. It was a lovely place, and they had only to open the gate in the garden wall to give their many visiting relatives quick access to the baths. Why, right now, her cousin, Christian Mallinckrodt, a nephew of her father, was here trying to get well. Both her parents had gone to Laach where he was studying management of public property to visit him and found him ill of a blood disease. So they had brought him back home with them.

Bernardine was doing everything the doctor had

suggested to the best of her nursing skill and knowledge. But that was not enough. There were two things still more important, Pauline had learned. They were love and prayer. Round-the-clock care was quite demanding, so Pauline had offered to help her mother. She was strong and healthy, but after a full month of school, homework, private lessons, household duties and helping as nurse's aide all combined, even she felt drained. She sighed. If only she could be like her mother!

Just then she heard footsteps on the stairs behind her and turned to see her father coming toward her, smiling broadly.

"Pauline!" he called. "Get ready to go to Borchen. Mother suggested that you and I go there for a little while. We will be leaving as soon as possible." He turned and hurried down the hall, as happy as a boy going on vacation.

"Yes, dear," said her mother, catching his words as she came from Christian's room. "Father and I thought it would be good for both of you to get away for a few days. This past month has been really hard on you. I think all the work and the way you are growing have been too much for you. He needs a change of scenery too, and you know how he loves Borchen."

"But Mother—" objected Pauline, touching her mother's arm.

"I know what you're going to say, dear," said Bernardine, taking Pauline's hand. "But don't worry. Just go. You have helped so wonderfully. I'll get along fine. The servants will help me, and Christian seems to be as well as we can make him. I want you to go."

"Oh, yes, if you think it's all right," said Pauline happily, clapping her hands. "I'll get ready." She ran to her room.

Borchen! No wonder her father was so excited. For him the country home and estate at Borchen were the garden of Paradise, and he loved the gracious little lady who lived there, his mother-in-law, as if he were her own son. As for Pauline there could be no better place than Borchen. There was so much fun, such a different life, and Grandmother von Hartmann was such a dear. She packed very quickly.

They had been at Borchen only a few days when the letter from Bernardine came. Grandmother read it to them after dinner as they sat in the cozy living-room: "My dear Mother, during the time Mallinckrodt and Pauline were on the way to visit you, Christian struggled with death. It was so sad I could not write. It's two days now since his sufferings came to an end. I do not know why God let me witness these days of pain and sorrow . . . . I am glad that Mallinckrodt and Pauline were not here . . . A sudden attack of pneumonia added to his physical ailments and cut short his young life . . . ." Grandmother's voice shook just a little on the last words. She had lost four of her own children in their youth, and she knew full well the impact of that grief. Pauline and her father stood up. It was time to go home.

Life at Aix resumed its old trend, but Bernardine was slow to rebound physically and emotionally after Christian's death. Both Mallinckrodt and Pauline tried especially hard to cheer her and give her time to rest. Gradually their loving concern was successful, and Bernardine seemed to be herself again. But the whole sad experience left Pauline with a vague, heavy feeling.

Meanwhile at school she was earning a reputation among her classmates that would last for longer than she dreamed. Soon everyone knew she was the inquisitive one, with a tremendous thirst for knowledge that kept her asking question after question in class and often with such innocence that others laughed at her, at least in secret. Everyone also knew that she was kind and loving to others—and that she was sincere. But most of all, everyone knew that Pauline was one girl who would not tolerate the least unkind talk about anyone and would try to find some excuse, no matter how small, for the one criticized. In fact, her defense of others became so well-known, it was a standing joke. "If there were a way to white-wash the devil himself, *you* would find it," the girls teased. But that was not all. Because of the way she walked and talked, her frankness, fearlessness, and long firm stride, they called her "our tomboy Pauline." She only shrugged and laughed.

She had good friends and was happy in their friendship. She brought a unique and pretty autograph book to school one day and asked many of the girls to write in it for her as a remembrance. Many of them did and were pleased that she had asked them. But there was one more autograph she just had to get—perhaps the most precious of them all: Luise Hensel's. She waited after class and walked with her teacher to her little room. With an admiration in her eyes that she could not hide, she asked, "Fräulein Hensel, would you please write something in my autograph book as a remembrance?" She held out the page hopefully.

Luise looked at Pauline thoughtfully and took it

31

in silence. She reached for her pen and inkwell and wrote carefully. She waited a bit as the writing dried, blotted it, then handed it back to Pauline.

A warm, good feeling spread over the girl as she saw the fondness in Luise's eyes. She took the page and eagerly read the lines:

> "In the heart's still, peaceful soil
> Ripens the beautiful seed of good.
> Faith heals the deepest wound of sorrow;
> Love smooths each path of thorns.
>
> May my dear Pauline remember with love
> once in a while her friend and teacher,
> Luise Hensel."

"Thank you, thank you," Pauline whispered, her fine blue eyes alight with a teenager's happiness in getting something personal from someone much admired. She put it safely in place and then ran home, leaping most of the way.

That evening after dinner she proudly showed the book with the many warm messages and signatures of friends to her mother and father. Bernardine smiled as she handed it to her husband.

"It's very nice, Pauline," she said. "You have something that will warm your heart often for many years. I must go up to see the boys now," and she turned toward the stairs.

Pauline watched as her father turned the pages. He smiled, amazed at the verses written by her young friends, some humorous, some sentimental. But soon the smile vanished, and his lips were straight and stern as he read the last page. Pauline half expected a question or remark, but he said nothing. He only nodded to her as he handed back the little book, and she took it somewhat puzzled. Oh well, the personal thoughts and wishes of school girls were probably not the favorite reading of men like her father, she thought.

"I still have homework to do, Father," she said, "so I'll go to my room."

"Oh yes, Pauline," he answered. "Don't work too long."

When Bernardine came down later, he said, "Luise Hensel seems to have a great deal of influence over Pauline and many other girls, for that matter. But I wonder how good that is for them. She fills them with such overly religious ideas. Those lines she wrote in Pauline's book are much too old for a young girl."

"But she *is* an excellent teacher, Detmar," said Bernardine mildly, "one of the best."

"That may be," he answered, "but I've also heard that because of her, about twelve or more girls so far have become nuns, and *that* is just what I—" He stopped, shook his head, and carefully tapped the burnt tobacco out of his pipe into the ashtray. There was no need for him to say more.

June brought Pauline's fourteenth birthday and also her farewell to St. Leonard's. She was told that later she would have private lessons at home with a professor. It was hard to say goodbye, but she knew there were several reasons for it. Mathilde her cousin, was going home to Büren, so she would no longer have a companion. Then, too, her parents thought that she was not coping well with the pressure of studies and activities at school; that she was too tense and too religious. Her mother had even written to Grandmother about her posture becoming bad. Because she was getting taller, she was bending

The home of Pauline's grandmother at Borchen

more and more over her desk every night in the wrong way. It was true: her right shoulder was protruding, and her left foot was making her whole body lean to one side. She wondered if she would ever stop growing and be straight.

Pauline was sure there would be times when she could see her classmates and friends from St. Leonard's again and even Fräulein Hensel. So she would not let herself feel totally cut off from them. She would try to make the best of the situation, but she wouldn't stop there. No, she would present the whole problem and how she felt about it where she had taken everything for the past seven years. She would take it to God.

Not long after came the one big joy that could lift her spirits. Hermann came whooping out one morning into the garden where she was reading, shouting: "We're going to Borchen! We're going to Borchen for a vacation!"

Pauline wasted no time asking him questions. She ran inside, got the word of confirmation from her mother, and started packing.

That afternoon the big blue carriage with its four strong, beautiful horses drove to the front door. After the goodbyes to Bernardine and the servants, Detmar, Mathilde, Pauline and the boys waved from the coach windows as it moved down the road. It would take several days to get there, but they would stop at the homes of relatives on the way. Pauline, Mathilde, and the boys were excited and happy, and so was Detmar in his own dignified way.

The pleasant summer days at Borchen slid by almost unnoticed. Sometimes the four children went for walks in the woods together, collecting butterflies and summer flowers. Sometimes they raced up and down the spiral staircase in the round tower at the back of the big country house of the von Hartmanns. They would very much have liked to slide down the sturdy straight bannisters at the front of the house, making it ring with their fun and noise, but Mathilde would stand at the bottom and shake her head when she suspected they were even thinking about it. At other times Mathilde and the boys, especially George, went to the farm buildings and fields to watch the men at their interesting work. Pauline would then often spend time alone, leaning over the bridge at the moat around the house, looking at the rippling reflection of the trees and herself in the water while the ducks glided lazily by. There, in the warm sunlit peacefulness, she could think and wonder and struggle in privacy with the dark doubts and nagging temptations against God and faith that had begun bothering her lately. Even worse were the guilty feelings she was having and the worry whether things she did were sins or not. Although God seemed far away at these times, she found that the only way to get relief was to pray desperately anyway, hoping there was a God and that He cared.

But when Grandmother and Uncle Carl, the head of the house, Mallinckrodt, Mathilde, Pauline and the boys and other von Hartmanns from nearby were all together, no one could be sad or troubled. Uncle Carl, her mother's youngest brother, was full of jokes and funny stories and kept everyone laughing. Being a master storyteller, he would then go on to give them exciting tales of the family's ancestors who had been knights and all their adventures and battles. Finally, he took the children to see a very old, magni-

ficent fortress built in the Middle Ages at Wewelsburg to protect the bishop of Paderborn and all the
people in that area. Pauline was captivated by everything he said and was strongly drawn to the history
behind it.

Before she realized it, fall had come and with it, all
the things she loved. There were apple and plum-
picking parties, outdoor potato roasts, and harvest
festivals. There were gatherings to see the start of the
hunt as the men and their horses streaked off and
homecoming parties to greet them as they returned
in the evening with their catch. Most of all, she enjoyed meeting and being with so many of her relatives, good, wholesome, affectionate people, to
whom her own heart quickly responded. Their
warmth strengthened her resolve to be loving and
cheerful with all.

Among the many cousins who came, there was
one whose acquaintance became a real gift for Pauline. She was Bertha von Hartmann, fourteen years
older than Pauline, who, in spite of the age difference, felt immediately drawn to her. She, like Pauline, loved nature and was deeply religious. They
both enjoyed wandering walks through the woods
and meadows while Bertha pointed out and explained
many of the wonderful plants around them. She was
also keenly perceptive and understanding, and this
made Pauline feel very comfortable with her. As the
days passed, Pauline found her more and more com-
patible and likeable so that by the time Bertha had to
leave, the two cousins had formed a strong friendship that gave promise of lasting. Still, Pauline could
not bring herself to tell Bertha of her inner pain and
temptations.

One sultry August afternoon, she was introduced to another guest of her grandmother's. He was Father Gossler, a Franciscan priest who came from the monastery in Paderborn. He was gentle and friendly and soon showed his strong devotion to God in a way that appealed to Pauline. Her grandmother told her that he was a convert to the Catholic faith and came from a noble Prussian family. He was known for his extremely penitential way of life and love of prayer.

Once when he came again, Pauline had the chance to ask him some questions in private. Hesitatingly, she touched on the doubts and the unreasonable guilt that harassed her. Patiently Father Gossler answered her and tried to strengthen her when her faith seemed to be crumbling. Sensing the agony of heart she was feeling, he steered away from giving her arguments and proofs for belief in God and held out only one remedy.

"Pray, Pauline," he urged. "Take the leap and throw yourself and your misery on God who is somewhere there in the darkness although you are not sure of it. Pray stubbornly, day by day, at least for nine days before Jesus in the Blessed Sacrament, even if you find it hard to believe that He is there. Only He, though hidden from you, can and will help you."

When he had gone, her grandmother showed her the little books he had written about Jesus in the Eucharist and gave them to her. Pauline took them gladly and even brought some home with her.

Bernardine was finally able to get away from Aix to spend a month with her mother and the family at Borchen. She came with Mallinckrodt who had returned home and had taken Mathilde back to her own home in Buren. Pauline could tell that her mother knew there was something bothering her and that it was about religion. She knew Bernardine was concerned, and yet she could not talk about it. She tried very hard instead to be cheerful and pleasant.

In late October they returned home, and by November Pauline was deep in study and lessons with the professor who came to teach her privately. She continued lessons in dancing and riding, attending the theater with her mother, and helping her nurse the servants when they were sick. Frequently too, Pauline helped her with planning and preparing for the dinners, parties, and teas that were so often given at their home. Although Mallinckrodt was serious in temperament, he was really fond of companionship and entertainment and loved to play the gracious host. Bernardine, too, loved company and pretty gowns, and took pride in setting a fine table, serving an excellent meal, and affording guests the most enjoyable evening possible. Pauline and George and Hermann would watch as the guests came in and were announced. They began to learn some of them by heart. They knew President von Reimann, who was soon to be transferred, and his wife; Dr. Sartorius and his wife; Franz von Savigny and Otto von Bismarck, two smart young men working their way up in government; Fritz von Coffrane, a friend of the family and an officer in the army, to name a few. There were also many other officers of the army and government, lawyers and judges, as well as relatives, neighbors, and friends. The young Mallinckrodts would listen to the visitors as they talked, and the boys declared they were going to be lawyers or judges some day. Pauline was now allowed to stay up longer and even take part in the dancing. But never did it cross her mind that some of these very gentlemen who went in and out of her home so freely would drastically affect her life.

Despite all her activity, Pauline's secret problems still lingered, surfacing when she was alone and tired. She tried to do what Father Gossler had said, going often to church to pray before the Blessed Sacrament. Then came a shock that aroused once again some of the worst doubts she had been trying to drive away.

It was early December of 1831. She had just finished a lesson with the professor and was walking with him to the door. Her mother came toward her from the living-room, a letter in her hand. Her eyes were slightly smaller and glassy as they usually became when she had been crying. Pauline moved toward her with sympathy.

"Mother," she said. "It must be bad news, I know. I'm sorry."

Bernardine took Pauline in her arms and hugged her as if she wanted to ward off something threatening.

"It's Mathilde, Pauline," she whispered in tears. "She died of typhus on the fourth of December."

The new year came in, cold and white, then melted into blossoming spring and fruitful summer. It was 1832, and Pauline had turned fifteen in June. She and her mother were extremely busy bringing food, medicine, and money to the poor in Aix from after her birthday in June until mid-August, when the family planned to take their annual trip to Borchen.

This time she was more sedate, joining less in the games of the boys and spending more time with Bertha. She was always glad when Father Gossler came to visit, and they could discuss what he had written in his little books about the Blessed Sacrament. Because of them, Pauline was beginning to feel a strong inclination to just be with Jesus in the Eucharist. For her His Presence was an oasis of security and strength in a desert of weakness and danger. With Father Gossler she was able to ask many questions, and seeing her quick mind and good understanding, he introduced her to the books of Fénelon and St. Francis de Sales.

Meantime her mother wrote to Grandmother, asking her to keep Pauline from too much contact with the priest. She was afraid that he would give his radical ideas about penance, fasting, and long prayers to Pauline and make even worse the girl's tension and tendency to be severe with herself in religious matters. But Pauline seemed not to be affected. Bertha was a good, balancing influence on her.

Fall came and the need to round out Pauline's education. Her parents decided to send her to a finishing school in Liège, Belgium, where she would be a boarder. Madame de Beauvoir from Paris was the head of the school and received Pauline there with the opening of classes in October.

It was not long before Pauline found the atmosphere of the school disquieting. The revolutionary ideas that were sweeping all Europe under the name of liberalism were at work here too, particularly regarding religion. Like her father, Pauline was attracted to liberalism which, in its pure sense, means freedom. But there was something in this type that repelled her. It was not healthy or genuine because it presented things without their true value. Students were permitted to attend religious services of any kind they chose on Sunday, but only *if they did not disturb the schedule of the school*. To Pauline this meant that the practice of one's religion was less important than the program of the school. She got the impression that having a religion was perhaps socially popular, but that it shouldn't be taken seriously. Also circulating on this campus were the notions contained in the publication called *Young Germany* and in the book of David Strauss, *Life of Jesus*, which presented Him as merely a famous human personality and definitely not God. Pauline felt like a fish out of water.

Then a strange thing happened. She discovered that she disliked the weak, diluted sham of religion being offered at this fashionable school far more than her doubts and temptations against faith and Church teachings, even with the suffering they brought.

Although she made friends as always, she was teased about her church-going, and that distressed her. At times she felt very lonely and starved for spiritual help. There was one girl, Jeanette, who especially liked Pauline. She tried to be a friend to her and drive away the loneliness. But Pauline knew that for the spiritual help she wanted, she would have to act independently. She did. She wrote to Luise Hensel, begging her to visit her soon. Luise came and listened to her quietly.

"Just keep going to church," she said calmly. "But also join the girls in their parties and be part of

41

the fun. And while you're there, make an effort to think of God often. Keep Him in your heart. As long as the parties don't become the most important thing for you—and I don't think they will—you have nothing to worry about."

Pauline relaxed and did as Luise advised. Next, she made up her mind to concentrate on improving her French, which her mother had frequently criticized. Gradually she found herself relating better with the other girls and more at peace within.

One afternoon she had gone off by herself to the school garden as she usually did every day to read and think in the calm quiet. She had chosen a bench in a secluded corner of the garden as her daily private spot and enjoyed the fresh air, the sunshine, the swish of the tree branches, and smell of the grass as she read. After a while, as she shifted position, clasping the open book on her knees with both hands, Pauline glanced up and saw with surprise someone standing a few feet away. It was a teacher, looking at her with suspicion.

"At last I've caught you," said the woman triumphantly. "I've been watching you sneak off alone every day away from the rest of the girls during recreation. I was wondering what you were up to, and now I'm sure I know. You're not quite the *little saint* you would have everyone believe you are, are you, Pauline Mallinckrodt? Give me that book!" she commanded loudly and viciously. "We'll find out what happens when Madame de Beauvoir sees the bad novel you've been reading in secret."

Before Pauline could hand her the book, she had already pounced on her and seized it. She turned it around, keeping the place Pauline had opened to, and began to read. Pauline watched her face. Slowly the color left it as her eyes went down the pages. Her chin came up, and her lips were pressed tightly together in angry defeat. She slammed the book shut and thrust it at Pauline, almost throwing it at her.

"Here!" she said, turning so forcefully that her skirt swirled out. She was gone in a few moments. Pauline held the book up and turned it carefully around, examining it. Did her Bible really look like a novel from the outside?

It was carnival time before Lent, and there was much excitement among the twenty senior girls of the school over the parts to be had in the carnival play. But there was something unpleasant brewing too. Some of these olders girls were upset and angry with one of the teachers and were spreading their charges against her among the rest. Their goal was to bring all twenty of the group into opposition against her and cause her to be dismissed from the faculty. They were asking each girl for her opinion and came finally to Pauline.

"I can't say anything against her," she said, "and I can't join you in asking for her dismissal."

The leader of the group gasped. "Pauline!" she fluted. "I can't believe you would say that! She's the one who tried to get you expelled and said you were reading bad novels, remember? How can you defend her?"

"She just made a mistake," answered Pauline. "She's really a good person."

As the girls left her in disgust, they met Jeanette. "Please let her alone," she pleaded. "Pauline will defend the good name of *anyone*. She says there is good in every person, and we must find it." The girls headed stubbornly for the office of the principal to place their complaints.

Madame de Beauvoir assembled the twenty girls and told them very seriously to put in writing in her presence, their opinions of the teacher in question. Very quickly the only sound in the room was the crisp scratching of pens across paper. In a little while Madame de Beauvoir walked out with the pack of papers, and Pauline was receiving hostile looks. But they didn't scare her.

The principal was elated. She had read all the girls had to say, and Pauline's defense of the teacher was superb. What a girl! thought Madame de Beauvoir. She knew of the teacher's suspicious and harsh treatment of Pauline and marvelled at the girl's noble action in return. This was worth celebrating.

So Madame ordered that the day's tea party where the girls assembled for French conversation each evening, be especially festive. She herself put the finishing touches on the table and greeted the students very pleasantly as they came in. They were surprised to find her so congenial and wondered about the outcome of their complaints. She talked with many of them, moving from table to table, until she came to a group with Pauline. She stayed with them and chatted with Pauline for sometime, pleased to see how much her French had improved.

She signalled for the girls' attention. "I have two announcements to make," she said. "The first is that the teacher you complained of has been justified. The charges against her were most ably answered by Pauline. Therefore, you will give this instructor your full respect and cooperation in the future. The second announcement is that you will all meet tomorrow to make final plans for the carnival, and Pauline will have the leading role in the play."

For an instant there was complete silence in the tearoom, and then came a burst of applause and happy girl voices, all talking at once. Jeanette squeezed Pauline's hand with joy. "Congratulations, Pauline! I'm so happy for you!"

But Pauline was so surprised and so glad at the double good news that she didn't know what to say. She could only squeeze Jeanette's warm hand in return.

The leading role in the French carnival play required dancing, and Pauline took the part well. She loved to dance and did it with vigor and grace. It was obvious that she enjoyed it. But her friends were surprised to hear that at the tea dances in her home, she always had a partner and never missed a number.

During Lent Pauline made a decision and prepared to go home at Easter—to stay. She would not return to this school. She said goodbye to Jeanette, the girls, and Madame de Beauvoir, wishing them well, and set off for Aix-la-Chapelle.

It was so good to be at home! She did not know how good until she had been away in an environment totally new and different. Yet, she felt different too, in a good sense. She knew she had been given a challenge and test, and she knew she had taken them and won.

She was sitting with her parents one evening, relating some of the events at school, when she felt the impulse to make her request then and there.

"Mother," she said, and then turned to Detmar. "Father," she said and paused. "I would like very

45

much to stay home after Easter and not return to Liège. I have improved my French and have learned enough from there. Please, may I stay here? I am almost sixteen."

Bernardine and Detmar looked at each other. "We'll talk it over, Pauline," said Detmar, "and we'll let you know later."

Pauline nodded and went out to look for Hermann. Neither of her parents was surprised at her request, and both were pleased with what their daughter had accomplished in six months at Liège. She was really a tall, well-formed young lady now with poise and a sweet disposition. She spoke French well and had excellent manners. Above all, she was good and unspoiled. All told, Pauline was a gem. There was no need for her to go back to Liège if she did not care to, they agreed.

Bernardine went up to Pauline's room to tell her the answer, but she was not there. As she turned to leave, Bernardine saw something that had fallen on the floor. She stooped to pick it up. It was Pauline's report card from Liège for the months of December to January, 1833, which Bernardine had already seen. She was about to leave it on her dresser when some writing in the margin caught her eye. It was Pauline's writing, but had been added since she and Detmar had seen the card. She looked more closely. "Spelling", it read, "6" and then "That makes me angry." A little lower: "Arithmetic, 5" and then "That makes me angry." Bernardine had to smile. Aha! Her daughter's pride was asserting itself. She looked at the other marks. Religion, Geography, Politeness all had 1, "highest of all"; Character, Application, History, all were 1, "equal with all other 1's"; Order,

Style, each was 2; Reading and Grammar, each was 3; Writing, Arithmetic, Needlework, all were 5. Five and six were not good marks, and Pauline obviously thought she deserved better for spelling and arithmetic. Bernardine laid the card down. She was glad the girl had at least given her anger an outlet by writing it out. Pauline was a gem, it was true, with a flaw or two that had to be polished away.

INSTITUTION DE Mᵐᵉ. DE BEAUVOIR.

BULLETIN des Mois de *Décembre et Janvier* 1833.

Classes   Mˡˡᵉ. *Pauline Malincrodt.*

Catéchisme, ...
1ᵐᵉ Religion, ... *1ᵉ de toutes*
1ᵉ Histoire sacrée, ...
1ᵉ Caractère, ... *1ᵉ Égale*
1ᵉ Ordre, ... *2ᵉ*
1ᵉ Application, ... *1ᵉ Égale*
1ᵉ Lecture, ... *3ᵉ*
1ᵉ Écriture, ... *5.*
2ᵐᵉ Orthographe, ... *6ᵉ . . .*
1ᵉ Grammaire, ... *3.*
Analyse, ...
1ᵉ Calcul, ... *5 . . .*
1ᵉ Histoire profane, ... *1ᵉ Égale*
1ᵉ Géographie, ... *1ᵉ de toutes*
1ᵉ Morale, ... *1ᵉ Égale*
Mémoire, ...
1ᵉ Style, ... *2ᵉ*
2ᵐᵉ Travaux à l'aiguille, . . *5ᵉ*
Fable, ...
1ᵉ Politesse, ... *1ᵉ de toutes*
1ᵉ Soins du ménage, ...
Dessin, ...
Musique, ...
Conduite générale, . . .

Report card of Pauline (age 16) from school at Liege in Belgium:
Marked are these subjects: Religion—1st of all; Character—1 (equal
to other 1's); Order—2; Application—1 (equal); Reading—3; Writing—5; Spelling—6 (this angers me); Grammar—3; Math—5 (this
angers me); History—1 (equal); Geography—1 of all; Ethics—1
(equal); Needlework—5; Politeness—1st of all.

Chapter IV

Sixteen! That magical birthday came at last for Pauline, June 3, 1833. Now she was indeed a young *lady*, not only in age but also in appearance. In a few months she would be presented to the circle of high society in Aix as the eligible daughter of the Vice-President. But there was plenty of time for that. Something else that pleased Pauline even more was to happen sooner: she was to accompany her parents on a trip to Switzerland.

She enjoyed the company of her mother and father more than ever before. They were treating her more and more like a young adult, and she was responding in the same way. She felt the pride they took in her and did everything she could to live up to it.

Pauline's experience of the Alps was awesome. Already a lover of nature, she found those massive giants of beauty, snow-capped even in summer, marvelous to look at and breath-taking to walk on, once she was up on them. Up there it seemed that there was no earth, just heaven and the mountain-top and God. Yes, she was convinced that if she did not sense God up there, she never would. She also enjoyed talking with the Swiss people and seeing the small villages that clung to the base of the mountains like children hanging on their mother's skirts.

Back at home, she accompanied her mother almost everywhere. They were living now on Theater Street, named so because it led directly to the beautiful theater of the city. This made it easy for Bernardine to attend more of the performances there with Pauline. Of course, there were still the visits to the poor and the social affairs held at her home.

Pauline noticed that Fritz von Coffrane, the tall, gentle, dignified officer was coming more and more frequently to visit and that each time he came, he joined her group and spent time talking with her. His former kindly, brotherly manner toward her was gone. In its place was an unmistakable admiring respect toward her that made Pauline stand tall and act every inch the lady.

Another cousin from Büren, Rudolf von Hartmann, had joined the Mallinckrodts in summer and stayed with them while he studied to prepare himself for a career in business. He took dancing lessons with Pauline and George and Hermann that winter too, and they had a good time.

With the onset of winter came the ball at which Pauline was formally introduced into the society of Aix. People were eager to meet the charming daughter of the Vice-President, so she joined the number of young ladies who made their début that year. Fritz was there too and was most attentive to her. Although he was much older than she was, Pauline felt attracted to him.

Besides the ball given at her home, it was customary for the debutante to visit many of the outstanding families of society in their homes. Pauline was not in the least thrilled with this and wished she could be excused from it all. "Our entire day was spent doing nothing but making formal calls—how amusing!" she wrote to Grandmother von Hartmann. Still, she knew her mother, and especially her father, expected it of her and would have been humiliated if she did not follow the dictates of the social class in which they lived. So she complied as gracefully and cheerfully as she could. But in no way would she put on airs. She was her frank, natural, friendly self and so enjoyed meeting people at receptions. The guests, in turn, were at ease with her and thoroughly enjoyed being with her. Though she still walked like a man, she danced very much like a lady, and for her, every minute on the dance floor was innocent relaxation.

The number of brilliant affairs to be held increased this particular year because of the prolonged stay of Prussia's crown prince in Aix. So Pauline found that there would be more than the usual round of socials she must attend, and many would include royalty. She decided to make the best of it, often trying, when she didn't feel like it, to be gracious and pleasant while dancing as preparation for Communion the next day or later. At times she was even able to pray silently in her heart on the dance floor.

Pauline continued going before the tabernacle to combat the old temptations that pestered her. She found that the only way to drive them away was by closing her eyes and repeating persistently, almost mechanically, the words of the Apostles' Creed, especially the parts she was doubting.

She had finished her prayer for the last day of a novena, as Father Gossler had recommended, and was kneeling silently in the pew. How long, Lord? she thought. Then without warning, a stupendous thing happened. She felt like a tremendous weight was lifted from her. She felt buoyant and light, almost floating. Her mind was crystal clear and sharp. But most of all, she felt as if a light that was a non-consuming flame was penetrating her and found that she was able to believe everything she had ever doubted, joyously and without the least trouble, with a certainty that made her strong and free! She knew the Lord had heard her and had literally poured upon her the Gift of Faith! She almost cried out with joy and crossed her arms on her breast as if to hug it to her forever. There was no need for that. The darkness of doubt would never touch her again.

Day by day she spent more and more time with her mother, learning her procedures in dealing with the servants, managing the household, nursing the sick, whether family or servants. From her Pauline learned also her father's likes and dislikes. The bond between mother and daughter grew even more loving and close.

Pauline's skill as a nurse was tested in the winter that followed. Her mother became ill with a nervous rheumatism for weeks, and even her strong father was sick for two weeks. She cared for them both lovingly, and then had a turn at being sick herself. When they had all recovered, the tea dances and balls for carnival before Lent started. This time it was somewhat wearisome for Bernardine as well as for Pauline.

Then, though they thought they were used to sickness by now, early June brought them the unexpected. George became very sick, first with a rash, then inability to move, to eat or to drink. But he had no pain. Bernardine thought it was rheumatism, although he continued to be unable to keep any nourishment. She nursed him day and night, keeping watch by his bed which she had placed next to the living room so that it was easier to reach him during the day.

But that was not all. One of the maids who had helped with nursing George also became ill and had high fever. Being a shy country girl, she refused to take medication from anyone but Bernardine who was already taxing her strength in caring for George. Mallinckrodt, too, was helping others in his own way, giving rides with his carriage to the sick and handicapped of the neighborhood, keeping up his usual schedule with his strong will despite any feelings of indisposition. To complicate matters, the cooks began giving Bernardine trouble, so Pauline stepped in and helped in the kitchen as much as she could.

By the first part of July, both George and the maid had recovered, but Bernardine was a sick woman. Not only were her strength and her resistance gone, but she had a high fever that came and went as well as attacks of severe stomach cramps. Pauline devoted herself to her mother, trying in every way possible to help her recover.

Adding to Bernardine's distress was the news that her husband had been passed over a second time by the authorities for the office of president. Von Reimann was leaving Aix for Berlin at the end of July, and Von Arnim, the new president, would take office the beginning of August. Characteristically, despite her poor health and keen disappointment, Bernardine gave a farewell party for twenty-six members of the von Reimann family. Meanwhile, she brooded over the slight given Detmar, knowing how much it hurt him and worse than that, the cause. Both he and she knew it was because he had allowed his eldest to be baptized a Catholic and all the children to be raised as Catholics, simply to please her. Her silent grieving over this made her illness worse.

Finally, Dr. Sartorius, their family physician, made a firm decision after speaking with Mallinckrodt.

"Bernardine," said the doctor in a very business-like way, "this really cannot go on any longer. I think you know as well as we that rest is not enough for you. You definitely need the baths at Schwalbach, so it's time we make arrangements for you to go there."

Bernardine, who had been sitting back in a recliner, sat bolt upright.

"But doctor," she protested, "there are baths right here that I can go to."

The doctor waved his hand as if to erase her objection. "Bernardine, you have gone to these baths and they didn't really help you. Those at Schwalbach are newer and better. Now please listen to us, and do as we ask. You will make everyone feel more at ease, knowing that you are getting the best we can obtain."

"But — " she began.

"I know, I know. You will need a companion.

53

Well, you shall have plenty. I shall go with you to Cologne, Pauline will go with you, and she will have her friend, Adelheid, as a companion. And Father Claessen will accompany you as far as Coblenz. So you see, it's all taken care of."

"Well," said Bernardine grudgingly, "if you think it is *really* necessary—"

"Fine! We'll leave next Wednesday, and I shall immediately take care of everything." He didn't tell her that he still had to ask all the people he had named, but he was sure there would be no difficulty. He was right; there wasn't.

Detmar, George, Hermann, Bertha, now eight years old, Rudolf and the servants clustered by the door to wave a final goodbye. Little Bertha did not try to hide her tears while the boys blinked and gulped theirs down. Detmar's face was unnatural, like a mask. Bernardine stretched forward in her seat as far as she could and as long as she could to see them all. Father Claessen, too, leaned forward in the carriage and pressed her hand, and Pauline, next to her, slipped an arm through hers.

The first stage of the trip ended at Cologne where Dr. Sartorius had ordered rooms for them at a hotel. He, Pauline, and the maid chosen by Bernardine, took Frau Mallinckrodt immediately to her room. She would need very much rest. The doctor gave his instructions and left. Pauline and the maid helped Bernardine to bed and with the little food she could take. After a while, Bernardine dismissed Pauline, whose face, so unusually serious and set, disturbed her.

"Go find Adelheid," she said very firmly. "You can have your dinner and then see something of this big city. I know Dr. Sartorius would not want you sitting up here. He'll show you around. Now go, dear. My girl here will take good care of me,'' she said, turning to the maid beside her.

Pauline could tell her mother wanted no argument, and knowing how strong and loyal the maid was, decided to give in. She would come back later.

She found Adelheid and the doctor. After dinner, he suggested going to the Rhine Promenade for a concert. It was a perfect summer evening, and music outdoors would be delightful. As they walked there, Adelheid became so excited over the colorful sights and elegant window displays they passed that she let out little squeals and laughs every now and then. Pauline was looking hard too, but her eyes were not on the same things. She was searching for military uniforms, and then for the faces above them, hoping that very soon she would find the right one.

Cologne was where Fritz lived, and she had hoped so much that he would hear they were in town and would come to call on them or that they might meet him somewhere near the Promenade. She was caught between a fluttering excitement over Fritz and a sobering guilt for even thinking of him while her mother was sick. Trying to manage the two feelings made her very distracted. She really didn't know what either Adelheid or the doctor had said. She had all she could do to keep up with them.

They arrived at the concert and found seats, but Pauline hardly heard the music. She tried not to be too conspicuous as she turned her head to look in every direction. Finally, she sat back disappointed. Fritz was not to be seen anywhere. She was so quiet and listless that Dr. Sartorius thought it best for them to leave the concert early and get extra rest. At the hotel, Pauline went immediately to her mother's room where the maid told her she was sleeping quietly.

Early the next morning, the doctor accompanied the group to the place where they were to get the steamer for Coblenz. Once they were comfortably settled, he said goodbye and left them to look after his patients in Aix. Father Claessen would stay with them till Coblenz and then put them on their way to Schwalbach.

The trip to the town was uneventful and tiresome. But at the end of it was something even more unpleasant. Because the baths were new, the accommodations for visitors were crude and available only in a farmhouse that was already overcrowded. There was no hotel. For people coming from well-furnished, comfortable homes this was truly a disappointment and inconvenience, but for a woman as sick as Bernardine, it was a dangerous hardship.

Pauline was really upset and impatient. There was nothing left but to turn to God, to make quick hard decisions, and to use her usual strong drive to carry them out.

Bernardine grew worse, and the doctor who was called diagnosed her illness as typhoid fever caught from some one she had recently nursed. The next two weeks were days Pauline would never forget. They were peaks and valleys of hope and fear as Bernardine seemed first better, then worse. Pauline was at her mother's side day and night, refusing to leave and tireless in her efforts to help her.

Finally, on the eleventh day, a rider was sent at dawn to Mallinckrodt in Aix-la-Chapelle. He must come quickly. Bernardine lay weak and wet with perspiration but conscious and clear-minded after a siege of delirium. She looked with love and sympathy on the young hands folded near her pillow and Pauline's head bowed in prayer—or was it fatigue?

"Pauline," she whispered hoarsely. The girl's face jerked up instantly.

"Mother!" she whispered back, and she felt surging over her a tremendous wave of love and admiration for this loving, unselfish woman who had given her life in many different ways.

"Soon you must take my place. Hush, *Liebe*!" she said as Pauline started to protest. "God is calling me home, and I must go. I want to go, Pauline. I want to go to our Father in heaven. Heaven, Pauline! How I have dreamed of it! And I will meet you there, all my dear ones."

She stopped and closed her eyes a bit. Pauline gently patted her face with a dry cloth and then moistened her lips with a wet sponge. As she finished, she saw her mother's fingers go to her rings. Slowly and with effort Bernardine pulled them off, first the left, then the right hand. She fastened them to her watch, hanging by her bedside.

"There, dear. I know it would be too hard for you and your father to do after I'm—" Pauline burst into tears and kept her from finishing.

She waited till Pauline had quieted down and then tried to lift the girl's face from the bedside. Pauline raised her head and looked full in her mother's black eyes. She knew she had something important to say, and she, Pauline, was ready. The words of this woman who had lived so well her faith and love for God and others and was now face to face with death, could be nothing but wise and true.

Bernardine stretched out her hand. Ever so lightly she touched the strong young face near hers.

"You are seventeen now, Pauline. A young woman. You must be the lady of the house. Oh—you can do it, but not alone. Keep God always before you. Let our family be united and in peace. Keep me ever in your memory." She stopped and waited a bit. Then she went on. "Care for your brothers and sister, for your father. Try always to give him joy. It will be hard for him when I am gone. Please ask Father Claessen, our confessor, to care for the children's religious training, Pauline."

She lay back with eyes closed, and Pauline motioned the maid away, thinking Bernardine would sleep. But soon she turned toward her daughter with a last mighty effort to speak. Pauline shook her head in a loving no.

"Yes, dear, let me talk while I feel I still have the strength. There are things I must tell you about the servants, the household, the budget. It will help you so much when you go back to Aix." So with tears in her eyes, Pauline listened carefully to the beloved voice giving careful directions for the future, and she tried to take some notes.

Then followed three days of severe suffering. On the last evening her father and Dr. Sartorius arrived, and the priest was called. Serenely, with simple, touching devotion, Bernardine received absolution and Holy Communion. With a contented smile and bright eyes she awaited the Anointing of the Sick, and her face showed real enjoyment as she felt the holy oil and heard the pardoning words. There was something intangible and beautiful coming from Bernardine's whole person, a deep joy that bordered on mute triumph and a peace that made everything seem lighter, easier, even the sickness and pain. Pauline was amazed at the way it was affecting her, too. Her entire being seemed to be filled with a contented, tranquil feeling, undisturbed at the notion of death that had bothered her previously.

She was kneeling beside her father, watching, when Bernardine pressed her lips to the crucifix held out to her, breathed once more, and then quietly left, to go with Him whom she had just greeted with a kiss. She had lived graciously; she died graciously. Nothing on earth could match the serenity of her face.

Pauline would never have thought it possible for two such conflicting emotions to co-exist in the same heart, and yet they did, right in her own. The definite, very real loss of her much loved mother was crushing and made her want only to cry in misery and pain. And it tore at her inwardly to see and hear the brokenness of her father, his powerful head and shoulders moving in soundless sobs, keeping watch by the body of the lady who had been his life. Yet, lifting her strangely within the very storm of sorrow, was a strong, steady joy—joy that her mother was forever happy, and a yearning, a longing to go there too, to be with Him as her mother was. Death no longer frightened her; in fact, her last hour would always be welcome because she wanted heaven so much.

They had to bury Bernardine there in Schwalbach, and the sad party went unhurriedly back to Aix. But between Pauline and Detmar there was now a stronger, firmer bond of understanding and support than before. Their mutual deep grief and their common love for Bernardine and the other children drew them together even more closely, now that she was gone.

Pauline was determined to make their home as pleasant and cheerful as possible and to carry on the warmth that her mother's love had given it. She resolved to fulfill her father's every wish as far as she could. She found that he, in turn, was most considerate and loving toward her. When she told him of the instructions Bernardine had given her, he immediately consented that she should arrange everything as her mother had said. After all, assuming responsibility for this household was a challenge for any one. There was, of course, Detmar himself, a government official, whose duty to entertain the elite was understood; then came George and Hermann, teenage brothers, full of life, fun and pranks; eight-year-old Bertha, about to enter classes outside the home; Rudolf von Hartmann, the cousin house guest, who was a student of commerce; and five servants who had to be directed. But Pauline could and did measure up.

It was customary that no social invitations be sent to a bereaved family or by them for some weeks after a death, and for this Pauline was grateful. There was so much for her to learn about managing everything, and it gave her time to do it without the pressure of having parties and guests. But she wrote often to Grandmother von Hartmann and even attended an occasional alumnae gathering at St. Leonard's, which made her feel good.

Quite unexpectedly and suddenly though, without any planning, there was a ball at the Mallinckrodt

Mallinckrodt family's coat of arms

home—in the attic. Directly across the street from their house was the home of President von Arnim, where a really formal ball was in progress. It was early evening, and through the fine, delicate draperies one could see the brilliant lights and the dancing couples. Suddenly, Frau von Arnim pulled back the draperies and opened the windows. The sweeping beat of the music and all its harmony floated temptingly into the room where Pauline was talking with a young friend. They looked at each other and grinned.

"I wonder if George and Bertha and Hermann and Rudolf are really studying up above us. They would have a wonderful view of that ball across the street from where they are. I think I'll see," said Pauline with a giggle. "I'll be right back."

She came back laughing and slightly out of breath. "They really think they could use some exercise. It'll make them study better, they say. And besides, when the music comes pouring through your window, doesn't it mean you should have your own private ball?"

"Yes," said the young lady. "Shall we?" and she held out her hand to Pauline as they went to join the others.

Later that evening when Mallinckrodt and Pauline were sitting downstairs as usual and the children and Rudolf were studying, Detmar blew a ring of smoke leisurely and watched it rise.

"I noticed this evening when I came home that the von Arnim ball was in full swing. I'm sure that didn't bother anyone in our house, did it?" He looked keenly at Pauline, with just the ghost of a smile on his lips. Pauline flushed a little but looked back at him and smiled.

"Why, no, Father, it didn't bother anyone at all," she said emphatically, guessing that he had seen and heard their private ball.

"That's good," he said, nodding at her, and his eyes twinkled.

Months later, a wintry day of March, 1835 blew in a rider with a surprise for Mallinckrodt, this time a pleasant one. It was a declaration by the king that, in recognition of Mallinckrodt's outstanding service to the state, he and his family would from then on enjoy hereditary nobility and would add the title *von* to their name to indicate their being raised to a class distinguished for service. They would now be called "von Mallinckrodt" forever. The declaration went on to state that Detmar was raised to membership in orders of merit as an honor for his faithful and excellent work. It was dated July 18, 1834, the day Bernardine had left for Schwalbach.

Pauline was happy for her father, but she knew he received the honor with mixed feelings. Its date surely twinged his heart with sad memories, and it was obvious the government was trying to recognize his excellence as a public servant and at the same time to compensate for refusing him promotion because he had dared to grant religious freedom to his children.

Pauline smiled a little to herself. She wondered what her hardy old ancestor, Evert Mallinckrodt, would say about the restoration of this title of nobility under such circumstances. It was he who, back in the fifteenth or sixteenth centuries, had given up that title for himself and his descendants on condition that his city, Dortmund, might be one of the free Independent Cities of Germany, not owned by any of the several lords. Actually, she mused, the title had first been given to the Mallinckrodts as early as 1241 and was verified again in 1349 when most of the family lived in a large castle called "The Wetter" on the Ruhr river. She recalled that the castle had been burned down by the people of Cologne during a bitter feud in 1445 and then later rebuilt by them.

Her father was descended from the Mallinckrodts of Dortmund, and they were well known in many German towns as members of the guild of cloth merchants who controlled and supervised the methods of cutting the products of the cloth industry. They had a coat of arms that had been passed down. She and the boys had studied it and knew it by heart: a golden shield with three black leaves whose points touch a red circle in the center; above the shield, a helmet over a flowing scarf, and two arms meeting above the shield, each with one finger upright in the same golden ring. It was all very interesting, and she could tell that the daring and high spirit of the old Mallinckrodts was very much alive in her father, her brothers and herself.

Bernardine had been the nurse in her home, so Pauline thought it only fitting that she should be the same when trying to take her place. She decided that the best way to do that would be to get professional training in dressing wounds and the use of home remedies and medicines. Within a short time she was going regularly to the local hospital for instruction and practice.

Meantime she was becoming more accustomed to her role as lady of the house, and she was learning another side of her father. Although still serious and exteriorly cold, he was very patient with her inexperience in trying to manage everything and was extraordinarily good to her. At times she was really touched by his tender consideration of her. Perhaps she did not realize that he was responding gratefully to the extreme thoughtfulness and constant care she tried to show him at every chance so that he should not miss Bernardine too much and grieve himself sick. After all, she loved him deeply. Then, too, the memory of her mother's final words to make him happy never left her. So, regardless of her likes or dislikes, she was always at his side, the constant companion.

Mallinckrodt faithfully kept his promise to Bernardine, and Father Claessen continued to come to the house for the children's instruction. Now it was little Bertha who took Pauline's place with George and Hermann. But Detmar himself staunchly maintained his own beliefs and religious ideas, and Pauline respected them as delicately as her mother did. But it was always like walking a tightrope and put her under continual stress.

With the close of Lent, Mallinckrodt considered the normal period of mourning over and decided to give a gentlemen's dinner party at Easter. He invited no less than thirty men, and he insisted that Pauline, the only woman present, take the place of honor as lady of the house. Presiding at her first dinner party at seventeen, with no other lady there, made Pauline nervous. But, her dear friend and teacher, Father Claessen, was present. "His calm and pleasant manner made me feel so secure that I lost all self-consciousness and embarrassment," she wrote soon after. That turned out to be just the start of many more such parties.

64

Each day Detmar was more and more pleased with Pauline and her attempts to manage the household, mother the children, and fulfill his wishes. It was time he decided, that she had a little vacation, a chance to relax, some time for herself. The month of May was half over and had made everything lovely. It was a perfect time to travel.

"Pauline," he said one evening as she sat near him sewing.

"Yes, Father," she answered, wondering what could be on his mind.

"Next week Mayor Zurhelle with his wife and Chief-Attorney Pakenius with his wife are going to Paris for a three weeks' tour—"

"Oh, how nice," she said, looking up for a moment.

"Well, I think it would be really nice if my daughter would go with them." He lit his pipe and waited. He had said it so slowly, so low and so matter-of-factly that at first Pauline did not really comprehend. Then suddenly, it dawned.

"Your daughter!" she exclaimed. "You mean that *I* should go to Paris for three weeks?"

He nodded, and a big grin spread over his face. He looked like a big boy giving someone a surprise he had saved.

"Oh, Father!" Pauline jumped up, almost dropping her sewing, and gave him a big hug. "That would be wonderful!" Then came the thought of the boys and Bertha. "But—"

"No buts. I want you to go, and I'll make arrangements for the children. We can go traveling too—to Borchen, Dortmund, Büren. We'll all be well taken care of and have a good time, and the servants here can have it a little easier."

So it happened, and Pauline was delighted, visiting the most beautiful city of Europe for three weeks. With the two friendly couples, she saw and admired the famous Louvre and its art, the majestic cathedral of Notre Dame, the site of the Bastille, the great triumphal arch, the Sorbonne University, the royal palace, and many other important things. She was perhaps most impressed by the Hôtel Dieu, one of the oldest hospitals in Europe, founded in 600 A.D. She was glad she had mastered French at school in Liège and was now able to use it.

It was mid-June when she returned home, refreshed and feeling quite grown-up. She had celebrated her eighteenth birthday in Paris and was now glad to get back. Yet she longed for the company and understanding heart of another woman. Though she was busy with many things during the day, she felt lonely just the same. She wrote to Grandmother von Hartmann, asking her to persuade her cousin Bertha to come to Aix and stay for a while with her. Bertha agreed, and it was a very happy young lady who welcomed her to the Mallinckrodt home.

The summer flitted by and with it many socials and dinner parties hosted by Mallinckrodt and his charming daughter, now well-known in the society of Aix. Bertha was impressed by the ease and graciousness Pauline displayed as hostess. She was equally impressed by Fritz von Coffrane's thorough enjoyment of Pauline's company and his candor in showing it. He was coming regularly now, to see Detmar, his distant relative, of course, but much more so to see and be with Pauline.

She noticed how her young cousin responded to

his attentions and wondered what her feelings toward him really were. But she would not ask. She would wait. It was too personal, and as yet, even to Pauline herself, probably not very clear. She felt sure that in time, Pauline would talk about it of her own accord.

One particular evening Pauline, with her father and Bertha, bade the guests goodbye at the door. She went to a parlor and from an open window stood watching Fritz as he talked with another gentleman guest by the front gate. The soft summer breeze flapped the curtain against her, back and forth, back and forth, until its rhythm started a sudden chanting in her head: Pauline loves Fritz! Pauline loves Fritz! She gasped and looked quickly around to see if anyone was there who could have heard it. Where did that come from? Was it true? Did she really love Fritz?

She looked at the tall, stately figure so perfectly groomed; his shapely head, bent now as he talked earnestly with his companion; his large, capable, well-kept hands. His face was visible only in general outline, but she knew every feature in detail: the high, broad forehead topped by thick, dark hair neatly combed and attractively touched here and there with silver grey; the straight strong nose; the deep-set dark eyes, so direct and keen and kind; the powerful cheeks and jaws, the clean-cut chin; the wide, expressive, sensitive mouth. But there was something that controlled his face, his movements, his voice, his whole person that drew her heart: the steel strength and discipline of an officer tempered by the remarkable gentleness, courtesy, goodness and culture of a man of high ideals. Fritz was serious and mature, an older man; steady and honorable. He was everything she wanted to find in a man.

By now he and the other man were gone. Once more the curtain hit her, rousing again the old chant, Pauline loves Fritz! Did she? Pauline put her hand on her heart. Yes, yes, she finally thought, I do. I think I do! What she felt now for Fritz was definitely not the little-girl affection she had for him when she was a child. Her woman's heart also told her that his serious and open admiration of her was not just that of a big brother. She was sure, then, of one thing at least: she did love Fritz. But then came looming into her consciousness like a huge shadow, what she had been suppressing all along—

"Pauline! Are you all right?" came a loud stage whisper and a rustle by the door. Pauline jumped slightly and twirled about. Bertha stood there in her nightrobe.

"Bertha! You scared me a little, Yes, I'm all right. I was just thinking."

"It's getting late, and when I saw your door still open upstairs, I was a bit worried," said Bertha. She put both hands on Pauline's shoulders and looked at her wonderingly. "You look troubled, Pauline."

"Oh, Bertha! I don't know what to say! I feel happy. I feel glad. But I feel troubled too. Does that make sense?"

"Yes, because that's the way we are, you know. Somehow we can be both happy and upset at the same time. Let's go up to my room and talk if you like, shall we?"

Arm in arm, they went upstairs, and Pauline told Bertha of her feelings for Fritz and of the affection she thought he had for her.

"And that's what makes you happy," concluded

68

Bertha.

"Yes."

"So what's the part that troubles you?"

"Well, Fritz is not a Catholic, and I don't think he has any intention of becoming one. My own religious beliefs are very, very strong and dear to me. I don't think—well, I'm not sure we could have a happy marriage. It takes almost an heroic amount of giving from one party and even then—" Pauline broke off, remembering her own parents' suffering.

"You're right, dear," said Bertha, patting her hand. "But now you must be very tired. So get some sleep and then you'll be more clear-headed and able to think about it better."

Pauline walked to the door, then faced her. "Bertha, what do you think about it? I trust you. Tell me."

"Well, Pauline, Fritz is a fine man, it is true. But he is too old for you, and most of all, according to what you just told me, I think there would be a constant heartache for both of you over something extremely important to both of you. And even if you and Fritz survived the struggles, what effect would the frequent tension have on your children? In my opinion, it would be very unwise to enter such a marriage."

Pauline nodded slowly, but Bertha could see that though her head said yes, her heart was still not convinced.

"Thank you, Bertha, and good-night."

"Good-night, Pauline, and sleep well."

The following week Pauline, with George and Hermann, began instructions for the sacrament of Confirmation which would be given August thirty-first. It was a warm afternoon of that week when Fritz came to see Pauline. He smiled as she came toward him with a look of surprise.

"Is there a shady spot in the garden?" he asked. "I would like to talk with you there."

"Oh yes, I think we can find one, Fritz," she answered and set out with her usual speed to go there.

"I hope I am not interrupting anything. I've wanted to do this for a long time, but I didn't have the courage till now. Is there something else you must do? Otherwise I'll come back some other time," he said in such a way that Pauline knew he really didn't want to be sent away.

"No, no, Fritz. It's all right. The children are playing their games, and the others are busy with their work, including Bertha, my cousin."

"Pauline," he said, facing her squarely, "I love you, and I want to make you my wife. I have loved you for a long time. I will do everything in my power to make you happy. Will you marry me?"

For an instant, there was silence. He stood looking down at her, seeing a rare and different kind of loveliness that appealed to him more than any other he had known. What he saw physically was a tall, well-formed young woman, stately in her maroon gown like a dark red summer rose, graced with the crown of her wheat-golden hair around her head. Her light blue eyes were sparkling with tiny green flecks of excitement. The face upturned to him was strong and supple with a prominent nose, a wide, shapely mouth, and sculptured chin. But this was not the unusual beauty that attracted him.

No, it was rather the totality of her superb personality, radiating a charm that he could see was far

Pauline as a young woman

from physical. In her clear gaze he saw straightforward honesty; in her smile, winning wholesomeness. Her very manner of being breathed utter goodness and unflinching courage. But over and above those was her magnificently warm, unselfish, and boundless love for others. It formed the expression of her face, enriched the sound of her voice. It flowed out from her thoughts, her words, her movements. Her presence brought the feeling of sacred mystery, of a brush with God. All these were blended, in her, into a beautiful whole that made her uncommonly lovely.

Pauline took a deep breath. "I can't answer you just now, Fritz. I must have time to think about it. You understand that, don't you?

He nodded. "Yes. But when can I hope for an answer?"

She hesitated. "The first week of September."

"That's a long time, Pauline, but I'll wait. Until September seventh, then." He kissed her hand and walked swiftly down the path.

She told Bertha about it before she told her father. Again, Bertha reminded her of his age, of their difference in religion, of the need to wait for others. Her father was curt about the matter. He saw no need at all for her to marry now. She was young, and Fritz was far too old for her anyway. Besides, the children needed her very much just now.

She listened to them both and seemed at times to even want to agree. But somehow she could never bring herself to formulate the word "No" even inwardly whenever she thought about her answer to Fritz. There was always the same insistent little voice saying that he was kind and loving and would be

71

good to her; that no one else was quite like him.

The one great distraction from her problem was her instruction and preparation for Confirmation, for which she really longed. She wondered what had happened to her drive and determination. At the mere thought of Fritz her heart seemed to melt like wax. Resolutely she prayed for the strength and guidance of the Holy Spirit, showing her weakness to the Lord and begging for His help to do the right thing.

August thirty-first came at last, and Pauline, George and Hermann took their places solemnly in the church. Just as solemnly the bishop confirmed each of them with holy oil, conditioning them like spiritual athletes and adults for the marathon of good that would last their whole lives long. The response of the Holy Spirit to Pauline's plea was tremendous. She experienced a pressureless power taking hold of her mind and will as she faced her problem and moving them sweetly but strongly to a definite decision. It was crystal clear to her now, and her will did no teeter-tottering. She knew what to say to Fritz.

To her great surprise, she felt a wonderful peace. Nothing disturbed her; she had not a care in the world. There was only a marvelous calm that she wanted never to lose. She truly felt that she had been entered and taken over by the Holy Spirit. She felt drawn to Him.

One week later she opened the door for an eager Fritz, and they walked together to the garden. He waited while she searched for the right words.

"Fritz, when you asked me to be your wife, I was thrilled and honored. I have thought about it very much...very much. And each time, there is the same conclusion: I cannot marry you." Her voice trailed off. With an effort, she spoke again. "I hope— I hope you will find someone truly deserving of you."

She could not look at him. She could sense the pain that was showing in his eyes and wished that she could relieve it.

"Why, Pauline, why?" he said in a low voice. "What have I done? Or is there someone else?"

"You have done only good things that I shall remember, Fritz. And there is no one else. I just feel sure that I'm not called to marriage. Please believe that." She was surprised at her calmness and knew that now she could never be swayed.

"I'll try to." He paused and cleared his throat. "I wish you happiness, Pauline. I shall never marry ....I will love you always....Goodby." He put on his officer's hat, stood for a moment looking at her, bowed, and was gone.

Chapter V

Quietly and quickly Pauline tiptoed downstairs, put on her hat, took her prayerbook and went out the front door. It was 4:30 A.M., and she hurried through the dark street to attend the five o'clock Mass. Every day she went to Mass, and several times a month she was permitted to receive Communion, which was a privilege. This was her favorite time of day. This was when she received the grace and strength and love necessary to do all her father expected of her, to control and cope with her teenage brothers, to mother nine-year-old Bertha, and to manage the large household efficiently. Even though she had been up late at receptions or parties with her father the evening before, she was up early for Mass the next morning. She could not and would not miss this meeting with the One who bore her up and was the secret of her cheerfulness.

Mallinckrodt liked to see her remain at home when she was not out with him. But that was no hardship, for she really did not long to go out on social calls. Since her cousin Bertha had gone home again, she had a good deal of time to herself each day after she had met with the servants about the day's schedule and had seen to the needs of the boys and of little Bertha. Her father had let to her the choice of occupying her time, so she used it for prayer and spiritual reading and caring for her poor. She read Father Gossler's books and through them began to learn how to meditate; through them too, her love for Jesus in the Eucharist was growing more and more. She read, at his recommendation, St. Francis de Sales' book on the love of God and felt her heart being stirred by it. The hours passed very swiftly, and she was never bored.

When Bertha came home from school, Pauline made it a point to spend time with her, talk with her, play with her, and above all, to hug her and show her the love of her mother who had gone away to Schwalbach and never returned.

With the boys, it was another story. They were full of fun and pranks, and she really had to think hard at times to know when it was proper to laugh at what they had done and when she should be angry. But whichever it was, she always laughed or scolded in such a way that George and Hermann had to know that it came from love. For her, love was the master key to handling children, but sometimes they stretched her patience to the breaking point. Then they would settle down—because Pauline was angry.

They called her *die gute Alte*: *die Alte* because she was *old*; the oldest of them all and therefore, the Boss, taking her mother's place; and *gute* because she was *good* to them and loved them even when she bossed them.

One evening, Pauline met her father at the door as he came home from work. She still had a half-knitted stocking in her hand. She laid it down and took his hat, coat, and umbrella from him. He found his big chair in the living-room and sat down with a big sigh of relief. She came back soon with his slippers. Overhead were lively sounds of moving.

"I'm glad your hard day at the office is over, Father."

"Yes, my dear, but it seems it isn't quite over yet. A messenger caught up with me on the way home and gave me another business letter. How are things here at home?"

"Good, Father, except that Bertha was coughing so hard that I put her to bed already. George and Hermann have done their chores and are playing in their room. I think you can hear them. Those two are never at a loss for a good time."

"Well, I'm glad they are real boys." He opened his letter, and she continued her knitting. The noise upstairs also continued.

Mallinckrodt was absorbed in his reading and Pauline in her thoughts when suddenly she became aware that the noise above had stopped. She went on knitting and waited. Still no sound.

Finally she stopped and said, "Father, it's very quiet in the boys' room. That seems odd to me. Usually, it means something is wrong."

"Well, take a look," he answered.

Pauline left her knitting on the chair and went upstairs. In a few minutes she stood at the top of the stairs very upset.

"Father!" she called down to him. "Please come

here right away! You must help me!"

Mallinckrodt rose quickly and started up the stairs.

"No wonder it was so quiet in there," she said to him. "Can you imagine what they're doing? They are squatting on the floor, trying to see who can spit the farthest! And they record it. They're so busy that they don't even hear me! Hurry, Father!"

He opened the door and stood there, watching the boys in silence, with Pauline beside him. George and Hermann went on, totally unaware of them. Pauline looked at her father. He started to move. Ah! At last! Now they were going to get it. To her complete amazement, he squatted down next to the boys, wrote down his bet, and joined them!

Pauline put her hands to her head and left the room muttering to herself. "I can't believe it! I don't know whether to laugh or cry. Our beautiful playroom! If Mother had lived to see this! But that's the way it is and that's the way it's going to be, I guess. 'Boys will be boys!'"

Although she accompanied her father to every social affair he desired and was a gracious hostess for all the parties he wanted to give, Pauline had no real interest in any of them. She much preferred to withdraw from contacts with rich and important people, enjoying her visits to the poor, her spiritual reading and prayer much more. Mallinckrodt knew this and was not at all happy about it. He did not want her to withdraw from social affairs. He saw that many flattering attentions were paid to her by both ladies and gentlemen at these parties, but also that Pauline was polite but not pleased by them. He had to do something to get her away from her preoccupation with religion and the poor.

Then came his chance. Bernard von Hartmann, a brother of Pauline's mother and a banker, came to Aix with his wife for a visit before going on a tour of Belgium. Pauline could go with them!

She was surprised and happy to go because she loved to travel. But she made up her mind before going that she would put the wishes of the others who were travelling with her before her own; that she would do this cheerfully and be a pleasant companion, not acting like a martyr. This would take some conquering of herself, but it would mean that she was truly living the love of God that she was reading about.

So in 1836 they went to Brussels, the capital of Belgium. She spent more than one day going from one fashion shop to another and from one jeweler to the next—with a smile. They saw there also the huge hospital run by the Daughters of Charity, like the one in Paris, and that made her decide. Secretly, in her heart, she was determined to be a Daughter of Charity, to give herself to God and to caring for others.

A new railroad from Brussels to Liège had just been finished, and the three of them had their first train ride. Pauline was delighted. It was like riding in an open coach but much, much faster.

In Liège, Pauline wanted to pay Madame de Beauvoir a surprise visit. But even before she had entered Madame's office, the lady recognized Pauline's long, fast steps in the hall and called in delight: "C'est la Mallinckrodt! It's that Mallinckrodt girl!"

Pauline was amused that Madame remembered her walk so well, and they talked of the old school days and even more of schoolmates. The conversation turned to Jeanette, Pauline's friend, who was in the town of St. Trond.

"I want to go there to visit Jeanette," said Pauline.

"*Ach!* Pauline!" said Uncle Bernard.

"Please, Uncle Bernard. I really must see her. I ask to go to just this one place." She could not say more because it was confidential. But Jeanette was very much in need of spiritual help, and Pauline would not fail her.

Uncle Bernard made some more objections, but nothing could stop her. Finally, he consented with much reluctance, and she visited with Jeanette.

Later Pauline wrote in her diary: "In some respects I have an unbending nature. However, this is not the first time I have been accused of being eccentric. So I am not worrying. Should I have the good fortune to carry out what I consider my vocation, then watch everyone look up! They will pity me and call me an oddity." She knew both the good and not-so-good sides of her own qualities.

From Liège they went to Namur, saw the Meuse and Scheldt rivers, then to northern Belgium, visiting the old and interesting city of Antwerp; Ghent and Bruges, the cities of lace-making; Louvain, the town of the world-famous university; Ostend, the port on the English Channel; and then over to the battlefield of Waterloo.

During the trip, Pauline was impressed by the beauty and wealth of castles and museums but much more by the institutions of charity. She was attentive at the theater and was just as excited at the races as those who had placed bets on favorite winners and was honestly disappointed when her own favorite jockey did not win. Uncle Bernard and his wife had to admit she was really a very agreeable companion.

On her arrival home, her father found her relaxed, but after some days he noticed that basically she remained just as religious and unworldly as ever. She tried very hard not to let her religious activities disturb him or even come to his notice if possible, and she sincerely made every effort to please him with love. But in order to accomplish both these things, she could no longer be her usual, outspoken, candid self. She had to carefully choose her words, and she noticed herself weighing what she was going to say and do in his presence. This dampened her normally spontaneous way of speaking to him, and he saw this. His reaction to this, in turn, was an odd mixture of coldness regarding her piety, with the most delicate and loving consideration for her personally. It was a strange and a subtle conflict between father and daughter who had the same unyielding, strong wills which caused them both to suffer.

Just when the tension was building more and more for Pauline, the Lord gave her the most precious gift of her life. Her confessor, Father Claessen, allowed her to receive Holy Communion every day. That made all the difference for her. The daily possession of Jesus, the intimacy with Him was a bit of heaven that fueled Pauline to go non-stop through the day, loving God, her family, all who crossed her path, even herself properly, with the love of His Heart given in Communion. It made her long more and more to give herself to Him and Him alone. She was twenty years old now, and the almost perfect balance of her maturity, physical, emotional, and spiritual, made her an exceptional person.

All this time while Pauline had been growing into womanhood, Aix-la-Chapelle had been changing very, very much. It was the Age of the Industrial Revolution. Machines had been invented for factories that could turn out many more times a day what the ordinary worker did with his or her hands. Greater production in a day or week meant cheaper prices but also lower wages. The ordinary worker had to choose between being the slave of a machine with cheaper wages or having no job at all. There was no such thing as a labor union or salary regulations. Women were forced to work in the factories and children too, in such bad conditions, that the stories of factory and child labor were distressing to hear. Children too small to work in the factories roamed the streets or waited in cellars while their mother, brothers, and sisters worked. Small owners were put out of business, and the middle class gradually disappeared. Meanwhile, those who owned the factories became richer and richer.

There were some among the upper class, however, who sympathized with those poor and intended to do something about their suffering. Mrs. Fey, a merchant's widow who lived in retirement with her daughters, opened her home in 1838 to a group who met to make plans to help them. Her idea was that the wealthy women of this group should forget about being class-conscious; forget that they belonged to the upper class and the poor to the lower class. They should go into the streets and the huts of the poor to help, instead of making only occasional visits to them or having charity bazaars where the ladies could be safe and clean, away from the poor.

Those who belonged to this group were graduates of St. Leonard's school; some were classmates of Pauline. There were the two sisters, Clara and Netta Fey, their cousins, Helene and Luise Fey, Francesca Schervier, Anna and Caroline von Lommessen, Minna Istas, and Leocadia Starz, and others. Clara, Francesca, and Anna knew Pauline well. So it was no surprise when Anna said, "Someone very important of this group is missing, and that is Pauline von Mallinckrodt." They agreed, and Anna was delegated to invite her to join them.

Pauline was completely delighted with the idea and accepted without hesitation. They all met at the Fey home together with Father Andrew Fey and some other priests of the city who were interested in social needs.

All were totally dedicated to the work of helping the needy, but each chose the way for which she felt she was fitted. The Fey sisters gathered the poor children of school age, begged for desks which they dragged to a place for meeting and taught the children. Francesca Schervier put all her efforts into caring for wayward girls and prisoners. Some of the ladies organized a soup-kitchen; others went from house to house, begging for clothing, textbooks, and other articles the poor needed. Pauline chose to serve the sick and the dying. At last she could put to use what she had learned from her mother and from the doctor at the hospital where she had taken courses. She worked as a nurse's aide in the Hospital for Men and in St. Stephen's Hospital in the section for poor, elderly women.

It was the old ladies at St. Stephen's who appreciated her the most. Many a night she spent with a poor dying woman or man, easing their suffering, praying short, comforting prayers, taking last messages. She arranged for a decent burial for each one.

Once in a while she would bring to the hospital a neglected little orphan she had found on the way in the streets and would give the child a bath and some clean clothes if possible. In fact, it was not unusual for poor children to show Pauline their heads sore with lice, hoping she would help them. She always did, taking them with her to the hospital or to their homes and spending hours cutting the hair, washing, and treating the infested heads. But her most precious gift to all was her radiant cheerfulness that made complaining turn to smiles and angry rebellion against suffering turn to self-control and trust in God.

At first the reaction of the upper class in Aix at the actions of these young women was shock and disapproval. Said one critic, "They are crazy, going into the homes and streets to the poor!" But later he called them "holy ladies." Even the poor in the beginning did not quite trust these fine ladies when they came to their homes but finally yielded gladly to their help. The people in general began to see that these women trained by Luise Hensel at St. Leonard's were generous and serious.

In fact, something exciting was happening to the whole Catholic Church in Germany. For some years, laws against Catholics had been made, and they were deprived of religious freedom. Gradually they were drawing closer to the center of Catholic unity which is the Holy Father and the Vatican. Realizing they had a strong leader in the Pope, they formed a united front in Germany, hoping to win their political rights. The government saw this and was alarmed. It immediately placed restrictions on the communication between the Pope and the German bishops so that documents or letters from the Holy Father to the bishops had to go through the government and only with its consent.

It happened that a professor by the name of Hermes at the University of Bonn began to teach heresy, saying that faith is built on doubt; that man's intelligence alone is the basis of faith. Pope Gregory XVI wrote a letter or brief condemning that heresy and stating that faith comes only from the grace of God; that it often goes above the intelligence of man but does not contradict it. The Pope's letter forbade the spreading of Hermes' teaching. Although this was a purely spiritual matter, the government interfered and would not allow the Pope's letter against the heresy to reach the people.

However, an intelligent gentleman of the Fey family wrote reports and documents exposing the error of the heresy. He had a devoted staff of young students and others who willingly made copies of his reports to be sent to the German bishops and professors. This was accomplished long before the government could stop Mr. Fey and his group. Later, those professors and priests who refused to teach the heresy lost their jobs at the university, and the bishop was refused residence in his own town. Pauline, of course, held faithfully to the teaching of the Pope, knowing full well from her past experience that faith truly comes from God and not from the human mind.

But that was only the beginning of Catholics' standing up for their rights and faith. Some time later, the Pope issued a letter about mixed marriages that was mild but required that the couple promise to have all children brought up as Catholics. The German ambassador at Rome named Bunsen interfered with this letter or Papal Brief and, before he sent it for publication, changed the part about the promise to raise children as Catholics. But through the Fey group of copiers, the Bishop of Trier learned of the forgery and warned the new Archbishop of Cologne about it. The government, however, ordered the archbishop to either bless mixed marriages *without* the promise or to resign. He refused to do both, and he and his secretary, Father Michelis, were put in prison at Minden. A year later the people found out about the forgery of Bunsen, and the sympathy of the Catholics for the bishop was strong.

As the news spread, people began to take action. In Aix-la-Chapelle a group of young women was formed that urged young men and women who were about to marry to consider seriously that the sameness of religion for husband and wife is the foundation of a really stable family life. They warned that over-confidence and merely hoping for mutual understanding in religious matters sounded assuring but rarely turned out to be real. This group was started by Bishop Laurent, who was its spiritual adviser according to the legal document dated February 5, 1838, and its president was Pauline von Mallinckrodt.

This was, without doubt, the greatest and most public point of conflict between Pauline and her father. It was his duty as an official to watch and restrain any reactions of the people against the orders of the state. Yet his own daughter was the leader of a group that was teaching the opposite of what the government denied. Still she was only being exactly like her father. Both had extremely strong iron wills; both had a passionate love for truth and honesty; and both would loyally carry out what each firmly believed to be right, regardless of feelings or amount of effort required.

Pauline had thought it all through painfully after Communion one day. For her the Pope was the spokesman for Christ and His Church. That, she believed was the highest and truest authority in heaven or earth. Besides, she knew only too well from experience the suffering that came from mixed religions in families and the need for children to be raised in the same faith. Though she loved her father deeply and would do anything to spare him pain, she *could* not possibly be a Catholic or a true Mallinckrodt by pretending to agree with the government's version of the Pope's letter or its treatment of the bishops. She stayed long after Mass that day, pleading for strength and love to do what was right with courage and kindness and especially the wisdom to find little ways of softening the blow for her father. But *nothing* would ever stop her.

To Mallinckrodt, on the other hand, it was and had always been sheer nonsense that the survival and renewal of the faith in Germany should depend on the Pope and the Vatican. The German Church had no need of Rome in his opinion. The whole matter so irritated him that he needed an outlet close at hand on which to vent his hostility against the Church, and he found one in Luise Hensel. He held her responsible for filling his daughter's head with all that religion, and he forbade Pauline, even though an adult, to visit her.

But loyal as he was to the state, and faithful as he was to his duties, he was even more a man of his own principles to which he held at any cost. One of those principles was freedom of conscience and religion, which, in his eyes, absolutely no one, neither king nor government could take away from any person.

Pauline hurried home late one afternoon from her work at St. Stephen's Hospital for the old sick women shortly after the news spread about her leadership in the Fey Circle against mixed marriages. She found her father sitting in his favorite chair, staring absently at the empty fireplace, an open letter lying in his lap. There was something a bit forlorn about him that was unusual and disturbing to her. It had the air of defeat, and Mallinckrodts never accepted defeat. She took off her shawl and went to him, kneeling by the side of his chair.

"Father—" she began.

"Oh, there you are," he said listlessly, patting her hand. "Well, they finally found someone worthy of succeeding von Arnim as the real president of Aix. I've been relieved of my duties as temporary president."

He handed her the formal, matter-of-fact letter that once more delivered the government snub. He sat back, hands over the sides of the chair, feet out. He would not bring up the question of why he was passed over again. It was too sore a spot for both of them.

But for Pauline, hiding it would not heal it. They had to talk about it. She read the short letter quickly and laid it down.

"Father, it hurts me very much that you were

passed over again. But it hurts me even more to know that it is because of me, your own daughter, that it was done. And yet—"

He had turned away his face and was holding up his hand as if to stop her words. Then he turned to her. "And yet, what you believe in is so strong and so important for life, according to your conscience, that it goes first, before anything else, no matter how personal," he said emphatically.

"Yes, Father," she said softly. "You *do* understand. And I am positive that you feel the same."

Mallinckrodt rose, tall and straight and imposing. He paced the floor a bit and then turned to her. Pauline too had risen, still standing by his chair.

"Pauline, you know that I have never accepted and cannot accept the teachings of the Catholic Church. You also know that I am a man of honor and of extreme loyalty to the state. *But*—" and he stopped as if to underline what he was going to say—" the state is not the watchdog of the family. It has no right to trespass on matters sacred to the family, especially religious matters. When it does, there is an old feudal law that says opposition by the people to the state's command is justified because the order is unjust. And so you have every right to belong to the Fey Circle opposing the state on mixed marriages—even though you are the daughter of the vice-president."

Pauline's eyes misted. She was deeply touched by his tremendous sense of truth and justice and his firm clinging to them, even though he was penalized for it during his whole career. He truly was a noble man and deserved the title *von* in his name.

She walked over to him and put her arm through his, looking up at him with shining eyes. "You're a wonderful man, Father, and I am very proud to be *your* daughter.''

Chapter VI

Boxes, big and small, stood piled and waiting. Floors and walls were bare. People were moving about in the big Mallinckrodt house, picking their way among the covered furniture and boxes, too busy to talk. Outside the sun was trying hard to warm the atmosphere, but it was still a cool day in June, 1839.

Pauline stood in the stripped living-room, tying a box on a table that was already wrapped. She looked up for an instant and saw her father moving something bulky toward the door. He looked positively happy. It was a long time since she had seen him so cheerful. Now at last, after many requests, he had received the king's permission to retire from government service, and he could hardly wait to go to Boeddeken. He would be seventy on his next birthday, and he wanted by all means to celebrate it by enjoying a well-earned rest from state duties.

So they were moving, and she would have to leave dear old Aix which had been her home for fifteen very important years, years in which she had grown from a seven-year-old child to a young woman of twenty-two. She would leave behind St. Leonard's and all her friends, St. Foillan's Church so full of sacred memories, Father Claessen, her long-time friend, teacher, confessor, and director. She would also have to leave her beloved poor and sick old ladies and men at the hospitals where she served. But she would do it cheerfully, for somehow she felt that this was what He, her beloved Lord, wanted for His own good reasons.

She would also have to leave Bertha, her little sister, because her father had decided flatly and without any explanation that Bertha was to remain at Aix in a Protestant boarding-school. Was it perhaps a belated reaction of his to having yielded previously to the Catholic education of his children at the cost of government displeasure? Pauline was not sure, but she felt much better when he asked Father Claessen to continue instructing Bertha in religion. He was still faithful to his promise to Bernardine.

George and Hermann were both away studying at the university in Berlin, and Rudolf had gone home. So it was just Pauline and her father, with the servants, who moved to Boeddeken on June twenty-third. The people of Aix-la-Chapelle sincerely regretted their leaving because they respected Mallinckrodt highly for his extraordinary integrity and other fine qualities.

Their new home had formerly been a cloister, first for nuns, and later for monks and lay in a quiet, peaceful valley surrounded by mountains that were covered with forests. The air was deliciously fresh, with a scent of moist earth and green life. Although many of the buildings of the monastery remained, they had been much changed over the 800 years that had passed. Most of the church was gone, except for the ruins of the semi-circular sanctuary. The part called the nuns' choir was still standing, as well as the cloister around three sides of the courtyard where the religious had walked under outdoor walks covered by a roof. Many farm buildings had been added close to the main one.

Mallinckrodt had many improvements made and was delighted with this country home. It was close to numerous relatives, and now that he was relieved of duties, he could entertain to his heart's content. There were many rooms for guests above the cloister walk, and he intended to keep them filled.

When Pauline saw how much her father relaxed and how much he enjoyed the company, she was determined to do everything in her power to make these visits and his days there as pleasant as possible. No matter how many the relatives and friends, nor how often they came, she would always be the cheery and obliging hostess.

She succeeded well, so well that all the von Hartmanns from Borchen, Büren, Bielefeld and Münster and all the Mallinckrodts from Dortmund and Paderborn loved to go to Boeddeken. Even her favorite cousin, Bertha von Hartmann, came frequently, which was always a joy for Pauline. Beloved Grandmother von Hartmann of Borchen had died two years earlier, leaving an unfilled place in the hearts of all her children and grandchildren.

Young Bertha, away at school in Aix, was surprised and a bit envious after reading the letters she received from her new home. Her father wrote: "Our house is becoming more and more cozy through the efforts of your sister." And later: "I cherish the hope of spending more happy days here with you, as I am now enjoying the time with your sister." When the boys went home for their holidays, they must have found it unusually lively and pleasant. George wrote to Bertha: "You should see what a jolly life we are having here in Boeddeken—even more so than formerly in Borchen. This is largely due to Father's congenial and outgoing attitude, a disposition such as I have never known him to manifest in Aix-la-Chapelle. As I come from Berlin to this happy group and meet with relatives who are such delightful people, I feel like singing a hymn of praise."

But there was another view of all this—Pauline's. She wrote to Luise Hensel: "Since we do so much entertaining here, I am living a life of many distractions, and the time which I formerly devoted to my beloved poor is now spent in useless conversation. Of course I know that God is served and glorified in any way, provided one acts out of pure love of Him. I know, too, that I might live a very holy life here."

She did find a way, though, to help her "beloved poor," and a way to satisfy her need for intimate contact with God. Because she gave of herself so generously day and night to providing the good times at Boeddeken, her father did not object to her going daily to Mass and coming later for breakfast.

She would walk or ride by horseback early every morning the two miles' distance to the little parish church in the tiny town named after the great old fortress-castle of Wewelsburg near it. There at Mass and Holy Communion she enjoyed the most precious moments of her day. She always brought along her basket full of medicines, bandages, and sometimes food and money because when she left the church, little hands would tug at her dress and shrill voices would beg her for help. So she would go to see grandmother who was short of breath, and to check for broken bones someone who had fallen, or to look at a father's cut from a scythe, especially when it was not healing. At times she would recommend calling the doctor but because she knew the physician from the city was slow to arrive, she would give all the medicinal help she could, adding food or money.

Then she would take the short cut home across the meadow, damp with dew, and hurry to change her wet clothes before going to the table where her father and the guests were having a leisurely breakfast and expecting her. Even then she would always arrive serene and cheerful, with a steady, even flow of happiness radiating from her toward everyone.

Both Pauline and her father loved this Boeddeken home; he for its country pleasures and she for its religious atmosphere. But they both knew, too, that in winter it would be impractical. Mallinckrodt had foreseen that and had bought the former home of Pauline's great-grandparents, the von Hartmanns, in Paderborn from the city officials for their winter residence. He had this house repaired and remodeled and the grounds around it beautifully landscaped. Very close to the house was the ancient Busdorf church in which were buried, among others, Privy Councilor Matthias von Hartmann and his wife, the great-grandfather and great-grandmother of Pauline. Matthias von Hartmann had been chief justice in the court of the bishop who, at that time, was also a prince in his own right.

It was to this old house, now redecorated, that one after the other, having completed their studies, George, Hermann, and Bertha gradually came home, living happily and contentedly with their father and Pauline. She, meanwhile, had refused all offers of marriage and knew in her inmost heart that her determination to dedicate herself entirely to God was growing stronger and stronger. But she was also sure that as long as God permitted her to have her father, it would be her duty to care for him and not leave him in his old age.

Just as she quickly found the poor at Wewelsburg near Boeddeken, so she lost no time in finding them at Paderborn. Her love for God in all His children, especially those who suffered in any way, was the radar that helped her to detect them.

Not far from the Busdorf church and her home was the ancient city wall of stone that made a sharp turn and continued on. Here was a neighborhood of low-roofed, miserable houses that leaned against the city wall, using it as their fourth and back side of the house. The poor who lived here, were, like those in Aix-la-Chapelle, ousted from their jobs of spinning and weaving in the north of Germany by the introduction of machines in their places. So they came to the city, looking for work without success or getting jobs in factories that paid almost nothing. Some of them had a little patch of land outside the city wall which they cultivated, hoping to raise some much-needed food they could not afford to buy. Pauline discovered them one day as she came upon a man near the city wall who was really sick. He needed

95

Pauline's winter home in Paderborn before she became a Sister

Part of the estate at Boeddeken

continual care, but she knew that the local hospital would not take him because only a limited number of beds was reserved for the people of the countryside. And there were many more like him.

Something had to be done, and Pauline, as usual, did it speedily, resolved to let nothing stand in her way. She pinned up posters in all the churches of Paderborn and in the synagogue, asking for ladies who would volunteer to care for the sick poor in their homes. Both the volunteers and the patients would be from all faiths or none. No one would be excluded. By November 21, 1829 twenty-four ladies had joined the group which was called "Active Members of the Association Caring for the Sick Poor in Their Homes." Two of these ladies were Jewish; one was the wife of the local rabbi.

Next she recruited households that would take turns in delivering meals for the patients. Then Dr. Hermann Schmidt, chief of staff at the hospital, whose wife had been Pauline's classmate, offered assistance. Paderborn was divided into regions corresponding to the principal churches, and under his direction, doctors were assigned to give free medical care to patients according to regions. Father Gossler, the Franciscan who lived in Paderborn, gladly offered his help in spiritual matters and became spiritual director of the association.

Pauline would not take the chairmanship of the association, not even of her section. She felt it was better for her to take orders rather than to give them. But she did accept the secretaryship, doing much of the paper work. She was able in this position to unite with the group some nurses who were willing to take night duty with the very sick poor. Since Pauline's days were completely taken up with other duties, she volunteered for night duty. After the first six months, the report of the main committee revealed that Pauline had spent more than one hundred nights with the sick and dying.

But soon there was angry reaction. There was in Paderborn an organization called the "Public Commission for the Care of the Poor," which had done nothing for those people along the city wall because they were ashamed to go the Commission and beg for help. Now, when news of the care given these people by Pauline's group reached the Commission, there were strong protests against the new association.

But Pauline was not in the least troubled, and she recommended to the others with whom she worked that they write a letter to the Commission, requesting permission to call themselves "Auxiliaries" to the Commission. "You will see," said Pauline in a letter to her sister Bertha, "eventually these gentlemen will give in to us and will make one concession after another." She knew they were only too glad that the work was being done, and as long as it was under their name, they were satisfied.

However, the daring young Fräulein von Mallinckrodt was not satisfied. There was something that still made her heart heavy and had to be remedied. It was the problem of poor sick mothers who were worried about their little ones. She explained it to the Ladies' Club when they met at the beginning of 1840.

"What adds to the suffering of these poor sick mothers, and indeed, must be of concern to us, too, is that their little ones not of school age are running about without anyone to care for them while their older brothers and sisters are in school. It seems to me that this sad situation could be changed if we would establish a nursery school just for these children and those of poor mothers who must work all day. We would need a lady to be on duty at seven in the morning to receive the little ones, one or more to pass the day with them and one to dismiss them only when their mothers come home," she said looking at them hopefully.

The ladies responded by renting space for the nursery school in the Alexius Garden which was standing unused in the middle of Paderborn. By May, the talking and happy laughter of small children could be heard behind the old walls of the garden, and soon curious folks were gathering to see what was going on. Quickly the news spread that the Fräulein von Mallinckrodt had opened a nursery school. Even the laundresses who rinsed their clothes on the banks of the Pader river had that as their main topic of gossip. Many families wanted to send their children there, but the pastor told them the school was only for the poor.

At first there were only eight children in the nursery school. Pauline was assisted by her aunt, Marianne, wife of her uncle Fritz von Hartmann, and by Frau Rintelen, a widow. They took turns with the children, but Pauline tried to be there as long as she could. They took children between the ages of two and six, gave them wholesome meals, taught them to pray and kept them pleasantly occupied. For this they rented the house of Herr Schulze. In nice weather they spent part of the day outdoors in the Alexius garden, singing and playing and enjoying the fresh air. Soon the number increased to more than twenty-four, and they had to find another place because the Schulze house proved to be too small.

Then they found an old building that had been bought for the hospital that would serve their purpose. Through Dr. Schmidt, they were allowed to use it free of charge. Pauline, with the ladies and children, moved there gladly. They had just become adjusted to the new location after four weeks when they were forced to leave. A fire broke out in the district and destroyed their building. So for the third time, Pauline was forced to look for a new location, and although it looked like the nursery was doomed to failure, she would not give up. Meanwhile, the number of children was growing.

Frau Hagemeier, a widow, was willing to rent a few rooms of her house to the nursery, and in November of 1840 they started to conduct the school there. But by Easter time in April, 1841 Frau Hagemeier had had enough of the noise of these frisky youngsters and their wear and tear on her property. She served notice to Pauline that her rooms could no longer be used.

But Pauline would not be discouraged. Without delay she made an appointment with the bishop and asked that her group be allowed to use some of the rooms in what was once the monastery of the Capuchin monks who had been turned out years before. The monastery had since then been returned to the Church. The bishop agreed to let her use rooms free of charge but only for a limited time since he intended to use the whole monastery for a seminary later on.

Pauline was really happy. At least there was a

roof over the heads of her poor children temporarily for the fourth time in one year. But she would need tact in using those rooms.

When the government had closed down the monastery and sent the monks away, they had allowed three old Capuchin Brothers to remain and spend the last years of their lives there. They occupied only a small number of rooms, but they were close enough to the rest of the house and the garden to hear the children. At first they were frightened and disturbed by them, but finally things led to a climax. Thoughtlessly the children chose to play in the patch of garden where Brother Lorenz had carefully and laboriously planted his celery bulbs which he hoped to sell at the market. He was furious. He knew the bishop had allowed the children to be there, and he could not very well scold the high-class lady to her face. So after she had passed him at his celery bed, he threw a stone in her direction, hoarsely muttering angry words.

Pauline caught the action and understood. She knew it was difficult for old persons who had had no contact with children for years, to suddenly get used to their noise. She also knew how much the celery bulbs meant to the old Brother. Selling them was the only means of income for all of them. That evening she sent some hot tea and white bread to him and the other Brothers, promising to do so every evening. That was fine. There were no more angry words after that.

Meanwhile, Dr. Schmidt, who was deeply interested in her work, gave her a donation of 100 Talers* from a brewery owner in town. He even advised her to add a school for blind children to the nursery

100

* In American money at that time, this amounted to about $69.00 since a Taler equalled about 69 cents. Both the German Taler and the American dollar purchased much more than now.

school. This excellent doctor was extremely compassionate to the sick he dealt with but especially to the poor. He cared for them without charge, not only trying to heal them but also to cheer them, considering even the most neglected as his brothers and sisters in Christ. He tried to hide his generosity from even his best friends. But the helpless sufferers in the hospital for incurables knew him and his wonderful kindness well. Some of these poor people had been rejected by society because of their deformities or disgusting diseases. But as he took care of them, he tried also to remove the bitterness from their hearts by a gentle hug or kiss on the forehead. It was no wonder that Pauline had such great faith in him and was eager to work with him in anything that would help the people they both loved.

About this time Bertha, the youngest of the Mallinckrodts, returned home from Aix to stay and was given a very warm welcome, especially by her big sister, Pauline. Soon she was with her at the nursery school, helping here and there, wherever she could be useful. She helped with teaching the little ones the alphabet, singing with them, teaching them their prayers and good manners. Then they needed help with their meal. They had a chance for a nap on little cots, and the very poor were given clean clothing. All were sent home clean.

Of course, all of Pauline's personal money was given for the nursery, but at times she needed more than that and took it from the household. Her father never objected although he knew where the money went. Once when she asked outright for a needed sum, he put a playful touch to it. Near her on the table was a silver plate. He picked it up and handed it to her.

"If you can hold that plate at arm's length for ten full minutes, I will give you a large amount for your nursery," he said teasingly.

"I'll hold it. You'll see," laughed Pauline, determined to do it with or without the money. She took the plate and extended her arm in mid-air while Mallinckrodt noted the starting-time. She could imagine how George and Hermann would tease if they were there now to watch *die Alte*, the Boss, stand the test.

Minutes passed, and her arm ached. The plate grew heavier and heavier, but Pauline held on. She thought of all the things she would be able to do for the little ones. Finally, her father came over to her and took the plate. Her arm fell to her side like a piece of lead that didn't belong to her.

"Congratulations!" he said, smiling. "You've earned the prize," and he handed her the plate with twice the amount she had asked for.

There were other ways she raised money for the school too. On weekends in nice weather when the family and guests were at Boeddeken, she would get all the ladies to knit stockings for the poor children.

When everyone got interested in cards, playing whist, the winners always donated the money they won to Pauline's nursery school. She also succeeded in getting managers of the theater and concert to give special performances for the benefit of the nursery. It happened once that not a single person came to one of these performances. The hall was empty, and her dreams of the Christmas she would give for the children were rudely popped. Pauline went sadly to the church and told the Lord how downhearted she felt.

As she rose from her knees, the sacristan came toward her with an envelope addressed to her. She opened it and found a generous donation from a benefactor. Not long after, other donations came in too, and the Christmas party for the poor came true. There was a lovely Christmas tree, trimmed with apples and cookies and lit with bright candles. Beneath it was the manger with the little Christ Child, Mary and Joseph and the shepherds. This was the center of attention, and the dear story was told again to the children. There were now about fifty of them. They sang carols in their hearty, unpretentious way with one or the other just a bit off-key, and then with big eyes each received a large apple, a cookie, some white bread, stockings, and some clothing. The grownups who were present were very moved by the children's singing and their joy as they received their gifts, which were necessities rather than toys.

Occasionally Pauline would be refreshed by going on the weekend to visit her cousin, Bertha von Hartmann, at her home in Münster. On this particular Sunday morning, Bertha was hostess to a small group of special friends. Two were very special. They were Professor Christopher Schlüter and his sister, Therese. He was a well-liked professor of philosophy at the University of Münster, a master of literature and the great books, and a deeply religious man. He was, however, gradually losing his sight and was already partially blind. Therese, much like her brother, was interested in the same things and was his constant companion.

Schlüter was the leader of a group of distinguished men and women who were interested in literature and religion. Luise Hensel, Pauline's cousin, Bertha, another cousin, Wilderich, who was a seminarian, were members of this group. Some were Catholic; many were of other denominations. But they all had one thing in common: all were drawn to this kind, wise, sensitive man who knew how to direct their search for truth and to open their hearts to understanding and acceptance of each other, no matter what their differences. They met either at his home or at the von Hartmanns' and discussed sometimes heatedly but always intensely, topics of deep meaning. At times he would read passages from great authors pertaining to their subject of discussion. But many times of late they knew he was quoting them by heart because he could no longer see the print.

Bertha had told Professor Schlüter much about Pauline, and he was eager to meet her. On this Sunday morning, though he could not really make out her face, he was impressed by her warm, friendly voice and manner. Before he knew it, in her earnest, open way she had steered them both into lively conversation about religious things.

Schlüter came away with perhaps a better vision of Pauline than those who could see. He was a man who was keenly aware of God in others. In her he saw a person of inspiring presence, a person in whom the life and power of the Holy Spirit were very vivid and strong. What she was, not what she said or did, struck him. Here was someone he would watch with interest. In the diary he always kept, he noted for this day: "Therese told me later she was surprised by Pauline's tall, stately, and wholesome appearance. Her face was not exactly beautiful but was extremely pleasant. Her eyes mirrored friendliness, cheerful unsophistication, and kindness of heart."

Busy though she was, Pauline did not lose sight of her sister, Bertha. She had noticed that although Father Claessen had continued to instruct her while she was in the Protestant boarding-school, there was still much about her religion that Bertha did not know. Pauline was convinced that religion which is to be really practiced is learned more by listening and example than by merely reading. So she spent time talking with Bertha about different spiritual truths, trying to fill the hunger of her sister's soul as she had tried to fill her own.

But these talks aroused in her a longing to know more about the spiritual life and to grow more in it herself, and she hoped some day for a chance to fill it. She had a friend, Ludwina, who had made a retreat under the direction of a Jesuit priest and had described it to her with great enthusiasm. Pauline knew that a retreat was going away for a few days to be alone with God, to think and pray with Him about one's life. She thought that perhaps she could make a retreat by herself, but she knew that her father would never approve of it. He was trying rather to remove from her life anything that would add to her religious activities.

It was mid-February, and Mallinckrodt had gone away on a trip for a few days. Pauline had just come from the nursery school when a visitor was announced. It was Ludwina herself, and she launched again into describing for Pauline the kind of retreat given by the Jesuits. It was called the Spiritual Exercises of St. Ignatius since the topics of meditations made by the retreatant were chosen and put in a certain order by their founder, St. Ignatius.

"Pauline, you really ought to give yourself a treat like this. It's a wonderful grace of God, something different from anything else you've ever experienced," said Ludwina persuasively.

Pauline leaned toward her and said softly, "Ludwina, you'll never know how much I have wanted to make a retreat. I've been thinking seriously of making one by myself, but—"

"Oh no, my dear. For your first retreat in the Spiritual Exercises especially you definitely need a director. Come with me," she said, taking Pauline's hand. "Come with me to Brede, and I shall see to it that you have your wish. You have a good chance now, and the ladies will manage the care of the children for the few days that you are away."

Pauline sat still, thoughtfully going over what Ludwina had just said. It was true. This was probably the best chance she would have of going away without leaving her father to himself. And Brede, the orphanage under Ludwina's charge, would have room enough for her to be alone and undisturbed and yet give her the means to contact Ludwina if she needed her help.

"You've convinced me, Ludwina. I'll do it. But I must write to Father and break the news first. Then I'll have to talk to Aunt Marianne about the nursery."

"Fine! Just do whatever you must do. Don't bother about me. I'm happy you are going." She picked up a book and settled down to read while Pauline went upstairs to write.

The next afternoon Pauline was on her way to Brede with her friend, eager for this new experience. Very soon Ludwina informed her that the Jesuit Father Tewes would conduct the retreat for her. Pauline was surprised and pleased.

In a short time she found that the Spiritual Exercises are for the soul exactly what physical exercises are for the body: hard work that reveals weaknesses, strengthens them, forms better habits, and generates a feeling of new life. The hard work was prayer and meditation. She saw her whole past life in a new light, found hidden faults and made firm resolutions for the future. Yes, she would start over and lead a better life, using the methods of St. Ignatius taught her by Father Tewes. Her heart was filled with gratitude to God for the special graces he had given her.

There was, however, one thing on which she disagreed with her director, Father Tewes. For the past three years she had been permitted to receive Communion every day. This was very unusual, and Pauline treasured it more than anything else in her life. Now Father Tewes advised her to omit Holy Communion on the mornings after a dance or entertainment to avoid scandal to others and because it was not a good preparation for Communion. He also advised her not to receive the Eucharist after much distraction with business or great hurry or during travel.

Pauline thought and prayed much about it. Finally, before the Lord, she concluded that she could not make any promise to stay away from Holy Communion. She would, instead, make special effort to think of God often during social affairs, being attentive to His presence in preparation for receiving Him the next day. She would also go to a church where she was not known so that she would not give scandal. "You know," she prayed, "that I am not attending these social gatherings because I enjoy them, but rather to serve You and to be cordial and helpful to others." She would try to keep returning to His presence with her thoughts even during business or other distractions in order to better receive Him the following morning. She needed Him so desperately. To her, Holy Communion was not a reward for holiness, but the absolute necessity for surviving.

No, she would not be stopped from daily receiving Him who was her life, love, and source of spiritual energy. It was a decision that took great courage at a time when customs were not easily changed, especially by a woman. Pauline was honest with Father Tewes about the matter. He later conducted several more retreats for her, and although not in agreement with her, he no longer forbade her daily reception of Communion.

She left the orphanage at the close of retreat completely renewed in mind and heart. On the way home, she went over her plans for all the things she was going to do. But as she stepped from the carriage at the door, Bertha greeted her with a worried face.

"I'm so glad you're here," she murmured. "Father is very sick."

Pauline was startled and a bit incredulous. "Very sick? What's wrong? What happened?"

Bertha shook her head. "I don't know. He came home from his trip feeling miserable and hasn't been up since. We called Dr. Schmidt."

Pauline nodded. "That's good. I must go to him. Here, Bertha, please take my things."

She started quickly up the stairs and met Dr. Schmidt as he came from her father's room.

"Thank God you're home, Pauline," he said, and

his usually pleasant face was serious. "Your father is a very sick man. He will need all the care you can give him."

"Dr. Schmidt," called Pauline anxiously as he started down the steps, "there is hope, isn't there?"

He turned and looked up at her. "I'll do everything I can, Pauline. You know that. But—I think you should notify George and Hermann to come home."

Chapter VII

George and Hermann came as quickly as possible. They and Bertha helped Pauline with caring for their father, and soon they all learned that he was suffering from jaundice. At times he appeared to be getting better; then he would again get worse. Finally, Dr. Schmidt told them there was no hope.

Pauline was grateful to God for allowing her to nurse him in his final illness, and she was grateful, too, for the presence and support of her brothers and sister. Silently she hoped and prayed that Mallinckrodt would ask for a priest and be converted, but he remained a staunch Protestant to the end. On April 4, 1842, while all his children knelt prayerfully around him, Detmar von Mallinckrodt quietly breathed his last.

Actually Pauline was not disturbed that their father died a Protestant. His Lutheran baptism was correct and made him a member of the Church. He had lived a good and upright life according to his conscience, which was all the Lord required of anyone. She was sure he had joined her mother in heaven. Nevertheless, she felt his loss more keenly than the others. Though he and she had often had serious differences, there was still a deep love and mutual respect between them that had grown more precious through the years. She would miss him sorely.

The sisters and brothers decided that for the time being, their way of life would not change. George would return to college, Hermann would continue his study of law and work on his thesis, which, he told her proudly, was the relations between the Church and State. Bertha would stay with Pauline, helping her more and more with the nursery school.

Dr. Schmidt and his wife were very kind to Pauline and Bertha, inviting them over many times after George and Hermann had left. The couple tried in every way to soften the sharp edge of the girls' grief and to draw them away from the many reminders of their father in the big, silent house.

On many of these visits to the Schmidts, Pauline learned much about handling the financial affairs of charitable institutions from the doctor, who was in charge of some. He shared with her his plans, his reports, and much information that pertained to such matters. He was a proficient business man, and Pauline was fortunate to have him as a teacher. She asked his advice about her own charitable works and in this way received an excellent business training that would serve her well in years to come. God was giving her the preparation she would need for her future work.

In February she had obtained corporation rights for her nursery school. When the enrollment in it reached 100 children, the government of the region of Westphalia awarded the school a grant of 400 Talers* which was to be invested in order that the school might have a source of profit. All the children had their own writing materials and playtime equipment. Each child also had a little parade flag and a personal identification tag to be kept in a particular place.

Pauline was not greatly surprised when, in June, Dr. Schmidt brought with him to the hospital two blind children whom he had found in the country-side.

"Could I entrust them to your charity?" he said to Pauline. "They are doubly poor, you know."

One look at their little faces was enough for Pauline. "Of course, Dr. Schmidt," she answered and took them with her to the monastery where the nursery school was. She made arrangements to have them live with the housekeeper there. She realized that they would need their own classes in order to learn. So she had Dr. Lachmann, director of the Institute for the Blind in Braunschweig teach her the Braille alphabet for reading and writing. He also showed her how to weave straw mats, to work with wicker, and to plait ribbon so that she could teach her blind children. She poured molds for the Braille reading boards, and for the study of geography, she embroidered a map by which the children could feel the raised outline of the countries and the mountains and rivers.

By December, the end of 1842, there were five blind children at the school and they were learning religion, reading, writing, arithmetic, knitting, handicraft and music. For this Pauline had the ser-

* About $276 in American money at that time, with greater pur-chasing power than today.

vices of Frau Schmidt, Dr. Schmidt's wife and her former classmate, who was a teacher of the blind. Pauline was glad to work with her.

Months before, Anna von Lommessen, another old friend and classmate, had written to Pauline, telling her about the group of women in Aix-la-Chapelle who had united to do the same kind of charitable work that she had started in Paderborn. They were doing well, and the movement had spread to other cities where ladies were doing similar work. Luise Hensel wrote, too, and invited Pauline to come to Aix-la-Chapelle. Both Luise and Anna invited her to unite all these groups across Germany into one large union. At the time, Pauline had written back that she really could not get away, having her father and the nursery school to care for. But now she wanted to see for herself how their project was going. So leaving the nursery and the blind in the capable hands of her faithful assistants and Bertha, she went for some days to discuss things with her friends.

To her pleasant surprise, she discovered that Anna had entered the Religious of the Sacred Heart and her sister, Caroline, had soon followed her. So Pauline decided to visit Anna in her convent at Jette, Belgium. It was a new and delightful experience for her to meet an old friend as a religious and talk with her. She also learned that Luise Hensel had gone to Cologne for a new type of work.

A retreat was begun at Anna's convent while she was there, and Pauline eagerly took the chance to make it. She knew without a doubt that God was calling her to become a religious, a Sister. But she did not know which kind, which congregation. Should she choose a life devoted totally to prayer and penance for the world or should she choose a life of charitable works among the people, making God known through the love shown them? Her natural disposition and feeling leaned strongly toward the works of charity, but she was not sure that this was what God wanted.

By the end of the retreat, Pauline's problem was solved. She knew God wanted her with Sisters who spent their lives working with and for His children in the world. She knew, too, that she had not far to go. The bishop had just invited the Sisters of Mercy of St. Vincent to her own city of Paderborn. Wasn't that a clear sign as to which congregation she should join?

The day after she had come home, Pauline could hardly believe her eyes when she saw the teacher of the kindergarten coming in to speak to her. The young lady had cut her hair and was wearing a religious habit. She said she was a member of Father Gossler's new Congregation of St. Clare and that the housekeeper wanted to become one too. Pauline looked at the dark dress with just a tiny tug at her heart. No one wanted to wear a religious habit more than she, but not under these circumstances.

The reports about Father Gossler were not idle gossip after all! He had advised ten wealthy girls and ten working-girls to form a community and live together in one house. He called them deaconesses, had them wear a habit, and follow a Rule similar to that of the Poor Clares except that they would go out among the people and nurse the sick poor and teach poor children. But, she further learned, her nursery school was to be their training school.

Much as she esteemed Father Gossler for his zeal,

spirit of penance, and knowledge of spiritual matters, Pauline felt she could not in any way go along with his project. He was, at the present time, her confessor too. Still she would have to, in all honesty, confront him on the matter of using the nursery school as a learning lab for his untrained girls. Besides that, he was starting a new religious order without the approval of the bishop, who was bringing another community of Sisters to Paderborn for the very work Father Gossler chose for his order. That work had already been begun and would be continued by Pauline's school and the bishop's Sisters.

She prayed and thought about it very much, and finally, with tears in her eyes, she wrote Father Gossler a respectful but firm and frank letter, stating her objections. She explained that, first, the money donated to the nursery school was for the benefit of the children, not for the founding of his new community. She could not, in fairness, take that money away from the purpose for which it was given. Second, if the nursery school were to be used as a training place for his young women, the attention would be totally on them and their learning instead of on the children and their learning. Also, the children would be getting a second-rate education because they were being used in an experimental school with unskilled teachers who were beginners. All this, again, would be definitely unfair to the children, and she could not permit it.

Pauline consulted her aunt, Marianne, about the housekeeper and the young teacher. Her aunt agreed with her that both would have to leave the Father Gossler group if they wanted to remain at the

Standing, left to right: Dina von Hartmann (later George's wife) and George
Seated left to right: Hermann, Bertha, and Pauline

nursery school. She called the teacher and gave her her choice. The young lady chose to leave the nursery. The housekeeper left without even discussing it with Pauline.

She was really in a sorry position now, but that very day she received a letter recommending a teacher who was coming to apply. The teacher herself came the next day, and Pauline accepted her at once. In a short time everyone liked her. Several days after that, a new housekeeper came too. Her name was Jule, and though she was rather gruff, she was very efficient.

Soon there was still another newcomer to Pauline's staff. She was fourteen-year-old Mathilde Kothe who had just graduated from the teachers' school for the blind. She had passed her examinations with honors and was eager to work with the blind children. Pauline looked at her. Her nickname of "little mother" really fit her. She was small in build and stature, gentle and delicate in her ways. Yet beneath her seeming fragility lay an unexpected strength of will and tremendous power of accomplishment that showed her potential leadership. She was an orphan, having lost both parents when she was very young. But the von Hartmanns of Büren had taken her into their home and raised her. At times she seemed somewhat serious, almost stern, but as soon as she was with the children, her loving concern for them made her sweet and pleasant. Pauline put her in charge of the blind children without hesitation.

Meanwhile the matter of Father Gossler and his new community was still unsettled. Pauline wrote again, telling him that she and her staff would do nothing without his advice, but would not subject the school to the authority of the president of the Ladies' Guild. She also offered to be a mediator of peace between Father Gossler and the bishop. However, at the very same time, the president of the Ladies' Guild was trying to have her removed as head of the nursery and school for the blind.

But Pauline was not frightened or upset. They could not stop her. Firmly and calmly she continued to direct both schools and to help with teaching the blind. In fact, one day in December, she brought home with her someone else who was blind, bringing their total number to six. This newcomer, though, was not a child, and yet, she was.

Pauline had found Margretchen peeking out from the window of her dingy home and decided that now was the time to help the poor girl. A few times before in warmer weather, she had seen her at her mother's vegetable stand and had promised herself that some day when she was able, she would care for that neglected one. Well, Pauline was now able, and Margretchen was right there. This was the time.

Pauline knocked at the door of the wretched house and asked the mother, Frau Feichtler, whether she might take Margretchen with her and educate her. The woman was only too glad to be relieved of the girl and gladly gave her consent. Pauline stretched out her hand to Margretchen, but the girl drew back. Half-blind and mentally retarded, she stood bent and awkward, with her head turned sideways and up, squinting cautiously at Pauline. She was twenty-three years old, but her face had the expression of a small child who was both hostile and suspicious. She did not trust people. It was no wonder. For over twenty years her mother had kept her in hiding, most of the time in bed. If she did happen to show herself, the roughnecks of the streets made fun of her, threw stones at her or pushed her. Beause she was alone so much, this forlorn human being did not know how to care for herself. She was unwashed, clumsy, and helpless.

Pauline took a step closer and bent toward Margretchen, speaking kindly and slowly.

"Come with me, Margretchen. I will be very good to you. I will help you and teach you. Your mother says you may go with me and stay with me. Won't you come?"

Margretchen's face relaxed. Her eyes looked down, but slowly she put out a grimy hand. There was something in that voice...something that she never heard before...something that sounded like someone wanted her! *Her!* She longed to hear that again—and again!

Pauline quickly took the dirty, moist hand, and together the stately young lady and the handicapped one went slowly to the monastery where the school for the blind was housed. Jule's eyes popped with disbelief, and even Mathilde showed shock when Pauline brought Margretchen in.

"Please set up a large bed in the room where the blind children and I sleep," said Pauline to Mathilde. "You will surely help her, won't you, Jule?" she continued, turning to the housekeeper. "We will need some clean clothes for Margretchen. I am going to bathe her and make her look nice. Don't worry," she called to Jule and Mathilde as she caught the glances they exchanged. "I'll take care of her myself every day until she learns how." She disappeared into the bathroom with her new disheveled, un-washed pupil. Jule turned away to help Mathilde with the bed, muttering something about leaving.

At supper that evening Mathilde and Jule received another shock—this time a pleasant one. Pauline, smiling and gracious, brought Margretchen to the table. The girl was positively transformed! Although she was still standing somewhat bent and leaning to the right, shyly stealing looks at her surroundings through squinting eyes, she glowed with cleanliness. Her brown hair was now soft, clean, and neatly combed but short because Pauline had to cut away lice-infested sections. Her face, neck, and hands were ruddy and healthy-looking. Her new, pink cotton dress and soft white stockings carried the pleasant odor of fresh clothing, and her new shoes were shining. If, in time, Margretchen could be taught to stand up straight and be less fearful, she would actually make a nice appearance with her chubby pink face.

Pauline soon discovered that she and Margretchen would have to eat alone until she could teach the neglected girl the basics of table behavior. She had to teach her also how to wash herself, to brush her teeth, to care for her hair and clothes and all the other details of caring for one's body. She taught her to say "Please" and "Thank you"; also how to walk, sit, and stand. Then she taught her how to knit, to pray—and to control her temper. For Margretchen was a very angry person whose hostility had grown over the years with each new experience of rejection, dislike, and frustration. That was all she had received. That was all she could give—except to Aunt Pauline. Ah, to her, Margretchen behaved differently because Aunt Pauline was so good. Margretchen found it easy to be good when she was with Aunt Pauline because her voice told Margretchen that she liked her.

Despite her mental handicap, Margretchen learned much in a few weeks although she still had far to go. She utterly resisted Jule's stern and strong manner, but under Pauline's kind, persuasive way she learned to carry water to the kitchen for Jule. At first she would talk to no one but Pauline, but gradually she learned to repeat what she heard, to spell, to read a little, and something about God. Even Margretchen's mother smiled when Pauline told her of her daughter's progress, and little by little she, too, changed under the influence of Pauline's kindness.

Meanwhile, the Sisters of Mercy of St. Vincent had come to Paderborn in answer to the bishop's invitation, and the sight of them made Pauline's longing for religious life even more persistent. Father Boekamp, who was confessor to the Sisters of Mercy, knew of Pauline's desire and strongly suggested that she enter that order. Without delay, she applied to the priest who was superior of the Sisters of Mercy, and it was agreed that after her return from the trip she was planning to take with her sister and brothers in six months, she would enter there. The order would also assume the care of her institute for the blind and the nursery.

Pauline heaved a big sigh of relief. At last! Her one great desire was soon to be fulfilled, and her blind children and her little ones would be taken care of too! Yet, it seemed almost unreal. Everything had gone so smoothly. Would it *really* be so easy as that?

Chapter VIII

With the start of 1843, Father Gossler went to Berlin for reasons known only to himself. His business was probably for his Franciscan superiors. He had wanted his sister, Antonie, to go with him, but she had preferred to stay in Paderborn with her mother and with the children of the blind school where she was a teacher of music. Gradually, the girls whom he had recruited to live in community as Sisters of St. Clare disbanded and returned to their homes and former work.

A little more than a year had passed since Mallinckrodt's death, and now his sons and daughters gathered to settle the inheritance and their future lives. They all agreed that the house in Paderborn should be sold since no one of them wanted to keep it. By common consent George was to take Boeddeken, and the rest of the family possessions were divided peacefully and to everyone's satisfaction. With some sadness, they all knew that they would have to separate and go their own ways, but before they did so, they wanted to take a trip together for the last time.

On July first, George dismissed the servants of the household in Paderborn and took care of the sale of the house to the officials of Paderborn. He told the others that he regretted he would not be able to travel with them since he had to enroll in the agriculture college at Eldena. That would be necessary if he was to successfully care for the Boeddeken estate. Pauline, Hermann, and Bertha understood and were content to make the trip as a trio. Pauline told her brothers and sister then of her intention to enter the Sisters of Mercy on her return. Although she certainly wanted to enjoy herself on this trip, she frankly admitted that her biggest interest would be seeing large charitable institutions and the way they were managed.

The three started out by going to Braunschweig, continuing through Germany's cities to Berlin, Leipzig, Dresden. Then on to Prague in Czechoslovakia, to Austria, to northern Italy, visiting Venice, Verona, Milan, Lake Como and Lake Maggiore. They returned through Switzerland and southern Germany, seeing twenty-six places in all. Hermann was the tour master, assisted by Bertha. But, of course, Pauline managed to visit the large institutions: hospitals, day nurseries, schools for the handicapped, hospitals for the mentally ill and the like. While Hermann and Bertha went to the theater or opera, "the Boss had to go to a charitable institution to see the latest method of drying laundry," Hermann would say.

Pauline carried a diary and took many notes on what she saw and observed in these institutions. She knew how much detergent they used in their large laundries; she watched the care and the amount of oil they used in filling the night lamps for the patients and in the schools for the handicapped. All this and many other items were carefully written in her book. She also carried with her, her trusty wicker basket that she had used at Aix and Wewelsburg to carry medicine and things for the poor. In fact, she never left home without it.

Unfortunately, she misplaced her diary one day, and off it went in another coach. Bertha and Hermann had a good laugh, which Pauline did not share. But she lost no time in mourning it. She started over in a new notebook recapturing her notations from loose scraps of paper having some of the scattered information and the rest from memory. But not all the notes were of practical things. Some were descriptions of the beauties of nature she saw in the valleys and mountains. One was a romantic account of an evening boat ride on the Danube river in brilliant moonlight. She and Hermann had remained on deck for hours while Bertha went to her cabin in fatigue.

What remained vivid in Pauline's memory was her visit to the motherhouse and hospital of the Sisters of Charity in Strassburg where the hospital had 1000 beds. She also visited the prison for women where the Sisters supervised the prisoners. Even more, she remembered the combined hospital and institution for patients of mental illnesses in Vienna. It numbered 4000 beds and was staffed by Sisters of Mercy and lay persons.

Most of all, she was impressed by their visit to the stigmatic, Maria von Mörl. This lady had the gift of the wounds of our Lord in her hands, feet, and side and suffered each Friday as He had. Maria's room was connected with a convent in the valley of Kaltern, and it was there Pauline, Bertha, and Hermann saw her on a Friday when she was re-living and suffering the Passion of Jesus. Although in past history some stigmatics have been known to be false, Pauline, Bertha, and Hermann came away convinced that Maria was genuine. Aside from the wounds and the suffering, there was a devotedness to God and a humility about her that made the supernatural very evident there. Pauline believed firmly, after seeing her, that God did reveal Himself to His people in these special ways.

The three had now traveled back from Strassburg to Coblenz and were surprised to be met there by their cousin, Bertha von Hartmann. She had an important message for Hermann. Although Pauline did not know the message, just the fact that Hermann had received it somehow made her uneasy. When they arrived at Dortmund at the home of their relatives, a letter from George reached them and broke the news of coming trouble. A family council was to be held at the home, first of Uncle Joseph von Hartmann in Büren, and then at Boeddeken. All were to go to both places.

Pauline's heart twitched. She was sure it had something to do with her plan to enter the convent. She was right. As much as her relatives on both sides had been in favor of her entering the Sisters of Mercy before, they were now definitely opposed. They had learned of an occurrence in the Congregation. A change which was justified had been made. They did not believe, however, that it was best suited to Pauline and her situation to enter there. All were strongly opposed to it.

Pauline was utterly shaken and confused. What, *what* would she do? Should she treat the combined opinion and advice of the whole family, especially her brothers and sister, who had her good so much at heart, as if it were a temptation of the evil one and enter anyway? Or should she stop short on her way to the one great desire of her life which seemed so very close and give it up? What did God want?

Because this was a decision for life and because it would affect her beloved blind children, she was most hesitant and restless. She did not trust herself; she could not talk to anyone in Paderborn because the priests had taken sides, both pro and con. At the same time George and Hermann, not understanding *die Alte*, were fearful that she might enter the Sisters of Mercy if she returned to Paderborn. So they hurried her away to Boeddeken.

Later she decided to go to Münster and consult Bishop Kellermann who had been in Professor Schlüter's discussion group as a priest. He listened quietly to her own hopes and ideas and then to the objections her family had given.

"Wait, Pauline," he said gently. "Do nothing just now. As time goes on, God will give you a sign. Wait for it. Look for it."

Now she would have to inform the superior of the Sisters of Mercy that she had changed her mind. So with a heavy heart, Pauline returned to Paderborn and told the priest of her decision. Without many words of explanation, she merely stated that her family strongly opposed her entrance and that she could not now decide to act contrary to their wishes.

That done, Pauline felt as if the whole world had fallen in on her. She was utterly depressed and felt very much alone. The happy family home and circle had been dissolved because of her and her plans. Now they were all scattered. She felt uprooted and miserable. There were inner conflicts still raging within her. She felt she could never be happy again.

Her relatives tried to be exceedingly kind to her. Many of them offered to let her make her home permanently with them, but she declined because she felt impelled to give her life to God and the service of others, especially the poor. This strong inclination made her choose to live in Paderborn rather than at Boeddeken. She accepted the offer of her Uncle Fritz von Hartmann, the banker, to live in his house there. Later, however, she moved to another house near his so as to be close enough for his protection but separate enough for independence.

Despite her heartache, Pauline continued to spend the greater part of the day with the children of the nursery and with the blind. As ever, her one great source of life was the Eucharistic Jesus, and she continued receiving Holy Communion every day as she had for years. Her school enrollment, too, expanded. Finally, one autumn day, Dr. Schmidt put a question to her.

"Couldn't we write a joint letter to President von Vincke to help us in our school for the blind? He is known for his willingness to aid all types of social programs. Perhaps he would even consider making our little school for the blind the beginning of a large one for the whole province of Westphalia."

Pauline became enthusiastic over the idea and

gladly collaborated with Dr. Schmidt in writing the letter to President von Vincke, who was head of the region of Westphalia in which they were situated. Their efforts were quickly rewarded. Soon they received a gracious answer, giving them an order to find out how many blind children of school age were living in the province.

She and Dr. Schmidt set to work to do this, and discovered that there were over 400 such children in the province. After receiving their report, von Vincke obtained a grant from the government for Pauline's school. By this grant the King permitted her to occupy the former monastery of Abdinghof which had been used to store the records of the treasury. He also approved the charter of the school. Pauline's heart was filled with excitement, hope, and gratitude as she saw possibilities for the school for the blind grow more and more.

Just when things had brightened somewhat, and Pauline's old cheerfulness seemed to have returned, another threatening event blackened the outlook for her. At the end of 1843, Dr. Herman Schmidt, her great benefactor and helper, was called to Berlin to become head of the medical department of the university there and a minister of the government. He had to go there early, and his family would soon follow. Not only would Pauline lose two dear friends, but she would no longer have the professional services of his wife, Pauline's former classmate and friend, Frau Maria, as the excellent teacher of the blind. She would also be without the inspiration, advice, and expert help of the doctor who had actually been the initiator of her school for the blind and material sponsor of the nursery. At the present stage of the institute for the blind, she could not very well afford to lose such a friend. But God had not asked her opinion or wish.

It was with sad hearts that Pauline and Bertha said goodbye to the Schmidts, who promised to continue to aid them both as much as they could. They offered their house to Pauline, saying she was most welcome to stay there if she chose. By July 1844, Pauline and Bertha did move there, but Pauline stayed only a year. Hermann, meanwhile, was working as a lawyer for the district government of Münster, and George was studying at Eldena.

The joint letter that Pauline and Dr. Schmidt had written to von Vincke bore more fruit the following year. Through von Vincke, Pauline's school for the blind received corporation rights from the King, and the Westphalian government promised a contribution of 4000* Talers to the school.

But it seemed that the Lord was focusing Pauline's trust and dependence more and more on Himself, for He was taking away, one by one, those on whom she leaned for help, joint effort, and support in her works of charity. Only a year after she had lost Dr. Schmidt and his wife, President von Vincke died. Pauline truly felt that God wanted her to lean on Him and only Him. She found release from her loss by putting her feelings on paper. "Dear Lord, the fewer external supports I have remaining, the more do I rely on You who are my strength. To You I appeal with serene confidence. Send me sufferings or joys as it pleases You. Only let me say at all times: 'God be praised.'"

As if in response to her loving trust and acceptance of His plans, the Lord pleasantly surprised her.

128

* $2,760 in American money then.

Doctor Schmidt, Pauline's helper and advisor in opening the Blind Asylum

President von Bodelschwingh

She received word that the provincial government of Westphalia had decided to grant her 50,000* Talers for the foundation of the provincial blind institute of Westphalia. It was to be named after von Vincke since he had died just a short while before his fiftieth anniversary of service to the government. Now the big question was, for Pauline, whether the new institute for the blind would be Catholic, Protestant, or of all faiths.

But this subject was really not of much concern to the man who took von Vincke's place. He was President von Bodelschwingh, who thought that Pauline's school for the blind should be considered part of the Protestant one in Soest. Pauline agreed that her school should be part of the Von Vincke Provincial Institute, but insisted that it should be the Catholic branch for those blind children who were Catholic. That became the topic of many letters between Pauline and von Bodelschwingh.

Almost unnoticed, the year turned into 1845. On May 20, the first wedding in Pauline's family took place. George married a young lady named Bernardine and brought his bride to Boeddeken. There was now another Dina in the family. The touch of joy was good for Pauline, and she was glad to be part of the family reunion at the wedding; for lately she had suffered the loss of so many dear ones. Yet she wrote in her diary: "I am often lonely, and how I long for the companionship of my family—but God knows how much good this trial will do for my soul. May He shape my life as it pleases Him, and as for my brothers and sister, I gave them entirely into His keeping."

There was still another joy ahead for Pauline.

129

* $34,500 in American money then.

Ever since she had first taken Margretchen to her institute for the blind, Pauline had personally cared for the handicapped girl and patiently taught her the basic habits of cleanliness and personal care as well as some extremely simple school lessons. But Pauline was concerned most for the poor girl's relationship with God. Margretchen, at twenty-six, had never received the sacrament of Penance and Holy Eucharist. Although she was mentally retarded and therefore not capable of serious sin, she did have a small child's sense of good and bad and was aware of wrong-doing, especially of bursting into fits of temper. However, Pauline wanted more for her than merely confessing her faults and willful wrongs. She wanted her to experience the Lord's love and forgiveness so that she, too, could learn to forgive. Pauline wanted her to have the wonderful feeling of being strengthened and of starting afresh, with everything that was ugly or guilt-ridden completely destroyed.

So for the next three years she took special time to teach Margretchen the necessary ideas of sin in general, of sorrow, of trying to make up for sin, of trying to do better, of love, and of prayer. Gently, patiently she repeated and narrated the stories that would carry these across to the girl. Gently, patiently, she questioned her about them. Finally, she succeeded in getting her to memorize the words for the beginning and end of confession and the sense to ask the priest for help.

The next step, of course, was to inform the priest who would hear Margretchen's confession and have him judge whether she understood enough to receive the sacrament of Penance. That priest was the pastor of the Busdorf church which was right next to Pauline's former home. His name was Father Karl Schmidt. He had been giving religious instructions to Pauline's blind children since she had opened the school for them, and so he was acquainted with Margretchen. In fact, Father Schmidt had serious doubts as to whether Margretchen would be able to learn and understand enough to receive the sacrament. Pauline had done her best to convince him that she could, but he remained doubtful.

It was May 30, and with the uneasy feeling of "butterflies in her stomach," Pauline waited with Margretchen at the school for Father Schmidt to examine the girl. Pauline was positive that Margretchen knew and understood enough. But would she show it sufficiently to Father?

The priest entered the room. He and Pauline exchanged greetings. He greeted Margretchen too, but—and Pauline's hopes went plunging down—the girl looked away and froze into silence.

Father Schmidt began to question Margretchen, but she sat perfectly still, hands in her pockets, head turned toward Pauline. He continued to ask, but without the slightest response. Finally, Pauline broke in.

"Father, may I please try to ask her a few questions? She is more used to me, you know. I'm sure she knows the answers. I think she is just frightened."

Father Schmidt sighed and sat back. He was obviously annoyed.

"Well, yes, I suppose. She is either frightened or just doesn't understand. Go ahead. Try."

Pauline touched Margretchen's hand and leaned

131

toward her.

"Come, Margretchen, you know about sin. Tell me what you know," she said softly and kindly.

Margretchen stirred and seemed to thaw into life at the sound of Pauline's voice. She squinted at her and took a breath. Then she answered slowly, haltingly.

"That's right," said Pauline excitedly and happily, and she patted the girl's hand. Margretchen, hungry for every crumb of acceptance and success, was quick to note the positive vibrations in Pauline's voice, and that spurred her on. She answered the next questions even better, and in a little while they had covered all that was essentially necessary. Although there had been many pauses and searchings for words, Margretchen had, in the last analysis, passed the test.

Pauline sat back and waited, her hand still on Margretchen's, pressing it with joy. Father Schmidt's face was an interesting mixture of surprise and disbelief. He cleared his throat.

"Yes...well...I suppose that is sufficient. Margretchen may make her first confession. I will hear her tomorrow....But that will be as far as she will go. There is no thought of her attempting to do more." He stood up.

Pauline ignored the last part. "Oh thank you, Father," she said. "I will bring Margretchen to the church right after Mass tomorrow. I appreciate your coming very much, Father, and so does Margretchen."

The next day Pauline waited and prayed outside the confessional as Margretchen received the sacrament of Penance for the first, but not the last time.

She hugged the trembling girl as she emerged, and they both praised God in loud whispers.

That night, after everyone, including even Jule, had congratulated Margretchen, and the other children around her were in bed, Pauline told her softly to kneel in her bed just before she got under the covers.

"You must try hard to learn enough to make your First Communion, Margretchen," she said in a low voice. "But for that you will need God's special help. So every night just before you get under the covers, say 'Dear Lord, help me to get so far.'" Margretchen nodded.

Six months passed. There was no stopping this loving lady who was determined that poor Margretchen should have the Lord just as she, Pauline, did. Pauline took the girl every day and painstakingly explained the difference between ordinary bread and the bread of the Eucharist. Each day before the lesson, she prayed to Jesus in the tabernacle very especially to help her as she tried to teach Margretchen about Him in His wonderful gift of Himself in bread and wine. In her turn, each night, Margretchen knelt in her bed and the blind children heard her pray simply: "That I may get so far; that I may get so far." Soon they were all joining her.

Once more Pauline dared to approach the priest about Margretchen. "Really, Father," she pleaded, "the girl knows enough to make her first Communion. Please come to hear her. I'm sure you will agree."

Father Schmidt yielded to Pauline at last and listened as she questioned Margretchen. She really did know that Jesus is God and that the bread over which the priest speaks certain words becomes the body and blood of Jesus. She knew the sacred words. She knew she must not eat or drink before receiving Him. She knew she must prepare for receiving Jesus by trying hard to be good. She knew, too, that receiving Him would help her to be good and would bring her to heaven.

At last, Father Schmidt was satisfied. Margretchen would be permitted to receive her First Communion at Mass on the feast of All Saints! Pauline hugged the speechless girl. What a triumph! Nothing was impossible to love. God had proven that. Margretchen's mother attended the Mass and with tears watched her daughter receive Communion.

Later Pauline wrote in her notes: "With humility and charity one can do *a great deal*; forbearance and patience, too, are important virtues." People had tried to warn Pauline about the futility of trying to prepare someone like Margretchen for the sacraments. But she could not be stopped. Her argument was: "Should an individual be regarded as a total imbecile because she has never been taught or even been in contact with human kindness? This child, too, has a soul, and I trust that grace can operate powerfully, even in the soul of one who is retarded."

The grace of God and the love of "Aunt Pauline" and her associates did work powerfully in Margretchen; enough to help her work and get along sufficiently well if not perfectly with others, to live in the institute for the blind for fifty-one years. She lived to be eighty-four years old.

On August 1, 1845 the bishop, Franz Drepper, made Pauline happy by allowing her to move into the monastery to live there so that she could be with her blind children day and night. Bertha, however, did not go with Pauline, but chose to live with Uncle Fritz, the banker, because she did not like Pauline's new home. Pauline lived there for a full year. Meanwhile, the children of the nursery also continued to come there during the day. Pauline had only one great concern and that was the physical, mental, and spiritual good of all these precious children.

Chapter IX

It was Easter time, 1845. Pauline was much engrossed with the progress of her nursery and institute for the blind in the Capuchin monastery. His Grace, Bishop Franz Drepper, was also much engrossed with progress in the Capuchin monastery but for a different reason. He was planning to turn the monastery into a seminary, and he had told Pauline that at the time he gave her permission to use it in 1842. He had already obtained the services of Countess Bocholz, who would be in charge of the household and was even now moving in. It came, then, as no surprise when Pauline received a message from the bishop telling her that by Easter, 1847, her quarters and those of the children at the monastery would have to be vacated. It would be no easy matter to find a new place for the two schools since there were now 120 children in the nursery and about eight blind children. With the staff of teachers and helpers, it would mean needing even more space.

For although the King had given her the old Abdinghof monastery to use for the schools, it was not really practical at all. The old farm house, upon being investigated, was found to be totally unsuited for classrooms, and the thought of renovating it was out of the question because of the great expense. Besides, there was neither a garden or a playground, which were absolute necessities. The only good that the old building could be to them was as a source of income from rent collected from occupants. Meanwhile, Pauline was sure that in two years' time she should find something somehow. She would have to.

Then came a surprise in late fall. On October 14, President von Bodelschwingh visited Pauline and her two schools in the Capuchin monastery. Unlike von Vincke, he envisioned the provincial institute for the blind as the house in Soest, which was Protestant, with Pauline's house merely added to it.

Pauline was greatly concerned about the religious denomination of her branch, resolved to oppose to the very end, if need be, that it should also be Protestant like the one at Soest. Previous to her work with the blind, she had certainly worked in charitable projects that were of mixed religions, and that had posed no problem for her since the organizations were private, and the children had been living at home. But now, with a provincial institute for the blind, which was public in the sense of being conducted by the government, and where the children lived away from home, parental rights were involved and must be protected. The parents who put their children in her branch of the provincial institute were Catholic and had a right to have their children instructed only in the Catholic faith. The parents of children in Soest were Protestant, and their right to have their children instructed in that faith was being honored. To force her branch to teach the Protestant faith, would be, to Pauline, an injustice she could not tolerate. So she had quickly written to von Bodel-schwingh, telling him her views and urging that her branch be Catholic. He had answered her objections just as quickly, without yielding in any way. But Pauline would not stop. She had kept on writing about it, hoping to influence him. Now the important man was here to see her. Would the meeting make things better or worse?

Von Bodelschwingh was impressed with what he saw and knew in a short time that Pauline was some-one to be reckoned with. He would have to find some way of breaking her influence.

Dr. Schmidt was doing his part for Pauline's cause in the legislature at Berlin. He agreed with her arguments. The blind children's parents certainly had the right of demanding that their religion be taught to their children. But the blind children them-selves should have their cross of blindness lightened by being taught *their* faith which would help them carry their burden more easily through their lives. Then, too, merely allowing the institute to be Catho-lic during Pauline's directorship was not enough to satisfy her. It must continue during the terms of all her successors. All this Dr. Schmidt kept in mind during the long drawn-out struggle in the legislature and between Pauline and von Bodelschwingh.

Despite her assertive nature and choleric tem-perament, which were certainly drawn into action by this conflict, Pauline was working constantly and carefully to moderate these characteristics. She had made it a goal to become more like Jesus whom she loved with her whole heart. Each month she spent a day in retreat, going over her conduct prayerfully, renewing her last retreat resolutions. She read the notes on her faults written from time to time. Those were what she must improve. For instance, she had been much too busy and had taken too little time for prayer. She had been impatient and had punished a child too severely. She had been upset and excited when dealing with the medical supervisor and had given him some sharp answers. Pauline determined that she would, with the help of the Eucharistic Jesus, be kinder and milder in dealing with others.

Pauline had also been concerned that Bertha would mature gracefully and be able to lead a happy Christian life in the world, independent of Pauline. She wanted this so that Bertha could manage successfully in the event that Pauline did enter the convent. But her worries on that score were soon over, for on April 12, 1846, Bertha now twenty, was engaged to Alfred Hüffer, a college classmate of Hermann's. Pauline was happy. Alfred Hüffer was a district judge and a Catholic of excellent character. "This man will lead you to heaven," she told Bertha.

By this time Pauline's patience with Berlin was growing thin, and since von Bodelschwingh had indicated he had no personal objection to having Sisters in her schools, she decided to try to get some. She left the schools in the hands of her sister, Bertha, and travelled with Anna Everken, her assistant, to Aix-la-Chapelle. There she would see Mother Clara Fey, her old classmate, and foundress of the Sisters of the Poor Child Jesus.

Although the first Sisters of Mother Clara were living in community, they did not yet wear a religious habit since they were still awaiting the approval of their order by the archbishop. Pauline and her companion were much impressed by the holy lives of the Sisters. She begged Mother Clara and their priest director to take over the management of the institute of the blind at Paderborn. But since they were just beginning and things at Paderborn were still unsettled, the Sisters advised Pauline to go on to Conflans to see Mother Barat instead.

Pauline and Anna did so and were graciously received by her. In fact, they spent three weeks with the Religious of the Sacred Heart there, taking part in their religious exercises and attending the instructions given in the novitiate. They were also allowed to read their holy rule. All this was to be of great help to Pauline later on.

Pauline was allowed to visit again with her good friend, Anna von Lommessen, now a member of this order. Her words gave Pauline so much encouragement that she was able to discuss with Mother Barat the possibility of their taking charge of the institute for the blind in Paderborn.

In spite of the many difficulties this would involve, Mother Barat agreed to do so provided Pauline could clear the matter with the government of Germany. She lost no time in writing to Dr. Schmidt who was a Privy-Councilor in Berlin, telling him of their willingness and asking his aid in getting the permission for a French order of Sisters to take the school in Paderborn.

But it would take some time before she could receive his answer. So Pauline and Anna thought it would be profitable for them to visit large institutions in Paris while waiting for the reply. Each morning they left Conflans for Paris and each evening returned there. They saw institutes for the blind, hospitals, homes for the aged, orphanages, convents, even the prison-house. They also visited some of the boarding-schools conducted by these Sisters. Between their tours and participation in the religious exercises at Conflans, the time passed quickly for them.

Finally, the answer came. Dr. Schmidt was sure that the government would not give permission for a French order of Sisters to take over the institute in Paderborn. Pauline, greatly disappointed, thanked the Sisters and began the journey home.

But she would not give up. They stopped again at Aix and once more begged the Sisters of the Poor Child Jesus to accept the institute for the blind. Both Mother Clara and Father Sartorius advised Pauline to follow their example and found a congregation herself for her work. Mother Clara told her that she had too few Sisters to take up the care of the blind.

"Mother Clara," said Pauline eagerly," please accept me into your congregation. Then I could care for the blind."

Clara looked at her long and seriously.

"Pauline," she said slowly, "I must say something that will be painful for you. But it is painful also for me. I know, though, that you will accept it as it is meant—sincerely and charitably. I must be honest with you."

She stopped and took a deep breath, then continued.

"I thought this over carefully and concluded that

141

if ever you or Anna von Lommessen asked for admission to this congregation, I would not feel competent to deal with such forceful natures as yours and hers, and there would have to be another place for me. I could not exact obedience from you because it would exceed my ability."

Pauline could scarcely hide the surprise in her face, but she accepted what Mother Clara said in all humility. There was silence for a moment between the two women.

Finally, Pauline said, "I understand, Mother Clara, and I'm grateful for your honesty. But I really cannot begin my own religious community."

"Perhaps you would like to apply to the Sisters of St. Charles Borromeo who have an orphanage and home for the elderly here in Aix. I will gladly take you to them," said Mother Clara.

"Yes, I would at least like to visit them," answered Pauline.

So she and Anna went with Mother Clara to the two houses of the Sisters of St. Charles. On the way back, Mother Clara turned to Pauline.

"Pauline, go to see Bishop Claessen of Cologne. He has been your long-time friend and the counsellor for your family. He has great influence with the Sisters of St. Charles. He was their confessor for years. Tell him everything, and I am sure he will advise you well," she said earnestly.

Pauline felt an urging to respond to Mother Clara's advice, and somehow she could not resist. Once more she and Anna prepared to travel.

They arrived at Cologne and took rooms at a hotel, going immediately to the residence of the auxiliary bishop. But Bishop Claessen was out of town.

Pauline, however, decided to wait for his return because she felt so much the need to talk to him.

She and Anna were doing their best not to be bored on the afternoon of the following day when a bellboy knocked at the door to tell them that the bishop had arrived at the hotel and wished to visit them. With that, Bishop Claessen stepped through the door, and Pauline gasped with delight.

"Come," he said, "you must be my guests. I will send the boys up for your bags. Stay at my house, and we shall have a nice visit. It will be like old times," and he smiled at Pauline in his familiar kind way.

That evening after dinner, he listened with full and sympathetic attention to Pauline's story of her call, her hopes, her frustration, her confusion, and Mother Clara's suggestion of the Sisters of St. Charles.

"Pauline," he said, as he sat gently tapping the tips of his long, fine fingers together. "I shall need some time to think over what you have told me and to pray for whatever guidance the Lord will deign to give me for you. Suppose you stay here for a few days and relax. I have a copy of the rule of the Sisters of St. Charles Borromeo which you can read through. It will give you a good idea of their life and mission."

Pauline needed no coaxing to remain there, and the two ladies enjoyed their stay. Pauline, again, was given another opportunity by Providence to learn still more about the rules of religious congregations by reading through the rule of the Sisters of St. Charles.

The bishop told Pauline early in her stay that, as

The first little Motherhouse in Paderborn

The first Blind Asylum in Paderborn

much as he esteemed the Sisters of that order, he did not think they were suited for the situation in Paderborn. They were a nursing order, used to large institutions. The institute for the blind was very small and undeveloped. Besides, he was sure that the authorities both of that order and of the city and Church would not agree to their transfer to Paderborn since the bishop there had already brought the Sisters of Mercy into Paderborn for charitable works. So there was no need for Pauline to go on to Nancy in France to the motherhouse of the Sisters of St. Charles Borromeo.

Pauline continued to wait while the kindly bishop prayed for light. After a few days, he met with her.

"Pauline, I have earnestly thought over the whole matter, have carefully considered it before God, and have arrived at the definite conclusion that it is best and God's will that you yourself remain with the work which, until now, He has blessed at your hands and has taken under His protection. Devote to the small beginning that necessary love, perseverance, and care which it stands so greatly need of for its continuance and growth. You know all the circumstances perfectly, and God has given you the confidence of the men desirous of assisting the blind.

"But go hand in hand with Holy Church. Upon your return home, speak to Bishop Drepper, to Vicar General Boekamp, to your pastor at the Busdorf Church, Reverend Father Schmidt. These men are acquainted with local conditions and the whole state of affairs and whatever they may not know of the latter, you can mention to them. Tell them what advice the Auxiliary Bishop of Cologne, after mature deliberation and prayer, has given you and ask them

144

whether they are not of the same mind: namely, that it would be good for you and those associates who wish to join you to dedicate your time and energy to the poor blind. Ask the Most Reverend Bishop whether to this end he is willing to give his approval and the blessing of Holy Church for the founding of a religious congregation. I trust that he will do so and that God will permit the views of these men to coincide with mine. And then just go ahead calmly and discreetly, but with determination. God will prosper the undertaking; but if, contrary to my expectations, it should not succeed, then come to me, I will assign you a sphere of activity in my diocese."

Pauline could not take her eyes off Bishop Claessen's face, and when he had finished speaking, she sat still, staring at him. Had she heard right? Had he really said to "found a religious congregation"?

As if he read her questioning mind, the bishop smiled and said, "Yes, Pauline. I said *'Found a religious congregation.'* God will help you." Pauline was still in something of a daze. This was a decision totally unexpected by her. Yet, the more she thought about it, the more it seemed the right thing to do. Best of all, it left her peaceful, which was the greatest sign that it came from God.

As they began their homeward journey to Paderborn, Pauline was filled with strange emotions which increased when she saw the city. As they rode through it, she felt an inner strength, a sense of certainty and pronounced vocation for the work she had begun. Here she would hear the voice of the bishop who would speak God's unmistakable will for her. She would go slowly but confidently forward.

The blind children were delighted to have Aunt Pauline with them again, and soon things were back to normal. But for Pauline "normal" meant concern for the immediate future, especially finding a place for the children of the nursery to learn and a place for the blind to live as well as to learn.

At last, she got an idea. She talked with her Uncle Fritz, the banker, and by contract, exchanged with him her holdings of the property in Minden for a small house of his and its garden right outside the city gate. It was an attractive, two-story structure. But it would already be too small for her great crowd of 120 nursery children besides the eight blind children and the staff needed to care for them.

It was decided that sixty of the poorest children among the 120 would be selected to spend the entire day at the garden house. The eight blind, the teacher of the nursery, the rest of the staff and Pauline, making twenty in all, would reside there permanently. This meant that there were eighty persons to cook for, and place for twenty beds had to be found. Pauline found it, and in September, 1846 they all left the monastery and moved into the little garden house.

Close to this house was another garden with a large house for sale. It was owned by Fräulein Seraphine Meyer and was also near the Kassel Gate to the city. Pauline had her eye on it immediately. It would make a good home for the blind, but—she had no funds to buy it. She knew it was no use to ask Hermann, who was the administrator of their father's estate, for the money. Although he was sympathetic to her charitable works, Hermann knew that the Boss had too big a heart and would give even when it wasn't prudent. So she wrote to von Bodelschwingh, asking for government money either to build a house or to buy the Meyer house. He flatly refused both requests. She would have to think of something else.

After they were fairly well settled in the Hartmann house, Pauline went to see Bishop Drepper. She told him of Bishop Claessen's advice and then waited breathlessly. The aging bishop received the news with no surprise and little enthusiasm. He told her to see her retreat-master, Father Tewes, and arrange to make a retreat. After that, she was to see his Vicar General, Father Boekamp, for further direction.

Pauline arrived home with mixed feelings. She was still at peace and confident in the Lord but a bit deflated in face of the bishop's coolness. But all that was forgotten for the moment when she came upon the sorry sight in the dining-room. The drawers of several cupboards were standing open with cloths and cutlery scattered about and many other things strewn around. Someone had broken in. Pauline immediately looked for the valuable silverware of the Mallinckrodt family. Part of it was gone. Some belonged to her sister Bertha, and Pauline was going to give her the rest as a wedding present. Fifty Talers that Fritz von Coffrane had sent Pauline for the blind were also gone. They would have to be more careful. Fortunately they were able to foil the burglars twice after that in attempts to steal the rest.

In November Pauline went to make retreat under the direction of Father Tewes. It seems that both he and the director of the teachers' institute wanted Pauline as the leader of their groups. Father Tewes was the spiritual director of many teachers who had formed an association in order to lead a more spiritual life. He hoped to start a semi-religious group of women teachers modelled after the Third Order of St. Francis with Pauline at the head. At present the chosen leader of the group was an excellent teacher named Agatha Rath. The director of the teachers' institute also wanted his prospective teachers under a woman's guidance. He felt that Pauline and her schools could give them that. Perhaps she would establish a boarding school for his students too.

During retreat Father Tewes told Pauline of his plan and asked her to seriously consider whether she felt called to head his project of a Third Order and whether she felt qualified to administer a model school for the newest findings and methods in education.

"Now before making any decisions, let us both resolve to do some serious and prayerful thinking from now until Christmas. Give yourself as a complete sacrifice to God, and at every Communion from now until Christmas, unite your prayer with that of Mary as you say 'Behold the handmaid of the Lord. Be it done to me according to Thy word!' The exact words are not essential, but try to make a total offering of yourself to God at least once each day," he told her.

Pauline's heart, during the retreat, was full of thanks for the goodness of God. She meditated much on the interior qualities that her congregation would and must have and was wonderfully happy with the vocation the Lord had given her.

"The call, Lord, is too exalted to have been chosen by myself. If You choose to make me Your instrument, You will enlighten Father Tewes to give me the right direction, and You will have the Bishop and the Vicar-General give me encouragement. All things must proceed from Holy Mother Church if they are to glorify You; without her sanction I should not dare to . . . .May I be one of Your chosen ones! . . .May all my actions henceforth flow from charity," she wrote in her retreat notes.

But once again a matter which had troubled her at her very first retreat with Father Tewes in 1842 returned. Would daily Holy Communtion be permitted in her congregation?

"In this matter as in all things else, I submit in advance to what obedience will ordain; whatever Father Tewes, and later, Holy Mother Church prescribe . . . .After having expressed my opinion, it will be my obligation to leave all the rest to God . . . .I realize that daily Communion cannot be the rule in a religious congregation, but there may be exceptions . . . .I implore You, dear Lord, let daily Holy Communion be permitted in our congregation."* These were her thoughts in answer to that burning question.

After retreat Pauline gave the Vicar General, Father Boekamp, the plan outlined by her retreat master for founding a religious order. He, too, like the bishop, seemed little impressed. But when Pauline told him that she was seeking the approval of the Church as a sign that this was really what *God* wanted, he responded more kindly. "We are witnessing new shoots and branches everywhere in the Church, so why should we not welcome another branch which will give joy to the Church?" he said.

Then she spoke to her confessor, Father Karl Schmidt, who, by contrast, was most eager to hear

149

---

* Later, on December 20, 1905, Pope Pius X permitted daily Communion for all Catholics who prepare properly.

her plans.

"We priests have a solemn obligation to encourage every good work which will add to the Church's glory. Far be it from me to stand in the way. Put yourself at the disposal of God....Your ardent longings have been instilled into your heart by God Himself....

"It is immaterial to me whether you follow your own plans or those of Father Tewes.... All our plans should be deeply rooted in God, so that even the failure of our most cherished wishes should never disturb our peace.... Give yourself wholly to the Lord. Ask Him to dispose of you and your plans according to His good pleasure."

She had discussed her future plans with the Church authorities, and now Pauline felt more at ease than ever, placing everything in the hands of the Lord who was directing her. Once again she became absorbed with her beloved work for the children.

Keenly disappointed about the refusal of funds to purchase the Meyer garden house for the blind, Pauline decided she would go from house to house to beg for money. But before she could do so, she and the blind children received a visit a few days before Christmas from an old priest who was very fond of children. He was Father Adami, and he knew that he had not much longer to live. He thoroughly enjoyed the children's company, especially those who were deaf-mutes or blind. His one great pleasure was to show them every sign of love possible.

Father Adami told Pauline that he wanted to remember these children in his will. He himself spoke of Fräulein Meyer's house, saying that because she was forced to sell in an emergency, the price would not be so high. Pauline was surprised and elated. That evening she told the children to pray for Father Adami each day because he was so good to them.

Actually, his feeling about his death soon came true. He died on January 6, 1847 at the very time when the children were praying the litany of the sick. That morning the priest's housekeeper called Pauline from the church to tell her of Father Adami's death and of the contents of his will. He had left 6000 Talers* to the school for the blind and a smaller sum for the nursery.

Pauline was delighted! She and the children would pray for that dear old priest for many, many days to come. Without waiting any longer, she immediately placed her bid on the Meyer house. It was just in time and only by a hair's breadth that she received the promise of the house, for another buyer had already put in his bid, too. With a touch of triumph she wrote to von Bodelschwingh: "I regret that this announcement will not meet with your expectations, but the Reverend Adami has willed 6000 Talers to the institute of the blind of Paderborn only. I have immediately used it to purchase the Meyer house as our new institute." Neither he nor anyone else could stop her.

* About $4,141.00 in American money at that time.

Chapter X

President von Bodelschwingh was downright angry over Pauline's purchase of the Meyer house and let her know it very definitely. In his own mind he planned to remove her from the control of the two schools she was conducting but merely told her that he would like to give her a lifetime honorary position on the board. She knew, however, that this position had no voting privilege and she would thus be made incapable of affecting any decisions. She sat down and wrote to him again, telling him she could not accept the offer of the honorary position.

"It was not for a distinction such as this that I renounced my former mode of life, the pleasures of society, and of my family. As far as the welfare of the children is concerned, I am willing to make any sacrifice. Indeed, I would not hesitate to withdraw entirely if I were convinced that they would fare better under the management of another. You will realize, I am sure, that I care nothing at all for an honorary position in the schools about to be reorganized. The only thing which appeals to me is participation in the activities of the schools." She sent a similar letter to Dr. Schmidt in Berlin. But he had been ill for some time.

Not long after, Pauline severed the school for the blind and the nursery from the aid and control of the Ladies' Guild. She paid from her own private means for food for the eighty persons and for the expenses of the staff. Other changes took place too. Jule, the housekeeper, retired, and two young girls were hired to help Mathilde, and Anna Everken also helped with the work.

In January, 1847 Father Tewes recommended to Agatha Rath, the leader of his group of teachers, that she give up her teaching job in Brilon and join Pauline. Pauline's vocation, he declared, was genuine. Pauline wrote to Agatha, welcoming her. "I can, of course, not offer you much more than suffering and a cross—but I can give you love, gladly and freely," she said.

Agatha was won over to the idea, but when she announced that she was leaving to go to Paderborn to teach the blind, the school board of Brilon offered to increase her salary and give her an assistant. But she refused their generous offer. When her carriage left Brilon, one of the little boys of the school ran a long way after the carriage, trying to persuade her to return.

Actually, only Father Tewes and Pauline's sister, Bertha, knew what Bishop Claessen had advised Pauline to do. The secret had been kept well. But it would not be long before it would be known to at least a few more young ladies.

The daily routine life of those in the two houses where Pauline and her helpers worked was pleasant indeed. Their genuine love spread its own brightness to the hearts of the blind and the nursery children. This love came from an almost tangible union with God that was fostered by Pauline and her associates. The atmosphere was vibrantly cheerful.

Uncle Fritz would occasionally visit his former garden house, especially on holidays. Pauline would set up tables under the huge evergreen trees, and he would tell the blind children some of his jolly stories or his spooky ones. Sometimes, in the autumn, they would have an outing in the woods. Another time they went to Höxter in a large hay wagon decorated with flowers and branches. There a teacher put some rooms at their disposal for two days. They even went on a boat ride down the Weser river.

One day, they had just returned from a lovely autumn outing. The children were laughing and talking as they jumped from the hay wagon into Pauline's waiting arms. A few other teachers who had stayed home were standing near the house, watching the happy group. One little blind girl, exuberant with the fun she had had, ran recklessly toward the teachers. She flung her arms around one of them and exclaimed, "Oh, if only you were one of the blind children, you could have been with us! We had such a good time!"

But for Pauline there was trouble ahead. The month of March took another dear friend from her. Bishop Claessen died in Cologne. He who had consecrated her to Mary at her First Communion and had later told her to found her own congregation was now with God.

Von Bodelschwingh, meanwhile, was busy with the Protestant branch of the institute for the blind at Soest. Pauline, too, was busy, writing to him about the annexation of her little branch of the institute in Paderborn, and the correspondence with him was long, wearisome, and seemingly useless. Often she was obliged to attend meetings with Bodelschwingh at Soest and Münster, and they were stormy ones. At last there were final agreements, concessions, and compromises to be made on both sides, but Pauline held fast to the right of her institute to be Catholic.

The government commission, headed by Bodelschwingh, finally opened the Protestant branch of the institute for the blind at Soest on March 15, 1847. It was then that Pauline presented to the commission the architect's plan for enlarging the Meyer house that she had bought for the blind. But they rejected both the plan and the estimated cost of it.

Pauline's strong sense of justice was keenly hurt by this treatment, and she inwardly rebelled against it. But she took her feelings in hand and managed them with prayer. "Your cross, O Lord, is our hope in life and in death. We shall seek the kingdom of God with courage and confidence," she whispered.

Ten days later Bodelschwingh discussed with Pauline the relation that her private institute for the blind would have with the provincial institute. That seemed to clear the air somewhat, and Pauline went away feeling that she had made her point about keeping her institute Catholic.

But her battle with Bodelschwingh was by no means over. With the coming of May, he informed her that he wanted half of the 6000 Talers Father Adami had willed to the Paderborn institute for the blind. That half was to go to the Protestant institute at Soest. Pauline really had to control her anger. She told him that there was no way that she could, in conscience, give him that money. Father Adami, a Catholic priest, had willed it to the blind children of Paderborn's institute and to no other. The money already belonged to Fraülein Meyer in payment for her house, and the matter was closed.

At times like these Pauline's lively temperament and strong will were severely tested. She was a person who reacted impulsively to people and situations, showing her joy, sorrow, humor, anger as they arose in her. So when she was involved in controversy, as was frequent now with Bodelschwingh, she found it very difficult to be controlled and calm, in spite of her kindness. Her struggle to control her temper was not a quick victory, and it took time until she achieved serene composure.

In August she transferred all the assets of her private school and the sum of her personal money to the Catholic division of the von Vincke Institute. This amounted to 18,600 Talers*. Final negotiations for affiliating her private institute with the provincial one took a favorable turn at last. The legal matters were completed; her institute would remain Catholic. The day for the opening of the Catholic branch of the provincial institute for the blind was set: December 6, 1847.

All during the autumn months, preparations for this big event were being made in the Meyer house. Many dignitaries such as the Prussian Minister von Florwell, President von Borries of Minden, the Lord Lieutenant of Münster, President von Bodelschwingh, Baron von Lilien-Borg, Proprietor Loper,

* $12,834 in American money.

and Count Rintelen of the Superior Court, and members of the Estates Commission were invited and had indicated that they would come. Pauline was quite excited and was very busy, arranging things.

"Pauline has a talent for organizing things of that kind. She is looking forward to the day as though it were her wedding day," Bertha wrote to her fiancé, Alfred Hüffer.

But Pauline was not to be there for the great event. On December 4, the members of the Estates Commission stepped into the von Hartmann garden house where Pauline and the staff were living with the children. She wanted to submit to them the inventory that would be turned over to the Catholic branch and to take them into the little Meyer house and its lovely garden purchased for the blind. Leading the way, she started down the stairs that led into the kitchen and suddenly stumbled. She fell a few steps, grabbed the bannister, and went down, with her foot twisted under her. A sudden sharp pain surged like lightening from her foot up to her head, and for a few moments everything went black.

When she regained consciousness, the gentlemen immediately helped her to sit up while she lifted her foot out and forward with great effort. She grimaced a little and decided it was better to remain seated on the steps for a little while. One of the men had already gone for the doctor.

When Doctor Everken arrived, he examined the foot. It was broken. He set it immediately, and then with Hermann, who had been called to the scene, carried her to her room.

"Fraülein," said the doctor," it is best that you go to bed with that foot."

"Yes, Pauline," affirmed Hermann, "you should."

"Thank you, gentlemen," said Pauline firmly. "But there is too much to take care of at present. Let me just stay here in this chair and rest for a bit. I shall be all right. I can go to bed after our business is settled."

Hermann knew from the look on the Boss' face that it was no use arguing. He nudged the doctor. "Let her do it," he said out of the corner of his mouth.

"Very well," said the doctor. "But you must put your foot up on that other chair and keep cold compresses on it to keep the swelling down. Those are my orders, Fraülein, and I ask you to comply."

Pauline nodded and gingerly raised the foot onto the chair they placed in front of her. Hermann went to get the compress.

Two hours later, she received the members of the Estates Commission and transacted necessary business with them until eleven p.m. She spent the night in that chair and the next day met again with the Estates Commission until everything was taken care of. She was much relieved when they left and she could finally, with Bertha's help, go to bed with her broken foot.

"Bertha dear," she said, sitting propped up with pillows, "have them bring the blind children here to me. I know they must be upset about my accident. If they hear me, they will feel better. Besides, I want to practice their songs one more time."

So the blind children gathered about her bed, and she told them that Aunt Pauline was fine. She would just have to be in bed some days while the broken foot mended.

"And now," she said brightly, "let's go over our songs once more. We want to do our very best, don't we?"

Then they sang, cheered by their beloved Aunt Pauline and wanting to please her. They sang as beautifully as only blind children can sing, with the keenness of hearing and sureness of tone, and sweet, bell-like clearness they alone possess.

"Very good!" said Pauline and she clapped for them. "Now go, children, and do your best—for the Lord."

Before the ceremony she had many visitors who expressed their sympathy. Not least among them was von Bodelschwingh himself who requested permission to do the honors of the opening in her place and told her he was sincerely sorry she could not be there to do so herself. But those that pleased her most were the visits of Bishop Franz Drepper and of Father Langenohl.

Father Langenohl had lived for a long time on her Grandmother von Hartmann's estate at Borchen, acting as house chaplain. He knew of her devotion to the Blessed Sacrament and realized that it would be very painful for her to be deprived of Holy Communion while she was confined to bed. He graciously offered to bring her Communion daily. This made her so happy that even her pain was eased.

Father Langenohl kept his promise and brought her Holy Communion each day, rain or snow. On Sundays and holydays, when he could not come because of other demands, two priests from the seminary took turns doing so at his request.

Someone also stayed with her during the ceremonies and refused to leave her. It was Bertha, her

Bertha, Pauline's younger sister

sister. In fact, Bertha stayed with her always and was there at her side day and night to take care of *die Alte* during all the long weeks of her convalescence.

The opening ceremonies of the Catholic branch of the von Vincke Institute for the blind proceeded with great success. The children sang, the speeches were given, the dinner for fifty-four was served, but not without thought of Pauline. In his speech, von Bodelschwingh praised her and Dr. Schmidt enthusiastically and was loudly applauded. At the climax of the dinner, he made a toast in honor of Pauline in which everyone heartily joined.

Later a contract was signed. It made Pauline the head of the school and Agatha Rath its head teacher. They were to be assisted by a board of three elected members which would include the Vicar General, Father Boekamp, as a permanent member. Pauline was the fourth member. She was given honorary status with lifetime tenure and voting privilege. It was the happy ending of an exciting event that Pauline would not forget.

Because her fracture was complicated, Pauline's recovery was slow, and she had to spend a long time in bed. The winter, too, was severe, and there was much ice and snow. Because it was impossible for the little children in the city to reach her school at the city gate, the nursery was closed until Easter.

But Pauline was uneasy and dissatisfied with that. She heard of a house which was for sale in a place called "Poor People's Corner" in the inner city, and she wanted to see it. Bertha and the others shook their heads, but Pauline insisted.

It would be no easy thing to take her into the city, but she wanted to go. So, tall and heavy as she was, they got her to the gate on a sled. Then, with the help of six people, they dragged her onto Uncle Fritz's sleigh, and all were on their way to the Pader river where the house was located. But Pauline soon saw that the house was unsuitable for a school, and since the very cold weather lasted longer than usual, the vacation was prolonged until it became warmer.

The coming of the new year 1848 found Pauline bound to her room with the disabled foot as before, but the lady herself was very busy. She was busy reading the rules of other congregations, learning how a religious community's life was regulated. She had obtained the rules of the Sisters of the Poor Child Jesus, of the Sisters of Divine Providence, of the Sisters of Mercy. These she studied carefully. With the help of Father Boekamp, the Vicar General, she obtained some of the early rules of monastic orders on which the rule of modern congregations was based. She discussed them with the Vicar General, and they agreed on choosing the Rule of St. Augustine. On this Pauline would base the rule of her new order.

As she read, she leaned more and more toward the idea of a new order rather than of leading a semi-religious union like the Third Order of St. Francis that Father Tewes was proposing. That was not for her. She remembered the words that Bishop Claessen had spoken to her as the representative of God: "Remain with the work you are doing and which God has so manifestly blessed under your direction." If she were to follow Father Tewes' group, it would mean consolidating teachers into a spiritual union, but there would be much more to do toward professional and personal rights and privileges. She would not be able to stay with her work for the blind, and she must. Nor could she expect her little congregation to both care for the poor and blind children and also work for the interests of a partly lay group like the Third Order. So, having settled that question in her own mind, she was able to tell Father Tewes that she could not take over his group and that she must stay only with the blind children.

Sure now of her own choice, she was not so sure of Agatha Rath. Agatha was a lady that Pauline highly respected and esteemed. She was an excellent teacher of the blind and a lovely person to live with. Pauline was experiencing that first hand right now. She knew Agatha possessed good judgment and allowed her to confer personally with Father Tewes. Pauline would find it difficult to part with her. But she had no need to worry. Agatha chose to remain permanently with Pauline.

Not only did Agatha remain with Pauline, but she also recruited another candidate for their budding order. This was Maria Schlüter, an experienced nurse from Brilon. She had served during the cholera epidemic in Silesia in the hospitals and was also a member of a small Franciscan community in Münster where she had been elected superior. But now she wanted to be a member of Pauline's group and gladly joined them in Paderborn. She was there only a few weeks when the bishop of Breslau came and asked her to consider returning to Münster. But she told him gently and respectfully that she was sure her future work lay here with the children and Pauline. Anna Everken, too, had thoughts of joining Pauline as a religious, but her health was very delicate. Pauline was not sure that Anna would be able to endure the demands that woud be made on her physically.

More and more they were drawn together as the year wore on. Pauline, Mathilde, Agatha, Maria, and Anna would sit together in the garden in the evening when the children were in bed and everything was quiet. Then they would sometimes discuss the habit they would wear.

"It must be nothing conspicuous," said Pauline, and she looked at Agatha in her neat and dignified teacher's dress. Anna caught her look and then remarked that Mother Barat, too, had worn a similar dress.

After a few more comments, they all agreed. Yes, they would adopt the uniform currently worn by all teachers as their habit. The little white bonnet Pauline was wearing would be a perfect headpiece over which a thin black veil could be added. To cover the frontal hair, a linen strip several inches wide would be inserted in the bonnet across the forehead.

"It would be nice to keep the white linen collar and cuffs," said Agatha.

"Oh yes," piped little Mathilde, "and do you know what? A large black cloak for street wear," she said smiling.

"And a white one for special, solemn occasions," said Maria, her eyes twinkling.

They were already observing community life, too. There were set times for spiritual reading and meditation, and they put limits on their outings and errands. Following the directive of the bishop, Pauline accepted the role of superior of the little community, and the others obeyed her most willingly. When she consulted them and asked their opinion, they gave it but preferred to act according to hers. Was it perhaps the answer to Pauline's prayer? Often she brought everything to God as she had learned years before as a child, and not the least was a plea to be able to get along with others. "Lord," she prayed, "let me win the hearts of those with whom I must deal." In September of 1848 the small community made a retreat together, and from that time on, they began to call each other *Sister*.

There was, however, so much trouble and unrest politically in Germany in 1848 that it was called the "year of the revolutions." In spring a revolution in Paris had overflowed the boundary into Germany and was brewing there. Then von Bodelschwingh, now won over to Pauline's cause, was concerned that the political trouble might cause harm and delay by the government to Pauline's plans for the institute of the blind and her new little congregation. Though he was a Protestant, Bodelschwingh was a man of Christian principles and truly wanted to see Pauline's religious community grow. Just when she had won him over, however, Bodelschwingh was promoted, taken from his local office, and called to Berlin as a member of the government ministry.

Once again she had lost a friend, and Pauline was somewhat disturbed. Her only solution was prayer. Often she could be seen kneeling before the tabernacle, a note in one hand, while she gestured with the other, presenting her problem as eloquently as possible before the Lord. "Dear Lord," she would say, "bend the hearts of the great ones of this world so that they may do whatever pleases You. Let me confer with You in all matters before transacting business."

With the coming of summer, things turned in

Pauline's favor for the nursery. Taxes on grain and other products were discontinued, leaving the house where the taxes were collected empty except for the living quarters of the guard. This toll house would be a good place to put the nursery since it was closer to the children's homes than her garden house. Pauline quickly applied to the city for renting the empty house. She also applied for a playground to be made near it. Hopefully now, the day nursery would no longer have to be closed in winter.

Two big events were yet to be celebrated by Pauline. In autumn, happy preparations were being made in the home of her aunt, Dina von Hartmann, for the wedding of Bertha to Alfred Hüffer. With happiness and gratitude, Pauline saw her little sister married on October 12, to this good Christian gentleman of kind and cheery disposition. No longer would she have to be concerned about Bertha's future. She was well taken care of, and Pauline was content.

Shortly after this was the solemn First Communnion of a group of blind children, for whom the day was very special. Pauline and her associates did all they could to make the celebration pleasant, devout, and memorable.

Now the bishop had a great surprise for Pauline, the other ladies, and the blind children. He knew how very difficult it was for them to attend early daily Mass at the parish church. First, they had to pass through a woods to the city gate. Then, they often had to wake the gatekeeper to unlock the gate and had to wait till he was alert enough to function. When there was rain, snow, or ice, it was practically impossible to lead the blind children safely through the mud or over the slippery ground of the woods and then beyond the gate, once it was opened.

So the bishop suggested that the small prayer room in the home for the blind be turned into a chapel with a permanent tabernacle. He himself came to offer Holy Mass for the first time in the little house and then left the Blessed Sacrament in the chapel. From then on, Jesus would stay with them there, would live with them. On his way out, the bishop placed the key to the tabernacle into Pauline's hand. She could only look at him with sparkling eyes and radiant smile. There were no words to express her joy at having Jesus under her roof and being His guardian. To have Him physically present was a little bit of heaven that would make any trouble or suffering very small.

Chapter XI

Pauline closed the envelope and addressed it. She laid down the pen and looked at the letter with thoughtful eyes. In it were documents and a petition for the corporation rights of her congregation from the royal government in Berlin. Once that was granted, the congregation would be recognized as a real, living thing by not only the Church, which had already approved of it, but also by the state. A little shiver of thrill went through her. This must get to the post office as soon as possible!

But there was more. The bishop himself wrote to von Bodelschwingh, asking him to use his influence with the Cabinet toward granting the first members of this order corporation status. He also called for Pauline and told her he thought it best that she present that letter to Bodelschwingh personally in Münster. She agreed and travelled to Münster where Bodelschwingh received her graciously and promised to urge the granting of her request in Berlin.

Then she returned to Paderborn to await results.

After some time she received a letter from Dr. Schmidt in Berlin, telling her that her application for corporation status was now before the Cabinet. He advised her to go there and support her petition personally. He invited her to stay with him and his wife while there. Pauline was happy to accept since his residence was at the famous Charité hospital with over a thousand beds. She hoped to learn much from visiting the hospital while she was there. Once more she took Anna Everken, Dr. Schmidt's sister-in-law, with her as her travelling companion.

The transaction of her business took several months, and Pauline saw and learned many interesting things about politics and people as well as institutions during her stay.

She had to be interviewed many times about her petition, but when all was over, she re-visited the Berlin Blind Institute and went on to see the large Bethany Hospital and the Catholic Hospital. The superior of the Sisters of St. Charles Borromeo at the Catholic Hospital talked over Pauline's plans with her and gave her many instructions and useful directives about her future congregation.

At last her application passed through all the necessary channels and was waiting only for the king's signature. At this point she could return home since nothing could now happen to frustrate her effort. It would merely take some time till the king arrived at the point of signing.

With deep thanks to Dr. Schmidt, Pauline left for home. Anna remained there with her sister and later joined the Religious of the Sacred Heart. But she always maintained a loving friendship with Pauline.

Her three associates, Maria, Agatha, and Mathilde and the blind children gave Pauline a warm, joyful welcome. It was good to have her home again. Three days later, in February 1849, the document from the Cabinet arrived, conferring corporation status on the little congregation that would soon be founded. Everyone was intensely happy and grateful.

It was only now that Pauline told her family everything: the future founding of a congregation that would care for the blind and the poor children; its having at last been granted approval by the bishop; and recognition as corporation by the state. All of them were glad, too, when they saw the happiness in Pauline's eyes.

Then came the times that all four ladies looked forward to. In the evenings, when they were alone and the day's work was done, they would sit together, fitting and sewing their religious habits. It was sheer pleasure to see the precious garments take form and to try them on. They looked at each other with knowing smiles, aware of the feelings they all shared.

In April, at the end of winter, the nursery was re-opened in the old toll house, and eighty children enrolled. Young Mathilde was put in charge of the nursery school, and it was in good hands.

Days ticked away, and soon it was August. Because the four women would be making retreat in preparation for their reception by the Church as religious, the nursery was given a week's vacation. Fraülein Franziska Rath took charge of the blind children. Judge Hüffer, Bertha's husband, who wrote music, came frequently and taught them new songs. Father Tewes explained to them that Pauline, Mathilde, Maria and Agatha were going to be Sisters and give themselves to God. They would wear different clothes and perhaps have different names, but they would still love and care for the blind children. Just this one week they would not be with them because they were getting ready for the big event.

Though Father Tewes had been disappointed that Pauline would not lead his group of teachers in a Third Order, he was still her friend and was glad to conduct the retreat for her and her three companions in preparation for the day of reception. The retreat would be held at the Hartmann garden house, now the new little motherhouse. The purpose was to become certain of God's call to religious life. Pauline was sure, but she was eager for the retreat anyhow.

The four Sisters entered the retreat eagerly. Father Tewes could hardly be called an eloquent man, but his talks on charity were down to earth, practical, and understanding. To the four women desiring to give themselves to works of charity, they carried great meaning. Their love for others was to be simple and warm. The one other great virtue necessary to keep the three vows of poverty, chastity, and obedience and their rule of life, he told them, was humility. Since they would be very active in serving others, the rule of cloister or of never being allowed to go out would not apply to them. But it was understood that they would not go out more than necessity or service demanded. They were to build an inner cloister, a cloister in their hearts which they would keep for the Lord and where they would meet Him frequently during the day.

Their title was given to them by Bishop Franz

St. Andrew, the Busdorf church, Pauline's parish church in Paderborn

Drepper. They were to be called Sisters of Christian Charity. Pauline thought the name was too ambitious. Who could deserve such a name? But, on thinking it over, she realized that charity was to be the very soul of the congregation, and that having it as their name, the Sisters would strive to excel in it. Therefore, she accepted it.

At last came the evening before the great day of reception. Pauline was at prayer, and as she prayed, the great cathedral bells began to play an evening song of praise. Soon those of the Busdorf church, her own parish church, joined them as if many harmonious voices were clamoring with joy in anticipation of the next day's celebration.

She thought of the blessing that the Church would bestow on her tomorrow, much like the blessing on a bride. It seemed to her that it would bring the same fruitfulnes to her spiritually as it did for a bride physically, for to Pauline the ceremony would bind her to Christ as firmly as matrimony bound a couple to each other.

"O Lord," her heart was saying, "if you will deign to impart this grace, bestow also upon me the necessary light and strength to raise unto yourself spiritual children who will surround your table like young olive branches . . . .Dearest Jesus, may charity be the fruit of this retreat. Impart to me a heart filled with love, not only for those of my immediate circle, but for all men everywhere."

It was eight o'clock on the morning of August 21, 1849, the feast of St. Jane Frances de Chantal. The Busdorf church bells were ringing, singing their praise of joy, Pauline thought, as she entered the church with her three companions. Accompanied by the organ's peals of deep, rich harmony, the four brides of Christ each in white dress and veil and carrying a burning candle, walked singly down the aisle with dignity and grace. Every head in the packed church turned, every neck stretched to watch each movement and hear each word of this moving ceremony. Not for many, many years since the closing of monasteries by the government had such an event taken place.

Bertha and her husband, Alfred, sat up front with George, his wife, and Hermann. Bertha was solemn and unsmiling. Now that the time had come, she was not at all pleased that Pauline was becoming a Sister. She turned toward the center aisle but looked gloomily at the faces on the other side of it.

Then, suddenly, she saw Pauline's face as she passed slowly down the aisle. She almost gave a little cry and quickly put her hand over her mouth. Pauline was radiant! Her face was positively glorious with a loveliness that could not be defined. Bertha had never seen her sister look so happy! How could she, Bertha, sulk when, after so many years of waiting, Pauline finally had what she wanted? Tears came to her eyes, but her lips relaxed into a smile. She could not help but be happy with Pauline.

Pauline and her companions went into the pews. Closest to them were the orphans of the Mercy Sisters and their own blind children who shyly touched their white robes. The rest of the church was filled with ordinary folks and dignitaries, the young and the old, the reverent and the curious.

Father Karl Schmidt, the pastor, ascended the pulpit. Briefly and clearly, he explained what the four women were about to do: they would begin a

172

new congregation of Sisters, give themselves to the Lord and His service, start their training in the religious life by receiving the habit and their religious name and entering the novitiate.

Then the choir began to sing the High Mass, celebrated by Bishop Drepper. All this time Pauline had scarcely taken her eyes off the crucifix and the tabernacle. Her soul was stirred to its depth and inwardly she was singing Mary's *Magnificat*. The Mass went on. Suddenly, it was time for the offering of their candles.

The four brides rose. One by one they gave their burning candles to the bishop, symbol of the total giving of themselves to their Lord and Lover. Then they stood waiting as the bishop blessed their habits. He presented each one with her blessed garments, which were carried by the brides into the sacristy.

There they put on their holy habits and returned shortly after to the sanctuary, kneeling before him. Then he called down upon them the Holy Spirit with all His gifts and solemnly blessed them. The new Sisters now returned happily to their places.

The bishop preached the sermon, and the Mass continued. At Holy Communion the Sisters received their Beloved, and He sealed the bond between Himself and each one with special love. For Pauline, that bond included her dear blind children.

A few moments later the four Sisters knelt again before the bishop, and he gave each one her religious name. Pauline would be Mother Pauline and superior of the little community. Mathilde would be Sister Mathilde; Agatha, Sister Maria; and Maria, Sister Elisabeth. Pauline surprisingly felt no fear or timidity, but instead experienced a surge of strength and grace for the office imposed on her. Still more, she felt as if the bishop were bestowing the blessing of fertility on her when he said, "And I entertain the hope that under your direction the Congregation will grow and expand."

Immediately Bishop Drepper appointed the Vicar General as spiritual superior of the small congregation and representative of the bishop for them. Then he handed Mother Pauline the Statutes and Constitutions which he had approved and urged the Sisters to keep them faithfully. Father Boekamp, the Vicar General, also addressed the people and the Sisters, extending congratulations to his new little flock.

Then the walls shook with the organ's vibrations of the majestic "Holy God," and all the people joined in the mighty, enthusiastic song of praise to the Lord for what they had witnessed that day. A new and sturdy little branch had budded on the gigantic vine of the Church and was already giving life to and bearing fruit for her members!

It was mid-morning, and the birds were chirping in the garden of the little motherhouse when the Sisters finally came for breakfast. The sun was warm and seemed to enjoy itself by flashing suddenly here and there through the trees into the smiling faces of the new Sisters whose happiness reflected as brightly as the whiteness of their coifs and the charming little bows under their chins. It was difficult to get used to their new headdresses as they turned to see all the garlands on the trees, on the outdoor table, on the door, and over windows of the house and heard the excited voices of the blind children nearby, waiting to greet them. One of the Sisters even jumped a

Mother Pauline von Mallinckrodt, Foundress of the Sisters of Christian Charity

little when the society of sharpshooters gave them a gun salute by firing salvos into the garden several times.

But the most touching moment came when the blind children gathered around them and sang the song they had learned for the occasion.

> "As the festive sound of bells
> Ring blue heaven's way,
> So, beloved brides of Christ,
> We greet you today,"

they sang as sweetly as they knew how. Tears moistened Mother Pauline's eyes, and she went over to them, thanking them in a voice full of emotion. Then the other three joined her, and soon the children's curious fingers were touching their rosaries, their capes, and veils and even encountered their coifs while searching for their faces.

"Aunt—I mean, Mother Pauline, where is your face?" called one little boy, clutching her black apron.

"Here, child," she cried, and laughing, put his hand on her nose and cheek.

Then the ladies gathered the children, and they withdrew to the Meyer house while the Sisters and the Mallinckrodts sat down to breakfast in the garden. After they had eaten, her three companions left Mother Pauline alone with her sister and brothers. They talked of many things: of their mother and father, of Bishop Claessen, of the good old days, and of days to come. Finally, Bertha, who was now quite converted to Pauline's being a Sister, gestured toward her.

"The new habit is very becoming, isn't it?" she said, looking at George and Hermann. George nodded emphatically, but Hermann shook his head.

"There's just a little something missing," he said, cocking his head as he looked Pauline over from head to foot. Then his eyes lighted mischievously, and before she could dodge him, he playfully and gently dented her coif in the middle at the top with his cane.

"Now!" he announced triumphantly, "that's it! Our Sister of Christian Charity has a heart around her face." He sat back and viewed his work with pride. The others agreed. It did look like a heart, and later, the other Sisters decided to adopt it as a permanent part of the habit.

The rest of the day was spent in quiet prayer and recollection by the four Sisters. They had begun their novitiate, which the bishop had limited, in their case, to one year.

Before she retired that night, Mother Pauline lingered over her notebook. What an unforgettable day it had been! How many feelings had filled her heart! She must never lose them. Carefully she wrote on the page for August 21, 1849:

"O blessed day! Goal of so many long years of desire! . . . I have attained what I sought. I am wedded to the Heavenly Bridegroom.—My most daring desires are fulfilled.—I rested a day in this blessedness. I rested a little with my Beloved and beside my Beloved.—Well did I realize that it could not last long in this earthly pilgrimage—it was a foretaste of heaven! The memory of such consolation strengthens for the battle and fortifies for the heat of the day—of the workday. A new life dawned.—A life in the Church and for God's holy Church in the strictest sense of the word."

The thirty-two-year-old Mother Pauline had fulfilled her dream by following the directive of God's

176

representative, Bishop Claessen. She was now a religious and the foundress of a new congregation. She had experienced the ecstasy. Now, as a realist and follower of Jesus, she knew there would also be agony. But she was not afraid. How could she be? She had Him who is the Way, the Truth, and the Life!

Chapter XII

It was night, and only the moon gave light in the little sick room. Mother Pauline sat next to the bed of the blind boy who was ill. Gently she patted a cool, wet cloth over the feverish face, watching him anxiously. Then she sat back and straightened herself, her eyes alert but tired.

They had chosen this one little room as the infirmary in the small motherhouse, and almost immediately it had been taken by this poor blind child. By day Sister Elisabeth nursed him, and by night Mother Pauline. How crowded they were, she thought. They needed another building for the blind so badly, but when would the committee in Berlin approve?

Mother Pauline shivered a little and drew her shawl about her more tightly. It was only November, and already the little von Hartmann garden house that was their motherhouse was showing that it was not meant to be a winter home. The wind blew so unmercifully in the chimney that it came close to destroying it. The drafts from wall to wall were so strong that Mother Pauline thought the house would fall apart. Snow came in under the window frames and drifted in neat low piles on the sills. Patiently she tried to wedge a cloth under the slim openings. But she had to be careful that she did not bump the bed and wake the sleeping boy. It was so crowded in the room, in *all* the rooms that one could scarcely move about. There were too many people for the little house, but what were they to do? Just bear it patiently, trying to share in the poverty of the Holy Family at Nazareth, confident that the Father knew of their need and would help in His good time.

She thought of the other three Sisters and herself and of their daily life. She smiled. There were three buildings with their personnel to be managed by four Sisters. Sister Maria taught the blind children in the former Meyer house; Sister Mathilde taught the eighty nursery children with the help of assistants in the toll house; Sister Elisabeth nursed the sick and supervised the staff for the cooking, serving, and washing in the motherhouse. Mother Pauline helped in all three places, keeping a caring eye on both the Sisters and the children.

But since they were novices, the Sisters had their religious duties too; some before they started their work early in the morning, and some after their work for the day was finished. The time with the Lord was precious and quiet.

Mother Pauline's thoughts went to the blind boys as she looked at her sleeping patient. At night the boys were taken to the toll house where they slept. The gardener also slept there as their supervisor and guardian. She would have to check whether the snow and wind came in there too. The blind girls slept in the Meyer house in the care of Sister Maria. Twenty blind children in all. Where would they put any newcomers?

President von Bodelschwingh had told her that they should take any and all newcomers since there were hundreds of blind children who were wandering about idle, away from home. Mother Pauline had told him she had no room and needed to build, but there had been no response. Yet she had made up her mind that, although as head of this branch she need not ask him everything, as a novice practicing obedience, she would not act independently of him in anything regarding the schools. Also, even though she was superior, she would consult the Vicar General in any matter concerning the Congregation.

The next day Mother Pauline took a letter from her desk and reread it. It was from Bodelschwingh. She had remembered it last night and resolved to answer it, no matter how difficult it would be. In his letter Bodelschwingh demanded that she dismiss a blind epileptic boy they had taken and said that the farmers of the town should take turns feeding him.

Mother Pauline sat down, took her pen, said a prayer, and began to write. As the words formed on the paper, she gained courage. She firmly but politely refused to send the boy away and begged to let him stay with the others until a place for him was available in the hospital for incurables at Geseke.

But that was not all. Bodelschwingh demanded that Margretchen be sent away too. Mother Pauline waited a while before she answered that. Finally on November 22, 1849 she wrote to him once more, pleading that Margretchen be allowed to stay. "She is now only rarely among the children, but generally in our house where she makes herself useful by carrying wood and water, etc. I fear that if she is sent to strangers, she may be beaten since she has so many irritating habits. We are used to her ways and will patiently continue to put up with her. Please allow her to remain with us, for we should like to have our institution become a refuge for the most unfortunate among the blind, where they can be taught to lead useful lives. The von Vincke division has as yet no facilities of the kind, whereas our little house is admirably suited to the purpose." Three months later she wrote to thank him for allowing Margretchen to stay.

The little house for the blind had only the most necessary rooms: classrooms, a girls' dormitory, and a tiny chapel. The cooking and the washing of clothes were done in the motherhouse, and all the meals were served there. Every evening when she was not on nursing night duty, Mother Pauline went to the home for the blind where she spent the night. Sometimes she was detained by business and found the children talking and laughing in bed when she arrived. In order not to frighten them, she would call in a kind voice, "Children, I am coming." She did not need to say one thing more. Her words were like a soothing hand, and everyone became quiet.

Bertha had been quite eloquent in her description of the lack of room in the little motherhouse at the time when Pauline had broken her foot and Bertha had spent days and nights caring for her in her tiny room. "The congestion is unbelievable!" she had written. "So many people crowded into such close quarters! My own existence seems comparable to that of a snail which carries all it needs upon its back. A basket which contains all my paraphernalia is constantly with me." She had always carried that basket with everything she needed, and into Pauline's room each evening an armchair had been brought in which Bertha slept. There was no room for another bed, and actually there was no other bed available.

Although Mother Pauline had not received approval for the new blind asylum from the committee in Berlin, she would not be stopped. She ordered work on the building to be started. The site for it was property that lay between the two garden houses, which were the motherhouse and the present blind institute. But there was also a new railroad being built just beyond the toll house at the gate to the city and the area between the two garden houses.

All that was fine, except for the Sisters and the blind children who had to walk there every day. The ground was strewn with rubble of all kinds: heaps of stones, iron beams, trestles, different kinds of equipment. The spaces in between were grooved by ruts and ditches. All of this made it difficult for the Sisters to walk back and forth in bad and good weather during the day and even harder to lead the blind children over the grounds especially when dark was falling. It was not unusual for a child to stumble and drag others into a puddle or a ditch or land on a stone.

Since the only entrance to the little chapel was through the dormitory of the little blind girls, all had to get up especially early on mornings when Holy

Mass was to be offered. Then Mother Pauline surpassed everyone else in speed and skill while getting the girls washed and dressed and ready. She helped them with arranging their beds neatly and seeing that their hair was nicely combed. All this had to be finished before the priest came through to the chapel.

Besides her work with the children, it was Mother Pauline's duty as directress of novices to give conferences and instructions to the other three Sisters. She prepared for these very carefully, but in a kindly way forbade the three to take notes on what she said. The spirit and thoughts of the foundress were not lost, however, because they are embodied in the many letters she wrote to the Sisters. It became quite clear to them that the three main goals of the new little community were the patient endurance of hardship, loving charity toward all persons, and complete acceptance of God's will.

Just about this time, an interesting request came to Mother Pauline. A lady named Fraülein Auguste von Cordier was part-owner of an island called Nonnenwerth on the Rhine river. A group of ladies including herself had already gathered there and wanted Pauline to take it over and make it part of her community. They wanted Pauline to go there and become their novice directress and superior.

Even Luise Hensel wrote, urging her to leave the work of her group in Paderborn in the hands of Sister Maria Rath. To Mother Pauline's even greater surprise and dismay, the bishops of Trier, Paderborn, and Münster were all in favor of the project. ·

Despite the approval of these important people whom she respected, Mother Pauline firmly and unhesitatingly said no. How could she leave the Sisters who had first joined her? "With what pitiful confidence I would inspire them by abandoning my vocation!" she wrote. "I hope for God's grace to remain until death in the Congregation of the Sisters of Christian Charity which has been established on a firm foundation within the Church." She also wrote to the bishop of Münster who had supported the idea so strongly, asking him what he would think of a superior who left those he himself had entrusted to her.

The year wore on into fall, and one Sunday after Mass, Pauline brought the blind children into the garden. All were laughing and talking, and some were singing. It was only then that Mother Pauline discovered she had visitors, Professor Christopher Schlüter and his sister, Therese. Mother Pauline was very glad to see them and sent for coffee and cake. They talked of mutual old friends, and then she told them about her new congregation and her plans for it. She went on to tell them about the new blind asylum that was to be built and of all the children in the nursery school and the blind institute.

Christopher's blindness had increased so he could not really see Mother Pauline's face, but her voice told him much. She was still sweet and kind, but her tone was much more quiet and sure, no longer excited and argumentative. Her old teasing way was gone, and in its place was a mellower, more tolerant sense of humor. He was glad to hear her once more and observe how she had grown spiritually and emotionally. Now he could write the final sonnet of the sequence he had composed about her.

Later, at home, he remarked to Therese as they spoke about their visit:

"It is fitting that God should call her. She has so much love that it would be impossible for her to give it all to one person." Then he handed Therese the last sonnet that he would write about Pauline. Her eyes caught especially these lines:

"His voice thy heart has won,
This life's short span thou wisely dost account.
The journey is begun.
The world and self upon
God's altar laid; unhindered thou canst mount.
. . . .
To all in sad distress,
The poor, the sick, the blind, thy charity doth give.
'Tis sweet to dispossess
One's self of treasure's stress,
Thy motto is: 'Alone for Christ to live.'
Farewell, farewell, to thee,
Thou God's own chosen one! In holy place
May memory's eyes still see
One who would like thee be,
Implore for him the savior's healing grace."

Indian summer came, and its gorgeous colors were everywhere. The weather was as mild as May's even though it was November. The four Sisters were in retreat, each preparing for the great event of the next day: pronouncing first holy vows. A postulant, too, was preparing to receive the holy habit. Bertha and her husband, Alfred, came to be with the blind children, and soon their merry shouts and laughter showed how well they were being entertained.

That same day Mother Pauline received a request from Father Wiemann of the Catholic church in Dortmund to send a Sister to teach in the public school for

Professor Christopher Schlueter, Pauline's blind friend

girls there. His parish had the long-standing privilege of appointing its teachers, so Father Wiemann had applied to the school board in Arnsberg, requesting approval to hire a Sister as teacher. But the school board was wary about it.

Pauline's father had come from Dortmund. For centuries the Mallinckrodts had been some of its leading citizens. Pauline's grandfather had been mayor of the town. But the Mallinckrodts were all Protestant, and she had been the first Catholic girl born in the Mallinckrodt family for years.

Catholic religious teachers had disappeared from Dortmund with the law of secularization of 1813. Before that, the town had lost almost all of its Catholics with the coming of Luther and the Reformation. Only seven families had remained Catholic.

Now, however, the descendants of those remaining seven Catholic families had grown into two or three hundred Catholic children, and they needed a teacher. For her father's sake, Mother Pauline wanted very much to send a teacher there, but she had only five Sisters. She would have to see.

The awaited day of November 4, 1850 dawned bright as the others. The bells of St. Andrew, the Busdorf church, were pealing again, calling the people to witness a ceremony even more solemn than that of the previous year. The four Sisters entered singly and knelt in the front pew, with the blind children to the side and their relatives and friends behind them.

Again the bishop celebrated the Mass. At the Epistle he blessed the four rings, and after the Gospel they went to the altar, expressing their desire to make their holy vows. Then the bishop intoned the

Litany of the Saints while the Sisters lay face down on the sanctuary floor.

When the Litany was ended, the bishop turned to them, now kneeling upright again, and pronounced over them a triple blessing. Each one was given a burning candle, and one by one, beginning with Mother Pauline, each Sister professed her vows of poverty, chastity, and obedience in a loud, clear voice. The Church allowed them to make the vows for only one year until the new congregation was approved by Rome. Later they would be permitted to make perpetual vows for life. But in her heart each Sister now silently added "forever."

Mother Pauline said her vows with utmost love and delight, folded the paper on which she had written them and handed it to the bishop happily. But when he, as the representative of Jesus Christ, placed the blessed ring on the third finger of her left hand, she seemed to be lifted out of herself, and she wanted the moment never to end.

The Mass continued to the Communion when the Divine Bridegroom sealed His bond with the four Sisters by giving them Himself in the Eucharist. It was then that Pauline's joy flooded her completely and her love poured itself out on her Beloved.

"Lord, You have been faithful to Your promise. You have superabundantly rewarded the sacrifice which I offered at the time of my confirmation . . . .Is it not too much to have given Yourself entirely to me? . . . .Truly, He who is the most rich, the most powerful, the most noble, has chosen me as His spouse . . . .I shall follow You in poverty, chastity, and obedience. You, my Beloved, shall be the only object of my soul . . . .And now, Love of my life, to all that I most willingly give You, together with my vows, I add everything else I possess: my health, my life, and may all be for love of You and for the welfare of souls in the practice of perfect charity. Give me the grace to know how I can best and most practically organize all things, that they may be pleasing to You, my Love."

The Mass ended with the glorious singing of the "Te Deum" and the Sisters, with the postulant who had received the holy habit and was now a novice, were escorted by the bishop and priests to the door of the church. There they received their congratulations, and Father Schmidt, the pastor, told Mother Pauline that he had been appointed their confessor.

Once again they went to the garden of their little motherhouse for breakfast. Everywhere were lovely decorations. Once again the dear blind children serenaded them as they ate and later crowded around to recite poems and tell them how they prayed for them.

The rest of the day was spent in peaceful quiet and prayerful thanks to God. It was the feast of St. Charles Borromeo, and so for part of the afternoon they listened to the reading of his life. Mother Pauline was deeply impressed by it and felt the flame of eagerness to serve others with love leap higher and higher in her heart. She knew they must steep themselves in love, for tomorrow they were to consume themselves in the works of love for others in whom Jesus, their Beloved, lived.

Chapter XIII

Mother Pauline stood at the window of the little blind asylum in the Meyer house and watched the movements of the working-men as they labored on the new building for the blind. Through the advice and personal approval of President von Bodelschwingh and through the loans made her by Uncle Fritz and others, combined with money from Father Adami's will and from the provincial relief fund, the congregation had finally been able to make the dream of a larger and better equipped institute for the blind materialize. Even though the building was unfinished, merely the sight of it made her happy. But there was more on her mind just then. Her negotiations with the school board of Dortmund and the business of the contract were not totally settled yet. But the date of January first when the board expected a teacher to arrive was not far off. She would have to talk to Sister Mathilde about it that very day. Of the five Sisters in the Congregation, Sister Mathilde would be the one most suited to go.

Mother Pauline went to the kitchen and sent one of the girls working there to get Sister Mathilde from the toll house. Her assistants could manage the children of the nursery for a while.

"Come in, Sister Mathilde," she said, smiling. "Please sit down." She, too, sat down, facing Sister Mathilde.

"You know that we have been considering sending a Sister to Dortmund as a teacher of the girls." Sister Mathilde nodded. "Do you think you could manage to fill that assignment? It would please me very much if you would go there. I have written often to the reverend pastor there, and he will be very kind to you and see to it that you have the help of the other teachers."

"Yes, Reverend Mother, I would be glad to go," said Sister Mathilde eagerly.

"Of course, you cannot live there alone. It would be too hard, and it would be better for you to have a companion with whom to share community life. So I will send Sister Clara, the novice, with you."

"Oh, thank you, Reverend Mother," exclaimed Sister Mathilde, "But I was wondering . . . well, I was hoping . . ."

"Yes, Sister dear. What is it?"

"Well, actually, Reverend Mother, I would feel much better if an older and more experienced teacher could be with me at the start. I have taught the blind and the kindergarten, but not older sighted children. I would be grateful for some guidance at the beginning."

"Ah, yes, I understand, Sister. I think that can be arranged. Suppose we send Sister Maria with you for a while at the beginning and then later Sister Clara can join you. How would that be?"

"Oh, that would be fine, Reverend Mother! Thank you!"

"Very well, then." She looked lovingly at the eager young face upturned to her.

"I must speak to Sister Maria. Go and tell her to come to me while you stay with the blind, Sister Mathilde. But take care that you don't fall on all that rubble on the grounds."

"Oh, yes, Reverend Mother," and in a moment the young Sister was up and gone.

Sister Maria came promptly, and Mother Pauline explained the plan to her.

"You could probably stay there a week or two till Sister Mathilde is settled. Then I will send Sister Clara, and you can return here. We need you here, you know."

Sister Maria smiled and nodded.

"I shall have to go to Dortmund before Christmas to find a place for you Sisters to stay," continued Mother Pauline. "While I am there, I may as well visit the pastor, Father Wiemann."

So it was settled, and Sister Mathilde began to prepare for the adventure of working in the first mission of the Sisters of Christian Charity, away from the motherhouse and the blind!

Mother Pauline went to Dortmund and found a place of room and board for the two Sisters at the home of Mrs. Elvert whom they would pay regularly. She also had a pleasant visit with the pastor and came home satisfied. When she opened and read her mail, she realized that at least temporarily, things were settled with the school board and von Bodelschwingh regarding Sister Mathilde's going to Dortmund as the first Catholic teacher of the girls in that school.

On December 31, 1850 Sister Mathilde and Sister Maria left for Dortmund as Mother Pauline, Sister Elisabeth, Sister Clara, and the blind waved goodbye. The next day and the following, the first days of the new year of 1851, Sister Maria presented Sister Mathilde to the school board, to the pastor, and to the men teachers of the school. All were very kind to Sister Mathilde and welcomed her. The male faculty gave her the school schedule and, in general, were as helpful as possible.

On January third, school opened after the Christmas recess, and 123 girls greeted and welcomed Sister Mathilde, their new teacher, with a song. The pastor, Father Wiemann, spoke briefly, saying that he was entrusting a cherished part of the Dortmund community to Sister Mathilde. She, in turn, expressed her joy at being able to work with these children and promised them her very best efforts. The children sang another song, and then the District Magistrate and the mayor both wished her God's blessing. The two assistant priests and the men teachers, too, wished her well in a very friendly way.

Because of the large number of girls, a plan was made for dividing them into two groups. Sister Mathilde would have the first group. Sister Clara would later take the second. The smallest girls remained in the class of Mr. Linpinsel. With the excellent help of Sister Maria and her own great patience and charity, hard work and perseverance, Sister Mathilde began the challenging task of teaching sixty some girls of various levels and ages. At Mother

Pauline's request, no fee was charged for the industrial classes in order to spare the poor children who were in a great majority in Dortmund.

At the same time, at home in Paderborn, Sister Elisabeth became very ill. She had been in delicate health for some time because she had been weakened very much by her unselfish nursing during a cholera epidemic before she entered the Congregation. The doctor later diagnosed her sickness as tuberculosis, and there was not much hope for her recovery. Mother Pauline needed Sisters so badly that she prayed fervently for Sister Elisabeth's cure. Yet she never failed to offer her to the Lord if that was His wise and good plan.

Many letters, meantime, had been passing between Director Pienenbrock and Mother Pauline about the Sisters taking charge of an orphanage at Steele. Such work appealed very much to her heart, and despite the lack of Sisters, she believed firmly that if God wanted her to do that work, He would provide the workers. Besides writing to Director Pienenbrock about the contract, she also notified von Bodelschwingh and Father Wiemann at Dortmund. Some young ladies were applying for admission, too, and she asked the Sisters or others who knew them to evaluate for her their suitability for religious life.

About mid-January Sister Maria returned home from Dortmund, while Sister Clara went there to help Sister Mathilde. With Sister Elisabeth ill, only Mother Pauline and Sister Maria were left to carry on the work in Paderborn. Yet the brave foundress was able to smile, especially when she saw that the new building for the blind was already under roof.

In February, Mother Pauline travelled to the orphanage at Steele by way of Dortmund, because she wanted to take Sister Clara along as a companion to the orphanage. She had humorously written that she would bring coifs, collars, and cuffs along for Sister Clara who would then need to bring only her comb and so forth, "along with her famous rose-colored nightgown."

They found the orphanage to be a spacious building having the chapel as the central point, with a wing for boys and one for girls on either side of it. It had been established by the last abbess, who was also a princess from Essen. After the nuns had been driven out, it was taken over by the government. The present director managed the institution very well. All was clean and orderly. The chaplain and the teacher of the boys would live in the boys' wing, and the Sisters would live in the girls' wing. There were 124 orphans. The Sisters would be expected to educate the girls, manage the household, and supervise all the boys outside of school hours. Mother Pauline was pleased with all she saw and was eager to send the Sisters there. But she could not do it till the necessary papers with the government and the Church were finally drawn up. Besides, the Sisters and children would have to first move into the new blind asylum and get settled before Sisters could be spared for Steele. On the way home, she stopped at Dortmund for a day's visit with Sister Mathilde and her pupils. She found all going well.

At home, however, day by day, Sister Elisabeth grew worse. Mother Pauline wrote to Luise Hensel: "If only she gets better. We need her very much. We love her very much. But I have offered her to God, and of course, a holy death is the goal of earthly wandering. But we do need her so very badly."

On Sunday, March 9, Mother Pauline visited with Sister Elisabeth and even discussed some matters with her. She seemed much better. Perhaps we shall keep her with us, she thought to herself. Then she left to go to the blind and read to them. Later as she was coming back to the little motherhouse, a panting postulant ran to her.

"Please, Reverend Mother, hurry! Hurry! Sister Elisabeth is dying!"

Father Schmidt, their confessor, was already kneeling by the bedside when she entered the sick room. She saw him lean close to Sister Elisabeth's ear and say distinctly, "When you see our Lord, speak my name to Him, Sister." Then he blessed her. Sister Elisabeth smiled weakly and nodded, whispering, "Yes, Father." He rose and turned to leave, saying he would come back soon.

Mother Pauline, Sister Maria, and Lisette stayed by her bed, praying so that Sister Elisabeth could hear them. They took turns leaving for supper and by evening all were in the sick room again with Father Schmidt.

Mother Pauline stooped down toward the pillow, speaking slowly.

"Sister Elisabeth, you will pray for our little Congregation when you get to heaven, won't you?"

The large eyes of the dying Sister turned to her. They were alight and happy.

"Yes, oh yes," she whispered.

Her breathing became heavy and difficult. Lisette took the frail shoulders in her arms and held her up so that she might get air more easily. Father Schmidt looked again at the young, pale face and put a crucifix in her hand. He raised his hand in the sign of the cross.

"*Ego te absolvo*," he said slowly. "I absolve you from all your sins in the name of the Father and of the Son and of the Holy Spirit."

Sister Elisabeth began to gasp. With each hand on either side, she sought to grasp the reassuring touch of Mother Pauline and Sister Maria. Each one took a thin hand and held it lovingly.

Tears ran down Lisette's face and dropped on Sister Elisabeth's.

"Don't . . . cry," she gasped. Then Mother Pauline saw Lisette relax with her precious weight. She gently laid the young Sister down on the bed. It was 11:45 p.m. The first Sister of Christian Charity had gone to God.

The Sisters and Lisette prayed the rosary for her, comforted by looking at her sweet, gentle face. The next morning Mother Pauline and Lisette dressed her in her habit and brought her into the green room. They laid her on the white-covered couch with her large white rosary in her hands. A particle of the holy cross and other relics lay on her breast. The venetian blinds were closed, and at the foot of the couch was a small table with crucifix and candles. Two kneelers were placed there for anyone wishing to pray. The blind children took turns by two's praying for Sister. Four days later Sister Elisabeth was laid to rest in a beautiful ceremony, accompanied by the children, Sisters, and many friends.

The saying of Scripture, "The Lord gives and the Lord takes away," was the most apt theme for Mother Pauline's little community during the next months. Before and after Sister Elisabeth's death,

196

young ladies joined the community, but in May, Sister Mathilde had to inform Mother Pauline that now Sister Clara was ill. It was feared that she, too, had tuberculosis. By June Sister Clara was back at the motherhouse in Paderborn to rest and profit from the fresh air and fresh food from the garden. Sister Mathilde had to carry on alone at Dortmund. But soon Mother Pauline was told of a young woman named Sophia Rengal who was interested in helping Sister Mathilde in school and even gave signs of wanting to enter the community. Not long after, Mother Pauline received a letter from her asking for admission to the congregation, and three other young ladies were also accepted into the postulancy, the first phase of religious life.

Sister Maria now became the directress of the young women who had just entered the community. During the weeks of July she gave them a course in preparation for teaching, entitled "Education and Management of Children." Fortunately it ended before the month closed because the week-long celebration of the feast of St. Liborius, the popular saint of the Paderborn diocese, competed for their attention. Not only were there outdoor processions and prayers but also music, drums, dancing, and carnival with merry-go-rounds and food vendors. Even the blind children enjoyed everything, especially the rides on the carousel.

After the course and the festivities, Sister Maria and Sister Clara went to the Lippspringe baths for a cure. Then Sister Maria was to study the Holy Rule and prepare instructions on it for the future novices.

Correspondence regarding the orphanage at Steele dragged on. There were letters to the assistant of the bishop of Cologne regarding permission to work in that diocese; to Berlin regarding the official contract; and letters to the director of the orphanage regarding both.

At the same time, work on the new blind asylum was nearing completion but not quickly enough to allow sufficient time to move in and get at least somewhat settled before the postulants were to make retreat. This was in preparation for receiving their habits and new names at the investing ceremony. It was set by the bishop for September twenty-second so that the new novices would be ready to go to the orphanage at Steele on October first.

Mother Pauline tried to assemble all the workmen and explain the situation to them. There were masters and craftsmen of every kind, and they promised to do their best so that the Sisters could move in by at least the following week.

They kept their word. On September 15, 1851, the motherhouse was transferred from the little von Hartmann house to the new blind asylum, and there were many happy smiles as the furniture and belongings were moved to that building. Soon the blind children, the postulants, and Sisters were in their new home. It made no difference that painters, carpenters, and locksmiths were still around. The Vicar General came and blessed the house. From his hands the blind, the servants, the Sisters all received Holy Communion. They were looking forward to the day when they would have Jesus permanently in the tabernacle of their chapel.

Not long after this, a plan made months earlier was carried out regarding the former little motherhouse. Clara, a cousin of Mother Pauline, had married Julius Zürmuhlen, but they had been unable to find a suitable home in the city. So by mutual consent they now moved into the small von Hartmann house, paying 100 Thalers for rent. The married couple was pleased, and so were the Sisters.

Having made the big step of moving into the new blind asylum, Mother Pauline and her staff had to prepare for the coming retreat of the postulants. After several letters, she finally persuaded Father Wiemann of Dortmund to conduct it, assuring him that it would be sufficient if he touched broadly on prayer-life, humility, love for others, and fulfilling the vows and rules. That would lay a foundation on which Father Berens, the Jesuit, could later build and add details.

The retreat went well, and the long-awaited day of investing brought a quiet ceremony in which six young women received the habits and white veils of novices and their religious names. Proudly they carried their long, white rosaries from the altar. Knowing that soon they would be going to the orphanage at Steele, they entered intensively into their novitiate.

Each day the workmen were finishing more and more of the parts of the house needing completion. The building was becoming settled and orderly, and Mother Pauline was eagerly awaiting the bishop's coming to say the first Holy Mass. Finally he sent word: it would be October twenty-ninth. In preparation, the Sisters fasted the day before, and when the children heard of it, they wanted to fast too. The next morning before Mass, everyone went to confession. Flowers and plants decorated the chapel and the house, and there was organ music. An uplifting spirit of joy and celebration seemed everywhere. The Sisters and children received Holy Communion, and after Mass, the bishop asked everyone to truly reverence the Blessed Sacrament that he was leaving there for them. Then he handed the key to the tabernacle to Mother Pauline, and each one left the chapel with a feeling of security and contentment. "Now all the labor and care entailed in the construction of the house seem to be well repaid. It has assumed its real worth. God is so unspeakably kind and merciful," wrote Mother Pauline to her friends.

That happy attitude was severely tested but carried her through the following weeks of November and early December. During that time Bodelschwingh received notice that the expenditures for the blind asylum had exceeded the estimate. Mother Pauline had miscalculated the costs, and Bodelschwingh was so upset that he wanted nothing more to do with Pauline's blind asylum. Despite his anger, she would not let him go. She had a loyalty, faithfulness, and charity that could surmount human faults in those with whom she had built relationships, whether in business or otherwise. Persistently she wrote to him, presenting her side of the case humbly and honestly. She did not lower herself, yet she was respectful and mild while at the same time forcefully and truthfully explaining why she had acted as she did. She did not hesitate to point out that other government officials saw no difficulty for the government to supply the necessary funds. At the same time, she repeated that she had never intended to offend him and begged for his continued supervision and care. He found her a person very hard to dismiss.

She also informed him that the government officials and the cardinal of Cologne had approved of the Sisters' taking charge of the orphanage at Steele. To her delight, she was able two weeks later to take four novices there to begin their work with the children. She would stay with them for some time, leaving the blind children at Paderborn in the care of Sister Maria.

It was four days before Christmas when they arrived, and they were gladly received. The director turnd out to be an extremely considerate, intelligent, and methodical man, easy to work with. The male teacher was just as congenial and pleasant. Sister Josepha, whom Mother Pauline had appointed as principal, got along very well with him in planning the schedule. The children, too, in a few days, seemed to love the Sisters. But already Mother Pauline could see that they would need another Sister to help Sister Clara with the little boys. She would have to write to the motherhouse for Sister Antonio.

Meanwhile she was busy showing the Sisters how to mother the orphans. With a cheery smile she energetically washed them and made it a pleasure for them to bathe. Carefully she examined their heads and found that twenty of the children had sores right down to their foreheads. These she had to conquer personally. So, despite all offers by others to take her place, she washed those heads each day and treated the sores. With special love she cared for those who were sick, doing the humblest little services for them.

But she had time for the Sisters too. In any free moment, she tried to make every Sister's work a bit lighter by helping. She cleaned, swept, ironed, and took over any housework that needed to be done.

What they loved most of all, however, were the evening recreations spent with her. She was so happy and pleasant that it was refreshing just to be with her. They would talk with her about the day's experiences and their difficulties, and before they knew it, the hard part seemed quite simple to handle. She had them looking forward to the next day eagerly with a challenge, the challenge that love can conquer *anything*! Just to be sure that this idea took strong hold in their hearts, she gave the Sisters a meditation every Sunday morning on charity and on love for the children.

It was always easy to tell where she was because she brought a spirit of joy wherever she went. Sisters, workers, children were left smiling and at ease. She knew how to listen totally, becoming the other person and entering that situation with her whole heart as it was told to her. Then she would comfort and offer advice and encouragement. But she corrected too, honestly and firmly; even then her love was unmistakable. When four months had passed and it was time for her to return to Paderborn, a sad group gathered to say goodbye.

Mother Pauline's first concern on arriving home was to consult Sister Maria about going to Steele as novice directress for the Sisters there. She told her that she herself, Mother Pauline, would care for the blind children. It would mean very, very much to have Sister Maria there with the novices. Her mind at ease, knowing that her beloved blind children would be in good hands, Sister Maria gladly agreed to stay at the orphanage for as long as she could be spared.

Even before Sister Maria's absence, Mother Pauline had spent as much time as she could with the blind, but now that was almost doubled. She took all her meals with them, gave them singing lessons, led them on walks besides teaching them. She was continually thinking of ways to make life happy and pleasant for them. On Sundays she read an interesting story to them for hours; she chatted with them. Frequently when they went on walks, she packed sandwiches and fruit, and no one enjoyed a picnic more than they. Then they would return home singing happily. During the week she saw to it that they had plenty of time for exercise and fun outside, and it was amazing to see how sure they were as they ran around the beautiful playground. Even at night she was with them, and around her bed were several little cots for girls needing special care and attention during the night.

Every summer Mother Pauline arranged to let them go to a neighboring estate where they could run and jump and play as much as they liked. On Christmas they would stand, awed, before the beautiful Christmas tree, carefully touching it as the Sisters described it vividly. They would hold their gifts almost reverently, fingering them over and over as they sang the carols in their unique way. On Easter there was an egg hunt outdoors with much scrambling and squeals of excitement. They could find those eggs with a speed that would put sighted children to shame.

Then there had come a seven-year-old girl who was so helpless that she could not even feed herself alone. She was almost a vegetable. Mother Pauline cared for her and worked with her as patiently as she had with Margretchen, never stopping until the little one was able to do what was required so that she could stay there.

It was just at this time that she heard the news about her dear friend, co-worker, and benefactor. Doctor Hermann Schmidt had died of a hemorrhage in Berlin. It was he who had suggested that she start a school for the blind. It was he who had brought the first blind children to her, pleading that she help them. He had inspired her life's work and had always been there to help her, even from Berlin. Now—surely he would help her more than ever—from heaven.

Chapter XIV

Sister Maria sat in Mother Pauline's office, absorbed in reading the paper she held. Three years had passed since the founding of their little congregation, and this was the list of the names of fifty young women who had applied for entrance during that time. Mentally she checked off the names of those who had been admitted. There were twenty, only twenty who had been accepted. She put the paper down and stared at it in her lap. How careful and prudent Mother Pauline had been! Despite her eagerness for more Sisters to fill the requests that were coming in, she had restrained herself and prayed much that she might rightly select those young women truly fitted and called by the Lord to be Sisters of Christian Charity. Her real concern was that she would not reject any one called nor admit anyone not called. It was far more important to have only a small number of Sisters really striving to *be* for God than to have many hurriedly-trained Sisters doing many things poorly. *Being* something for God is greater than *doing* something for Him.

Sister Maria nodded silently as this thought crossed her mind. The door opened, and Mother Pauline came in.

"Ah, Sister Maria!" she said. "I am sorry to have kept you waiting. Oh!" as she caught sight of the list in Sister Maria's hand. "Going over our congregation? Our whole big congregation?" They both smiled.

"We must send three Sisters to Solingen. I have promised them. But then we must stop. We may not and cannot take any more schools until our novices have had two complete years of spiritual and professional training." She looked searchingly at Sister Maria, alert for her reaction.

"I was just thinking that very thing, Mother, as I went down the list of our Sisters. I feel very much at peace when I see how careful you have been to admit only those girls who show the qualities required by our Rule. How could anyone who is moody and changeable or easily depressed possibly work successfully with the blind or with children in school or with the poor?"

"Even more, Sister Maria, how could she survive in community life? But most of all, a girl must be willing to give up her *self-love* and *self-will* so that she can joyfully make God's will her own. Only then can she be effective for God. Besides that, I think it is only reasonable to ask that anyone wanting to live a life of charity should be loving, simple, and well-mannered. And—she should show this by being natural and friendly. I do not like to see young girls walking around with their eyes down. It looks artificial.''

She paused and was silent so long that Sister Maria looked at her curiously. She rose and went to her.

''Mother Pauline,'' she said softly, touching her gently.

''Yes, yes, Sister Maria. Don't be alarmed. It's just that I was a little overwhelmed suddenly by our great inexperience in the formation of the spiritual life. We have plenty of sincere good will, but we need wise direction so very much.''

To her great delight, the Jesuit priests returned to Paderborn that year of 1852 and opened a house of studies there. Mother Pauline was quick to request their services for her Sisters. Father Minoux was one of the first Jesuits to respond. He came to celebrate Holy Mass, gave the Sisters inspirational talks, and offered to give them retreats. These were so excellent that Mother Pauline thanked God over and over for sending him to them.

Father Minoux was also particularly suited to give her advice regarding the training of the Sisters as religious and as teachers. A learned and kindly man, he was superior of the Jesuits, men religious whose main apostolate is education. So Mother Pauline listened gratefully to his suggestions and often asked him outright for guidance.

''Take others the way they are, Mother, not the way you want them to be,'' he told her. He also cautioned against *too many* devotions and penances. He emphasized the importance of professional training for future teachers and impressed this on Mother Pauline. However, he pointed out that not everyone should be given exactly the same program of studies and that individual Sisters should be trained according to their abilities.

Soon the Jesuits sent the Sisters an excellent teacher of theology, and in the spring of 1853 courses for teaching Sisters were also given by the Jesuits with preparation for the exams required by the state for all who would teach.

But that was not all. Through Father Minoux Mother Pauline was able to keep her promise to Father Tewes and offer a retreat for the association of teachers of which he was chaplain. Seventy attended the retreat given that summer, and the Sisters gladly gave up their beds and slept on straw ticks to accommodate the unexpected large number who came. This was just the beginning of many more such retreats. The bishop was very pleased, and Mother Pauline struggled for words to express her immense joy and thanks at having so many of her hopes fulfilled.

As the numbers of the blind children and of the young women entering the convent increased, it became very clear that a new motherhouse was needed. Both groups could no longer share the blind asylum. So Mother Pauline began to plan for a new building to be erected on the site of the first little motherhouse, the von Hartmann house. She called on her brothers, George and Hermann, to help her. She needed the cooperation of Hermann especially since he was the administrator of her part of the family inheritance, which would be used to pay for this project. Work on the new motherhouse began in 1854, and because construction in those days was slow, continued for more than twelve months.

The winter that year was extremely severe, and

the poor were unusually miserable because of it. Mother Pauline had instructed the Sister who answered the door that no poor person who asked for help was ever to be turned away. Each day that Sister gladly gave something to each person who came. Whenever her supply was gone, she would go to Mother Pauline for more. Each time, Mother Pauline would smile happily and remark how good God was to let them give something to the poor. At last one day, the Sister in charge of finances told the Sister at the door that Reverend Mother had very little money left. But she felt she had to follow instructions, and so she went to Mother Pauline for money to give the poor who were waiting.

Mother Pauline put down her pen, opened her drawer and the box in it. There was nothing. She opened drawer after drawer and box after box. Finally she put a silver piece and some pennies in the Sister's hand. "Here, Sister, this is all we have," she said with a brave smile. The Sister hesitated. "Yes, take it," said Mother, "they need it more than we. God will take care of us." Obediently Sister took it, but there were tears in her eyes, and she stopped in chapel with the money on her way to the door.

A few hours later, Mother Pauline sent for the Sister. As she entered her superior's room a little worried, Mother Pauline turned to her, beaming.

"Look, Sister!" she cried. "Look what happens when you trust! The good God has helped us. Sister Josepha sent us a large sum of money from Steele and six woolen blankets. Tomorrow we can begin helping the poor again!" And she squeezed the young Sister's hands with joy.

Day after day the site of the old Hartmann house

was a very busy place, and already the frame of the new building was visible. Workmen were all over, and action was in full swing. Things looked promising.

Mother Pauline turned from the window and the view of the construction across the road and sat down. She was pleased with the progress they were making on the building, and it gave a little more verve to her mind and her hand as she set to work. She had not been working very long when there came an excited knock at her door.

"Come in," she called.

"Reverend Mother," said Sister Crescentia, puffing, "please come quickly! Two of the workmen are fighting! They are using their tools to fight with and someone's going to get hurt badly!" She put her hand on her chest and tried to catch her breath.

"Here, sit down, Sister," said Mother Pauline, pushing the chair toward her. "You say an Our Father for the two hotheads, and I'll see what I can do."

In a few minutes she was hurrying across the road and onto the grounds of the building site, looking for the fighters. As she turned a corner to go to the back, she found them, each dancing about with shovel raised, waiting for the other to strike.

"Gentlemen!" she called. They paid no attention to her, keeping their eyes riveted on each other, wary of the least movement.

"Gentlemen, *please*!" she said again louder, and she looked with concern at what she was carrying. Then, as they still ignored her, she stepped boldly between them.

"Here!" she said and stretching out both arms,

210

thrust a mug of beer toward each of them. "You must be tired and thirsty. That's when a person gets more easily upset. Have a drink, and you will feel better—and then shake hands, won't you?"

For an instant there was a scowl and then surprise on the men's faces. They both stood still with their shovels lowered. Then as they stared at the nun between them, holding out the beer, they began to grin. Slowly one reached for the mug, and then the other.

"Good!" said Mother Pauline, smiling and patting the second man gently on the shoulder as he took the beer. "Now—drink to each other!" and she gave him a tiny push toward the other man. Both dropped their shovels and strode toward each other. "Here's to you!" she called as they clinked the mugs together and drank. She started to move away, still watching them. The last time she looked they were patting each other on the back and finishing their beer.

As she walked back to her room, Mother Pauline reviewed the incident with the two workers and realized that it was not merely her personal power that had so easily influenced those angry men and stopped that fight so quickly. No, it was something much more than that, something she treasured more than anything else in the world—the power of Jesus given to her in Holy Communion each day. It was His tremendous love working through her that had pacified those men. It was His love that fired her with energy to serve all—the Sisters, the blind, the children, the poor, officials, clergy, businessmen—without tiring. It was His love that comforted and sustained her in hardship and sorrow—His love,

211

found always in daily Holy Communion and in visits to Him, the Eucharistic Lord reserved on the altar of their chapel. She knew she must have this for all her Sisters. She must ensure it for those still to come. The Sisters who had joined her until now were receiving Holy Communion daily, but it was not the usual practice in convents. Nor was it usual for every convent to have the Blessed Sacrament in its chapel.

Though Mother Pauline was ready and willing, with her Sisters, to accept every hardship and forego many things, she would not permit that the Sisters in any place be without daily Holy Mass and the Eucharistic Jesus reserved in the tabernacle. For it was this alone that would strengthen them to continue on faithfully and this alone that would enable them to act, not with mere human kindness, but with the love of God Himself—true charity. "The Blessed Sacrament is my life, my bliss; to it I owe the grace of my holy vocation," she had written to Luise Hensel. *Vocation*, for her, was *charity*, and the Eucharist is the source of charity, its life-support. Without the Blessed Sacrament, the Sisters would be deprived apostles. Yet at this time the custom of the Church did not permit what she wanted.

Bishop Drepper, who had fully accepted and helped her and her young congregation, made no reply to her requests for daily Communion and reserving the Blessed Sacrament in their convents. But this did not stop her. She continued her pleas to the bishop, and when he did not answer, she turned to the Vicar General, Father Boekamp.

"Every congregation has its own special and distinguishing mark. Do ask the most Reverend Bishop to allow ours to continue in an atmosphere of joyful, vigorous and refreshing activity which will emanate from the intimate companionship of Jesus in the Eucharist. Needless to say, we shall submit to the decree of the most Reverend Bishop, but in so doing, our congregation will be burdened with a painful sacrifice, the most acute sacrifice which can possibly be imposed on us whose hearts are aflame with love of the Blessed Sacrament. The spiritual characteristic of our congregation must be one of health and vigor, strength and proficiency in accomplishing works of mercy. Were you to deprive us of the Blessed Sacrament, we should be like soldiers who are sent to battle without weapons or means of defense."

Still there was no answer, but Mother Pauline did not give up. She kept pleading with the Highest Authority, the Lord, to grant her petition. But this was only one of the many intentions that kept her on her knees. It was not unusual for her to spend hours before the Blessed Sacrament, kneeling upright and totally absorbed in her conversation with the Lord. The Sisters often grew tired just seeing her there so long, but she became relaxed and energized with the power that came from letting God love her.

That love was the wine that soothed and strengthened her as people, places, and projects all crowded at once into her consciousness, clamoring for attention and fulfillment, and "shattering her nerves," as she wrote in a rare instance. There was, for example, the bishop who had asked that she take the cathedral school, and she had sent Sister Augustine. There was Dortmund, begging for another Sister in the school. There were her many letters to Jesuits, asking for a chaplain for the orphanage at Steele. There were the plans for the Gothic arches of the new chapel and for the bell tower that had to be revised by a Jesuit Brother. There were the pros and cons she had to hear and consider about the arches during the revision. Then came the death of the little son of her brother, George, who needed comforting. Quickly following was news of a robbery at the orphanage at Steele and of the arrival of a chaplain there in the person of Father Ferrenberg since the Jesuits had refused to send one. These were a few of the things she had to handle.

One of her main concerns was that the poor who came to the motherhouse for food be respectfully treated and well-fed. In winter they were to be shown into a warm room, not kept near the door. For years certain sick and elderly people received their midday meal daily at the convent. Besides these, there were thirty to forty and fifty needy persons coming hopefully every day for a meal. Some ate at tables set up in the corridors; others were given carry-out meals for their families. Naturally, feeding so many people entailed extra and almost constant cooking by the Sisters. Only when the city finally opened a food distribution center were they able to return to a more normal load of work.

Often Mother Pauline went down to meet the poor to see that they were cared for. What she gave them probably filled and satisfied them more than the food. It was her gracious and respectful bow as she greeted them, giving them dignity and a sense of worth. One old beggar who slept in a shepherd's hut on grounds near the motherhouse property was always delighted when he saw her coming. It was the highlight of his day. "In the whole world there is not another lady who would greet a poor beggar in such a way. She treats me as if I were a king," he told the Sisters as he took his plate one day.

At the same time the affairs of the young congregation developed and increased. She had now three Sisters in Dortmund where a convent was being built. Requests for Sisters came from Lippespringe and Corbecke, but always haunting her was getting the approval of the government and the Sisters' passing the state examinations for teachers. Her good friend and adviser, Father Minoux, was transferred but was replaced by another excellent Jesuit, Father Haslacher. Then, too, so eager was the pastor at Solingen to have her Sisters come that he was already building a convent.

In November of 1854 Mother Pauline took Sister Clara and Sister Alfonsa to Solingen, and, she wrote, "they were followed by schoolboys who were astonished by the amazing creatures called nuns." She also had to transfer two Sisters from the orphanage at Steele and had to write for another chaplain since Father Ferrenberg was ill and was leaving. Soon Father Klein took his place.

Now an idea very dear to her heart was ripe for action. She would work very hard to get Brothers, a group of men religious, not priests, whose lifestyle was similar to the Sisters', to teach and supervise the boys of the orphanage and of the Blind Institute. It would mean hard work and patience, writing many letters to officials of the government and to the superiors of the Brothers and to the bishop. But that did not matter. The project was worth all the trouble.

Word came that Father Ferrenberg had died, and now Sister Maria was ill, with the ugly question mark of tuberculosis hanging over her. She learned that

Sister Boniface's teaching load was far too heavy, and her health was in danger. She had to warn Sister Mathilde to rearrange classes.

Debts harassed her more than anything, and she had plenty of them with the new motherhouse and chapel. Often she wrote to Hermann, begging for money from her inheritance, "very much and very soon," as she once added.

But money was not the only thing she wanted from Hermann. A retreat for laymen was being conducted by the Jesuits at her institute, and she was very persuasive and loving in her letters to George, Hermann, and Alfred, her brother-in-law, inviting them to make it. It would be during Holy Week, and they would have an excellent chance for their Easter confession and Communion.

With each passing day, she realized more and more that she would have to give up her direct involvement with the blind and give her full attention to the formation of the Sisters and to the many affairs of the order, both religious and secular. She would have to appoint a superior for the Blind Institute. The question was who: Sister Mathilde or Sister Anna? She would consult with the Sisters who were superiors in other houses. But, leaving the blind would cost her dearly. They were her first love and always would be. To be without the chance to serve them, without their company, without their personal response was for her to be without the warmth of sunshine, without the vigor of fresh air.

But she would do it and do it *gladly* even with the ache in her heart. She would do that and far more difficult things because of a love that penetrated and pulsed in her, far greater than the first human love for the blind. It was supreme love. It was love for God. For Pauline, God was so lovable that there was *nothing* she would refuse Him. She had only one goal in life: to please Him, and that meant doing His will, whenever and however He showed it to her. Doing His will became a powerful, lovely refrain constantly echoing in her, moving her mind and heart, her thoughts and actions, her body and soul to the marvelous rhythm of God. It saturated her consciously and subconsciously. She said it and wrote it literally hundreds of times.

So when, after much trouble and effort and letters on her part, Bodelschwingh wrote to say that the Brothers would not be allowed to teach the boys at Steele or the Blind Institute, she was keenly disappointed. But she adjusted to it quickly when she recognized it as the will of God working through others. Well, she could not get the Brothers, but she would at least get a wash machine and mangle for the Blind Institute.

As more and more requests for Sisters came in, *always confronting* her was the vision of not having enough money to support them, to educate them, or to care for them in sickness and in old age. She needed Sisters with good health, with talent, and with a dowry. Even if they had no dowry, she needed them and would take them. Since the salary paid to teachers in elementary schools was low and insufficient to support the community, she was leaning toward accepting the request for Sisters in the high schools where the salary was better. However, she would have to prepare the Sisters for that teaching level, and it would be neither quick nor easy.

In spite of her disappointment and troubles, she

kept looking to the Lord and trusting Him. "He has never deserted me when I trusted Him, and He will never do so," she told the Sisters confidently. She really worked hard to be cheerful and even-tempered and to overcome depression. So when Hermann generously answered her plea for money, her usually bright smile became almost brilliant.

She was half-amused and half-alarmed when she learned that the school boards at Minden and at Arnsberg feared having religious as teachers to the point of panic. They were convinced that the Sisters would obey only the bishop and totally disregard the state and its requirements. Even worse was the fact that other towns shared this belief.

About this time Bishop Drepper became critically ill. Mother Pauline was allowed to visit him, and with loving respect, she told him of the Sisters' prayers for him. Then in answer to the one desire that never left her, she dared to make a last request.

"Your Grace," she said gently but distinctly, kneeling by the bedside in mantle and folding her gloved hands, "you have been a real father to our little congregation and have brought us this far. Our new motherhouse chapel will soon be ready. Will you give us permission to dedicate it and to reserve the Blessed Sacrament there?"

She picked up the prepared statement granting these permissions and held it out to him eagerly for his signature. The priest who was his secretary brought a dipped pen, put the paper on a desk pad in front of the bishop, and propped him up as he took the pen. Slowly and with great effort Bishop Drepper signed his name, and Mother Pauline sighed noiselessly with gratitude and relief as only the crisp sound of the pen on the paper broke the silence in the room.

"Thank you, thank you, Your Grace," breathed Mother Pauline, controlling her great joy. She bent again near the bishop, lying now with closed eyes. She *must* ask. The last blessing of a dying bishop would be especially powerful, like Jesus'.

"Please, Your Grace," she pleaded, close to his ear, "may we, your daughters, have your blessing once more?"

The dying bishop opened his eyes, gave her a little smile and slowly raised his hand. His assistant priest took it and gently helped him trace the cross, saying the words aloud as Bishop Drepper moved his lips too, his eyes fixed on Mother Pauline. She was deeply moved. This man of God had truly, with her, brought her religious family into existence. He would surely never forget them. That evening Bishop Drepper died.

Not far from the new motherhouse ran the new railroad of the province of Westphalia. Summer had come, and the railroad was finished, ready for the inspection of King Frederick William himself. The ceremony took place at Paderborn, and the king, with his officials, was invited to the Blind Institute for a visit.

One of the ladies of the staff at the little home for the blind was stationed as a lookout and soon came puffing excitedly to Mother Pauline who was putting finishing touches on the hair-dos and clothes of the children.

"Reverend Mother, they're coming!" she trilled.

"Very well. Thank you, Martha. Come, children. Hold hands. We must take our places." She led them quickly to the little hall at the front door.

The children ranged themselves on both sides of the door as they had practiced. Mother Pauline and the Sisters, wearing the white mantles and white gloves used for special occasions, stood among them. The other members of the staff joined them. The blind children were silent but fidgety, sensitive to the excitement in the air that one could almost touch.

Then he was there. The king strode in, and although the children could not see him and his party, they could sense how splendid he looked in his fine uniform and shining medals, from the rustle of his clothes, the click of his boots, the slight clank of his sword, the crisp smell of very special fabrics, climaxed by the sound of respectful voices greeting him in the flurry of air as he passed.

The king smiled as he glanced at the garlands and wreaths on every window and door and sat expectantly in the big, finely-cushioned armchair set for him. Everyone grouped around him, and the children sang a song of welcome. His eyes went from face to face as they sang. When tiny Caroline Hille stepped forward and said a poem in his honor with the lovable enthusiasm of a child, her blank blue eyes fixed straight ahead, he blinked back the tears in his own eyes and cleared his throat.

Again he was deeply touched as other blind boys and girls came forward, unafraid and simply, to offer him handmade gifts for the queen. He noticed that their dignity quite matched his own as they bowed to him carefully and solemnly.

Then the king rose and spoke to the children gently and lovingly. He thanked them and their teachers and the staff for the pleasure they had given

220

him and for the gifts for the queen. He knew the children would become fine men and women, and he would be happy to help them whenever he could. He shook their hands, patted their heads, saying good-bye to them as he left. Even as his coach pulled away, he called goodbye to the waving children who could only hear the whirr of the wheels and the clap of horses' hoofs. The king went home enriched that day.

Mother Pauline treasured the document signed by Bishop Drepper on his deathbed and guarded it carefully as she, the Sisters, the postulants, and the staff moved to the new motherhouse in November, 1855. About a month later, December 28, Bishop Freusberg consecrated the new chapel and left the Blessed Sacrament there. One of her biggest dreams was finally fulfilled.

Now that Mother Pauline had left the Blind Insti-tute for the motherhouse, someone else would have to be in charge of the blind. Although it was very hard for her to leave them, she knew that her time must be totally given from this point on to the forma-tion of new members, cultivating the spirit of the congregation, as well as handling its government and financial matters.

The general choice of the other superiors for the head of the Blind Institute was Sister Anna. If only it were possible to still work with the blind, Mother Pauline would gladly have worked under Sister Anna. But the new infant community was growing more and more, and so she resolutely turned her full attention and energy to caring for that in all its phases.

Chapter XV

Hermann suddenly stopped tapping his pen on the fine antique desk and swung his chair around to face George. He had been visiting his brother and his sister-in-law, Dina, for a few days there at the beloved old estate of Boeddeken, and it had brought back many dear memories—memories especially of his father and of Pauline. More than once nostalgia had gripped him, leaving him staring at some familiar thing for several minutes while images of the past flashed on his memory. He sighed. He would have to be returning to Berlin soon, and it was high time that he re-focus on the present with all its challenges and circumstances.

He tipped his chair back and dangled one foot. "You know, George," he said, "the Boss seems to be doing quite well. Now, as of the end of 1855, she has 45 Sisters, and they are teaching 1000 students in three schools outside of Paderborn. Her congregation has been recognized as a corporation by the government, and she is preparing to work toward papal approval of it. They are going to take over another school in Sigmaringen too. All that only six years after she founded the order!"

George had put down the paper and was puffing on his pipe. "Yes," he answered. "I think we can be proud of her. She didn't even accept all the women who applied for admission."

"I know," continued Hermann. He laughed softly. "She has also made up her mind to put the finances of the motherhouse on a firm foundation and is pressing me to sell her shares in the mines. Beginning with January, she wants the Blind Institute to be self-supporting and the day nursery to be independent as soon as possible. She may not be a wizard at math, George, but she doesn't let that stop her from taking charge of her business affairs."

She doesn't let *anything* stop her in *any* affairs," remarked George dryly. "She's a remarkable woman, Hermann." Their eyes met. They both shook their heads and laughed.

It was not far into the new year of 1856 when Paderborn received the news that Professor Conrad Martin, who taught religion at a high school in Bonn, would be its new bishop. Those acquainted with this priest knew him to be extremely intelligent, deeply prayerful, and devoted to those in his care. Very soon after he was consecrated bishop, he became a great friend of the Sisters of Christian Charity.

The Blind Institute was now thriving under Sister Anna's excellent direction, which left Mother Pauline free for other things. Besides handling the many practical problems of human relations, school situations, convent needs and expenses of the Sisters working in all the missions of the congregation, Mother Pauline was busy teaching French to the Sisters of the motherhouse and planning a formal program for the educational and spiritual development of all those in training. This she intended to carry out as soon as possible.

She was interrupted one day by a surprise visit from Bishop Martin who had brought a stranger with him. Even before he was introduced to her, Mother Pauline knew from the gold chain and cross outlined against his black suit that the visitor was a bishop. But she was surprised to hear that he had travelled all the way from the state of Illinois in the United States of America. He was Bishop Junker and had come to ask her to send some Sisters to his diocese in Illinois to teach in the schools that his Catholic people had built there.

Mother Pauline's face lit with her marvelous, transforming smile. She knew English well enough to understand Bishop Junker, and Bishop Martin helped with answering him. She also knew that since Bishop Martin had brought him to her, he approved of her sending Sisters to Bishop Junker's diocese.

"Your Excellency, I am honored that you should ask for our Sisters to teach in your diocese in America, and believe me, I would like very much to send you some Sisters. But at this very moment, I have no Sisters. Every single one is already committed to a post or promised to one. And—it is important to me that we have the approval of the Holy Father on our little congregation before we take missions across the ocean."

Bishop Junker looked at her for a long moment, then he nodded and said, "I understand, Reverend

Mother."

Suddenly it was already May, and news of her Uncle Fritz's death reached her. Another dear ally who had helped her from her teenage years on had gone. But she would be the last one to begrudge him heaven.

Things were far from better in Witten. She had had to withdraw all the Sisters from the classrooms because the school board believed they would not comply with the state and would take orders only from the bishop. She had allowed Sister Agnes to stay there for the sewing classes, but now it was necessary to discontinue even that and have her leave there by July and return to Paderborn. It was sad that such misconceptions could continue to exist.

Disappointment and frustration soon faded in the bustle of preparations for the investing of new novices and the coming visit of President von Bodelschwingh. Mother Pauline needed to set the date for the investing ceremony early enough with Bishop Martin, and she was concerned not only that the novices' habits be well-made and finished on time, but that they themselves would be well prepared spiritually. Then she and Sister Anna would have to make a thorough check of the Blind Institute and ready the blind children for the questions that Bodelschwingh would surely ask.

It was a warm day in late August, and Mother Pauline sat wearily at her desk, her hands limp in her lap, her eyes closed. Close by stood Sister Maria, viewing her with alarm. This was not at all like Mother Pauline.

"Reverend Mother," she said quietly, "you need rest and fresh air. The pressure of so much business over these past months, especially disagreeable business, has been sapping your strength. I'm afraid you have nervous exhaustion."

To her surprise, Mother Pauline said nothing. She yielded immediately to Sister Maria's touch and walked with her to a chair near the open window.

"Thank you, dear Sister," she murmured. "I'll be all right. Perhaps later I'll take a little walk in the garden."

She breathed deeply, and the stirring of a sudden tiny breeze felt good on her face. She became acutely conscious of the quiet around her and then smiled as the cheerful, staccato little chirps of birds punctuated the air. She had not noticed them for a long time.

She sat listening, relaxed, for a while. Then she rose and went downstairs. As she passed the kitchen on her way to the garden, the voice of the Sister came to her, clear and strong.

"Oh no, my boy. Your price is too high. The berries grow wild right out there near us."

Mother Pauline turned quickly into the kitchen and strode toward the Sister at the kitchen door with that long, heavy step of hers. At the sound of the walking, Sister turned and moved toward Mother Pauline, revealing the figure of a boy holding a bucket of berries outlined in the doorway.

Mother Pauline looked at the boy keenly for an instant and saw the poor, faded, patched clothes, the thin face and arms, and the big, blue, disappointed eyes.

"Dear Sister," she said kindly, "The price is too high? I don't think so. Not if you consider the long stooping and picking that are quite difficult. I know from my own childhood when I picked berries in the woods in Borchen to please my grandmother."

She looked down and nodded understandingly at the boy. His blue eyes brightened so much that it made her smile at him in her wonderful way. It seemed to him that she was smiling all over, not just with her lips, and that it made her almost glow. He smiled back happily.

"Please, Sister, bring a dish with milk and a spoon and some sugar," said Mother Pauline. As the Sister passed her, she whispered, "Pay him for the berries, too."

Then she scooped some berries generously into the bowl with milk and gave the rest in the pail back to Sister.

"Here, child," said Mother Pauline, "sit down at the table and eat some of the berries first before you go home. You should enjoy them after you stooped so long in the burning sun to pick them."

The lad could only clutch the spoon and look from the big dark berries in the milk to her shining eyes. He didn't know what to say. The light in her eyes did more for him than even the taste of the luscious berries. It made him feel good and very happy, ready to go out and pick *anything*!

She watched with pleasure as he ate. He was sitting on the kitchen chair, his feet hanging inches above the floor. He was obviously relishing the fruit, but kept his eyes on the Sister who was emptying his pail. She handed it and some money to Mother Pauline.

The boy slid to the floor. "Thank you," he said softly. "Thank you very much."

Mother Pauline gave him his pail and put the money carefully and gladly in his free hand.

"Goodbye now, and thank you, too. God bless you, dear child," and she patted his head. She had hardly said the words when he was out the door, sprinting exuberantly on his way home. The Sister joined her at the door and together they stood looking after him.

"Things like that always refresh me, Sister. You, too? Don't worry about the money. God will provide. Meantime, we'll have some delicious berries for supper."

With the coming of the new year 1857, Mother Pauline realized that not only must she devote all of her time now to the revising of the Constitutions of the order but that she must also withdraw to a special place in order to do it. So she met with Sister Maria and the older Sisters and asked to have a small, secluded room on the top floor of the Blind Asylum as her working place.

"Please, dear Sisters, allow me to work there undisturbed as much as possible. But, of course, if there are pressing problems that you feel you do not want to handle alone, please call me. I'm sure, though, that you can take care of most of them. I ask your prayers that God will help me in this important work."

"Of course, Reverend Mother," said Sister Maria.

"Since I will be needing help and advice, I shall be consulting Bishop Martin and Father Roh," continued Mother Pauline. "They have already been kind enough to assure me of that."

Since the Church required that congregations of women founded at that time base their rule on one of the early monastic rules, Mother Pauline chose the rule of St. Augustine for women religious. However,

Hermann von Mallinckrodt, Pauline's youngest brother

there were other rules called Constitutions that she wrote to accompany it. These showed a remarkable blend of the spirituality of St. Ignatius and of St. Francis de Sales. Pauline was well acquainted with the writings of both saints, and their main spiritual qualities were very evident in herself. Her final work was a truly beautiful example of the influence of three great saints on a single rule of life for religious women.

Besides giving much of his time and learning for the revision of the Constitutions, Bishop Martin also gave the Sisters instructions on theology during the winter. For that they were very grateful. Just the chance to receive more solid learning about God was precious, but to be able to get it from so learned and devout a teacher without having to leave their house and go out in the cold was almost too good to be true.

The Sisters could not, however, keep bad news from finding its way to Mother Pauline's room, secluded though it was. There had been first, the death of her faithful former helper, Aunt Marianne, the wife of Uncle Fritz, who had himself died only recently. Months later came the word that faithful Sister Josepha had contracted consumption. Sister Xaveria would have to replace her as Superior at the orphanage in Steele. Now, in April, there was an outbreak of smallpox in Dortmund, and all the Sisters had to be vaccinated.

Hermann offset those worries with the exciting news that he was going to Rome and would keep in touch, sharing his experiences with Mother Pauline and the Sisters. Besides that, permission was given, in answer to her request, for the Sisters to go from door to door collecting money for a new nursery. All this good news was like a quick transfusion of vitality, and Mother Pauline went back to her work on the Constitutions with new energy.

She worked so diligently that by February of the next year, 1858, she had finished the Constitutions in rough form. Carefully Bishop Martin went over them with her. Later, the Sisters were called to a chapter at the motherhouse where the Constitutions were presented to them. They listened carefully and discussed the Rules enthusiastically. Mother Pauline called a second chapter at the orphanage in Steele for those Sisters who had been unable to attend the first one. Here they objected to only one point of external discipline, which was removed. Mother Pauline was happy to see how well the Sisters had received her labor of love.

Now it was time to send the Constitutions to Boeddeken where Father Trippen, George's chaplain, would translate them into Latin before being taken to Rome for approval. They would have to be ready by July when Bishop Martin was scheduled to leave for the Vatican.

Having finished the heavy task of writing the Constitutions, Mother Pauline was able to direct her thoughts to planning for the immediate future. She would have to reserve Sisters for America and Sisters for the hospital in Witten. Then she concluded transactions for taking over a school in Witten and one in beautiful Sigmaringen. She bought a house in Sigmaringen for the Sisters' convent, and since it was so far away from the motherhouse, the Sisters would have to stay there for retreat. She also had to plan dates for the Sisters to take the teachers' examinations, assign to suitable schools those who passed the tests, and send their certificates for teaching to them after they arrived. She also needed to make a plan for building a nursery, for raising still more of the needed money, and obtain the bishop's approval.

It was in the midst of all this business and planning that her heart and mind were suddenly caught up in that same detaching and inviting fascination with heaven that she had experienced at her mother's death. April 28 had dawned, and with it a new life for Sister Josepha. Dear, good Sister Josepha had died that day, and Mother Pauline was both sad and glad. Sad because she would indeed miss her; glad because Sister had reached all that made life worth living. Mother Pauline had obtained permission from both the civil and church authorities to bury the Sisters in the garden. So the little black house that stood in the garden was changed into a chapel dedicated to St. Joseph. There a burial vault was prepared, and the caskets of both Sister Josepha and Sister Elizabeth were carried to it. The burning lights of the Sisters and postulants and the singing of the blind children made it beautifully solemn and reverent. At the grave Father Schmidt spoke some fitting words, and then all went back to the motherhouse chapel to make the Way of the Cross for the two Sisters.

In conducting all of the business necessary for administering the congregation, Mother Pauline tried to counterbalance her natural tendency to dominate by telling the Sisters repeatedly that she was open to their opinions. A person actually in the given situation is much better able, she declared, to make the right judgment than one who is not.

Yet for some reason, she found that of late she

was frequently not open to the opinions of her brothers. Even worse, there had been some sharp words and unpleasant feeling between herself and them, a thing that had never happened before in all the years she dealt with them.

Just the other day they had both come to the motherhouse to give her their opinion on a matter she had earlier presented to them. She had needed to consult with them about a growing problem that would require using a substantial part of her inheritance, and Hermann was the executor of this money. Because more young women were applying for admission to the congregation, and more ladies were coming to join in teachers' retreats, the motherhouse was too small and crowded to adequately accommodate them all. They really needed more space. But Mother Pauline felt she had a solution that would require no building.

Far away there was for sale a large, ancient monastery with wide, rambling grounds. She had gone to inspect it and had come away dreaming of the fine motherhouse and boarding-school for girls that it would provide. There young women could be trained as religious, the young Sisters could study, and other Sisters would teach the girls. The school would yield a welcome income.

George and Hermann had listened attentively to the plan and had gone away promising to study the whole idea carefully. Soon they were back to give their evaluation of it. It was not good. Hermann had remarked to Bertha, "*Die Alte* has wonderful ideas, but her arithmetic is as bad as ever." He had come to advise against the plan.

Mother Pauline could hardly believe it, but as

Hermann laid out both the pros and cons with George nodding solemnly in agreement, her hopes had vanished. Yet, true to herself, she had some questions to ask. It was then as she heard them answer that she had noticed a disturbing change. Hermann was really sarcastic, and George was curt and abrupt. She saw that there was nothing to be gained by further talk. To them the project was impractical, and Hermann was unwilling to invest her money in it. She thanked them both and took them to the door. They seemed like two strange businessmen.

After they had left, she stood for a few moments with her hand still on the knob. She was very disappointed, but even more, hurt and confused. What was wrong? What had she done? She began to walk, not knowing where, absorbed in thought. After a while she stopped and looked up. There was the altar. She had come into the chapel to the one Friend who loved her no matter what she did. It was as if her feet had gone there by habit.

She looked long at the tabernacle, pleading for some insight. Slowly it began to come, and then more rapidly, as scenes from her last two visits to Boeddeken flashed before her in quick succession. Two things stood out in her memory like ugly blurs: the frequent exchange of blunt, disagreeable words and the sound of raised, irritated voices. She recognized them only too well. The words and the voices belonged to her and George and Hermann. She covered her face with her hands.

With a shock she realized the great changes time and circumstances had made in her and her two brothers. How could she possibly not know that with

George von Mallinckrodt, Pauline's oldest brother

their particular professional training, experience, and present lifestyle so unlike hers, their view of things would have to be totally different? After all, they were not Sisters. Perhaps that was it! Perhaps the constant deference, respect, and yielding of the Sisters to her as their superior had made her over-sensitive and vulnerable to any sort of frankness or disagreement. She knew that she herself was extremely candid, even blunt. Probably, without realizing it, she had spoken to George and Hermann with that "strong determination" Father Roh had told her was a good quality, but *without* the mildness he had said was so necessary. Yes, she had been too assertive, and at times, even vehement. That she had to change. But she also knew that in some of those matters she had discussed with her brothers (not necessarily the purchase of the monastery) that she was right. They concerned things relating to the congregation about which she had far more knowledge, experience, and intuition than George and Hermann.

There was, for example, the instance of Sister Bertha's dismissal. This novice was a dear friend of Mother Pauline's sister Bertha and was intelligent and pious. Yet, even after a prolonged novitiate, she had still shown signs of restlessness and dissatisfaction. With the best of will Mother Pauline could not in conscience allow her to make her vows and so had to ask her to leave. Sister Bertha did so reluctantly but peacefully. Bertha, however, was far from peaceful, crying much and complaining to Pauline. When that failed, she asked for Hermann's intercession. He tried, but Mother Pauline was firm. She knew they both meant well, but they did not understand all that convent life required. Her decision was right, she knew, but perhaps she should have been more gentle in giving it.

As she knelt before her Lord and saw herself in His revealing light, she surrendered one more foothold of her ego. She prayed for pardon and for courage blended with mildness.

"Divine Master," she went on, "take me into Your school of love—I so want to learn from You. Teach me the art of self-denial, and above all, I beg you to make me lovable in all my contacts, that I may never hurt or wound anyone, but let me become all things to all men. Lord, fill me with love and humility that I may please You."

She went straight from the chapel to her desk. She had to somehow rebuild that good relationship with her brothers as soon as possible. Quickly she took paper, dipped her pen, and began to write fast and urgently, her hand driven across the page with love. She told Hermann and George how miserable she felt, how she regretted those unpleasant incidents, and that she loved them both very much. But, at the same time, she was straightforward and unyielding in whatever she felt was right. Of self she would always let go; of right, never.

"Forgive me everything whereby I have pained you or shown myself disagreeable toward you," she wrote . . . . "Let us avoid as far as we can those topics on which we mutually disagree or let us treat them with particular discretion so that we do not cause one another any heartache. Each of us has his own interests; you have yours and I have mine. The direction of the congregation is my concern and, with that in mind, I will not allow myself to be dissuaded from upholding those principles which in my opinion will serve its flourishing development. Permit me to continue undisturbed in my task just as I permit you freely to manage your affairs....And if occasionally we give one another some good advice, let us try to do so in such a way that we do not offend each other... Let us therefore both forget all the unpleasant happenings of the past and begin the New Year with renewed brotherly and sisterly love and trust."

A week later, she was laboring carefully over another letter, a most important one, to Bishop Conrad Martin. It was a formal petition, requesting him to present to the Holy Father, Pope Pius IX, the Rules and Constitutions of the Sisters of Christian Charity, and to ask for the Church's approval of them. She included a brief history of the congregation, ending with its current status after ten years of existence: 68 Sisters, 11 missions, and 1,444 students under instruction. The bishop was pleased and promised to fulfill her request.

A little later, her response to a Sister who was superior in a developing school showed how much her regard for the ideas and choices of others had increased. She had learned from her recent experience with her brothers, and she had grown even more by her surrender to the Lord, begging Him to temper her powerful will with His love. Yet, she was not dictatorial. She wanted to be firm, but she feared being harsh. After stating her views and objections forcefully, she told the Sister not to accept them simply because Mother Pauline was her superior. No, she was to consider them only on their own merits. Then she, the Sister, was to make the final decision. Mother Pauline respected her judgment and left her free to act. But with that freedom went full responsibility for the outcome, successful or unsuccessful, which the superior must bear. To Mother Pauline obedience was a call to maturity and full personhood.

One morning early in February, there was some excitement as the Sisters and the blind children said goodbye to Bishop Conrad Martin. He was leaving for Rome. They would miss him but were happy at the thought of what he would do for them in Rome. Meantime, he left the Sisters a replacement for his homilies and instructions with meditations on the Gospel. He had written these himself and had given them to Mother Pauline for the community.

As they thought and prayed over Scripture, the Sisters must have been struck by the loving concern of Jesus especially for those who stray, for it soon found an echo in their own apostolate. Two Sisters began going every Sunday to the prison at Männchen where they visited the women prisoners, serving them in any way they could. They prayed with and for them, or just encouraged them, listened to them, cheered them. Before long, the women came to love the Sisters. In fact, because of their influence, some of the prisoners asked for the priest, received the Sacrament of Penance and found peace and forgiveness along with the resolve for a better life.

It would soon be time again for the ceremony of investing new novices, and that meant preparing them for it by the customary retreat. Pauline was full of the love of God and very enthusiastic about religious life. Naturally loving and out-going, she could hardly keep all that enthusiasm to herself. She simply had to share her vision of what it means to be a Sister of Christian Charity. What better way than by giving a retreat? So she began to carefully plan the conferences she would give to the young women who would become novices.

After the close of retreat and the investing, business matters sent Mother Pauline to the convents at Dortmund, Witten, Solingen, Anrath, and Steele. She was able to complete everything in two weeks. Then she went on to Sigmaringen, which was still farther away, and spent a full week there.

Her reason for staying so long was that the annual retreat for the Sisters of Sigmaringen was being given at that time, and she wanted every Sister, including the cook and housekeepers, to make the retreat. But someone would have to cook and clean and do the laundry in their places. That would be no problem. Mother Pauline smiled, took off her cuffs, and put on an apron. What was a Mother for? It reminded her of the good old days at Aix when she had managed the family household. She soon made friends in her hearty way with the girl from the orphanage who had come to help, and together they swept and dusted, washed and ironed, and tempted appetites with tasty meals. The Sisters gathered around her happily when retreat was over, glad that she would stay for another week to visit with them and settle her business.

The trees were budding, and it was May when she got word that the bishop was returning from Rome. He arrived on the sixth, and practically the whole town went out to meet him. The mayor and city officials welcomed him at the train while the priests and a large crowd waited for him at the city gate. Various societies waving their banners, groups of people and children awaited him along the streets as a procession led him to the cathedral. There the Sisters of Mercy and the Sisters of Christian Charity with the blind children and many more people waited inside for the bishop. He had given an address at the train station and now gave another to the happy crowd that filled the cathedral. At last a carriage took him to his residence where his brother and relatives were waiting to greet him.

That same day the bishop sent the document of approval of the congregation to Mother Pauline. He knew how eager the Sisters were to receive it, so he lost no time. Mother Pauline called all the Sisters of the motherhouse and of the Blind Asylum together so that they could see it. It was called Decree of Praise, and Mother Pauline read the translation of it aloud.

Toward evening the Sisters went to the bishop's residence to thank him for the decree.

"We are very grateful to you, Your Excellency," said Mother Pauline, "for obtaining this decree for us. I think their faces tell you how happy we are about it," and she motioned to the Sisters standing around her.

The bishop nodded with a smile.

"After I presented your Constitutions with the request for approval, they were examined by two consultors who made a report on them to the Holy Father," he said. "Some days later I was given this Decree of Praise for you, and at that time I was allowed to petition for approbation of the Constitutions. I was told that it would probably be sent in one year." He leaned forward a little for emphasis. "That, my dear Sisters, is unusually fast. Normally it takes about *ten* years to get such approbation after receiving the Decree of Praise."

They were all most pleasantly surprised. But the bishop was not finished.

"Besides the Decree of Praise," he said, "the Holy Father has agreed to bestow on your congregation the additional beautiful title, Daughters of the Blessed Virgin Mary of the Immaculate Conception, in honor of the dogma he recently proclaimed." There were little sounds of awe and joy in the group, and then a moment of silence.

"And now," he went on, smiling broadly, "I have something else for you, something that did not come from Rome."

The Sisters all looked at Mother Pauline expectantly, but she only shrugged a little and looked back with raised eyebrows and questioning blue-green eyes.

Bishop Martin picked up another paper and held it out to Mother Pauline.

"This is a document from Berlin stating that government gives permission to your *congregation*, not just to individual Sisters, to teach in the public schools of Germany from now on," he announced with such triumph that the Sisters clapped almost involuntarily. Mother Pauline had worked hard and waited long for that as well as for the approval of Rome.

"We hardly know how to thank you for everything, Your Excellency," said Mother Pauline, her voice strained with emotion. "I can only promise you that you shall be always remembered in our prayers gratefully."

Buoyant with all this good news, Mother Pauline turned now wih even greater zest and drive to the work awaiting her. More and more change was taking place in labor and industry with the introduction of machines. This, in turn, was changing the educational scene, especially for girls and women. There was an ever growing demand for high schools for girls. But this was also creating more classes and divisions in society. At first Mother Pauline had been reluctant to place her Sisters in these schools, but she saw that it was unwise to resist any longer. In fact, she realized that here was an opportunity for a greater apostolate with youth. So she agreed to have her Sisters take over the high school for girls at Constance.

This would be a boarding-school, and the building would need renovation. Mother Pauline knew this would be expensive. The congregation would be able to do only the most necessary. So the girls would have to bring their own beds, but she did not worry about that.

She was far more concerned that each Sister who was to teach those teenagers had a genuine love for them. She was convinced that without love, no real teaching can take place. It was absolutely necessary that each girl be seen by the Sisters as a unique and valuable image of God. Each must *feel* accepted because education begins in the emotional sphere. It depends on winning the hearts of the students; it is built on charity and self-sacrifice.

However, along with love there must be authority which places the consequences that follow reasonably from wrong acts or choices made by the students. At the same time, those in authority should help the girls come in contact with inspiring ideals and let them react freely to them. Ideals appeal strongly to the basic goodness in young people and help them find direction. She knew that a healthy tension for the teenagers would be created by the guidance of authority on the one hand and the attraction of ideals on the other. She felt strongly that there should be no repression of originality or natural talent in the girls. This would make them independent within a wholesome framework and teach them to make their own decisions, respectful of the consequences. But experience had taught her that only a combination of patience, calmness, authority, and a just application of consequences by teachers leads young people to self-direction and responsibility. All of these she would demand of the Sisters assigned to teach them.

As life in the congregation moved on, she was immensely pleased to hear that permission to keep the Blessed Sacrament in the chapel of the Sisters had been granted for both convents at Constance and Solingen. The list of people to whom she must write letters of thanks was getting longer and longer because of all the kindnesses shown the congregation since the Sisters had moved into those two houses. But for her it was a labor of love and little enough return for all these people had given.

For some time there had been forming in the back of her mind the vague notion of planning a new motherhouse and novitiate wing with perhaps a boarding-school. But it soon became a very real need. When Mother Pauline saw the congestion caused by the coming of so many Sisters and lay teachers for their retreat and found that the Sisters not in retreat would have to give up their beds and sleep in the beds of the blind childrn who were away, she knew without a doubt that it was high time to start planning. She did so, but after consulting her council, she decided that it was better for the community to merely enlarge the motherhouse and add the novitiate wing but not the boarding-school.

There was another project very dear to her, a dream she had had for a long time that she finally realized had to be abandoned. She let it go only with great reluctance, not thinking that, as a result, the pain of it would soon be doubled. She had always hoped that some day a group of Sisters with the desire and the needed qualifications for perpetual adoration of the Blessed Sacrament could be set aside in a house chosen for that purpose. One Sister in particular, Sister Clara Pfänder, longed to be a part of such a group. She had been the community's first postulant, invested on the day that the first four Sisters had made their vows in 1850. She was the novice sent to help Sister Mathilde at Dortmund in the Sisters' first mission. She had devoted herself generously to every other assignment given her by Mother Pauline, waiting all the while for their mutual dream to come true. Her goodness and fervor, especially her love for the Eucharistic Jesus, had endeared her to Mother Pauline. Yet through the years her longing for a different religious lifestyle grew, and when it became clear that perpetual adoration was not feasible in the congregation, she felt she had to seek another community.

Mother Pauline understood her need and made every effort to help her find what she was looking for. Finally, after letters had been written to several orders and Sister Clara found none to enter, Bishop Martin thought it best for her to leave by October, 1859. Sadly but lovingly, Mother Pauline said good-bye to her. God surely had other plans for Sister Clara, and Mother Pauline would not stand in her way.

Chapter XVI

There was perhaps no other person in Pauline's religious life so uniquely fitted to help her grow in holiness than Bishop Conrad Martin. His position as her immediate head in the Church, whose word she regarded as Christ's very own, assured him her complete cooperation and reverent respect. His personal qualities of great learning and sharp intelligence, with little tolerance for opposition, offset by his deep piety and love for God, increased that respect. Even more, his genuine care for the congregation, his continual interest in all the Sisters, his frequent coming for religious ceremonies and purely social visits, won her confidence and love. But above all, he had become her personal spiritual director at her own request when Father Boekamp's appointment as such ended with the death of Bishop Drepper. To her Bishop Conrad Martin was the representative of God and the Church, father to the congregation, and her spiritual guide.

It was only natural, then, that true to her upbringing, Pauline should treat the bishop with a great courtesy, amounting almost to formality. But she turned it into sheer graciousness with her genuine warmth and sincere simplicity. Her conduct toward everyone, but especially toward him, was remarkable for balance. She was humble, but dignified; frank, but prudent. She was friendly, yet delicately reserved. She was always polite and attentive but so natural and relaxed that there was never any strain. She was loyal and obedient to him, true to her inner principles of right and justice.

Bishop Martin, on his part, had studied Pauline and knew well what sort of person she was. Her candor made her quite transparent while his experience and understanding of people let him see qualities in her not otherwise so obvious. More than once on meeting her as he came into the convent, he had been struck by what he saw in her face. She was usually very serious and very reverent in her bearing, her clear eyes reflecting a quiet inner adoration, like one keenly sensitive to the presence of God within her. In the very next instant, though, as soon as she noticed the bishop or anyone else, her face would relax in a magnificent smile, radiating a joy and love that were mirrored in her shining eyes and set her glowing with the loveliness of God.

The bishop was very aware of Pauline's deep love for God and her unswerving determination to do His will at any cost. He was also aware of her equally deep humility that would allow the grace of God to do painful but splendid things in her. He saw a woman of great soul, capable of heroic virtue. So he was silently pleased, like a spiritual father, with each sign of her progress and resolved to continue to draw her on and on to perfection.

Frequently, after he had celebrated Mass, he would think of some small way to test her virtue or make her grow in it. She always rose to the occasion.

One particular cold, crisp January morning the bishop was giving the Sisters an instruction. He stopped and pointedly questioned Mother Pauline. She rose and answered him as best she could. He paused for a moment and then accepted her response. There was a slight titter of amusement among the Sisters, and afterward they teased her about it. She took it good naturedly and later even wrote about it in one of her letters to the Sisters.

Another time the bishop stopped Mother Pauline as she came out of the room where everyone went for his conferences. Two other Sisters were walking with her as they met him. He handed her a notebook containing outlines which he had prepared for the Sisters for meditating on the Sunday gospels.

"Perhaps the Sisters will find these helpful," he said. Then quite deliberately and well aware of the presence of the other two Sisters, he said casually, "By the way, Mother Pauline, how are you getting along with your meditations?"

"Very poorly, Your Grace," she answered simply.

He nodded but said nothing. He knew very well that those outlines were of no help to her. She was far beyond them and greatly advanced in her prayer life. He suspected that the Sisters knew that too, but the important thing was that Mother Pauline remain humble so as to keep her intimacy with God and to realize how far she had yet to go.

So he continued—challenging, testing, advising,

Bishop Conrad Martin

correcting, even reproaching her, but he was always met with her courteous, unruffled acceptance. She had a way with him, and Bishop Martin took more from her than he would from others, listening to her questions, opinions, and ideas more readily because of her utter sincerity, her openness and humility.

Meanwhile, Pauline was trying to control the spurts of growth in the healthy young congregation. It was February of 1860 when she finally wrote to a bishop and to a priest in the United States about their request for Sisters. In reply to the letter of Bishop Junker in Alton, Illinois she wrote that she was glad he had obtained other Sisters to work in his diocese. She regretted that she did not have enough Sisters to send him, adding that her congregation did not have official approbation of its Constitutions as yet. To Father Bartels of Teutopolis, Illinois she wrote that she was preparing Sisters to go to America, but they could not go till they received the Church's approbation of their Rules. She suggested that he get other Sisters as Bishop Junker did.

Almost as if in answer to her reason given to the two American clergymen for not going to America, there came from Rome the following month three sheets of corrections to be made in the Constitutions. These corrections could be made at the Sisters' discretion and then returned to Rome. Mother Pauline was happy about it, for three sheets were considered minimal, she told her cousin Bertha.

The Sisters were busy with a variety of activities, and at the motherhouse many of them took the course in nursing given there by Dr. Everken. The number of Sisters increased too, and by April of that year there were more than eighty of them.

This was, of course, a blessing, but for Mother Pauline, it was a mixed one. She was more than glad to have the Sisters, but she badly needed money to support and educate them. Many had been accepted without dowries because their families could not afford to give them. By this time, Pauline's own inheritance and the dowries of the few young women who had brought one were practically gone, and the congregation was really heading for financial trouble.

So Pauline turned to what she had not been too proud to do before: begging. Humbly, affectionately, and tactfully, she wrote to her uncle Bernard von Hartmann, asking him to remember the congregation in his will. She wrote also to her cousin, Hugo, the banker, with whom she often did business and from whom she made loans. She instructed the postulants and novices to ask for something by way of dowry for the congregation. Outside of uncharitableness, probably nothing distressed her more than owing money. "Debts torture me intensely!" she wrote to one of the Sisters.

Naturally, she wrote about this to Hermann, the administrator of her inheritance. He was now a representative of the House in Berlin. Her letters told him eloquently how very much the paying of debts concerned her. But in June she had another reason to write to him, a more pleasant one. He was finally engaged to a fine young woman named Elischen von Bernhard, and she congratulated him heartily.

In the middle of the summer Bishop Martin asked Mother Pauline for Sisters to take over the care of the housekeeping in Paderborn's seminary, and she consented. They were to start their work there in the fall. But there was still more that they would start.

Despite her anxiety regarding her own resources for paying bills, Pauline had not the slightest doubt about God's ability to do so. She trusted Him completely, totally. So if He indicated that He wanted the Sisters to work in a certain place, she would send them there, confident that He would see to it that they had sufficient means to carry on His work. With that in mind, she accepted the care and education of orphan girls at Höxter and a girl's school at Viersen as new places for the Sisters' apostolate in the fall.

It was the last week in August when Pauline went with George, Dina, and their daughter, Marie, to Hermann's wedding. She smiled happily and fervently thanked the Lord as she heard Elischen and Hermann exchange their marriage vows. At last they were all settled and taken care of—her brothers and sister. It was true that they were all adults, perfectly capable of running their lives, but somehow she still felt responsible for them. Three months later, on a trip to Düsseldorf on business, Pauline visited the newly married couple. She saw very quickly that Hermann and his wife were genuinely contented.

The blind children were counting the days till Christmas, and Mother Pauline was doubly busy with preparations for it. But she suddenly had to stop it all when she got word of her sister. Bertha had been sick for some time and had gone to Meran to recover. Alfred wrote to say that she was not getting better; that actually, she could not get better. Both Bertha and he needed her. Would she come?

Sister Maria and the other Sisters understood and sent her off, promising to take care of everything. Nothing of the usual Christmas celebrations for the children or Sisters would be skipped, including the adoration of the exposed Blessed Sacrament with the lovely prayers and hymns.

Pauline prayed for Bertha as the train jolted along. She had never thought as she mothered her little sister growing up that this youngest of them all would be the first to die. Her heart ached for the five little ones who would lose their mother. And Alfred! Dear, devoted Alfred. How he would miss Bertha!

The slow jerks of the train as it came to a stop at Eisenach interrupted her thoughts, and she realized that she would have to stay there overnight. It was very cold, and as she walked to the Half Moon Hotel to register, she was more than grateful to thoughtful George for the muff and foot warmers he had insisted on sending her. She stood by the window of her room looking out and could not help thinking of the young Saint Elizabeth who had come to this town as a refugee but helped the poor here so many years before. There were still several letters that Pauline had, by all means, to write to some Sisters that night yet. So she lit the candle on her writing table and began, but even as she wrote, her mind kept going back to the saint. It seemed only natural to mention her in the letters. Finally she had to stop when the candle sputtered at its stump and threatened to go out.

Pauline arrived at Meran and found Bertha very sick. Tenderly she cared for her and did everything she could to make her comfortable. She remembered how Bertha had waited on her, Pauline, when she had broken her foot. It was important that they get Bertha back to Paderborn as soon as possible, but they would have to wait until she was stronger. Meantime Pauline herself caught a bad cold and felt miserable. That did not matter. They had plans to make. Alfred sent George a telegram, directing him to get the upstairs rooms in Paderborn ready for Bertha and a nurse, to move the children into other rooms and hire a tutor for them. Then he took Pauline aside and looked at her pathetically.

"Pauline," he said huskily, "please, please stay and go back with us to Paderborn. I'm afraid to try to bring Bertha back by myself. I'm afraid I may do something wrong or not do enough. I must get her home alive, Pauline." His voice broke, and he put his hands to his face.

Pauline looked at him wih compassion and patted his shoulder. "Of course I will go back with you, Hüffer," she whispered. "I will help you, and we will get Bertha home safely, I feel sure."

On December 20 the doctors said Bertha could travel. Pauline and Alfred bundled her into the rented carriage with pillows, blankets, furs, foot warmers and hot water bottle. Although they passed through cold that was sixteen below zero, Bertha never felt it even once. They traveled three days by carriage, arriving at Innsbruck. They rested half a day and then took a train to Munich. From there Pauline went on ahead to Paderborn to take care of business and arrange things at home for Bertha. Alfred and Bertha rested for a day in Munich and then went by train in stages back to Paderbon. Finally, they were home on the Thursday after Christmas.

Pauline, the children, Lisette the maid, the servants, and the children's tutor were all waiting to welcome them. Bertha was in good spirits and was delighted to be with the children. George had seen to the rearranging of the rooms. Pauline stayed on, doing what she could to help Bertha get settled. Then she said goodbye temporarily, telling Alfred to notify her if she was needed. It was December 30 when she finally returned home to the motherhouse.

The new year was only a month old when Pauline saw, as she visited, that Bertha was failing. Pauline loved her with a mother-sister love that rebelled against her inability to help Bertha. This only intensified her prayers as she painfully and totally released her sister into the hands of the all-wise God. They took Bertha to Niederbach, and it was there she died on February 28, 1861. She was buried at Boeddeken in the family plot around the picturesque chapel of St. Meinolph which George had rebuilt.

As month followed month, the Sisters' financial state did not improve very much. Mother Pauline resorted again to asking people outright for donations. She sent two pleasant, strong young Sisters to France to beg for the orphanage at Höxter. It was so badly in debt and so poor that Bishop Martin had said he would fully understand if the congregation did not take the care of it. Just hearing the words *poor orphans* and *difficulty* was enough for Mother Pauline. Needy children always had instant entrance into the tenderest spot in her heart, and the mere mention of the hardship was a challenge that aroused her fiery spirit. Yes, they would take the orphanage, and somehow they would keep it running.

So Sister Scholastica and Sister Seraphine left for France in June and travelled from place to place, begging for the orphanage. They tried to keep in touch with Mother Pauline, hardly able to give her an address because they kept moving on. From time to time they sent her sums of money they had collected.

Delighted as she was with the money, she was far more concerned about the Sisters, so that by January, 1862, she decided they must come home regardless of success or failure. Her letter reached them at La Salette where there was a report of the appearance of Mary to two children of that area. She thanked the Sisters warmly for the 2000 francs they had sent a while ago but then begged and finally ordered them to come home as soon as possible. They had endured many hard things and were surely exhausted. She could not wait to see them again.

The Sisters did start home and were back in Germany by February, 1862, stopping on the way to see their parents at Mother Pauline's suggestion. They also went to a few more places for some last donations for the orphans and were finally caught in Mother Pauline's enthusiastic embrace at home in Paderborn, the first day of March.

She looked at them with such love and admiration that the two young Sisters were somewhat embarrassed.

"Because of you and your loving self-sacrifice, we were able to pay off a good part of the debt of the orphanage," she said. "Neither the children nor the Lord will easily forget that."

She had, all this while, been keeping an eye on Bertha's children and husband, Alfred, and was glad to hear that they were well and were enjoying a visit from Hermann, his wife, and little son, Meinolph. Hermann's term of office had expired, and he was waiting for the elections that would soon be held so that he could again serve in government.

Her most immediate and frequent means of contact with the Sisters was by correspondence. Her letters were often a combination of news, business, spiritual advice, and even correction. Still, they were very loving no matter what their content, for she was unashamedly affectionate. Frequently she ended a letter by saying that she loved the Sisters very much and almost always signed herself "With love, Sister Pauline." A constant loving manner toward others was so important to her that if she felt she had been too severe in correcting a Sister, either orally or in writing, she would apologize, not for the reprimand, but for the way she had given it. Then she would fast as a penance for her harshness.

It was natural for her to speak and write in a cheerful, positive way. Hearty down-to-earth encouragement to goodness and holy living was always somewhere in her letters to the Sisters, especially when there was some hardship or sacrifice entailed for them. Once, when she had to transfer a Sister cook from a well-liked place to another, she told her that she was getting a "kitchen with gaslight!" Later on she added, "Become very lovable," something that she herself tried noticeably to practice.

All her life Pauline was extremely sensitive to the least presence of sin, especially in herself. But it was not the heavy burden of guilt she had had as a teenager. No, she was now much more conscious of having displeased and offended God who is all lovable and loving. That is what grieved her: offending the One she loved with her whole being; the One who deserves only the best that a human being can give, and without reward, simply because He is who He is.

The thought of having hurt the Beloved and of the price *He* had paid for those very sins and all others was part of her reverent attention to God dwelling in her as she went about her work. It not only set her aflame with love for the Lord and His people, but leaped up hungrily in her, demanding some unmistakable signs of sorrow and reparation to the meek, uncomplaining One who had taken our punishment. So Pauline felt herself very much attracted to bodily penances of various kinds, not for the sake of suffering, but for the discipline they would give her tendency to yield to her lower self. She knew, too, that uniting her acts of penance with the passion and suffering of Jesus would make them redemptive, helping to save herself and those for whom she offered them.

At first Mother Pauline was zealous in practicing bodily penances and allowed the Sisters to do so too. But as the community grew and with it the many demands on the Sisters in the classroom, in their spiritual duties, in the effort needed for persons of very different characters and backgrounds to live together in love and harmony, in their necessary dealings with priests, parents, lay teachers, city officials, she wisely shifted the stress on physical penance to other forms of self-denial. She knew the Sisters were under sufficient bodily strain from their various duties, and at times from fatigue, poverty, cramped quarters, and the like. There was no need to add more and cause physical breakdowns. It was far more productive of health and holiness to restrain one's temper or selfish wants or hurt pride. It was good penance and couldn't hurt one's health. More and more often, she was able to touch the Sisters inwardly and draw out the best in them through her wonderfully creative power that came from being united with the ever-creating God.

"Become holy, " she said to one Sister, "through patient bearing of this or that little or big unpleasantness....Should someone say an unkind word to you, do not rate it too highly. If you accept it in a friendly manner, you will receive great merit from God and gradually win the hearts of all, and besides, you will be pleasing to the eyes of your divine Bridegroom, Jesus Christ."

Pauline was convinced that a Christian, and certainly a Sister, should bear suffering patiently, uniting it with the passion of Jesus in reparation for sin. But that did not stop her from being most sympathetic to anyone who was sick or sorrowful. She saw to it that every available means was used to help a Sister who was ill no matter where the patient was. Often she would send a Sister or assign one already there to nurse the sick one, giving herself the problem of finding someone or some way to perform the duties of the Sister she had sent. She wanted the services of a good doctor to be secured and his directions to be followed regardless of extra work or effort. If ever she lived out her title of "Mother," it was at times like these when she was all tenderness, kindness, and concern for the sick child or Sister. Yet her compassion was never a flabby, sentimental thing, filling the patient with self-pity. No, it was loving but strong, cheerful, and challenging, trusting in the power and wisdom of the Lord.

Mother Pauline visited the sick without fail, and if she was too far away, she would write to the ailing Sister and her superior fairly often, expecting progress reports. Even then, nothing could stop her from going to a distant convent if a sick Sister there, who was troubled, had asked to speak to her. More than once Mother Pauline would have just arrived in the Paderborn train station from a long journey and heard of such a request. She would immediately board the next train for that place, ignoring her fatigue or hunger. It often meant another full day's travel there and still another to return. That did not matter. To comfort one of her Sisters in body or soul or both was real satisfaction of her unending yearning to love and serve others as her Beloved had asked.

People, of course, were her biggest love, but any creature of God had a claim to it. The Sisters were careful not to let her see a trapped mouse because she would feel sorry for it. She was very fond of the big black dog they had put at the gate because there was so much stealing at night. He was a good watch dog, scaring newcomers and alerting the Sisters with his noise. He barked and howled so much that he frightened Bishop Conrad Martin when he came for Mass or for giving the Sisters instructions on the Psalms. So they chained the dog, but that didn't keep him from enthusiastically showing his affection for the Sisters by jumping up with his paws on their shoulders. Some of the Sisters would squeal with fear, but Mother Pauline was delighted with it. She would laugh and talk to him, patting his head and trying to keep him from licking her face, denting her bonnet, or mussing her bow.

By April some Sisters who were able to write neatly and beautifully were busy making twenty-five copies of papers that were to be taken to Rome by the bishop on May 15 when he would travel there again. There was much Latin involved in the copying, and it required very careful work. These papers had been requested by the Church authorities in Rome in connection with approval of Pauline's congregation and were, naturally, very important to all the Sisters.

When Bishop Martin returned in the latter part of June, he did not bring the decree of approval they all wanted so much, nor had they really expected it. It was too soon for that. But he did bring something else.

Mother Pauline called the Sisters together excitedly, and when they came, a little breathless, her eyes were shining, and her lips were flashing that splendid smile. She was holding a document that she lifted up in a gesture of triumph.

"Just think, dear Sisters," she exulted. "Bishop Martin has brought us the written permission from the Holy Father to have the Eucharistic Jesus in the consecrated hosts reserved in *every* convent of our congregation!" She paused, filled with joy. "That is the most wonderful, priceless gift we could ever receive!" she said finally, voicing the thought and feeling of them all. They carefully cherished the document, and Mother Pauline was always quick to inform bishops and pastors that the Sisters of Christian Charity possessed it and its precious permission.

The usual events of examinations for teachers, the ceremonies of investing and first vows of the Sisters came and went quickly in late July. But, as often happened now, there were also more new buds of apostolate sprouting on the healthy young vine of Pauline's congregation, requiring much attention and care. So many calls for Sisters were coming in from various areas that she could accept only a few and frequently had to write regretful letters of refusal, hoping the recipients would understand.

Having already sent Sisters to Viersen for the elementary school, Pauline felt that she could not refuse to send those needed to staff the high school that would open there in the fall. Then there were Crefeld and Magdeburg, two more places to which she had merely promised some Sisters in the future. But she didn't reckon with the powerful effect of urgency that spiritual need and poverty were sure to have on her.

She did very much traveling that summer. She saw and heard of the many Catholics in Magdeburg, who were poor not only in body but also in soul. Most of them had never had any contact with one of the mere three priests assigned for 3000 people, and they were living their difficult lives in a cloud of religious indifference. They badly needed Catholic schools, they needed residences for the Sisters and for the teachers of the boys, and, of course, they needed money. Their want was great and immediate, and it conquered Mother Pauline. There must be no delay. Plans for four classrooms of an elementary school, for a high school for girls, for a school for the poor, and for a sewing school must be made at once. Teachers must be prepared.

Her assistants were in sympathy with Pauline's urgency and enthusiasm for Magdeburg, but they looked at her with respectful bewilderment. *Where* would they get the money for all that? Pauline had had to write not long ago to her banker cousin, Hugo von Hartmann, to borrow money so that the community itself could operate.

Pauline saw the questioning eyes all around her. They only made her more determined than ever to open the schools in that town. Money? They had no money? Well, that would not stop her!

Slowly she rose, and as the Sisters looked up to their tall Reverend Mother, they saw in her eyes the gleam of that old Mallinckrodt spirit and the shining light of unquenchable trust in God that were always there when she met an obstacle.

"Don't worry, dear Sisters," she said, lifting her head. "God will help us. I'll beg. I'll write to the royalty and beg. We shall get the money. You'll see."

As always, she wasted no time and began her many begging letters in late July. Besides writing to the pastor of Magdeburg about the situation and to those connected with the St. Boniface Society which might possibly donate money to the project, she began with a most humble and courteous plea to His Majesty, Emperor Ferdinand, for aid to his poor Catholic residents. Since Magdeburg was in the diocese of Bishop Conrad Martin, it would be best to send the money to him.

By September she had written to the Queen in Berlin, and to Countess Nellessen, Father Hutmacher, Canon Prisac, Lingens, a lawyer, and Dr. Hahn, all of Aachen. By then she had appealed also, in her most respectful and persuasive way, to the Archduchess and Princess Sophie of Austria, to Count von Galen in Münster, to Mayor Kaufmann of Bonn, and to Countess Goldstein of Düsseldorf. She never tired of writing the same words of description, explanation, and pleading, over and over again, keeping always in mind the position and means of the person she was addressing.

She had no sooner finished those when it was necessary to begin writing letters of thanks. Besides the donations of the royalty, an unknown benefactor sent 10,000 francs to Bishop Martin to be used as he pleased. He gave it to Mother Pauline to take along when she would bring the Sisters to begin their work in Magdeburg on October 7. She intended to open both a private and a public elementary school there at once and in spring to add a high school.

She had ordered furniture for the convent which would come only later, but she wrote to the pastor, saying that she was sending bedding for the Sisters to his address in advance of their coming. She also asked that the housekeeper buy twelve bushels of potatoes for the Sisters' winter supply and that there be enough straw in the house to fill four bedsacks and four pillows.

Pauline was just as urgent about the personnel for Magdeburg and was unusually brief in her courteous written request to Bishop Martin asking permission for Sister Augustine to pronounce her first holy vows although she had been a novice only seven months. Because of Sister Augustine's "sterling character and great experience gained through many years of blessed labor" previously in the same area, Mother Pauline considered her "especially suited for the school in Magdeburg." She asked for the bishop's dispensation from the remaining months of novitiate for Sister Augustine because she had "distinguished herself by great zeal in the religious life."

But there were many other things on her mind as well during this time. She was concerned about who would take the teacher examinations and the preparation for them. There was the three-day retreat to be arranged for the ceremony of investing of new novices. With the taking of new schools in Magdeburg and Crefeld and the addition of new classes in other places, many transfers of Sisters had to be made. Over these she and her assistants thought long and hard, trying to put into open positions the Sisters best qualified for them with regard, at the same time, for their health and the harmony of their local community life. Then, of course, there were the send-offs and farewells. After that, officials were coming to inspect the blind asylum, and they had to get ready.

With regard to the blind, Pauline and the Sisters had a plan for the little old blind asylum they had moved out of—a creative plan. It would be just right as a home for ten blind adults. But the house would have to be repaired, and that would cost 1000 Thalers. Somehow, somehow they would manage it.

Weeks earlier a request had come to Mother Pauline for Sisters to be sent to Crefeld, and she had come very close to refusing on the advice of Father Roh, S.J. But it was Father Wiemann who had prevented her and scolded her for thinking of refusing such a sphere of activity. The biggest Catholic parish in Germany! Did she realize that? It was plain that neither she nor the priests of a religious order understood how a Catholic pastor in the middle of such a Lutheran district as Crefeld felt. Not only must the Sisters go there, but they must go next month, in October, otherwise the Catholic children would be lost to the Church. They would go to the Protestant schools because the present principal and teachers of the Catholic school were leaving. So once again, Pauline yielded, and now Crefeld was waiting, expecting Sisters to open three classes for girls.

As she and her councillors sat together, Pauline

smiled and threw up both hands defenselessly when Crefeld was mentioned.

"I took it," she said, "out of sheer trust in God. He will help. I am certain of it because He gladly helps the poor and the weak and the little ones and in a way that shows His power. Anyone who trusts in Him has built on a firm rock."

Somehow, as she spoke, the words that seemed so ordinary and even trite, carried to the Sisters who were with her a feeling of strength and security as if, indeed, there was suddenly a rock beneath them.

In spite of her unsinkable good spirits, though, Pauline was quite drained and physically ill by December. She admitted to attacks of rheumatism, but admitting to it was all she would do. She was treated like a princess, she said, with the loving care of the Sisters, and what was left of her illness was not worth mentioning. It would take more than that to stop her.

Chapter XVII

It was 1863, and vibrations of startling ideas were crackling into action in different parts of the world. In America, Abraham Lincoln was daring to free the slaves. In England, the very first professional training for women nurses was being offered by Florence Nightingale. There, too, John Henry Newman, famous Anglican, had converted to Catholicism and was defending it superbly. In France, the poor, uneducated teenager, Bernadette Soubirous, who had seen Mary, the Immaculate Conception, was promoting prayer and penance while in Germany, members of the Workers' Union were joining the Marxists.

But there were other shock waves pulsing in Germany. Pauline had jolted the rich and surprised the poor by giving herself and her money for poor children, for the sick poor, for the blind, and for founding an order of religious women that educated also the sighted poor, orphaned, or spiritually deprived. Nothing had been able to stop her from achieving all of these, but very close to her and her Sisters now were the pulsations of a dangerous mind that was appearing just then to be innocently patriotic.

This was Otto von Bismarck, the ambitious young politician who had often attended the Mallinckrodt parties at Pauline's home in Aix-la-Chapelle. He had become Prime Minister of Prussia in 1862 and had enlarged it by annexing three provinces of territory near it in two wars. Some day, according to his plan, all the independent provinces of Germany at this time would be united into a single nation under the rule of Prussia. But for the moment Bismarck and his ambitions seemed far removed from Mother Pauline and her work. If there were throbs of danger, she certainly did not feel them—as yet.

Spring was emerging shyly, pushing tiny leaves forward and nudging brave buds open in the chilly air to flirt with the warming sun. Sister Walburga walked slowly in the garden outside the mother-house, appreciating every little thing that grows. She had been called here just a few days ago by Mother Pauline to act as her assistant in place of Sister Cecilia, who was very sick with consumption. She reached under her black apron and took the long rosary with its large white beads from her side. It would do her good, body and soul, to pray her rosary out here in the fresh air, and there were so many things, especially new ones, to pray for. They flashed quickly across her mind as she made the Sign of the Cross.

There was the school at Oschersleben—that poor, poor school that Bishop Martin had urgently asked Mother Pauline to take. The dear Lord knew they would need almighty help for that. There was the orphanage at Solingen just recently accepted by

Mother Pauline, and there was the high school for girls at Dortmund to which she had recently agreed. Each of these had its own needs and problems besides the obvious ones of requiring suitably trained Sisters and enough of them. Then there was the necessity of always having some Sisters sufficiently skilled in French and English in order to teach them. As for English, they would need a good number who could speak it when the day came to go to America. Of course, one always had to pray for more young ladies to enter. But even more than young ladies, they needed the room in which to house them. They had been forced to turn girls away because they had no room! Last, but not least, they had to pray for the sick, especially the sick Sisters whom they really could not spare.

Sister Walburga finished her rosary and went immediately to Mother Pauline's office. The door was slightly open, and she could see the strong, serious face marked with a look of appeal as Pauline bent over her pen and paper. Sister Walburga knocked lightly.

"Come in, dear Sister, come in!" called Pauline, as she looked up and smiled. The inner glow of God's love lit her eyes, her lips, her whole face, making the whiteness of her heartshaped coif seem even whiter.

"Can you guess what I'm doing, Sister Walburga?" she asked lightly.

"I can see that you're writing letters, as usual, Reverend Mother, but judging from the look on your face, I'd say that you are—"

"Begging! That's right. I'm getting to be an experienced beggar but it's worth it. This time it's for

Oschersleben, and I have an enlarged list of royalty as my target. Look." She handed Sister Walburga the names.

"Reverend Mother! You mean you really wrote and begged from Queen Victoria of England and Empress Eugenie of France?"

Pauline sat back very straight in her chair and gave a soft, deep chuckle. "Oh, yes, and not only those. I wrote also to Queen von Bragance of Baden, the Queen Widow of Saxony—"

"And Queen Amalia, Prince Albert, Prince George and Princess Marie of Saxony," interrupted Sister Walburga, reading down the list.

"Yes. Why not? And then to four bishops, the Cardinal of Prague, and some influential priests. We can't forget them." Her remarkably revealing eyes were twinkling. "All these people have very good hearts, you know. Usually they aren't aware of these needs and must have someone tell them. Their donations will be coming in not every long from now—and then, I start writing thank-you letters."

It was Sister Walburga's turn to chuckle. "Reverend Mother," she said, shaking her head, "you are—"

"Ach, Sister Walburga, that's nothing. It's the least I can do for God's poor."

Sister Walburga nodded. "If there is nothing special you would like me to do, Reverend Mother, I'll continue with my regular work," she said and turned to go.

As she walked to her room, she wondered just how many letters Mother Pauline had written. She knew that whenever Reverend Mother transferred a

Sister from a school, she wrote courteously to the pastor and the superior of that place, telling the reason, if possible, the name of the Sister replacing her, and her qualifications. She knew too, that Mother Pauline frequently wrote letters of spiritual instruction, advice, encouragement, and correction to both superiors and individual Sisters. Letters for teacher certification, for matters of inheritance, dowry, mortgages, purchase and sale of property were also written by her. Then there were letters about religious affairs: obtaining confessors for the Sisters, arranging for retreats, for the ceremonies of investing and of pronouncing vows. Lastly came all the purely social letters of news, loving concern, thanks, and good wishes to the Sisters in each house and to her own family members.

Sister Walburga had never really listed them all in her mind like that before. But when she thought about all the hours Mother Pauline spent in prayer, her reading to the blind and personally providing recreation for them as well as the many business trips she had to make, her interviews with Sisters, clergy, officials, visitors, friends, and relatives, Sister Walburga actually gasped aloud. The total activity and self-giving of this Mother of theirs was enormous! Years later, she learned that Pauline's correspondence alone amounted to 3,500 letters.

Some of these letters she wrote to well-to-do families, fighting for the rights of several individual Sisters to their inheritance or dowry. True, she was always very polite, reasonable, and cordial, but she was nonetheless a fighter, firm, direct, tenacious, refusing to weakly stand by and lose what was rightfully theirs. It was not only because the congregation needed the money, but more importantly, because of the contempt the family cast on a daughter who chose to give herself to God by refusing her her part of the family goods. Surprising as it may seem, the same great flame that set her burning with unconditional love, made her aggressive with unyielding zeal for what is right. She had the tenderness and unselfishness of a great lover as well as the grit and steel spirit of a true fighter. Better still, she knew well when and how to use the qualities of both.

About this time, Mother Pauline wrote to Sister Mathilde about some difficulty of hers and told her frankly to "try another procedure." What was it? Just Mother Pauline's old standby and her favorite one: trust in God. Sister Mathilde was to put herself in His arms; to deliberately act cheerful, not depressed. God always helps those who trust in Him and at the right time. Regarding a troublesome Sister, she reminded Sister Mathilde that that Sister was already an older Sister and was very susceptible to love. "Love begets love," she told her, and "trust awakens trust." It was no marvelously new advice, but rather a pointed, unmistakable reminder of very old but often neglected facts on human nature.

Pauline's main concern in education was the Sisters' treatment of the children, and after Sister Mathilde's report, she told her: "Just love the children very much." In that way, Sister would regain their hearts. Then too, it was unthinkable that, as daughters of Mary, the Sisters would try to train children without involving the Mother of God. "Recommend to her all your children, each individual child, and the naughty ones with special fervor and love," she advised, adding like a wise mother, "You should not

270

strain yourself and undermine your health by too loud speaking and too much worry."

As the donations for Oschersleben came in from the royalty, Mother Pauline was very busy with preparations for opening the school there. Repairs were badly needed on the convent quarters, walls around a garden would have to be erected, drain pipes and chimneys would have to be fixed, and a new school building of two stories would have to be built since there was now a request for the housing of ten to twelve abandoned orphans on one floor. Teachers for the boys would have to be hired too, since it was not feasible to get Brothers to come as had been hoped.

But she had to take time for celebration too, at the motherhouse, especially late that summer when the daughter of the Countess Stolberg received both her First Communion and Confirmation from the hands of Bishop Conrad Martin in the Sisters' chapel. It was not at all unusual for him to bring distinguished people there to the Sisters for a visit or celebration of some kind.

Not long after that, in August, the prelude to the building of the long-awaited and much needed new wing of the motherhouse began. Mother Pauline had received word earlier from Rome that from now on the novices were to spend their full novitiate of two years at the motherhouse and no longer on mission in the different convents. That meant the Sisters had to build immediately. They simply had no room, and they would need a larger garden too. So the men with the wrecking equipment started on the trees in the garden, then on the barn, and the cattle disappeared. The mayor kindly sent word that he would quickly give the Sisters a building license. But the workers lost no time. They began construction that same day.

Pauline turned, as she often did when trying to meet the financial emergencies of the community, to her banker cousin, Hugo, for a loan. She pledged him the community's banknotes of the Savings Bank and promised to also use incoming dowries to repay him for the amount she borrowed to cover the cost of the new wing. From the civil authorities she made a request, too, for a collection to be made in the Westphalia district for the benefit of the orphanage the Sisters were conducting at Höxter.

But the demands she was making on her nerves and physical strength were too much even for her strong body, and Pauline was definitely showing signs of burn-out. At the invitation of George and his wife, Dina, she went for a rest to Boeddeken, the dear old lovely estate where she had lived with her father after his retirement until his death. The fresh, country air and the atmosphere of prayer, serenity, and quiet that still clung to the whole place from the centuries of religious life faithfully lived there first by nuns and later by monks, soothed and strengthened Pauline. In a few weeks she was back home, ready for new challenges.

Building was halted during the winter of 1864, but it gave Pauline and the Sisters time to devote their attention to something just as important and pressing: making corrected copies of their Rule according to the revisions indicated earlier by Rome. Mother Pauline was also busy asking various bishops in whose dioceses the Sisters were working, for testimonial letters to the Holy Father about the Congregation of Sisters of Christian Charity. These would be sent to Rome with the revised Rule through Father Liemke who was going there after Easter.

By April of that year, planning and screening for more than one project became necessary. Happily, applications of young women desiring to become Sisters continued to come in, and Mother Pauline carefully examined them, accepting some, rejecting others. Outside, plans for a beautiful new and much larger garden were being made. The diocesan architect, Mr. Bergman, was designing Stations of the Cross and planning their location in the garden. News that a well, already dug sixty-six feet deep in the garden, was close to yielding water made it easy and exciting to go the necessary sixteen or twenty feet more for that good, clear liquid so badly needed. When it was finally found in abundance, Mother Pauline's eyes sparkled like the precious spring water, and she set aside the first pitcherful to be offered with the wine to the Lord the next day at Holy Mass.

Already six years earlier, Mother Pauline had obtained permission for making a small cemetery for the Sisters. Now they would enlarge it, and Mr. Bergman would construct a lovely mortuary chapel on it also. This chapel would be dedicated to St. Conrad, the patron of their own Bishop Martin. Through the Archbishop of Freiburg Pauline obtained a relic of St. Conrad for the altar of the chapel, for the bishop, for the Sisters, and for herself. She hoped that Bishop Martin would consent to be buried there in the lower vault so that the Sisters would have him, their spiritual father, among them. But he only smiled at the suggestion and said nothing.

Just as the bareness caused by winter's stripping

was filled with May's soft green leaves, thick grass, and bright, hardy flowers, so did the skeleton beams of the new wing begin to broaden into full-fledged walls. Soon the completed shape of the new west wing was rising into view, and there were often smiles of eagerness when the Sisters looked out the window toward the setting sun.

But there were tears and sadness too. Mother Pauline tried to comfort George, whose little daughter, Paula, died in August, 1864, but her own heart was almost numb with sorrow as she saw five of her Sisters die within seven months. One of them was only twenty-one years old. Now, besides Sister Cecilia, who had consumption, Sister Maria was very sick with typhoid fever. Shortly before Christmas, Sister Maria died with majestic peace, conscious to the end. In her, the second of the original four Sisters had gone to heaven, leaving Pauline without her beloved faithful "Sister of Good Counsel," as she had called Sister Maria because of her last name, *Rath*, meaning counsel or advice, which she had so devotedly given with all her other services. Pauline had now to ask Sister Walburga to take Sister Maria's place as assistant, leaving Sister Cecilia's place open for the time.

But joy had its turn, too, in their lives. It was a happy day indeed, when the property of one of the Sisters was sold for 16,000 Thalers, and it was applied to the debt for the new wing. Months later everyone was even more delighted to watch the face of the Sister cook as she saw the water being pumped into her kitchen pots by machine! Even in cold November, the visit of Queen Augusta caused a warm, happy flutter of excitement among the blind children as she came to see the institute and presented Mother Pauline with a beautiful crucifix as a remembrance.

But as November, 1865 was drawing to a close, so too was the life of Sister Cecilia. She died less than a year after Sister Maria, causing Mother Pauline special sorrow but giving her still another chance to surrender herself to the Lord's will, so sacred and precious to her.

As she stood looking down at the still face of Sister Cecilia, Mother Pauline said, "I love and esteem every one of our Sisters. But of all, she was the most loved, and she was an exemplary religious. May the name of the Lord be adored, loved, and praised in all His dispensations!"

Very shortly after, she called Sister Mathilde to the motherhouse to take Sister Cecilia's place as novice directress, and asked Sister Augustine to also replace Sister Cecilia as Mother Pauline's secretary.

As the new year 1866 unfolded, Mother Pauline and Sister Mathilde, Sister Anna, Sister Walburga, and Sister Augustine were looking forward more and more eagerly to April 25. It was then that they were to begin the three months of preparation for pronouncing their final, perpetual vows. It was called tertianship or the third novitiate, a time of formation for the Sisters in addition to the two years of novitiate they had had earlier. Originally Mother Pauline had wanted also the superiors of all the missions to join her and her councillors in the tertianship. But civil war had broken out between two of Germany's independent states, Saxony and Prussia, and Bishop Martin thought it best that the superiors remain at home with their Sisters during this time of unrest.

The tertianship would be twelve weeks of prayer, silence, spiritual reading, reflection on living the three vows of poverty, chastity, and obedience, and on community life. There would be time for walks in the garden and for needlework. The last four weeks would be a thirty-day retreat conducted by Father Behrens, S.J., ending with the ceremony of total self-giving to the Lord through final vows. From then on, the other Sisters would take part in the same program, with a different group coming for it each year.

It was during this tertianship, on May 1, starting at six o'clock in the morning, that Bishop Martin went through the new wing, blessing it. He blessed also the new St. Conrad chapel and consecrated its two altars. Next he blessed the cemetery and the many statues of saints and apostles set in its wall as well as the statue of Mary poised gracefully on a tall stone pillar in the center of a circular flower bed farther into the garden. Then he blessed the first small mortuary chapel dedicated to St. Joseph and even the garden. The Sisters and Mother Pauline looked around at the new buildings, the garden, the walls, the statues and smiled contentedly. Everything was lovely, and it was so peaceful. Gone were the pounding and banging of construction, the noise of workmen. The Sisters could truly walk with God in the living stillness.

But as Pauline and her companions enjoyed the days of quiet and prayer spent almost completely in St. Conrad chapel except for meals and sleep, the noise of civil war outside increased and spread. People were afraid that the region of Westphalia, where Paderborn was, would be invaded by the fighting. If that were so, some of the Sisters' missions would be caught in it. Finally, when the bishop heard that there was battle near Sigmaringen, he decided to cut short the retreat so that Mother Pauline could encourage and help her Sisters and make plans for those in danger. He set the date for final vows on July 16, the feast of Our Lady of Mt. Carmel.

The most solemn and important act of the five Sisters' religious life was also the most private, simple, and quiet. Besides the Sisters of the mother-house and blind asylum, the only guests were the blind children. There were garden flowers everywhere in the upper level of St. Conrad's chapel, leaving a faint fragrant scent to mingle with that of pure beeswax burning in lighted candles. Outside, a huge willow tree drooped its many long branches over the entire chapel like the fingers of God caressing it. The large heavy stones of the chapel walls resisted the summer heat, cooling the air inside with a slightly damp mustiness. Over all these was a general hush of reverence.

Bishop Martin, presiding, sat before the altar, facing the Sisters who knelt before him, one by one. The keen ears of the blind children recognized the voice and intonation of Mother Pauline as she solemnly, and with all her heart, pronounced the words that gave God everything she was and had—forever. They listened carefully as Sister Mathilde and the other three Sisters followed, doing the same. Then came a tremendous surge of joy through everyone, as it always does when someone witnesses or performs the highest human act of worship one can give to God. For these Sisters, the bishop pointed out in his sermon, had joyously performed the very act of dying by giving God everything for always. Their act was as final as death, and they would carry it out each day. But in doing so they would just as certainly be free to live a new life, the life of their Spouse, the risen Christ, in God. They spent the rest of the day in quiet joy with Him, the Beloved, as the perfect close to an extraordinary time in their lives.

Re-entry into the old routine was not easy, but for Pauline it was made even more difficult by sudden confrontation with the confusion, restlessness, and fear caused by the war. Close to the motherhouse the railroad thundered by all day and all night as it carried military goods and fighting equipment to the soldiers. With its noise in her ears and its echo in her mind, she tried to make plans for safety of the Sisters.

Then, suddenly, the war was over. Prussia had won against the other German states. Its flag was now flying over more and more territory, and all seemed to be at peace. But Pauline knew that, along with the Prussian flag, the power of its prime minister, Bismarck, was rising too. What did that mean? She wondered.

Before the unexpected close of the war but after the close of the tertianship, Mother Pauline had wanted to visit the convents and interview the Sisters. She knew, though, that her traveling at wartime would be unwise and that in some places she would not be able to get through. So she had written to each house, asking every Sister to write to her by August 12, telling Mother Pauline whatever she felt she should about herself, the house, school, etc. All the letters were to be sent to Mother Pauline unread by anyone else. She promised that she would do her best for the Sisters, but that, of course, she would not be able to satisfy everyone.

Before long, the letters began coming in, over 150 of them, and Mother Pauline was extremely busy reading them and noting all the facts and personal data on individual Sisters and situations that would have to be taken into account when transfers were made. Besides that, she was handling the necessary business involved with taking over a school in Soest the following year.

It was becoming quite evident that in numerous missions the Sisters were carrying heavy teaching loads, spending long hours with very large classes and receiving a very small salary. The salary was so small, in fact, in more than one place that the Sisters often did not have sufficient food. Their energy was being sapped by the heavy demands of their classes without the means of replacing it. It was more and more difficult to teach well, and there was no longer any joy in it. The Sisters were becoming weak and ill long before their time.

So Mother Pauline wrote respectfully but bluntly to the pastors and school boards of these places, describing the difficulties of the Sisters. She explained the need for a bigger salary not only to buy enough food for the Sisters but to help the congregation which had to pay for their education, for their medical care in sickness, and finally to support them in their retirement after they had spent themselves teaching in the schools where authorities did not pay them enough to live on. She sent a similar letter to Soest and to every new school the Sisters were about to take.

By the early part of December it was obvious that

Pauline's own health was breaking, and the Sisters were somewhat relieved when they saw her accept the invitation of George and Dina to go to Boeddeken for recovery. She discovered there that she felt very well after a good sleep, and that probably that was the only remedy she needed. She returned home to the motherhouse early in March, resolved to retire early every evening. When she did so, she found herself much refreshed, and the doctor praised her. But he strictly forbade her to fast even though it was Lent.

As Pauline was trying to regain a hold on her strength and work schedule, her heart beat faster with delight at the reports about Hermann's activities in the German parliament. He was clashing repeatedly with no less than the prime minister, Bismarck, voice to voice, speech to speech, boldly declaring himself the representative of justice in defense of the rights of the Church.

In June of that year, 1867, was the 1800th anniversary of the martyrdom of Saints Peter and Paul in 67 A.D., and Bishop Conrad Martin was going to Rome for that celebration. Mother Pauline and the Sisters had sent their revised Rule and letters of testimony about their congregation from various bishops to Rome with Father Liemke much earlier, so they were hoping and praying that the bishop would return with good news.

At Höxter things were booming. There was an elementary school, an academy, the orphanage, all to be staffed by the Sisters of Christian Charity. A new building that would house the Sisters of the elementary school and the needlework school was being constructed near the orphanage. Best of all,

Mother Pauline had succeeded in getting the contract of the Sisters drawn up in the name of the congregation, rather than of individual sisters, with a better salary than before.

Not far away from the motherhouse in Paderborn was a facility called Bath Island where people with respiratory problems were treated. It was something of a resort, having amusements and a promenade on which to take leisurely walks outdoors, besides the rooms for treatment. It was necessry for each person to have an admittance card which was expensive. Since so many of her Sisters were having lung or chest trouble and too many had been lost to consumption, Mother Pauline wrote, begging for the use of one room for one or two hours for the treatment of several Sisters. They would take turns and would not use the amusements or promenade. She asked for one card to be issued to the congregation at a reduced fee, but nothing ever came of it.

About mid-July she received a visitor who had come from America ten years before to ask for Sisters to teach in his diocese. It was Bishop Junker from Illinois, and she admired his persistence.

"You promised me, Reverend Mother," he said, smiling, but his voice was low and serious.

"Yes, I know, Your Grace," she answered, and her voice was just as serious. "Surely you will remember that I told you we were waiting for the Church to approve our Constitutions before I could send Sisters to you. We have been preparing. The Sisters have been studying English, we sent revised copies of our Rule to Rome, and now—" her face lit with a bright smile, "I think that in a short time we shall have what we have been waiting for. Then we can make final preparations. I ask you please to wait one more year, Your Grace. Then the Sisters will come."

Bishop Junker pursed his lips, raised his head, and looked up at a corner of the ceiling as if considering.

"Well, I guess I'll have to wait," he said slowly, "but remember, Reverend Mother," and he pointed his finger emphatically as he spoke, "I asked you first, so I get your Sisters first."

Mother Pauline laughed softly. "Of course, Your Grace. I gave my promise, and I shall keep it."

It was almost as if her words to Bishop Junker about the Constitutions were prophetic. Bishop Conrad Martin returned from Rome several days later, bringing the Church's approval of them for ten years! To obtain this so soon was indeed an unusual thing, and knowing how much this meant to the Sisters, Bishop Martin solemnly handed the document to Mother Pauline in St. Conrad chapel.

Quietly she prayed, "My soul is filled with gratitude as I praise God. Dear Lord, throughout the fifty years of my life you have showered me with your benefits. Now there remains for me only to observe the Rules and Constitutions to the best of my ability and to die a happy death. Amen."

Pauline thought the matter of going to America was shelved, but she was mistaken. In August there, before her, stood another American bishop. He was from Natchez, Mississippi, and he had a very large diocese with only seventeen priests to serve the Catholics scattered among people of other beliefs. He needed Sisters. She told him she would consider it but had already promised Bishop Junker first. Now without a doubt she knew that all the Sisters who had studied English and she, too, had better start reviewing it in earnest.

The days of fall had just begun when city officials began to pressure the Sisters to install gaslight in the motherhouse and blind institute. Pauline told them that they would have to wait until the director of the blind institute, who was in Berlin, gave his consent to install it. Then and only then would she consider it for the two houses.

Things were at last ready in Soest, and in October the Sisters began to teach in the school there. For weeks before, Pauline had been eyeing the tall gray stone house across the street that Mr. Vollmer had built but left unfinished. He wanted to sell it, and she wanted to buy it. She could put it to good use. Finally, all necessary transactions were completed, and she purchased the house toward the end of October. It still needed a roof and some other minor details, so she made arrangements for its completion.

But that was the last thing she would do for some time. It was the evening of October 31 when some of her councillors found her. She was so weak she could not move at all, and her general condition was alarming. They called the doctor, who later said she had suffered a slight stroke and needed complete rest if she was to get well. All the Sisters of the motherhouse and blind asylum and the children were told about it, and prayers for her recovery were offered almost ceaselessly.

When she was able to be moved, Bishop Martin ordered her to Boeddeken under the care of another Sister and of good, faithful George and Dina. The winter snow brought not only beauty and blanket to the soil of the hills of Boeddeken's entire valley but also a soothing hush that made one feel relaxed and cozy. Pauline prayed and rested and relished the leisurely reading of one of her favorite spiritual authors, St. Francis de Sales. She read again his book on the love of God called *Theotimus*, resolving to focus her love on Him more and more.

But George and Dina and her Sister companion found it difficult to keep her totally at rest. Occasionally during her three months' stay at Boeddeken, she went back to the motherhouse briefly. She still did not have full use of her pen fingers and asked another Sister to write for her as she dictated. That was the way she wrote to Father Minoux, S.J., telling him of her realization that she would have to let go of some of her duties, especially those of superior of the motherhouse. She was sorry to do so because that position gave her a chance to serve the Sisters she lived with personally, something she dearly loved. Working only with the matters of the congregation in general and with those concerning the various mission houses of the Sisters would isolate her from the care of local matters and of the Sisters in her house. But common sense told her it had to be done, and when Bishop Martin and her confessor both expressed the same thought, that settled it. Pauline appointed Sister Mathilde as superior of the motherhouse promising her that she, Pauline, would obey her promptly.

In early December she again visited the motherhouse and with help wrote a letter asking authorities for permission to build a new and larger day nursery along with a larger playground for poor children on city property with the condition that if the congregation ever closed the nursery, the Sisters would pay the city the tax value of the property. The present building was in very bad condition and was too small. Caring for poor small children had been Mother Pauline's first project, and it was very dear to her. She had to do everything she could to save and improve it. She was successful. The city granted her request, and back to Boeddeken she went where George, Dina, and her Sister nurse were waiting for her.

Another year had already begun when she returned to Paderborn, feeling much better and fairly well restored. It was February, 1868, and it didn't take her long to settle into her routine. She had been looking with great interest at the fine old monastery of Holthausen built by Cistercian monks in the twelfth century near Büren. It was now the property of the Baron von Brenken who had two sisters with the Sisters of Christian Charity. According to certain terms of inheritance, he could not sell the monastery, but he was willing to rent it for a very reasonable price. Mother Pauline was delighted. Its location in the country was ideal as a place of quiet and rest for the Sisters who were recuperating from strain or illness and for those studying in preparation for teachers' exams. Now, at last, she had a place to send them.

Birds were chirping luring calls, and hardy plants were pushing up, ignoring the April chill as Sister Mathilde walked from the garden into the motherhouse with the novice who had brought the message. Mother Pauline wanted to see her. She knocked at Reverend Mother's door and went in almost immediately as she heard the instant response.

"Ah, come in, come in, Sister Mathilde! Sit down," said Mother Pauline warmly. Her tall figure was blocking the window, but Sister Mathilde could see Pauline looking down at her affectionately. As her eyes examined the dear face turned up to her, Mother Pauline recalled the day eighteen years ago when she had asked this same Sister Mathilde to go to Dortmund as the first teaching Sister of Christian Charity at their first mission. Time had not marked her face much since then. She was a real pioneer, and now it was time to ask her to be part of another first.

"As you know, Sister Mathilde, I asked the Sisters some time ago to write to me their honest feelings about going to America. Many said yes, and some said no. I am glad they were so frank."

"Yes, Reverend Mother," came the soft answer.

"I just wrote to the houses telling the Sisters that the names of those chosen to go are listed with their offices and duties. One or other can still be chosen. But they should be happy for their vocation to go to America. It is a great grace to help in spreading God's kingdom, don't you agree, Sister Mathilde?"

"Oh yes, Reverend Mother!" said Sister Mathilde emphatically, eyes a little larger, still waiting patiently for anything more yet to come.

"I told them that those assigned for America will leave their mission houses in the autumn of this year and spend the winter at St. Joseph House, which will be ready by then, I hope. It would be an excellent chance for most of them to make tertianship and pronounce their final vows before going overseas. Those who do not make final vows will be prepared to foster a deeper spiritual life adapted to their particular assignments. And—"

"Yes?"

"I would like you, Sister Mathilde, to go with them as superior in our first American mission." Pauline stopped and waited. Sister Mathilde took a deep breath, "Yes, Reverend Mother," she said, nodding. But that was all she could say.

Mother Pauline smiled and patted her hand. "Thank you, dear Sister. Then it would be best for you to come to St. Joseph House in the fall too, to live with the group and get to know them all well. You will leave for America probably in the spring of '69. Bishop Junker of Alton will be your sponsor, and I have asked all the Sisters to pray for our missionaries to America."

The Sisters were able to move into St. Joseph House much later than expected, but they finally had the whole building and the chapel blessed by Bishop Martin in mid-December. Twelve vacancies had been made by the Sisters destined for America who were now at St. Joseph House. Three more were created by the illness of Sister Scholastica, Sister Andrea, and Sister Ida, and so it was utterly impossible to take new missions anywhere. Mother Pauline had to firmly decline as many as thirteen requests and turn her attention to filling the current empty posts.

The winter had set in with full strength and brought in the new year appropriately with snow and cold. Pauline had moved over to St. Joseph House and found it quite pleasant to be there.

Then came the surprise. Mother Pauline tapped on Sister Mathilde's door and opened it.

"Reverend Mother! Come in!"

Pauline entered, carrying a white paper. "I just received this," she said, motioning with it. "I thought you should be the first to know. Bishop Junker is dead. Without him to sponsor us there is no point in going to America. Nor do we yet have permission from Rome to start a new novitiate in America which we would certainly need. So I shall have to write to Father Bartels, the bishop's assistant, to offer our sympathy and tell him that we cannot go to the United States."

"Somehow the Lord did not want us there yet," said Sister Mathilde, shrugging. "And Bishop Junker couldn't wait any longer, Reverend Mother."

In May Mother Pauline directed a tertianship at St. Joseph House and another one in summer. In June Bishop Martin advised her to reassign the Sisters who had been destined to go to America. In order to pay the debts on the new buildings, she had, in early spring, distributed some 2000 tickets among her relatives and the Sisters of each convent. They were to sell as many as they could. Later, she borrowed 10,000 Thalers from her cousin, Hugo, offering him property, dowries, inheritances, and savings of the congregation as security.

Before long, the Sisters were looking at the calendar with almost as much unbelief as Mother Pauline. It was August 21, 1869, and the congregation was twenty years old. Somehow it didn't seem possible that so many years had passed since that day when she, with Sister Mathilde, Sister Agatha, and Sister Maria had received their habits as the first Sisters of Christian Charity. But, as Pauline looked around at this St. Joseph House and across the street at the enlarged motherhouse, as she saw the list of Sisters' names and the addresses of their houses, she knew without doubt that it was true. There were now 250 Sisters working in twenty missions. If she had had room for them, there would have been more Sisters; and if more Sisters, she could have accepted more missions. But it was as God wanted, and she was content.

But she admitted to Provincial School Inspector Schulz that she was really afraid of the teachers' exams this time and afraid for the Sisters taking them. She told him that she very much needed certified administrators for her schools and asked him to please be considerate.

Much to her relief, the Sisters she sent to Münster passed the teacher examinations there and were certified. If they had failed, she would have had to close the girls' school in Höxter. At the same time she was able to send Sisters to Unna, a new mission, for a girls' school there.

Because the Sisters had received the title "Daughters of the Blessed Virgin Mary of the Immaculate Conception" from Pope Pius IX, they had made it a custom to celebrate the feast on December 8 with great reverence. But this year, 1869, just before he left for Rome to attend the very important General Council of Vatican I, Bishop Martin added something new and more solemn to this custom. He said that in every house the Sisters should annually spend the two days before and the feastday itself in retreat. This would be in preparation and thanksgiving for the renewal of vows for one year which all Sisters, except those already under perpetual vows, were invited to make before the superior of the house on the feast of the Immaculate Conception. This year it would be the same day as the opening of the General Council in Rome. Pauline urged the Sisters to be as fervent and prayerful as possible so that this ceremony might be always remembered and passed on to Sisters of the future as something very special.

There were only a few more days before Christmas, and the bright white of newly-fallen snow in the sunlight was reflecting on the morning paper that lay on Pauline's desk. Her councillors were all there, having just finished a meeting. Sister Augustine couldn't resist looking at the paper because something had caught her eye even though it was upside down. She was squinting against the bright sun rays, unaware that anyone was watching her.

"Here, let me turn it for you," laughed Mother Pauline, as she moved the paper right side up toward her councillor.

Sister Augustine blushed a little, stopped squinting, and grinned. So did the others.

"Oh, excuse me, Reverend Mother. I couldn't help getting interested when I saw the word *Mallinckrodt*. See?" And she picked up the paper, pointing to the name at the top of a column in the middle of the left side.

Pauline took it from her and began to read rapidly. Sister Augustine and the other Sisters waited. After a few seconds, she turned to them, beaming.

"It's about Hermann and his speeches in the parliament again. He is afraid of no one and keeps fighting for truth and justice, for the rights of Catholics and the Church."

"God bless him, Reverend Mother," said Sister Anna.

"I must write to him and his wife, Elizabeth, and

tell them how we read about Hermann and how proud we are," finished Pauline. "Thank you, Sisters."

As they left the room, Sister Mathilde whispered to the other three, "It seems to me that Hermann has a match in his sister, Pauline. When she takes on a cause, you can be sure it is for right and justice."

"And she doesn't give up until she wins. She's polite and patient, but—smart and daring," added Sister Walburga.

"But I think you're forgetting something," remarked Sister Augustine. "Reverend Mother has two qualities that are even more important and more difficult in any type of conflict: the power of self-control and knowing when *not* to fight."

Sister Mathilde, Sister Anna, and Sister Walburga looked at her thoughtfully. "Yes, I suppose you're right," said Sister Anna as they walked away.

Sister Augustine thought of a passage in one of Pauline's latest letters. To her it was a proof of real wisdom and courage.

" . . .under the present circumstances," Pauline had written, "where agitation regarding education and schools seems geared to a volcanic eruption, it would not be prudent to fight for one's principles in a single individual case. It may be better to permit a small wrong in order to avert a possible greater one. We hope that other, better days are in the offing."

Were they? Only time would tell.

Chapter XVIII

Queen Marie of Saxony looked from Mother Pauline to the superior of the Gray Nuns and back again.

"Surely you will not hesitate to take the orphanage now, Reverend Mother Pauline."

"I assure you, Reverend Mother," said the Gray Sister, "we would be grateful and relieved if your Sisters would take it from us."

"And I, too, if you would take the school for girls of noble families who have become poor. Neither the Gray Nuns nor the lay staff of either school can meet the demand for more teachers," said the Queen.

"Oh yes, Your Majesty, we will take both," answered Mother Pauline. "But I have a suggestion to make. Why not open the school for girls of noble families to the wealthy as well as the poor? In that way, the school would have income from those who are able to pay tuition."

The Queen and the Gray Sister looked at each

other and then nodded. "Yes," said the Queen. "That is indeed a good idea. We shall do that. Thank God at least two of the very old Catholic institutions in Dresden will remain open. You shall have my full support, Reverend Mother Pauline."

Mother Pauline thanked Queen Marie and left the royal city of Dresden to return to Paderborn. That was in June. Hardly a month had passed when, on July 19, 1870, Napoleon III of France declared war on Prussia. A week later Bishop Martin returned from the General Council of Vatican I which had been interrupted. All the bishops of the world went back to their people, preparing to explain to them the doctrine of infallibility which had been defined by the Vatican Council. However, some dissatisfied Catholics in Germany who refused to accept this doctrine started a movement called "Old Catholics" and were joined by a brilliant theologian, Dr. Döllinger, who continued to teach error. These people were a great help to the government's Liberal Party which, though basically godless and anti-religious, was particularly hostile to Catholics. For the people of Germany, conflict was everywhere: between nations, within their government, and even in the Church.

The Sisters had been preparing also to take over an orphanage and home for the aged in Herzogenrath the following month of August. But not long before they were to come, the mayor of the town notified Mother Pauline that the convent was to be used temporarily as a military hospital and asked her to send Sisters to nurse the wounded. At first, she declined because the Sisters were trained chiefly as teachers, not nurses. But after she talked with Bishop

Martin about it, she realized that even though all the nursing orders of Sisters were already engaged in caring for the soldiers, there was still a great need. Without further objections, she immediately sent Sisters to work at the two military hospitals at Herzogenrath and Solingen. There they served so well that they were later commended and decorated by the government.

Bismarck's plan to attract the states of southern Germany to the northern ones, which made up Prussia, was working beautifully. Armies of soldiers from the southern states were joining those of Prussia and together they defeated the French at Sedan September 2. Napoleon III and Marshal MacMahon surrendered and were taken prisoner with hundreds of French soldiers. Two days later, a new French government was formed at Paris which deposed Napoleon III as emperor and recalled scattered French armies to continue fighting the Germans. For years in the past, French soldiers had been posted in Rome to defend the Holy Father, but now they had to go. That was all that Victor Emmanuel and his soldiers in Italy needed. They quickly took Rome and the Papal States, leaving the Holy Father untouched but a voluntary prisoner in the Vatican.

To Pauline the whole thing was very sad and ironic, and her tremendous reverence and loyalty to the Holy Father made her feel his imprisonment keenly. If only there was something she—or someone—could do!

Meanwhile she was busy making arrangements to send Sisters to the two schools of Queen Marie in Dresden. One afternoon in the chilly fall, she returned to the motherhouse from her errands for this project, bringing with her a poor man. His face was thin, and his hair hung long from under his beaten hat. His clothes were shabby and ill-fitting, and as they entered the convent, he stood a little behind Mother Pauline, embarrassed.

"Good afternoon, Reverend Mother," said the postulant who was helping the Sister at the door. She smiled brightly but looked from Mother Pauline to her unusual companion with some surprise. Quickly she caught a whiff of whiskey as the man coughed.

"Good afternoon, Sister," answered Pauline. "This gentleman was sitting in the cold by our gate, and I invited him in. Please go to the kitchen and get a cup of coffee for him. I shall bring him to the parlor. Come, sir," she said, turning to the man. "Follow me," and she led the way.

"Please sit down," she said, motioning to the most comfortable chair. As he sat down a little unsteadily and rather sheepishly, she took off her long cloak, laid it across a chair, and set down her packages.

Outside the door, she met the postulant with the cup of coffee.

"There is no milk in the coffee, my dear," said Mother Pauline. "He cannot drink it black."

"Please, Reverend Mother, I could not find any milk at all in the kitchen. Anyway," and the postulant grinned as she looked up at the kind face above her, "black coffee will do him good. It will sober him up."

Pauline's blue-green eyes glinted hard, and the postulant gulped a bit.

"Dear Sister, how can you say a thing like that?

Who knows *why* the man is drunk? Perhaps he has had nothing to eat all day and bought some liquor to get warm. And, of course, on an empty stomach, it affected him. Be very careful not to judge rashly. Go and call Sister to make him a good meal."

Now it was the postulant's turn to be sober, and she went as fast as she could without spilling the coffee, to find the cook.

Mother Pauline looked into the parlor. "Please make yourself comfortable," she said to the man. "I'll be back shortly." In a little while she returned, carrying the coffee with milk and talked with him until the postulant came to bring him to the guest dining-room.

While he ate the hot meal, she went to the kitchen and asked that food be packed for his family. Then she looked for one of the workmen and explained the situation.

"Please take him home," said Mother Pauline. "It is almost time for you to stop work anyway." The workman nodded. "God bless you," she added.

By the middle of October everything was ready, and she arrived at the beautiful royal city of Dresden on the Elbe river with twenty Sisters, some for the orphanage and some for the boarding-school for girls of noble families. Queen Marie was delighted.

For two weeks Mother Pauline stayed there to help the Sisters settle in and adjust. It was not easy. The Sisters were embarrassed by the constant presence of the queen at all their activities. Her daily supervision, even though she was kind and meant well, put them under some stress. Then too, everyone was aware that Sisters were banned in Saxony by law, and they had to be very careful not to be seen on the streets. Through Mother Pauline's concern, arrangements had been made that they could go to church without going outside, and all their spiritual needs would easily be taken care of by the parish chaplain and the chaplain of the queen's court. By the time she left, the Sisters were beginning to cope with the whole situation.

It was the eve of All Saints' Day when her train pulled into Kassel early in the morning. Because of the transporting of thousands of troops, no train connection with Paderborn was possible for her then. She knew the city and was glad that she could attend Mass and receive Holy Communion. Then, as she came from church, she got the idea! A German officer who had boarded the train at one of the stations had told her that four days ago the French general Bazaine had surrendered at the Metz. 83,000 French soldiers had been captured, and among those taken earlier, many were dying in the barracks because disease had broken out. Emperor Napoleon was being held prisoner by the Germans in a castle at Wilhelmshöhe, and—her own mind added—another very important person was still prisoner in the Vatican at Rome. Surely something could be arranged, she thought.

She had plenty of time. She would go to Wilhelmshöhe. As she travelled, she was thinking, thinking intently, formulating some possibilities for freeing the Holy Father. Perhaps her own country's officials would exchange Napoleon for the Pope and then free him. Or, better still, when the war was over in the near future and Napoleon was released, he could lead in battle any willing French prisoners freed by the German general, Moltke, for the purpose of fighting and defeating Victor Emmanuel and his troops in Italy. That way they could restore to the Holy Father his freedom and the Papal States. Then the French could return to France as victors instead of dying of disease in the German barracks. Of course, she would have to present this idea to both Napoleon and Moltke, but of that she was not afraid.

Pauline arrived at the castle in Wilhelmshöhe and walked up to the first Prussian soldier in the long line of guards stationed spaces apart up to the door of the castle. He saluted her respectfully, and after her request, escorted her to another German officer, who listened politely. Although they did not show it, the other soldiers were surprised and impressed and wondered about this tall, dignified lady in the long black cloak and the white, heart-shaped cap with the bow, who came alone and was so completely at ease.

At last she found herself inside the door, where another soldier stood at attention. Again, she made her request.

"Would it be possible for me to have an audience with His Majesty, Emperor Napoleon?"

The soldier brought her to a waiting-room and told her to be seated. He would take her request further. After a while, he returned.

"It is not possible for you to have an audience with the Emperor himself, Fräulein von Mallinck-rodt, but his secretary, Pietri, will see you." The soldier bowed and left.

Surprisingly, it was not long before Pietri appeared and greeted her courteously. Now that the chance to really present her idea had come, Mother Pauline felt a glow of excitement. She immediately began to describe in excellent French her suggested plan for the release of the Pope, and her enthusiasm grew as she spoke.

Pietri listened politely, admiring the courage and loving loyalty of this humble religious woman before him. He knew she did not realize that Napoleon was no longer emperor in the eyes of France and could hardly lead an army in its name, even if the French soldiers were released by Moltke, which was unlikely. He tried to explain that the plan could not be carried out, much as he regretted it. He thanked her for coming and wished her a safe journey home.

As she left that castle, Pauline suddenly saw clearly that her plan was, indeed, an "air castle," as she wrote months later to Hermann, and that "no one had the slightest intention of helping the Pope." But if she was disappointed, she was far from defeated because she knew without a doubt that God needed none of them. He could and would do all things well. So the soldiers she passed on the way out saw no difference in her. Her head was just as erect, her shoulders were just as straight, her step was just as long and firm as before. In fact, there was something soldierly about her!

When she arrived home, she told only Bishop Martin of what she had done and of her plan. He smiled and shook his head a little sadly, not because of what she had tried to do, but because Christ's Vicar was so treated by heads of state. He had to admit that her plan was creative and courageous, even if impractical.

Somehow, though, despite her efforts to keep the whole affair secret, the word got out that the "Ultramontanes"—those who were working for the freedom of the Church from the interference of liberal state governments and believed in the Church's authority—were in operation again. Months later the newspapers carried sarcastic reports about them, and Pauline was labelled as one. It was said that she had pleaded with the French Empress Eugenie for the release of the Pope.

Hermann wrote to Pauline, inquiring about it. She wrote back, telling him the whole story and saying that there had been a large coach in front of the castle when she went to see Naploeon but she did not know whose it was. She had never even seen the empress and did not know her at all. She had tried to be cautious and secretive, but if people were laughing at her, no matter.

Hermann was rather proud of her and told her that many others were very pleased with what she had done. Catholics were holding meetings in Aachen and in Berlin for the defense of the Church, and a petition for it had been sent to the King of Prussia, now crowned emperor of the whole of Germany, both north and south. The cardinals of Rome, called the Roman Curia, had themselves been communicating with a German archbishop about perhaps giving refuge to the Holy Father either in Fulda or Cologne. Even Bismarck was asked about the possibility of the Pope's receiving refuge from Prussia. As one might expect, he replied, "Such a turn of events would be unheard of, though not impossible insofar as it might even be useful to us. The Catholics would recognize us for what we are in truth: the only power on earth which is able to give sanctuary to the head of their Church."

Many Catholics of Germany sent messages of loyalty and obedience to the Pope, and later Mother

Pauline did the same. She thanked him, declared that she and all the Sisters accepted every decree of Vatican Council I, and told him of their sorrow that the Papal States had been seized. Most of all, she told him how honored they would be if he would choose to make his home temporarily with them in Paderborn. They would gladly give him St. Joseph House as his residence. The letter was signed by all the Sisters, but the offer was never taken.

Pauline was home from Dresden only about a month when, on the last day of November, she had a severe fainting spell. Both the doctor and Bishop Martin ordered her to Boeddeken for a rest, ignoring her protests. But even they did not realize what she was yet to face.

It was spring of 1871, and she had returned early in the year. She stood with Sister Anna, looking at the cracks in the walls of the very house she had offered to the Holy Father. The war with France was over except for the signing of the treaty, but the heavy artillery carried so often on the trains at such great speed past St. Joseph House situated near the tracks, had taken its toll on the building. The repeated powerful vibrations had shivered its walls, and they had split.

But there was a totally different kind of split that made Pauline happy. This time it was in the political parties of Germany's legislature to which Hermann had been elected. Because Bismarck, the chancellor, had cleverly annulled several laws of 1849 that guaranteed freedom of religion to every German and was working for a national German church cut off from the Pope and completely under the authority of the government, many Germans banded together and formed a party that was between the Liberals and the Conservatives. It was then called the Center Party, and one of its leaders was Hermann von Mallinckrodt, along with von Windhorst and von Savigny. This party proposed that freedom of religion and freedom for church organizations be stated in the constitution for the new German empire and that Germany make a protest to Italy about the taking of the Papal States.

Hermann in particular made some fiery speeches in parliament defending the Church.

"Since when did the Church become an institution of the State?" he said. "Did Octavius or Nero or von Döllinger establish the Church? Or is its authority from its Divine Founder who sent the Apostles . . .without the authority of kings? Let me quote a speech from Chancellor Bismarck himself made in 1849: 'If we continue in this manner, then I yet hope to see the crazed ship of state crash against the rock of the Christian church.' Now, gentlemen, I don't like to see the ship of German empire taken over dangerous reefs—so why do we not dismiss the second mates now?"

His bold quotation of Bismarck struck home, and everyone knew the "second mates" were the antireligious Liberals.

Bismarck retaliated quickly. In July he dissolved the Catholic department of the Ministry of Culture and of the Ministry of Public Instruction. He gave further orders that no more agreements were to be made by the German government with religious congregations for taking over schools. That caused even the Conservatives to break with him. Then Virchow, speaker of the Liberals, actually gave a name to their struggle against the Catholics, calling it the "Kulturkampf," the culture war. War was once again declared in Germany, this time against many of its own citizens, trying to destroy their values, their way of life, its very meaning.

It was a war of wits and minds, of beliefs and ideas, of teaching and learning, but the Catholics would not give up. In the very face of this hostility, Mother Pauline dared to open another school in Dortmund. Though the authorities would pay the salary of only one teacher, she would pay the rest. The next month, August, she heard that the Notre Dame Sisters were forbidden to teach, and she knew there was trouble ahead. But she laid her mind, her heart, and her hand in God's and waited calmly with Him for what was to come. The 250 Sisters working in twenty establishments in thirty-two different activities belonged to Him. He could use them as He pleased. He is so wise and knows so infinitely much more than those who work for or against Him.

The Catholic bishops of Germany met at Fulda and during their general assembly addressed a letter to the emperor, asking for freedom of the Church from state interference. Letters from priests and from Catholic families flooded the Department of Education, some reaching the Emperor. But the only answer they received was from the Commissioner of Education, Falk, who said that they sounded as if the government was breaking laws by ordering what it did!

Soon Falk declared that no more teachers belonging to religious congregations might be engaged, and Pauline prepared herself to receive word that her Sisters were dismissed from the schools. In a very short time laws were passed expelling the Jesuits and other religious orders of men.

"We are in God's hands, and we shall leave ourselves trustfully to His guidance," she told the worried Sisters at the various convents and seeing her stand before them, strong and serene, gave them courage. But Pauline was not a woman who would sit and wait for disaster to strike. She believed firmly that God helps those who help themselves, so she hurried to save whatever she could. She went to Dresden, Magdeburg, Oschersleben, Sigmaringen, and Constance, meeting with various persons and trying to make arrangements so that the convents and property owned by the Sisters would not be confiscated by the government.

Next she travelled to Berlin on business regarding Dresden. But she also managed to get an appointment with Dr. Falk, the Commissioner of Education, who was very active in carrying out the wishes of Bismarck. As she waited to see him, she prayed that somehow there would be a way for the Sisters to remain in the schools.

"Dr. Falk will see you now, Fräulein," said a young man, who worked there as a clerk.

"Thank you," said Pauline, bowing slightly and following him to the Commissioner's office.

"Fräulein von Mallinckrodt, I believe," said Falk, intoning her name in an unpleasant way and rolling it slowly over his tongue somewhat like a lion licking his chops.

"Yes, Dr. Falk. Thank you," answered Pauline, as she took the chair to which he motioned her.

There was an instant of silence as the two surveyed each other. Falk noted her ungainly shoes that were totally eclipsed by her gloved hands, her erect posture, the graceful flow of her worn black cloak, the dignity and poise of her head. His look was stopped by the intensity of hers, the pallor of her face and the whiteness of her coif emphasizing her glowing eyes and charming smile.

"Dr. Falk—" He was startled a little by her voice and moved slightly, resettling in his chair.

"Dr. Falk, I have come to ask you if there is not some way the Sisters can remain in the schools where they are. Our congregation was recognized as a corporation and given corporation rights by the royal government in 1849. Since 1850 the Sisters have taught in the provincial blind asylum and many schools with a fine record and no complaints. If you examine the reports, you will see that they have merited praise. We have taken great pains to see that the Sisters are excellently prepared to be good teachers. Surely you would want to retain such teachers in the schools." Mother Pauline was bending forward slightly and eagerly watching his face.

Falk had taken off his glasses and was tapping them gently on his left hand.

"Yes, it would be a shame to lose such good teachers," he said, narrowing his eyes. "But, my dear lady, that is not necessary. All that you and your associates would have to do is take off that religious garb and be like other women, and you may remain in the schools. Now, that isn't so—"

Pauline knew instinctively it meant more than just changing dress. She rose slowly to her full height, almost looking down on Falk, who had also risen. He could feel her indignation and stepped back involuntarily.

"Never!" Her voice was low, but the two syllables punctured the air. "Never will we give up our holy vocation, Dr. Falk. I hope you will be able to find the great number of good teachers in such a short time, as you will have to, to replace the Sisters. Good day, sir." As he took a breath to answer, she had turned and was gone.

As soon as she arrived home, she wrote to the emperor, telling him of the blow delivered by the decree of the Minister of Education and of her unsuccessful interview with him. She begged His Majesty to repeal the law and allow the Sisters to continue their quiet activity in the schools. She asked for an audience with him too.

But she did not stop with that. She travelled back to Berlin and saw the cabinet councillor of the empress and then the cabinet councillor of the emperor, Herr von Wilmovski. She also had an interview with Minister Count von Eulenberg, who was very gracious. She was forced to merely leave her card for Bismarck, who was not at home, but she won the sympathy of Countess Hacke, lady-in-waiting to the empress. Pauline asked her to tell the empress of the Sisters' situation. A few days later, she wrote to the countess, begging her to speak with the Grand Duchess, who was probably responsible for the Sisters' remaining in Constance, and request that the duchess plead with her father, the emperor, to keep the Sisters in the schools of Prussia. As citizens of Prussia, they should not be deprived of their only means of earning a living.

Yet, much as she tried to continue the apostolate in her own dear country, Pauline was ready to give it up without a tear, a single complaint, or show of worry the instant it became clear that God was asking it. For she loved Him unconditionally. She loved Him more than herself or any work of His. She knew from experience that He mysteriously brings good out of even the deliberate evil deeds of men and women whom He created free; that He knows what He is doing and wants only the best, despite obvious failure and tragedy. So she was not depressed or sad. She did not fret one moment over the loss of precious work and places because it was not her own will that she was seeking. Whatever God, her beloved, wanted was the driving force of her life, the sole reason for her existence. He had only to indicate His will, and she would strain forward gladly, with all her strength, to do it, bitter or sweet.

Pauline was sure that those who harm others usually act blindly. She was equally sure that criticizing them accomplished nothing except to offend the Lord who commanded us to love our enemies. As trouble increased, and the Sisters, with sad hearts, were forced to leave their life's work, no one was allowed to make angry or unkind remarks about those responsible for it. In fact, if it did happen, it became one of those rare occasions when the Sisters saw a stern Mother Pauline.

"You must stop that, once and for all!" she would say sharply.

During a visit one day with Pauline, a friend, loyal to her and the Sisters, began to use harsh and angry language about someone who had hurt Mother Pauline and her work. The feelings of the visitor were so strong that she talked on and on, rapidly and impulsively, condemning the offender. Suddenly she stopped, abruptly aware that her words were not being well received. She looked at Pauline closely and made a tiny sound of surprise. There were tears in Pauline's eyes!

"Please, my dear," murmured Pauline. "Such words do no good."

"Oh, Reverend Mother, I'm sorry," she said apologetically and put her hand on Pauline's arm.

Because she was so intent on doing God's will, Pauline was quick to find His least expression of it. It was, then, no surprise to her that calls for her Sisters were coming not only from North America but from South America as well. To her, these were messages from God, loud and clear, pointing out new places where He wanted to send the Sisters rejected by their own government. In answer to a request from Bogota, Colombia, she was ready to send six Sisters, who were now at the motherhouse studying Spanish. Bishop Martin had given his approval, and she was waiting only to receive acceptance from the bishop of Bogota and word from the Colombian consul regarding a contract and travel information.

Then from Dresden came news that roused mixed feelings. The Sisters wrote that Queen Marie was not the only one watching them at their work in the two schools. They had discovered that spies from totally anti-religious groups in the city had found their way in and were observing the Sisters and the students at every activity. At the beginning their reports had been surprisingly favorable, even full of praise. But later, there was open combat.

Besides that, Sister Walburga, the superior at Dresden, wrote that Queen Marie had received a letter from Emperor William which stated that it was not possible for him to grant the Sisters of Christian

Charity an audience as Mother Pauline had requested. But he had asked Dr. Falk to explain the problem to him and decided that he could not make an exception and allow the Sisters to teach in the public schools. However, they would certainly be allowed to do their original work according to their statutes: teaching the blind, the poor, and the orphaned. They would also be permitted to teach in private schools according to standards of local authorities. The letter went on to say that the emperor had ordered a message conveying this to be sent to Fräulein von Mallinckrodt. Pauline was pleased to read this, but she was cautious about rejoicing. She had received no such message as yet.

There was, however, another message and a sad one. Hermann's wife, Elizabeth, fondly called Else, was dead, leaving him with five children. The oldest was only eleven. Pauline could sympathize with his grief and personal loss. Just recently Hermann and his family had moved to Grandmother von Hartmann's house at Borchen at the invitation of the widow of Uncle Hermann von Hartmann. She had given Pauline's brother, Hermann, the house and estate on the condition that he allow her to live there for the rest of her life. Hermann, Else, and the children had been happy with the arrangement. But now he would have to make a definite change. As a member of the legislature, he had to be away very much in Berlin. He could hardly expect his elderly widow aunt to care for the children and raise them, nor could he just leave them to themselves. Some months later, he married Thecla, the youngest sister of Else, and Pauline was glad. Thecla had often been with the family before and would be a good mother and wife.

The law requiring the expulsion of priests in religious orders now began to be enforced, and the Jesuits left Paderborn much to the sorrow of the people. Pauline shook her head and smiled grimly at the strange joke that was taking place. While the Church was celebrating for the first three days of November the 1100th anniversary of the introduction of Christianity into Germany, the government was expelling from Germany one of Christianity's leading groups, the Jesuits!

Although life for Catholics in general and especially for bishops, priests, and Sisters was becoming very difficult, Mother Pauline knew that they should try to go on as normally as possible, including the small affairs that might otherwise be omitted in times like these. Since there was a lottery in Paderborn to raise money for the cathedral, the Sisters of the motherhouse bought a ticket. They needed money badly too, and Mother Pauline wrote to the convents, telling the Sisters the number of their ticket. They should please pray, that God willing, their ticket might win the prize.

At times Pauline's personal experiences were very revealing to her. She was made well aware that in spite of her courteous, loving ways, she did not please everyone. In fact, it became painfully clear to her that she actually riled some people, and one priest in particular. But she never took offense or felt rejected. Rather, she humbly admitted her limitation, regretted it, and looked for a solution. Since she was very conscientious about keeping careful account of finances, she had gone to this priest to ask for a receipt for offerings she had given him for

Masses for the dead. Somehow she angered him, and she left after a few minutes. But she would not do without the receipt. So she wrote to Sister Walburga:

" . . .I think it is necessary that you write an amiable letter to Reverend Father Rector as soon as possible. The conversation was so unpleasant that I feel very bad about it. I am not the right person for him, and therefore I do not like to go to him. You know it is difficult for me to say the right things to him."

Thoughts of America pressed on her more and more as things grew worse in Germany. Toward the end of November Pauline went to Würzburg to visit her friend, Dr. Berghaus, to get information about going to the United States. He had lived there for twenty years, still had a house in New York, and had travelled in the States very much. He could tell her about things like the climate and give her names of persons who could help. He told her as much as he could to help her prepare the Sisters she would send there, but he strongly advised that she go to America herself.

Almost each day another letter came from one of the missions saying that the contract of the Sisters was not renewed and that they would have to leave by April 1. It had been announced in the legislature in Berlin when it met in November that Dr. Falk had ordered all Sisters out of elementary schools. Hermann had immediately challenged it, speaking for two hours. He showed how that order violated the original German constitution of 1850 and read the letters of protest from people where the Sisters taught. Then Mr. Stross, a Protestant, rose and pointed out how foolish it would be to put the Sisters out. The state would lose three thousand teachers at one stroke, and it would be hard to replace them. But when all was said and done, the votes showed that the anti-Catholics had won.

In Paderborn, Mother Pauline faced the group of Sisters she had called together: her councillors and the senior Sisters of the motherhouse.

"I'm sure that you have been thinking much the same as I lately—that when our good Sisters start coming home from their closed schools, we will not have room enough here at the motherhouse for them all. We must find still another house besides St. Joseph's," she said.

There was a low murmur of agreement from the group.

"It seems to me that the house where the Jesuits used to live, the von Kettler house, would be a good place," Pauline continued. "We could rent it, and since some of the Sisters will be going to America, there will be room for others returning at different times. What do you think?"

The sisters were pleased with the idea.

"Very well. Then we shall have to discontinue the rental of Holthausen because we cannot afford it. That will give us the furniture we need for the old Jesuit house. I'll arrange to have it brought from Holthausen. By the way, what shall we call this house? I should like to call it the "House of Divine Providence," said Mother Pauline, looking about for signs of approval. She waited; then the Sisters clapped and smiled. Yes, that was it.

Chapter XIX

Sister Augusta stood with Mother Pauline at a window of the Gutenberg castle on the second floor, looking at the lovely scene stretching below. In the distance, behind the rolling lawn covered with trees and flowers was a chain of mountains towering like gorgeous giants with arms invisibly linked. The nearby beautiful countryside was in tiny Lichtenstein, whose prince was allowing the Sisters to rent the castle for their boarding-school. They had had to leave the school at Constance and sell their house. But because of the prince's goodness, they were able to carry on their work in this peaceful place.

Mother Pauline smiled and turned to Sister Augusta, who was pointing out the window enthusiastically.

"You can see Switzerland and the Alps from here, Reverend Mother! This is really an ideal spot, isn't it? God has been very good to us to provide us with such a place. The Sisters and children will be happy here, I'm sure."

"Yes, God's ways are so mysterious," answered Pauline, "but in all He does He is adorable." Then she added seriously:

"But what hard and sad times and catastrophes are still ahead of us? In the end, the dear Lord Who ruled the world for so many years, has the most practice. His mastery will show itself, for He is the almighty and all-wise God."

Both were quiet and thoughtful for a moment. They could hear the sounds of voices and of furniture being moved below.

"Come, Sister Augusta, perhaps we can help them a little," said Pauline as she turned quickly toward the stairs.

Back in Paderborn there was moving and settling in to be done at the House of Divine Providence, too, and Pauline hurried to get it ready for the Sisters who would be coming back from closed schools. She welcomed each Sister there with a warm embrace and did everything possible to cheer them all. She knew how much the Sisters longed to stay in their classrooms. She also knew that government authorities had tried and were trying to persuade them to leave the congregation. But they had remained loyal, and she treasured them! She must make things as pleasant as she could for them. As she looked about the house, she knew it was cozy and comfortable. But—there was no income, nothing steady to support them. America was waiting, and some would have to go there soon.

Pauline laughed a little to herself as she made an interesting exchange of service at Anrath. From the school where, by government order, she watched the Sisters close everything and leave, she went with others to the building where, in the same town, by request, they were opening a home for orphans and the aged. The Sisters didn't mind if the government was a bit illogical.

Since the house of the congregation at Viersen would have to be sold, Pauline was working on that and similar matters as usual, one evening, at the motherhouse. Suddenly, she was startled by a fire alarm from outside. She went from window to window, trying to discover the direction of the blaze. She had plenty troubles of her own, but she could not ignore those of others, especially something so terrifying. Finally, she saw in the extreme north a very red section in the black sky and thick clusters of nasty smoke rising against it. She knew that section—densely crowded with houses and people, poor people! Some of her Sisters were in that area too.

In a moment she was out of the room and in the corridor, almost bumping into two Sisters who came running toward her.

"Reverend Mother, there's a fire—"

"Yes, I know," she interrupted. "Come with me, Sister, please," she said, taking the first one by the arm.

"Tell Sister Augusta and the others that we two are going to the fire," she called to the second as she looked back.

They were grateful to find that their Sisters and house were safe. But Mother Pauline and her companion moved on quickly to the place of the fire.

There was general confusion and grief. Little children were running, crying while their parents tried to rescue a relative or some belongings. Fire workers were working frantically to bring water to the spreading flames, often stopped by panic-stricken people or animals. Almost that entire section of the city was burned to the ground that night.

Mother Pauline tucked up her long black skirt, pinned back her veil and cape and set to work. She brought frightened, wandering little ones back to a safe place under the care of someone older. She stepped into rubble and helped needy families salvage some possessions. She led their animals to safety if she could and beat out embers that would not die. She comforted those who had lost the little they had, wiping their tears and her own. The two Sisters worked until early morning and came home at last, leading a sad group of people to the motherhouse. During the weeks that followed, Pauline gave food and shelter to many of the fire victims.

Somehow the money and the Sisters' credit stretched, and one day she actually saw precious traveler's checks resting in her hand. She would need them for the Sisters who were going to America soon and for her own trip there later.

Then the historic day came. It was April 8, 1873, and she stood at the dock in Bremen with Sister Xaveria and her seven companions, who were bound for New Orleans in America. They were excited, glad, and sad all at one time. They had said goodbye to their families some time ago, and now came the hardest part: to say goodbye to Mother Pauline.

She embraced each Sister, almost lifting her in a gesture of support and encouragement. She whispered loving words, calling down God's blessing on every individual. But the Sisters' farewells were wordless because only tears came and a huge lump in their throats that blocked clear speech.

Pauline and her companion waited, watching for the black veils and white bonnets to appear on deck. Then they waved their white handkerchiefs until their arms were tired and they could no longer see the Sisters on the departing steamship.

Meanwhile more Sisters returned to Paderborn from four other closed schools, and their convents were sold whenever possible. Pauline was extremely busy writing letters of thanks and farewell to the pastors of places the Sisters had had to leave. She also wrote asking for letters of recommendation from various religious orders in Germany that already had some members and houses in America where she and her companion might stay as they travelled about the United States.

To her surprise and real regret came the news that President von Bodelschwingh, with whom she had dealt so often over the years regarding the blind asylum, had died suddenly. She immediately wrote to his widow, sending prayers and genuine sympathy.

Then she came to Sister Walburga's letter, and her pen began moving vigorously across the paper in answer. Sister Walburga was a versatile person and an excellent character. Mother Pauline had entrusted her with various offices and responsibilities. However, as much as she loved her, she very much wanted to see her become holy. So she did not spare her when she read of Sister Walburga's extreme attachment to Dresden and her tremendous difficulty in leaving it.

"Your letter was painful to me," Pauline wrote her. "It shows a sickly soul. God has permitted

317

events to happen as they are. His Hand will guide us, and He will dispose everything for our best, if only we surrender ourselves to Him and His guidance wholly and devotedly. Until now, He has taken good care of us; He will do this in the future too."

Almost as proof of those words came the happy news of the Sisters' safe arrival at New Orleans. What a welcome they had received! Father Bogaerts had met them at the ship with a delegation of people who had clapped and given them flowers with the sweet scent of magnolia and orange blossoms. The climate was very warm, but so were the hearts of these people! He had put them in carriages drawn by decorated horses, and they were taken to St. Henry's Church. As they alighted from the carriages, Father had laid letters from Germany in Sister Xaviera's hand, and she held them up to show the others. Little girls in white dresses and veils and little boys in white suits, with the parishioners all around, stood before the church door and bowed to the Sisters. One little girl had come forward, curtsied, piped a little speech of welcome and offered a bouquet to the nearest Sister. Then the church bells had begun to ring loud and joyfully, and everyone went in to thank God. There was a mighty hymn of praise, and then benediction of the Blessed Sacrament. The Sisters had come at last!

About three weeks later, on May 22, Mother Pauline and Sister Gonzaga, her companion, stood ready to leave for their trip to America. Pauline had to say goodbye to everyone—each Sister, each blind child, the gardener, the ladies in the laundry, and especially to Margretchen, whom she had to assure over and over that she would return. Meantime Sister

Mathilde would take her place, managing the affairs of the congregation.

At the train station were Hermann and Alfred, who gave her some medicine for seasickness. She had seen George and Dina earlier.

"We are sailing on the ship, *Hermann*, you know," she said to Hermann. "That's a good sign. Thank you for everything," she said to them both as she stepped high onto the train that would take them to the harbor of Bremen.

On May 24 they boarded the ship and two days later were in the harbor of Southampton, England. They were allowed to go into the city, and Mother Pauline was delighted when the people she spoke to in English understood her. Their friendliness encouraged her to keep practicing her English. She was equally happy to learn that they could attend Mass and receive Communion the next day in that city.

After they left Southampton, the long part of the journey began, and for days the Sisters saw only that tremendously vast ocean in all its moods and faces. Sometimes in was greenish-blue, sometimes very blue and other times dull gray. Some days it was gentle and serene, lapping soothingly, and other days it was stormy, wild, and rough with high, foaming waves. Mother Pauline and Sister Gonzaga spent most of the time on the deck, and often they were seasick. But after a few days they became more accustomed to the rolling motion and tried to enjoy the fresh sea air. They sat on deck, praying, reading, studying English, writing letters, and watching the sea gulls. Mother Pauline was reading *The Vicar of Wakefield* to improve her English. When she finished that, she would read *Ladybird*.

At last came the thrill of landing in America! It was June 7, and their ship was welcomed into the New York harbor by a German sister ship, the *Bremen*, whose band was playing loudly for the passengers of the *Hermann*. But Pauline and Sister Gonzaga were completely taken up with the beauty of the harbor until they realized that there was no one there that they knew. For the first time they felt strange and alone. Then a kind stewardess took them to the customs office and afterwards directed them to the Franciscan Sisters at St. Mary's Hospital in Hoboken, New Jersey, where Pauline's friend, Franziska Schervier, who was foundress of those Sisters, had told them to stay.

It was very warm, and Mother Pauline found the heat intense—the opposite of two days before on the boat, when there had been hail and cold, and they had been near an iceberg.

On her list of convents in America, Pauline found that of Religious of the Sacred Heart in Manhattanville, New York. The two Sisters made their way there and visited with Mother Baden, who was also from Germany. They had their first experience of an elevator and went up to the fifth and sixth floors. Later Father Frederick, a Jesuit, met them at the convent and gave them a tour of New York City.

"It's enormously large," said Pauline in amazement, as she surveyed the crowds of people and seemingly endless streets with so many large buildings. Father Frederick smiled.

The Sisters were delighted with the huge lawn and wooded area called Central Park that spread through New York City for the pleasure of the people. They were astonished by Broadway Street and the other streets of stores and shopping and were fascinated by the long lines of carriages, waiting for pedestrians to cross the wide streets. But Mother Pauline felt that New York City was not the place for her Sisters to establish themselves.

They travelled next to Wilkes Barre, Pennsylvania, where they were met by Father Nagel who had written to Pauline earlier, asking for Sisters. The Sisters were constantly in wonder at the beauty of the land and at its size. "Pennsylvania is twice the size of Germany," she wrote home. They visited Father Nagel's frame church and were greeted there, too, by girls and boys in white.

From there it was natural to stop at Scranton, the diocese to which Wilkes Barre belonged, and meet Irish Bishop O'Hara, who greeted them in German. He would be happy to accept the Sisters in his diocese, he said. When Mother Pauline agreed to send Sisters, he said the pastor would announce in German to the people that the congregation was going to open a parochial school and a boarding-school in Wilkes Barre.

At the request of a priest, the Sisters stopped at Melrose to pay a visit to Archbishop McCloskey. They had heard that he was not at all eager to have foreigners in his diocese; so they went there with hesitation. But the archbishop was surprisingly friendly and spoke with them in French, telling them he would welcome them. So Mother Pauline agreed to take a school there since it would be annexed to New York.

They went next to Philadelphia and were impressed by the general appearance of the city and by the beauty of the cathedral and celebration of the Mass.

There were thirty altar boys in a semi-circle around the sanctuary, and the singing, the vestments were exceptionally fine. They had met Bishop Wood and were given a tour of the cathedral, which had many chapels. Mother Pauline was especially drawn to the one dedicated to our Lady with its white marble statue of Mary tinted blue by the light from a stained-glass window behind it.

But the hustle and bustle of city traffic was almost too much for the Sisters. The noise and movement of the wagons and horses, of horse-drawn trains in the streets, of steam trains, and of boats used to go to different sections of New York were really stressful, pulling one's attention in many directions at once. However, Pauline was most pleased with the great courtesy policemen showed to ladies and Sisters who could not find their way through the lines of wagons. These officers would lead the ladies by the arm through the traffic, making way by simply waving their short sticks.

On the train to Baltimore, Pauline wrote home despite the jolting, saying how beautiful America is and that they liked it *very* much! She and Sister Gonzaga were becoming quite americanized. She noted that they often saw Negroes, whom she seemed to watch with great interest.

They arrived in Baltimore very early in the morning, so early that the doors of the church they had come to, were still locked. They were grimy and tired from their train ride, so they sat down on the church steps, waiting till the doors were opened. Soon a little old lady came to the church, and the Sisters talked with her. When they heard that she lived close by, they asked whether they might go to her house

Pauline's travelling basket and her Office

and wash. She took them there gladly and gave them fresh water in a tin basin. Then they all returned for Holy Mass and Communion. When the Sisters learned that the bishop of Baltimore was not at home, they continued on their way.

Pauline purposely arranged the trip in such a way that they would be able to see Washington, D.C. So it was with real pleasure that they hired a carriage on leaving the train and asked the driver to take them to the most notable places. He did so very obligingly. They drove past the White House, the Congressional Building, the Treasury Department, various monuments, and other beautiful places. Sister Gonzaga was genuinely awed by the Treasury Department and the thought of all the money it housed. Mother Pauline declared that the Congressional Building surpassed by far all buildings of its kind in Germany, France, Austria, and other parts of America. She learned too late that they could have gone into the Congressional Building to observe the Congress at work.

On the train once more and bound for Cincinnati, the Sisters decided to take a sleeper this time. They had been so tired and dusty on their last train ride. At first they rather enjoyed it—sitting on the seats facing each other and having at the other end of the compartment water and soap and towels. When the Negro porter began to make up their beds, they watched him curiously. But their curiosity soon turned to discomfort.

Sister Gonzaga was uncomfortable knowing that she was above Reverend Mother, but she grew even more uncomfortable from the heat, the jerking motion, and the lack of air. By five o'clock she was up and out of the berth and found Mother Pauline up too. After the porter had closed their beds and opened the windows, they felt better and leaned their heads against the seat back to doze a little. No sleepers again ever in summer, they agreed.

In Cincinnati the Franciscan Sisters met them and took them to Archbishop Purcell. He introduced them to the board members of an orphanage for which Sisters were wanted. The Franciscan Sisters would not accept it because they do hospital work only and were hoping that Mother Pauline would take it. Since all spoke German, the meeting went smoothly. The orphanage was large and well-situated with beautiful gardens, and Mother Pauline was inclined favorably to it. But she could not as yet make a commitment to the board, saying only that perhaps in the future it would be possible to send Sisters.

On July 1, Mother Pauline and Sister Gonzaga boarded a steamship called the *Shannon* and left Cincinnati, sailing down the beautiful Ohio River, destined for New Orleans. It would be a trip of 1600 miles and slower than by train, but more pleasant. A doctor they had met earlier on the train had told them it would be better for them physically to go by boat since it would give their bodies a chance to adjust to the increasing heat gradually.

It was a ten-day trip, much quieter than on the ocean, with a magnificent expanse of water, especially at Cairo, where the Ohio and Missouri Rivers flowed into the Mississippi. Such a vast amount of water other than the ocean was almost incredible! The Ohio was a clear green, and the Mississippi a muddy yellow. The changing scenery on either side of the rivers was equally magnificent—hills, luxuri-

324

ant woodlands, small towns, valleys, mountains, farmhouses, log huts. It was hard to believe that so much land was all one country!

As they travelled farther south, it grew more exciting and warmer. They soon discovered the reason for all the noise and fireworks on July 4 and became almost envious at the celebration of freedom everywhere. They stood long at the railing of the ship, looking at the sugar and cotton plantations and the workers as they passed. There were Negroes among the passengers on board, and the boat stewardess was a Negro.

By the time they had reached Memphis, the heat had increased and the Sisters had become well acquainted with mosquitos. While they stopped there, Mother Pauline sent a telegram to the Sisters in New Orleans, telling them the time that they would arrive there.

As the *Shannon* came into the port of New Orleans, Mother Pauline and Sister Gonzaga looked eagerly around, but there were no white bonnets and bows to be seen. They were earlier than expected, so they sat on their baggage and waited. There was plenty of activity a little farther down where many black men were unloading cotton bales. The two Sisters were very much absorbed in watching them.

Suddenly, somewhere behind them, someone called, "Reverend Mother!"

Pauline jumped and turned, and then ran joyfully to the arms of Sister Xaveria while Sister Gonzaga was caught in the embrace of the other Sisters.

In a short while they were home in the big, airy convent with its enclosed garden, close to the school and church. This was St. Henry's! It was hot, and there were mosquitos, but there were also luscious fruits and exquisite flowers, and friendly, generous people.

Mother Pauline and Sister Gonzaga spent ten days with the Sisters, seeing firsthand how happy they were. There were over 100 children in school, and it was obvious that they loved the Sisters. Pauline could tell that the Civil War and political conditions had caused suffering here. There were many black people, and when she saw the large black, beautiful eyes of their little ones looking at her wonderingly as she passed them in the street, Pauline longed to tell them that God loved them and that some day she would have a school for them too.

Before long, it was time to start the homeward trip, and Pauline said a joyful goodbye to the Sisters. She had seen in each place she had visited in America how the Church was growing and was even splendid in this great land. She experienced a wonderful sense of triumph—that little men like Bismarck could never really crush the Church. It would go on long, long after him! So her joy overcame her sorrow at parting, and she encouraged the Sisters in New Orleans to become holy and work for God's glory.

The two travellers boarded a train this time for the first part of their return trip. They were bound for Chicago, and it would take fifty hours to reach it. But no sleepers for them. They preferred to relax in their seats, and in that way, saw alligator swamps and many more things they might have missed. At one stop, the priest who was the vicar of the Nashville diocese came on the train and joined the Sisters. They had a pleasant conversation with him, and later on, he bought a box of delicious peaches for them.

Finally the long train ride was over, and they were in Chicago. It was a new Chicago they were seeing, rebuilt after the great fire that had swept it only two years before. The Sisters stayed downtown at the Sherman Hotel since this was merely a stopping point and they would be continuing on shortly. They had not seen so many elevators, and over the beds there were nets as protection against the mosquitos. The next morning they went to the fancy dining-room for breakfast. Mother Pauline, very satisfied with her roll and coffee, was amused as Sister Gonzaga heartily enjoyed the American breakfast of meat, eggs, coffee, and hot bread.

Once more on the train, they rode as far as Detroit and visited there with Mother Barat's Sisters, Religious of the Sacred Heart, learning interesting things. From Lake St. Clair they went on and took a carriage to Niagara Falls. There they carefully descended 200 steps, and at the bottom, stood breathless at the gorgeous sight before them. Endless floods of crystal water rushed with tremendous force over the cliffs, forming gigantic transparent sheets of lovely, white, liquid lace that foamed and boomed and roared as they plunged to the faithful rocks below. Mother Pauline and Sister Gonzaga welcomed occasional spray from the falls as a kind of souvenir. They only smiled at the two young girls who were on the platform with them because the looks exchanged between the girls and Sisters said everything. It was difficult to hear over the noise of the falls, and the sight really made one speechless. Later Pauline wrote home that, to her, Niagara Falls was the most beautiful sight in America.

Buffalo was the next stop on their journey, and

they had the opportunity to visit Jesuits whom they had known in Paderborn and who had been expelled. They were particularly happy to see Father Behrens, who gave them good advice about settling in America.

By July 27 the Sisters were back in Wilkes Barre. Before returning to Europe, Mother Pauline wanted to buy some property for establishing an American motherhouse. But she wanted the advice and permission of the bishop. While waiting for him, she wrote to Father Wigger of St. Louis, who had asked for Sisters for his school. She told him that he could get them later through the provincial superior who would reside at the motherhouse soon to be built in Pennsylvania.

Finally, with the bishop's help, Pauline bought six acres with a small woods in Park Hill, which overlooked the Susquehanna River and was in a lovely valley. This land would provide for a convent and school. Through the bishop Pauline was able to get a good architect, who promised to send the plans for the buildings to Paderborn.

For the time being, Pauline's mission was accomplished. She had seen her Sisters in their first American mission and had become acquainted with a good deal of the land, its conditions, and its people. It was good and beautiful, and she praised God for giving the Sisters this new home and new opportunity. Now she must go back to the fatherland and send more Sisters.

Back in New York, she and Sister Gonzaga went through piles of mail. It saddened her to see so many requests for Sisters that she could *never* fill. The Catholic newspapers had carried stories about her visit, and this had filled parishes with hope. Especially hard for her to refuse were three requests for Sisters to start schools for Negroes. The black people had been freed from slavery, but they were not wanted in schools with whites.

On August 2, Mother Pauline and Sister Gonzaga set sail for Bremen and arrived there on August 14. Two days later they were home in Paderborn, with many things to narrate.

Chapter XX

It was good to be home, but there were important things to do, and Mother Pauline lost no time. She set to work immediately to prepare for sending more Sisters, this time to Wilkes Barre. It had been decided that Sister Mathilde was to go as provincial superior, but she became ill. So Pauline asked one of the group to stay back and travel with Sister Mathilde to America later.

So for the second time that year, 1873, Sisters of Christian Charity left their beloved homeland, Germany, to settle in America. In late September Mother Pauline took ten generous Sisters, eager to do God's work in another land, to Bremen and cheerfully waved to them on the ship as it rode out to sea.

More and more her thoughts kept going back to those now staying at the House of Divine Providence, mentally listing them one by one as ready or not for going overseas. She smiled and stopped as she thought of one name in particular. It was Luise

Hensel, her dear old teacher. Yes, they had invited her to spend her retirement there with the Sisters after she could no longer work and her mother had died. Luise had spent the last years caring for the sick and poor at Wiedenbrück just as she had taught her students to do, and now Pauline was glad she could show her gratitude to this very special lady by offering her a home.

In that same house were the Sisters who had been destined for South America and were studying Spanish. They had heard nothing really certain, so Pauline wrote to a Religious of the Sacred Heart in Chile, asking for definite word from the bishop there and for possible financial assistance for travel.

Although the Sisters at Dresden had tried every possible means to stay, the blow finally came, and they, with the children, had to leave the royal schools there. Baron Veith kindly offered his castle in Bohemia to them as a place to stay. Mother Pauline travelled with Sister Walburga, the superior, to see the cardinal archbishop of Prague and obtain his permission and blessing to move there into his diocese. By January 4 of the new year, 1874, they were gone from Dresden.

The Sisters in America were travelling too. Sister Stephania and Sister Sixta had first visited Sister Stephania's father and brothers who had settled in America earlier. They were delighted to see her again, and Mr. Busch, Sister's father, accompanied them to New Ulm. There they conferred with the priests of the parish who wanted Sisters for their school. Aware of the poverty of the congregation because of the loss of their income in Germany, the great cost of travelling to America, and of supporting

331

those left behind, Father Knauf offered to advance the Sisters' salary if they came.

Mother Pauline was pleased and impressed with the report of the two Sisters and accepted the mission at New Ulm. She appointed Sister Stephania as superior and Sister Sixta as her assistant. However, she would not be able to send the intended five more Sisters until spring.

Letters from New Orleans told of the Sisters' homesickness as well as their struggle to get accustomed to the climate. They had been ill in the summer and the fall but were all right now. Father Bogaerts wrote, praising the work of the Sisters and asking that the Sisters buy the house he had given them. It had been the priest's residence, and he was now renting a few rooms elsewhere for himself. A rectory was being built, and he would need the money.

Mother Pauline understood his need but replied that she had no money at all for this purchase, not even for the first payment. She suggested that the Sisters there, with the permission of the bishop and consent of other pastors, go from door to door accompanied by a lady, asking for donations to pay for the house. There was no money to build a motherhouse in Wilkes Barre, either, and the Sisters were renting a small house near the present convent for the girls who would become postulants and novices.

"Our banker is Divine Providence and we know that God will not forsake us, but you surely agree that God does not easily hand out large sums," she told Father Bogaerts.

At Wilkes Barre the generosity of their neighbors saved the four Sisters. There were three in the elementary school and one in the high school. They had little money and were living on stale bread and black coffee until someone found out. After that, the people sent them food every day.

Meanwhile in Germany things were growing worse. More and more Sisters were returning to Paderborn, expelled from their schools. Parents of the students were angry, but it did no good. Suddenly the congregation was notified that the Sisters were to be out of Witten by the first of April. At the very same time word came that the Franciscan Sisters wanted to hand over the mission at Ancud, Chile to the Sisters of Christian Charity. Best of all, the Chilean government was willing to pay the sum of $700 travelling money for each of twelve Sisters and one priest! Mother Pauline was happy to accept. She was told that the consul of Chile residing in Paris would give his help.

But conditions were growing more and more tense as the German people reacted angrily not only to the expulsion of the Sisters from schools but also to the May Laws passed a year earlier against the bishops and clergy. According to those laws, seminarians had to study in state universities, taking courses set by the government. Appointments of priests to various positions in the dioceses made by the bishops could be vetoed by the government, and other decisions made by the bishops regarding matters in their dioceses could be disregarded and taken over by a government court.

Instead of defeating Catholics, these laws strengthened and brought them together more than ever. The bishops refused to cooperate in following those laws. Priests supported their bishops and obeyed them, even though many were put into prison or fined. The Center Party for Catholics in the German legislature increased its membership to ninety-one. Catholics all over began to rally publicly around their bishops, fearless of the government.

So it was that on April 8, 1874, the day after Easter, something very unusual happened in Paderborn. Before this, from time to time, groups of people had come to the home of Bishop Conrad Martin, expressing their loyalty to him and to their faith. On the feast of the Annunciation in March, the total number of those in various groups had been estimated at 5000. But on this day there were about 15,000 men from different parishes and deaneries that came, group after group, to the bishop's house and garden to publicly show their unshakeable faith.

There was such a crowd that some men put ladders on the garden wall and climbed in and out because they could not get through the entrances. But all was done in perfect order, and there was no trouble of any kind because they were all united in one great positive effort. They also wanted to hear those who spoke enthusiastically to the bishop for them, affirming their allegiance to him as representative of Christ for them and professing their faith in all the Church teaches.

Pauline knew that her brother, Hermann, and her brother, George, with his son Hermann, were there with those groups. She also knew that her brother, Hermann, was right in the middle as usual, close to the speakers, encouraging them to openly give witness to their faith. Inwardly, her heart was glowing with pride and excitement.

But at the beginning of May when the parliament

adjourned, Hermann announced that he was resigning. He had served long and well in the service of his country and the Church. He had suffered much during his career because he was a strong, faithful Catholic, but he had not given up or complained. He was not embittered when someone had sent him a noose to hang himself and told him to do the country a favor. He had continued on and had fought well for freedom, truth, and justice. Now it was time to retire.

Von Windhorst and his companions in the Center Party tried to persuade Hermann to stay. They could not imagine a session without his strong voice and honest, convincing words.

"No, my friends," he said decisively. "I cannot speak any more. There are no more words for me to say."

Before leaving Berlin, he went by open carriage to pay a few calls to friends and say goodbye, but he came home that evening with a bad cold. By late May he was seriously ill, and Thecla sent a telegram to Pauline.

At first Pauline hesitated to leave the Sisters, but Bishop Martin urged her to go. So she caught the next train to Berlin. Two stops later, George boarded the train and joined her for the trip. She needed only one look at his face to know that he, too, was sick, really sick.

"George," she said, putting her hand on his arm. "I don't think you should go. You are sick, and you may get worse. You know that Hermann won't thank you if you or he or both of you get worse. Please—go home. You can come later when you feel better."

George looked at her but said nothing. His eyes

335

looked sick, and he gave no argument.

Pauline went on. "Listen to *die Alte*, please? One last time? I'll tell Hermann everything and give him your love. Go, George, go," and she gave him a tiny push.

At last he stood up and moved toward the door of the train. He turned then and waved, trying hard to smile. A few minutes later, the train stopped, and Pauline saw him get off. All the rest of the way she prayed for her two brothers.

When she had arrived and Thecla had brought her to Hermann, he turned his head toward her and smiled weakly. Over the years she had spent many, many hours with the sick, and her keen eyes could tell that she had come just in time but that George would not see him again.

She knelt at his bedside and looked at him lovingly. Again he turned his head toward her and said softly, with an effort, "Pauline, please say the rosary with me."

Suddenly there was drawing in her throat and warm tears were rising to her eyes. She swallowed hard and pressed her teeth together to prevent crying. It had been first her mother, then her father, then Bertha, now Hermann. Little, mischievous Hermann, always daring and wanting to win. In a blur she saw the fine white head, the classic nose, the bright dark eyes like her mother's, the firm mustached lips and shapely chin with its well-trimmed white and black goatee. This was the noble parliamentarian Hermann. Even in America they knew of and admired him, and now he was waiting to go to God.

She began to pray, making each word audible and meaningful for him. She saw his rosary in his left hand, moving slowly over the beads. Thecla came in, but Pauline paused to tell her to take a rest, that she would stay with Hermann.

Later that evening he became delirious, talking excitedly about politics and the Church and finally saying goodnight to his imagined colleagues. Pauline tried to cool his forehead and calm him, and at last he seemed to fall asleep.

In the morning he was awake and clear but extremely weak. He looked about, and Pauline knew he wanted his whole family. They gathered around his bed, and with his eyes he embraced each one. He put back his head and seemed to be reviewing his life. Then he whispered something. Thecla bent to catch it.

"I have never fought with dishonest weapons," she repeated.

They gave him the pad and pencil and his glasses that he reached for, and slowly he began to write. After the third word, the pencil toppled, his head sank, and there was one long, satisfied sigh. Two of the three words on the pad were legible: *freedom . . . justice*. He had fought for them and for truth all his adult life. Now he would enjoy them forever.

All of Berlin mourned his death. Even his enemies praised his courage and unyielding defense of what he considered right. Thousands walked in his funeral procession, the poor with the rich, the powerful with the weak. Pauline and the Sisters joined them at the Paderborn station to Borchen. From there the pall-bearers carried the coffin to St. Meinolph chapel at Boeddeken where the first blessing was given. Then back to the dear old home at Borchen where many workers and farmers came for the repeated blessing on their beloved employer. Pauline, the Sisters, and many, many more walked back again across the fields to the family plot at Boeddeken behind the coffin. She led the rosary and bravely intoned some songs. At last, after a fitting sermon for an outstanding son of the Church, Hermann was laid to rest with the other Mallinckrodts.

But for Pauline, there was no stopping. Bismarck had thought he could cripple the Church, but he had miscalculated. He had reckoned without God or His devotees, like Pauline, and so, for him, things were not going well.

Early in June Mother Pauline again brought a band of fourteen Sisters to Bremen to set sail for America. Some would stay at Scranton, others would go on to Williamsport, Danville, Nippenose in Pennsylvania and still others to New Ulm, Minnesota.

Although she was, to some extent, successfully counteracting the Kulturkampf, Pauline still could not escape its blows or pain. One day in early August something happened that exceeded any other event in the nearly one thousand years that a bishop had resided in Paderborn. A crowd had gathered around the bishop's house, and people were shouting angrily because Bishop Conrad Martin had been placed under arrest and was to go to the local prison. He was sentenced to be there because he had appointed a pastor without government permission. When the bishop appeared at the door, there were sympathetic calls to him from the crowd, and those closest to him went up the steps and would not let him enter the carriage. The Sisters could hear noise and the shouts in the motherhouse chapel where Mother Pauline had asked them to go to pray for the bishop.

When the bishop finally got into the carriage, there was no one who would drive him to the prison, not even a worker from the post-office. Finally, some poor man from outside the town was seized, not really knowing what he was supposed to do. He was forced to drive the bishop to the prison, and people said he was pale with horror.

The crowd followed the carriage all the way, and when it arrived at the prison, some tried again to prevent the bishop from getting out. But eventually the officials got him through the crowd and into the prison, slamming the door against the cries and protests. That day, August 4, 1874, was a sad day in the history of the town.

For the Sisters, however, there was soon a day of double joy and celebration, for on August 21 was the silver jubilee of the Sisters of Christian Charity and of Mother Pauline. Twenty-five years ago, she had founded the congregation and had been invested as a religious. Of the first four Sisters, only Mother Pauline and Sister Mathilde were left, and Sister Mathilde was in America. But at breakfast that morning she had surprised Pauline with a cable of congratulations and love. The Sisters overseas, knowing how hard it was to get enough money for travelling across the ocean, sent some as a gift to Mother Pauline for those who would be sent to the Americas later.

At home, the Sisters tried to find a suitable personal gift for Mother Pauline on her jubilee, but it was difficult because she would accept very little. She wanted to be poor like Jesus, having only the necessities to live and do her work. Those necessities also had to be simple and inexpensive. She was firm in keeping her heart free from desires for earthly things. So she refused the new habit she found hanging in her closet. Her two present habits, worn and mended, as well as her two pairs of coarse shoes, were sufficient for her. One thing, however, she was glad to accept and that was a bust of her dear brother, Hermann, which they had placed in her room when they decorated it for the occasion.

To please them that day, though, she did wear a crown of silver leaves for a while and modestly sent to all the convents a photograph of herself previously taken for the occasion at Bishop Martin's written command. It was the only photograph of her as a Sister they would have. She was quite sure that Sister Anna and Sister Juliana were responsible for it, probably having asked the bishop to send her that order, but she forgave them. The picture was a fine one, with Mother Pauline standing tall in her long black cloak, white rosary in her hands, and at her feet, her usual wicker basket which held her prayerbooks and sometimes provisions for her trips and the poor. But the Sisters said no photograph could capture the beautiful expression that they always saw in her face and her whole person.

Only once that day did her expression change briefly to a shadow of sadness when a message from the prison came to her with the good wishes and blessing of Bishop Martin. How she wished he could be free!

Her smile quickly returned when the blind children came to congratulate her. It was just at that time that two young boys, who often served for Mass and other devotions at the motherhouse, came to deliver a message. They were the sons of a gentleman who gave professional services to the Sisters and was very interested in the congregation. The boys knew nothing about the jubilee and were very curious as they saw the blind children standing in several rows around the stone table near the grotto of St. Paul in the motherhouse front garden. The blind were facing Mother Pauline, who stood behind the table with another Sister, and was leaning forward with her hands on the table. She was listening intently as the children recited poems and sang pretty songs for her in their clear, unique voices. She looked with great love and kindness at each dear face with its sightless eyes and, after the performance, she shook hands and spoke with each child.

The two altar boys were still staring at the scene when the Sister portress, who answered the door, came over to them.

"Today is Mother Pauline's silver jubilee. Twenty-five years ago she became a Sister and founded our community. Go and congratulate her, boys."

For a moment they stood there, blank and as if frozen, but finally they went to Mother Pauline and congratulated her.

"Thank you very much, boys," she said and shook the hand of each one heartily. But something in her face told the boys that she was embarrassed by all this and did not want to be the center of attention. She turned quickly, saying, "Come along to the party for the blind children, boys," motioning to the back.

Each of the two brothers gladly led several of the blind children through the garden to the outdoor tables in the open space next to the St. Conrad chapel. This part of the garden was separated from the street by a wall with niches having statues of the twelve Apostles.

The children were hardly seated, and Mother Pauline had begun to serve them herself, when it started to rain.

Pauline looked up to the sky and said, "Dear rain, please wait until the children have finished."

But the dear rain grew heavier. So the two boys helped Mother Pauline and the Sisters push the tables under the large trees whose branches were heavy and thick with leaves. The children enjoyed the cake, coffee, and fruit and laughed when an occasional raindrop wet their noses or a bite of cake.

After lunch the children were taken to a class-room where the party continued with happy chat-ting, laughing, piano playing, and singing. Mother Pauline went to each group of children, sitting down to talk. She drew even the shyest child into the conversation by gently asking a few questions.

The older altar boy was impressed by Pauline and watched her with interest. He was sitting near her in one group and could hear her clear, penetrating voice, always so well controlled and pleasing in tone.

That evening she announced a delightful surprise to the community. Starting at six o'clock in the morning the next day, there would be a pilgrimage to St. Meinolph's chapel at Boeddeken and a picnic in the woods. The Sisters were also invited to be the guests of George and Dina von Mallinckrodt at the Boeddeken estate during the day. No one wanted to miss this outing.

Bright and early next morning there were three large farm wagons from Boeddeken standing in front of the convent gate. They were gaily trimmed with garlands and green branches, waiting for their happy cargo. Forty of the younger Sisters, including novices and postulants, set out on foot for St. Meinolph's, and all the rest climbed into the wagons with their lunch. It was the biggest community celebration ever—with 106 Sisters in all. It was also one of the loveliest trips ever—through the beautiful Alme valley with its sunny meadows and cool woods full of chirping birds, clear brooks, and bright flowers.

At ten o'clock there was Holy Mass in St. Meinolph's chapel, and although there were too many to fit inside, the young people gladly stood outside under the shade of the huge linden trees, looking through the open door. A Brother, who was a hermit and lived in one of the huts near the chapel, served the Mass. Then everyone went to the woods to relax and eat lunch. Later little groups went to pay George and Dina a visit.

By sunset everyone was ready to start for home, and this time there was a long line of wagons and carriages waiting. George had asked the neighbors to add theirs to his so that no one would have to walk home. So all the Sisters rode home in the dusk, hushed by the solemn stillness and magical beauty of the woods and valley as twilight touched them gently and artistically with summer evening loveliness. It was an especially precious memory of the homeland for the twenty or more Sisters who would soon be going overseas.

All too soon the important days came for Mother Pauline and her Sisters. On August 11, she accompanied ten more Sisters to Bremen where they took the boat bound for the United States. On September

12, she went with Sister Gonzaga and a group of twelve Sisters to Bordeaux, where they boarded the steamer to go to Ancud, Chile. They stayed at the ship's railing a long time, trying to keep a glimpse of Mother Pauline and her companion in view. Then they turned to find seats on the deck and to pray the rosary for a safe journey—and for the grace to cope with the homesickness that seemed to have started already. They would be the first Sisters of Christian Charity in South America, and Sister Gonzaga would be the provincial superior there. Now the congregation would have an English province in North America and a Spanish province in South America.

It was only some weeks later that Mother Pauline found time to answer the request for sending Sisters to St. Petersburg, Russia. A young lady, along with some other noble ladies, was interested in entering the congregation if they could do charitable works there. Mother Pauline was certainly interested but said that she would want to go to St. Petersburg with another Sister first to be sure that the Sisters would be allowed to wear their habit, work peacefully without government interference, and could communicate with the motherhouse in Germany. They would also need the approval of the bishop in Russia. If the ladies should find another congregation more to their liking, Pauline and her Sisters would gladly step back. The only thing that matters is that God's work is done. But nothing more was heard about St. Petersburg, and Mother Pauline left it in God's hands.

On the last day of October came the good news that the Sisters had arrived safely in Rio de Janeiro and were now on the last part of their journey to Chile. This spurred the Sisters to offer still more prayers for continued safety on their trip.

But Pauline was equally concerned about the missions at home, and in late November she went to Coblenz for an audience with Empress Augusta that she had been fortunate enough to obtain. The empress was there with her whole court of grand ladies, but Pauline was not frightened. Almost unconsciously she rose to the occasion with the same dignity and self-command she had been used to as lady of her father's house with guests of high rank. She spoke eloquently to the empress, pleading for her aid in obtaining permission for the Sisters to remain in Crefeld as teachers in that school.

Empress Augusta was very gracious and spoke kindly to Mother Pauline, and so did some of the princesses and duchesses. But despite the courteous and kind manner came the same sad message: there was nothing the empress or her ladies could do. The Sisters would have to go.

Pauline bowed and thanked them and turned to go. No one could have guessed that she had received a hard blow. Her head was up, her step was long and firm, and there was a smile on her lips. God had let her know His will, and she accepted it lovingly.

As she left the court, the empress and her ladies gazed after her. Then someone said slowly what everyone else was thinking: "That lady is worthy of wearing a royal crown herself." But Pauline was content. She was sharing the crown of her Beloved, and it was made of thorns.

Chapter XXI

The wind was lightly tossing Sister Walburga's veil about as she watched the girls playing in the castle garden. Like the Sisters and students at Constance, they had had to leave their school and go to a castle. She smiled wryly. It was a peaceful, happy scene but very misleading. No one would ever guess how much heartache, uprooting, and moving the girls and the Sisters had endured till they finally arrived here at Mühlhausen. They had been forced to leave Dresden, but Count Veith, who had three daughters attending the school at Dresden, had offered his castle at Kosteletz to the Sisters. So they had packed everything, obtained the consent of the girls' parents, and gone with the children to that castle.

With the help of all the willing hands, they had unpacked, settled in, and organized living quarters and classrooms. They were managing fairly well even though the castle was small. But it did not take long for the reputation of the Sisters to spread and soon the enrollment increased beyond capacity. They had to find larger quarters; there simply was not enough room. At last Duke Lobkowitz offered them his castle near Mühlhausen, and once again they moved, hoping that the Duke would not be forced by government authorities to recall his generous offer.

Sister Walburga looked around. Most certainly it was delightful here, but for how long? Was it safe? Mother Pauline was talking about starting a novitiate here. Was that wise?

Five months had passed since Bishop Martin's imprisonment. Mother Pauline had visited him twice and had been happy to hear that he would be released. But at the very time they were releasing him, the authorities demanded that he sign a document of resignation as bishop of Paderborn. He would not so much as touch the paper, let alone sign it.

"No state authority gave me the office of bishop," he said, "and no state authority can deprive me of it."

Two weeks later, January 19, 1875, he was taken to the prison at Wesel. When the people of Paderborn heard that he was to be transferred to Wesel, they wanted to bid him farewell and give him one last sign of their love and loyalty. They came in big crowds to the depot, but authorities had barred the platform of the train. So they lined up along the railroad tracks.

The Sisters of Christian Charity, led by Mother Pauline, also came to show their loyalty to the bishop. When they could not find a place, they marched over to the freight depot and stood on the ramp over which the animals were taken into the box cars. Here

347

they received the blessing of the bishop from his window of the train as it passed them. Now there was neither bishop nor vicar general in Paderborn; in fact, there would soon be left only three bishops in all of Prussia.

In February Mother Pauline went to Wesel and was permitted to visit Bishop Conrad Martin. His personal valet and friend, Hubert, also visited him. They brought him as many personal articles as they could, and most of all, told him as much as possible about his flock in Paderborn and his whole diocese—his priests, his people.

But if the Church was tightly confined in one place, it was spreading out freely in another. By now there were fifteen foundations of the congregation in North America with some eighty Sisters in all. There were eight houses in Pennsylvania; one in New York; one in Michigan; one in Iowa; three in Minnesota; one in New Orleans. Since neither the bishop nor his vicar was in Paderborn, and Pauline's nephew, Hermann, the son of George, was going to Rome, she was giving him the papers petitioning for the erection of a novitiate at Scranton in North America and one at Ancud in South America. He was to present them to the Holy Father for her.

In her report to the Congregation of Bishops and Regulars at Rome, Mother Pauline wrote:

"I must proclaim with the greatest gratitude that the means used to bring harm to us, in God's hands became instruments of blessing. How greatly our field of activity has been extended!"

Indeed it had. Word came from the Sisters enroute to Chile that they had gone through the Strait of Magellan and landed at Valparaiso. From there they went to Ancud, where they were welcomed by the bishop, the officials, and the people. They were now in their new convent and would have a novitiate, an academy, and a boarding-school there. In Puerto Montt not far away there was a little hospital where some Sisters would work and some elementary schools for colonists where others would teach.

So it was that sorrow and joy, sorrow and joy were constantly shifting in the Sisters' hearts, and sometimes one became the other as the sufferings of the Kulturkampf made possible the successes of new establishments in the two Americas.

When Mother Pauline saw that the property of Bishop Martin was seized as soon as he had been taken to Wesel, she knew that the property of the Sisters would be next. She immediately contacted her brother, George, who had the proper papers drawn up, and then sold the motherhouse and St. Joseph House to him. They could not take away the property of private citizens who were not members of a religious order.

At the end of May, Pauline and the Sisters experienced another bitter-sweet event. The last solemn ceremony of clothing the new novices with their habits was held in the chapel, the auxiliary Bishop Freusberg taking the place of imprisoned Bishop Martin. Where would the next ceremony take place? Would it ever be here again?

Two days later the Convent Laws were passed. According to them, all convents had to be closed within six months and all convent property had to be taken into custody by the state and managed by it. Mother Pauline had foreseen this and had already sold the convents belonging to the congregation in

Solingen, Höxter, Magdeburg, Oschersleben, Sigmaringen, Anrath, and Crefeld to private citizens, just as she had done with the motherhouse and St. Joseph House.

It came as no surprise that the Franciscan Fathers were expelled a month later and that their monastery was seized and closed. With sad hearts the Sisters and children saw them leave.

The month of August had hardly begun when Mother Pauline received word that Bishop Martin had secretly left Wesel and fled to Holland. To the German government he was now a traitor and a reward was offered for his capture. German officials told those in Holland not to give the bishop asylum. Pauline, however, determined that somehow she would help Bishop Martin.

But the work in the Americas had to continue, and the need for Sisters had to be filled. Inspired by the tremendous faith and generosity of their Mother, thirty more Sisters left from Bremen for the United States, knowing that they would never see their country or their loved ones again. Their hearts were strong with faith in a good, wise, all-knowing God who held them in His hands.

All this time while on her many travels for business, Pauline had also gone more than once to Belgium, looking for a possible place to set up headquarters for the congregation and a novitiate. As it was, Himly, the government official who was harassing Pauline about the congregation's ownings, declared that the Sisters would have to pay rent to the owner, George, or leave. Then when the Sisters from Crefeld came back to Paderborn homeless, Pauline knew it was high time to get a house in Belgium.

Autumn was really upon them when she accompanied six more Sisters to Bordeaux for the long trip to Chile. At that time of the year and on that route, the sea was not kind to voyagers. But the brave Sisters took their courage from the Lord whose plan they were carrying out and from Mother Pauline whose trust was unquenchable. Her next plan was to meet Sister Hildegardis in Belgium where they would search for a place of residence.

Although Bishop Conrad Martin was a wanted man, he had succeeded in remaining free but hidden in a castle at Neuberg, Holland. It would be daring for anyone to visit him, but danger and difficulty could not stop Pauline. She seemed to thrive on them. So it was not surprising that she did manage to visit the bishop there at the castle. She had a plan to bring him to a place of refuge and safety.

Just before Christmas, Father Stamm, the bishop's secretary, was suddenly arrested by the government. He had tried, up till now, to keep the bishop informed of the matters of his diocese, but now, he too, was gone. In Paderborn there was no one left in Church leadership to whom the people could look. Even the priests were leaving town to live elsewhere.

The end of the year brought another sorrow, not so much for the Sisters as for the children involved. Word was received that the Sisters must leave the orphanage at Steele. Who would care for the orphans? Mother Pauline was hoping that Miss Anna, with whom the Sisters had worked, would take charge.

Although the outlook was grim for the new year 1876 that was dawning, Mother Pauline was doggedly persevering. She would not give up. No mere

351

opposition to Catholicism would keep her or her Sisters from doing the work of God. She willingly paid the bill from George for the rental of the mother-house and St. Joseph House. She also sent three young ladies who wanted to join the congregation to the novitiate that she had dared to start at Mühl-hausen where the Sisters had recently moved with students from Dresden.

But the long arm of the ever-present Kulturkampf was always reaching out for her, and soon she had trouble again. The Sisters from the school at Solingen had left there, and the convent was sold. But in mid-February Mother Pauline had to travel to Berlin with Sister Lioba to try to keep the government from seizing the houses at Steele and Solingen. On February 22 she was again in Berlin to face Himly in court, where he had three suits against the Sisters. Three days later they won all three, and the orphans at Höxter were jubilant. Their orphanage had been one of the three suits, and they had prayed as never before that the Sisters would win the suit.

The orphans of Steele, however, were not so fortunate, and Sister Agnes reported to Mother Pauline that they were all gone. She would see to it also that everyone at Solingen left by the set date.

It was decided that stoves, bedding, and furniture from Solingen should be divided and sent to Mühlhausen and to Weltrus, another house they had started in Bohemia. Some would be set aside for a house in Belgium which Mother Pauline had found-ed. It seemed excellent for her purposes. She had discussed it with Bishop Martin when she had visited him for the second time in Holland, and he had agreed that it seemed wise to purchase it. So she was going to Brussels with Sister Agnes, and they would further investigate the possibilities of buying this house and estate in a small town called Mont St. Guibert.

Bishop Martin also consented to Pauline's going to Rome after Easter with Sister Adalberta and a group of ladies. At first he had planned to go himself, but he feared the Italians might turn him over to the authorities because of the warrants out for his arrest. So he put aside the idea and gave Pauline recommendations for interviews with various people in the Vatican. She then promptly wrote to her nephew, George, the son of Bertha and Alfred Hüffer, who was in Rome, asking him to get lodgings for her group.

Pauline's main reason for going to Rome was to obtain final and permanent approval of the Church for her congregation. It was one of her dearest desires, and all the Sisters were praying for it. Another idea she had vaguely in mind was possibly opening a house in Rome where both the Sisters and tourists could stay.

But before she went there, she had business to transact elsewhere. She was planning that when the Sisters were sent away from Crefeld, they would go directly to Mont St. Guibert in Belgium and start a boarding-school there. She also planned to pay for the Belgian property, at least in part, with the money gained from the sale of the convent in Crefeld.

Sister Agnes met Mother Pauline in Brussels at their usual meeting-place, the home of Sister Agnes' sisters, who owned several lace factories. One of the sisters in particular, Johanna Luig, had been their guide for all their previous business trips in the area and would be so now. She had also made contacts and carried on some of the business for Mother Pauline in her absence.

As they went from office to office, Johanna was very surprised to see the change in the way the different officials treated Mother Pauline this time. From at first having been cool and barely civil to her and her companion, they were now perfect gentlemen, pleasant, attentive, and polite, even accompanying her to the door when she left. It was the old law of action—reaction. Mother Pauline had been, as usual, every inch a lady, a truly Christian lady. She had been dignified, gracious, yet humble. She had explained her plans and intentions with unmistakable honesty, and her warm, hearty courtesy toward them was so sincere that their own unfriendliness made them feel awkward. Doormen tipped their hats to her and were honored when she shook hands with them. There was something about her that called out the best in all of them, that made them feel they truly had worth and compelled them to act like it. But her kindest smiles and bows were for the poor she met, especially the children.

That evening the Luig sisters were invited to a fine social affair but were concerned about their two guests. Mother Pauline and Sister Agnes assured the ladies that they were only too happy to relax and spend the evening together.

"Don't bother about us," said Pauline. "We feel very much at home. Just go ahead and get dressed. We want you to look your best."

In a few minutes Johanna was standing before her, holding two gowns.

"Mother Pauline, I really don't know which of

these to wear. You used to dress for parties and balls. What do you think? Which of these is better for me? The pink or the lavender?" And she held a part of each dress up to a shoulder.

Mother Pauline laughed softly and put both hands on her knees.

"Johanna, dear, it's a very long time since I had anything to do with gowns—but, well, let me see—" and she stepped back to get a better look.

"I would say the pink, Johanna. It blends much better with your complexion and coloring. It's a lovely dress."

"Thank you, Mother Pauline. The pink it shall be," smiled Johanna, and she hurried off.

Pauline had hardly sat down again when the other two came in. Sister Agnes arched her eyebrows in surprise and smiled at Mother Pauline.

"Since you gave Johanna such good advice, would you help us too, Mother Pauline?" said the first one of the two. She didn't wait for the answer. "Should I wear a sash with this dress or not?" She held out a wide, beautiful velvet ribbon in both hands.

Pauline folded her hands and looked thoughtfully at her.

"You know," she said, "the cut of your gown makes it flow so beautifully that a sash would spoil its lines, my dear. I would say that you don't need it."

"And I, Mother Pauline," called the third sister. "What about me? Should I wear this lavaliere or these long, long pearls?" She held both pieces of jewelry up to her neck.

Mother Pauline supported one elbow in the other hand and rested her chin on the front of her folded

355

fingers. She tilted her head first to the left, then to the right.

Finally she said, "The lavaliere looks right to me. It's exquisite yet simple, in perfect proportion for the space of your neckline. It's decorative without being overdone."

A little later three gowned ladies with gloves presented themselves with smiles to Pauline and Sister Agnes. Both Sisters smiled approvingly, rose, and led them to the door.

"You look lovely," said Sister Agnes. "Don't they, Mother Pauline?"

"I think you'll be among the most charming ladies there," said Mother Pauline. "But remember—what *really* matters is that you are pleasing in God's eyes." Then she smiled and said, "Have a good time, and God bless you."

Next day, with her business in the city completed, Pauline and her companions went to the public sale in Mont St. Guibert for the estate of Madame Demeurs in order to prevent its purchase by anyone else. At last they were able to start the process of buying the house and estate, and Pauline promised payment to the representative of Madame Demeurs as soon as the convent at Crefeld was sold. After much searching and much discussion, she was close to having a safe and peaceful refuge for her Sisters. But there was, oh, so much yet to do regarding that house in Belgium.

Pauline was very grateful to the Luig sisters for their hospitality and to Johanna in particular for doing so much of the preliminary business. As she said goodbye to them, she took Johanna's hand and leaned forward, looking from one face to the other and said, "God has blessed you with prosperity now, my friends, but the day may come when He will also bless you with hardship. It is then that you must believe and see yourselves held lovingly in His hands, for He is in command. Accepting what He wills with trust will bring you deep peace and contentment, and they are more precious than all the riches of the world."

After World War I, when they became poor, Johanna and her sisters remembered those words vividly and discovered how true they are.

Two days after leaving Belgium, Mother Pauline was on her way to Rome with Sister Adalberta, two of her nieces, and two lady friends. It was dark when they arrived in that great city, and they were met by Father Felix von Hartmann and Dr. George Hüffer took the ladies to the Hotel Minerva nearby.

Next day as they walked across St. Peter's Square, Pauline was filled with many emotions. A great thrill went through her, filling her with joy and pride as she looked at the huge church before her that was the center and heart of Christianity, drawing people of all nations to itself. It seemed like a colossal mother, stretching out to her children enormous welcoming arms formed by the curve of massive pillars on each side of the square. Pauline held her breath a little, reverently conscious of each step she took on those cobblestones. She was on sacred ground. She knew that on the very soil beneath those stones where she walked, martyrs had bled and died in agony and shame for the unseen God they so firmly believed in. For this had been the circus of Nero where crowds were entertained by the suffering and death of human victims. Pauline could almost hear the groans and prayers of the dying.

When they entered St. Peter's Church, she and her group were overwhelmed with the grandeur and immensity of it, its walls, ceilings, dome, statues, paintings, and precious works of art. There were many side altars along the walls besides the great main altar with the magnificent canopy in the front. At one of these side altars Pauline and her companions attended Holy Mass and received Communion that day and all the days of their visit in Rome. Later they visited the special chapel where the Blessed Sacrament was kept and honored. Wherever they went Pauline was fascinated not only by the wonderful things around her, but also by the people passing her, people from many different countries, speaking many languages, in different dress. She felt very small yet very honored to be a part of the tremendous family of the Church, a tiny part of Christ's Body, which was so incredibly large with such very different members, yet all pulsing with the one same holy life, all believing the same faith!

Later that day Mother Pauline, Sister Adalberta, and the ladies were part of a group of one hundred pilgrims scheduled to have an audience with the Holy Father, Pius IX. The Pope moved graciously from one group to another, and when he came to Pauline and her group, he mistook her and Sister Adalberta for Carmelites because of their white mantles which they wore for this special occasion. Dr. Pick immediately introduced them as Sisters of Christian Charity, and Pauline added in French, "Daughters of the Blessed Virgin Mary of the Immaculate Conception," the title the Pope himself had given them. He smiled and extended his hand. Mother Pauline took it with great respect and with emotion kissed his ring, the sign of the successor of St. Peter.

"Your Holiness," she begged, "please grant a blessing for our whole congregation and for each individual Sister," and her face beamed as she heard him pronounce the blessing.

Later the ladies of her party went sightseeing, but Pauline would think of nothing else until she obtained what she had come for—final approval of her congregation and its rule. So she and Sister Adalberta went without delay to the office of Bishop de Montel who had helped Bishop Conrad Martin years before in obtaining the first approval.

The bishop listened quietly to Pauline's request and saw how very much it meant to her.

"Reverend Mother," he said slowly with his soft Italian accent, "I would gladly help you to get this final approval, but I must tell you honestly that it cannot be at this time yet."

Pauline had been leaning forward eagerly but now sat back against the chair in silence. She looked at him wordlessly.

Chapter XXII

"You see, Reverend Mother," continued the bishop, "your congregation has spread to new countries and new cultures, and with it has gone your Rule and Constitutions. The Church must now see how that Rule fits those new cultures and the native Sisters who must live by it. Perhaps it will need to be changed. If so, that must be done before it can be given final approval. Besides that, we must also have a letter from the bishop of each diocese in the world where your Sisters are, reporting on their work."

Mother Pauline nodded and rose slowly.

"I understand, Your Grace. Thank you," she said, bowing. Without further discussion she left with Sister Adalberta.

That afternoon she went to the Gesu Church of the Jesuits where St. Ignatius, their founder, was buried. She felt a strong spiritual bond with him since she had received so much guidance in writing the Constitutions from Jesuits and they had directed and advised her and her Sisters in the spiritual life so very much. She prayed at his tomb a long time, voicing her keen disappointment. After the evening meal at Campo Santo, she went to the cemetery, which was very close, whose inscription overhead read "Teutones in pace"—"Germans at rest." It was truly quiet and restful there, and she prayed not only for those buried there but for her beloved country. Somehow the edge of the day's sorrow was softened for her.

Next morning as she was absorbed with Jesus after Holy Communion and Mass at St. Peter's, one thought kept flashing in her consciousness very clearly: Go to see Cardinal Ledochowski. No one knows better than he about the conditions in Germany. So she followed that urging and obtained an interview with the cardinal.

"Reverend Mother Pauline von Mallinckrodt," he said warmly. "It is a pleasure to see you. Unfortunately, I can tell you only what Bishop de Montel said. But—" and he raised his finger and his voice, "I think we can do something. We can at least apply for approval of your Rules and Constitutions for another ten years. Let us do that."

He wasted no time. The cardinal drew up the necessary paper immediately, sent it to the proper authorities, and personally called on the people concerned. Within two days Mother Pauline had the document of approval for ten more years in her hands.

After that, everything was sheer joy. She and her group visited the seven main churches of Rome, marvelled at their architecture and art, prayed fervently at the shrine of our Lady of Perpetual Help in

St. Mary Major for the persecuted Catholics in Germany. They went up the Holy Staircase believed to be ascended by Jesus at His trial, visited the Mamertine prison where St. Peter and St. Paul had each been held separately. They saw the spring of water that appeared miraculously, with which Peter had baptized his jailers. They saw the places where Peter had been crucified and Paul beheaded. They walked with awe through the catacombs guided by Monsignor de Waal, who showed them the tombs of the martyrs St. Cecilia, St. Agnes, St. Emerentiana, and others. Each visit to the shrine of each martyr gave new strength to Mother Pauline to face and bear the special kind of persecution in her own country.

Most frequently, though, she knelt with Sister Adalberta to pray below the main altar at the tomb of St. Peter. It was over this spot that Constantine, the first Christian Roman emperor, had built a basilica and placed the altar because, according to Latin inscriptions found there, the body of the first Pope had been hurriedly buried in that place after his crucifixion nearby. Surely, she thought, the lovable, impulsive Apostle who was head of the Church at a time of constant danger, heresy, and persecution and told his people to endure and rejoice in being tested and tried, would never leave Catholic Germany's cry for help unanswered.

Pauline and her companions also had the chance to visit Pompeii and Florence as side trips from Rome, and in Florence she had the pleasure of talking with Father Beckx, the Superior General of the Jesuits.

The climax of the whole Roman visit was another audience with the Holy Father, this time a private one. His kindliness put her completely at ease, and she felt so serene that she could have knelt there before him indefinitely. After she had been introduced, Pius IX leaned toward her. His eyes, like shiny rich black olives, made a striking contrast to the pure white of his hair and skull cap, and the cross on his white cassock dangled as he bent forward.

"Tell me, my daughter, how are things with you in our beloved Germany?"

Pauline had never shed a tear in four years of suffering caused by the Kulturkampf. But now suddenly, for some reason, she was so deeply touched by the sympathy in the Pope's voice, that she had to struggle to control herself.

"Your Holiness, we have lost all but a few missions for the blind, for orphans, and the aged and our motherhouse in Prussia. We were able to transfer two boarding-schools to Bohemia and one to Lichtenstein. All the Sisters from the other houses had to come home. But, Your Holiness,—" and here her face became radiant with her smile—"we have sent over one hundred Sisters to North and South America to work for God's kingdom."

As Pauline looked up into his face, she saw that the Holy Father's eyes were moist, but that he, too, was smiling.

"We have now, by God's grace, a motherhouse with a novitiate and nineteen schools in the United States and a motherhouse with a novitiate, two hospitals, and four schools in Ancud and Puerto Montt, Chile, Your Holiness."

"Chile!" exclaimed the Pope. "Ah, that is good. I have delightful memories of the time I spent as a young priest working in Chile. Keep up your good work there and in America—and in your own dear country. Remain steadfast, my child, and may God help you."

"Our Bishop Conrad Martin wishes to be remembered to you, Your Holiness, even in his exile. He says distance and prison walls cannot prevent his prayers and blessings for his people," said Mother Pauline.

The Pope clasped his hands in an upward gesture. "Bishop Conrad Martin! How is he? When you see him next, tell him I congratulate him on his bravery and perseverance in the hard struggle."

"Most gladly. We are buying a house in Belgium, and soon I shall invite him to make it his home with peace and safety as long as necessary. And now, please, Your Holiness, grant a blessing and indulgence at the hour of death for each Sister of Christian Charity." Pauline handed the Pope the document, and he took the offered pen to sign it. Quickly she passed it to Sister Adalberta and silently held up rosaries and medals for him to bless.

The Holy Father smiled, blessed the religious articles, and then put his hands on the bowed heads of the two Sisters.

Once more Pauline looked up to him lovingly. "Thank you, Holy Father, for everything, but especially for giving us the title of Daughters of the Blessed Virgin Mary of the Immaculate Conception."

He smiled again and said, "May you be ever true to it. Now go in peace, and may the Lord bless you." He moved his hand once more in a cross, and both Sisters rose to go. Pauline would never forget those moments of face-to-face encounter with the Vicar of Christ.

The very next day the group departed from Rome for the homeward trip, stopping at Naples, Ancona, and Loreto, inside whose church the little house of Nazareth in which the Holy Family lived is said to be preserved. They also visited Venice, Triest, Vienna, and Prague. From there, Mother Pauline and Sister Adalberta left the group and went on to Weltrus and Mühlhausen to visit the Sisters and novices in those houses.

At last they arrived back in Paderborn where happy Sisters and blind children welcomed them noisily. They were home for Pentecost, and Mother Pauline spent hours telling them all about the trip and answering questions. But, best of all, she gave souvenirs of Rome to everyone: relics and rosaries to the Sisters, medals and statues to friends and the children.

While she was gone, the purchase of Mont St. Guibert had been completed, and Madame Demeurs, the former owner, was going to hold a public auction of her furniture. Mother Pauline wanted very much to be at that auction to buy some of that furniture for the house. She worked all night so that she would be able to travel to Belgium in the morning.

Fortunately, she managed to get some suitable pieces of furniture for the house and asked the Sisters from Crefeld, who had been assigned there, to clean and arrange it. Her next stop now was St. Trond, also in Belgium.

Meanwhile Bishop Martin had been forced to leave Holland also, and this time he had taken refuge with the Franciscan Fathers in St. Trond. When Mother Pauline was announced, he was surprised but happy to see her and to receive from her the Holy

Father's greeting and message. Then came the moment she hd been waiting for.

"We have bought the estate in Mont St. Guibert, Your Grace," she told him happily, "and we invite you to make it your home for as long as necessary. Everything is ready, and you can stay there safely. No one need know who you are except the bishop of the diocese at Malines. Give us this honor, Your Grace."

The bishop was pleased, but before he could answer, Pauline went on eagerly.

"Since we will have a boarding-school for girls, we would be happy if you would act as our chaplain and religion instructor, Your Grace. We call it St. Joseph School. To everyone there you will be known only as L'Abbé Martin or Professeur Martin. Please say that you will come."

Now he was immensely pleased and relieved.

"I will gladly accept your invitation, Reverend Mother," he said, "to stay at Mont St. Guibert as chaplain and religion instructor of your school. When shall I come? And what about Hubert?"

"Oh, Hubert is also most welcome, Your Grace. And we would like you to set the date of your arrival."

"Very well, Reverend Mother." The bishop paused for a moment, thinking. "I should like to arrive four days from now, June 12, in the afternoon," he said.

Sister Angela was just sweeping up the last bits of dust by the large, curving staircase at the main entrance of the imposing gray stone three-storied house in this lovely spot of Belgium. It was she who would take care of the bishop's two rooms upstairs and would serve his meals. Although everything was ready upstairs, she wanted to be sure that all was presentable at the entrance too. She looked around. Two other Sisters were dusting in the parlor and in the dining-room.

Suddenly one came running toward her from the parlor, untying her apron strings.

"He's here, Sister Angela! The bishop's here! From the window I saw him get out of the carriage!" And with that she disappeared through a door to call Mother Pauline. Before Sister Angela could do anything else, there was a heavy knock at the door. She put down her broom and dust pan and opened the door. Facing her were Bishop Conrad Martin in the ordinary street clothes of a priest, his secretary, Father Stamm, and Hubert, his valet. Unpredictable as usual, the bishop had arrived earlier than expected.

A little nervously Sister Angela quickly straightened and brushed her apron and then bent to kiss the bishop's ring.

"Hearty welcome, Your Grace!" she said, stepping back to swing the door wide.

Just then, to her relief, Mother Pauline came into the entrance. She hurried forward to greet her distinguished invited guest—the persecuted and courageous bishop of her diocese, Paderborn. She was pleased beyond words that at last he was here—in exile, yes, but where he would be safe and surrounded by love.

"I cannot tell you how glad we all are that you have come, *Monsieur l'Abbé*," she said, emphasizing the two last words for everyone to hear. From now on, Bishop Martin had to be addressed only by the title used for a priest, and in Mont St. Guibert that would be by the French title she had used. As long as he was here, no one must know of his position as bishop of Paderborn. He was now merely the chaplain and teacher of religion in the girls' school. He smiled, extended his hand to her, and nodded understandingly.

After some refreshments, Pauline took the three men to the chapel for a visit and then to the second floor where the bishop's bedroom and sitting-room were. These were in the immediate front of the house and had a most pleasant view. Outside the bishop's bedroom was a balcony, the only one of the building. Mother Pauline opened the doors leading to it and ushered the bishop and his two friends outside to the pleasant scene. The summer breeze swept past them and surrounded them as they stood at the railing looking down.

Mother Pauline took a deep breath, and so did Bishop Martin. She merely pointed below in silence. The building stood high on raised ground and was surrounded on all sides by a lovely park, trees growing thick and close together to form a huge, natural enclosure for the house. Once the road in front of the house reached the trees, it was impossible to see it any longer. Some ten or twelve feet from the front steps the land sloped gently but steeply down into a pretty lagoon that mirrored the soft waving of the trees around it and seemed to ripple in time with their swaying. A canoe or two sat waiting at the sides for some students who wanted a smooth, leisurely ride. In the distance one could hear the blare of a train as it crossed the property far away.

"Isn't it peaceful, Monsieur l'Abbé?" murmured Mother Pauline to the bishop.

Before he could answer, Father Stamm broke in.

"It's excellent. It's ideal, Your Grace—I mean, Monsieur l'Abbé! I shall be able to contact you here easily."

Bishop Martin looked from Father Stamm to Hubert, who just stood there, smiling contentedly. Then he turned to Mother Pauline.

"Yes," he said, "it is excellent, Reverend Mother, and I thank you. Now where is the school?"

"Oh, that is farther back on the grounds, behind this building. Suppose I take you there a little later. I would like to get the keys and see that things are ready." She waited for the bishop's approval.

He turned from the balcony and started to go in.

"Very well, Reverend Mother. We'll wait for you here. Meanwhile Hubert and I can start to unpack."

It was not long before the three men were again following Mother Pauline, this time across the spacious grounds behind the house. To the left was a large garden of flowers and vegetables. To the right was a number of older buildings of different sizes.

They veered sharply to the right and continued walking until they saw on their left an old but sturdy two-storied building in the shape of a U. They turned around and found its open end facing them; a wing to the left, a wing to the right with a connecting wing between them in the back. The open end of the U was the courtyard, and Mother Pauline pushed open its gates for the guests.

"This building was here even before Monsieur Demeurs bought the estate and built his fine gray stone house," said Mother Pauline. "We have renovated the left and right wings. Both will have bedrooms for some Sisters and all the girls, and here, in the right wing, will be the chapel upstairs with dining room and classrooms downstairs. The middle wing has rooms for storage and possibly a kitchen and laundry. This is where one enters the school," she said and opened the door in the center of the wing on the courtyard side, bringing them all inside.

She led them down the corridor whose strong wooden floors creaked a little under them to the far end of the wing whose outside they had just seen and into a large bright room filled with desks. Hung on hinges on the walls of both sides of the room were high windows with fancy handles that opened inward. They were not new and had obviously been there from the beginning.

"This is most likely where you will teach, Monsieur L'Abbé," said Mother Pauline. "How fortunate our students—and we Sisters—will be to have you!"

A few days later, on the feast of the Sacred Heart, Bishop Martin blessed the house and the chapel tucked in the woods of the old town of Mont St. Guibert, which dated back to the year 850 A.D. and could boast 1000 years of Catholicity.

Content that the bishop was safely established, Mother Pauline was constantly on the road throughout the month of July, handling business of every sort but especially matters for the departure of another group of Sisters to North America. By August 5 eighteen Sisters were ready, and once again, she inspired them with bravery as she brought them to Rotterdam to board the ship. It seemed that her great heart began to beat in their own as she embraced each one and that her unsinkable spirit sped to them from her waving handkerchief and buoyant voice as she called over and over, "*Aufwiedersehen.*"

These were exciting times, and a week later she was in Mühlhausen in Bohemia at the castle where the Sisters still taught some students, but now where also several German young women who had entered the congregation earlier received the habit of Sisters of Christian Charity and their religious names. They would now begin their novitiate there at Mühlhausen. The transplanted SCC branch was sprouting!

Pauline's happiness was doubled when she returned to Mont St. Guibert in Belgium a month later for the very same ceremony. She had the great joy of seeing five young ladies receive their habits and their names from Bishop Conrad Martin, who took special delight in giving them. Pauline and her work would not be stopped no matter what Bismarck did. The Lord would see to that.

Yet He did not shield her from continuing blows of the Kulturkampf hammer. On November 7, making sure that the Reverend Mother Pauline von Mallinckrodt was at home in Paderborn, the royal sub-prefect, Mr. Jentzsch, called on her at the motherhouse. Politely but firmly he served her notice that the motherhouse and St. Jospeh's House, now called Hospital since it housed the sick Sisters, would have to be closed by January 1, 1877 by order of the government. Pauline protested, telling him that the Sisters were aged and sick and that it would be dangerous to move them.

Mr. Jentzsch knew the Sisters well and had no ill feelings toward them personally. But he was a loyal servant of the state and had a duty to do. He tried hard to justify the action of the government, but he was plainly embarrassed and finally just handed the document to Mother Pauline.

"You will have to sign this," he said, "as proof that you were duly notified."

She took the paper, sat down, dipped her pen into the inkwell, and began to write. Never before had she written her name with such pain.

It was that same pain and a sense of outrage that made her pen fly across the paper two weeks later, finishing a letter of protest and request to Dr. Falk, now Minister of Ecclesiastical Affairs and Public Instruction. She made copies of that letter to be sent to at least six other officials. She explained the condition of the Sisters, their lack of income and begged that the government order be recalled as an "act against humanity."

There was someone else who was ill at this time, in fact, was dying and had a claim on Mother Pauline's attention. It was the faithful gardener who had worked at the motherhouse for twenty-seven years, living in the modest quarters given him on the motherhouse grounds. It was he who had planned and cared for the large garden and planted the rows of beautiful linden trees that led to the Sisters' cemetery which he had designed.

Pauline went to be with him in his last hours, praying with him and comforting him, thanking him and telling him that the bishop was safe now in Belgium. She could not and would not tell him that the motherhouse he loved so much would have to be closed. So he died peacefully, assisted by her prayers and presence.

She had also been notified that five law-suits against her congregation concerning property were being held by the government, all of them on one day, November 24, in the Court of Appeals. Her comment was: "We will earnestly ask the good God to direct everything according to His holy will and good pleasure, and we shall praise His holy name in sorrow and in joy."

Besides the five suits against the Sisters of Christian Charity, the government also had a suit that day against the French Nuns and the Salzkotten Sisters. But of the seven cases of court proceedings, all seven were won by the Sisters, and the praise of the Lord was loud and strong that night in many convents, but especially in those of Pauline's daughters!

The season of Advent in preparation for Christmas was by now well along, and the Sisters at the House of Divine Providence could see that Luise Hensel was busy sewing lovely clothes for the figures of the Christmas crib. But they could also see that she was growing weak and ill. They called the doctor, and by December 17 they called Pauline, who came quickly to her dear old teacher.

Lovingly she cared for Luise who was now bedridden. She prayed with her and read to her, fed her, talked with her.

"You know, Luise," she said softly as she bent over her, "you laid the foundation for my spiritual life and taught me much that led me to God. The Lord will welcome you with open arms."

Luise smiled a little, opening and closing her eyes with great effort as if the lids were very heavy. Gently she squeezed Pauline's hand.

Some time before, she had written a poem called "Müde bin ich, geh' zur Ruh,"—"I'm tired and I go to rest." It had been set to music. The next day she died quietly with her hand in Pauline's, but there

373

was an eagerness in her face. She was truly tired and wanted to go to blissful rest. They sang the lovely words at her grave, and once again Pauline was homesick for heaven.

Chapter XXIII

Breakfast was over, and with Sister Wunibalda, superior of the motherhouse, Mother Pauline walked with key in hand to the outer door of the chapel where the people were accustomed to enter. It was New Year's Day, 1877, and the chapel had to be closed to the public. She looked across the street to St. Joseph Hospital. In a little while they would have to bring the remaining sick Sisters from there to the motherhouse, which could no longer function as a motherhouse. It would be called Mallinckrodt Manor, with George as its owner. Since St. Joseph Hospital also belonged to him and would now be empty, he would rent it out.

Pauline locked the outer chapel door and gave the key to Sister Wunibalda. Then she went to supervise the moving of the sick Sisters from St. Joseph House. It ws a slow, sad, laborious process. By late afternoon all was done. But George and his lawyer handed in a written protest to authorities, and Pauline wrote, begging that the sick Sisters be allowed to stay in Mallinckrodt Manor.

From there she went to Bohemia to the house in Mühlhausen where the Sisters had a castle school and a novitiate and to Weltrus where they had another school. Both houses were doing fine, and she was very pleased with the novices. Bohemian was a very difficult language, but fortunately, they had a young Bohemian lady with the Sisters as a teacher for the girls and the Sisters.

Much as she liked the Bohemian houses and the novitiate there, Mother Pauline knew that it would be a financial impossibility to increase the number of Sisters on the staffs of the two schools and to allow the number of novices to grow. There just wasn't enough income to support more. Besides, Bohemia was really too far away to keep sending young women who wanted to become Sisters. Now that the motherhouse had to be closed, the novitiate and teachers' training school for the young Sisters would have to be moved out of Germany. Belgium would be a better place for both, but the house at Mont St. Guibert had room for neither.

However, there was a congregation of Sisters who owned a fine convent and school in the town of Alsemberg not far from Brussels and wanted to sell it to Mother Pauline. They were no longer able to staff it. She liked it very much and was particularly pleased to see that it would have room for a novitiate and a teacher-training school as well as a boarding school for girls of low-income families. There was also a school for Flemish children in the village which was taught by the Sisters of the convent and would be included with the others.

The buildings were large and in good condition, and the whole complex was U-shaped. There was an overhead passage connecting the house with the impressive village church that stood behind the convent so that the Sisters and children could easily attend Mass from the church choir. In the church was a beautiful shrine to our Lady who had appeared in Alsemberg many years before and had caused it to be widely known as a pilgrimage town.

Because of the shape of the building, it would be easy to keep the novitiate and teachers' school separate from the girls and their school by the various wings. The property had two pretty gardens, and the building had its own chapel where all could visit Jesus in the Blessed Sacrament. Best of all, the price was not too high, and Pauline hoped they could purchase it. Once again, Johanna Luig was handling the affair, and Pauline was confident all would go well.

She returned to Paderborn then for an important happening at the former motherhouse. It would be a secret one. At dusk on March 6, seven young women were clothed with the habit and given their religious names in the almost empty chapel of "Mallinckrodt Manor." The most ordinary and simple hymns were sung to avoid any sign of a special occasion. Kulturkampf or no Kulturkampf, the congregation had to go on, and Pauline was not one to be afraid of risk. The next morning the new novices were on the train, bound for the neighboring country where they would have a home and could freely enter their novitiate in peace.

The government had ordered that an inventory had to be taken of all furnishings in the former motherhouse, so Pauline set to work with the Sisters, carefully cataloging everything after the novices left. Numerous things had been sold for a nominal price to George and friends of the Sisters who would keep them until the time when the Sisters could return to the motherhouse once again.

Meanwhile things were progressing in Belgium and in North America. At Mont St. Guibert there were twenty-five full-time boarders, two part-time boarders and eight day students. Bishop Martin was convinced that Mother Pauline should move out of the motherhouse in Paderborn completely and make her residence at Mont St. Guibert. From there, he said, she could easily visit the sick Sisters temporarily allowed to remain at the emptied motherhouse in Paderborn and could frequently go to the schools and novitiate at Alsemberg if they were ever established there. Deep in her heart, she knew he was right, but she had to wait for the right moment.

Reports from the United States were encouraging. The Sisters of Christian Charity now had twenty houses there: eleven in Pennsylvania, two in New Jersey, one in Michigan, four in Minnesota, and two in Louisiana. Besides these, a motherhouse where the provincial and her assistants could reside, where young women could enter the postulancy and the novitiate and make their vows, and where, as young Sisters, they could be trained as teachers, was being built in Pennsylvania!

But, as usual, local events in Pauline's own dear country tinged those joys with sorrow and now jolted her attention onto unpleasant things. Himly, the persevering opponent of the congregation, had now brought five lawsuits against it into the third stage of prosecution in Berlin, hoping that this time he might win them. Pauline handled that news as she always did—quietly placing the suits and their outcome in the hands of God. She travelled to Berlin to consult her lawyers about them, but far more important to the congregation than the lawsuits were the beautiful words she wrote to the Sisters about them: "Let us try to gain the victory through meekness, patience, humility, love of God, and a forbearing love of our neighbor. May holy prudence guide our words and actions. Let us forgive our adversaries, and let us beg God to take us under his protection."

Her next move was to write to Dr. Falk, pleading that the sick and aged Sisters at the former motherhouse in Paderborn be allowed to stay there permanently. To move them would mean their early deaths, she declared, and as citizens who had rendered a lifetime of service to teaching German youth, they deserved to spend their last years in their home without displacement. A few days later, she received a letter, a consoling one, but not from Falk. It was from the Cardinal of Mecheln welcoming her and her Sisters to Alsemberg, the miraculous shrine of Mary.

Then came a new challenge. A Sister from New Zealand came to Belgium to see Pauline, asking for Sisters to go as missionaries to that country. They would be given free transportation, a home, property, and an apostolate there. New Zealand! That would be real missionary work. What a wonderful chance for the Sisters to spread God's kingdom! Mother Pauline was really excited about it. They would need permission from Rome, but that was not impossible. Perhaps she really could find some Sisters to send!

At the end of March, there seemed to be some sign of hope for the Sisters at the motherhouse. The district official, Jentzsch, came to visit the sick Sisters there and evaluate the situation. His coming was the first response to Pauline's request for the Sisters' permanent residence there, and it made her optimistic.

All this time Bishop Martin's advice that she move completely out of the motherhouse in Paderborn and set up headquarters in Belgium had been quietly working within her. Now suddenly, after Jentzsch's visit, it seemed to her to be not only prudent but also very urgent, leaving her with thought and energy for only one thing: packing all and settling in at St. Joseph School in Mont St. Guibert. She called Sister Lioba, her secretary, and together they started to pack many things from Mother Pauline's office and Sister Lioba's room at the motherhouse, finally adding a few personal things of their own. Sadly the remaining Sisters watched box after box come to the main door. They made no effort to hide their tears as the blind children surrounded Mother Pauline and Sister Lioba to sing for them one last time, and men and women members of the board of the blind institute came, one by one, to say goodbye. It was April 4, 1877 when the congregation was officially moved to Belgium.

Hardly a week had passed after Mother Pauline's return to Belgium when news came, both bad and good. The Sisters were forced at last to leave the orphanage at Steele and would need to be reassigned and placed. This was, as a matter of fact, no surprise to Pauline, and she did have a plan. But the sorrow of the orphans and of the Sisters was very real to her and was increased by the fact that she could do nothing to lessen it.

The good news was that the lovely convent-school complex at Alsemberg was now theirs. The purchase of it was finally concluded, and very positive things could soon start happening. Mother Pauline was back and forth between Belgium and Germany, and soon large transports of furniture were arriving at the convent-school in Alsemberg from Paderborn. By the beginning of May, some boarders from Brussels had already come, and the Sisters were finding it a real challenge to teach these girls in French.

But the students liked the classes and the excellent food and board they were receiving, and favorable word was spreading rapidly, promising a good enrollment in the fall. The Sisters were also conducting the village school in Flemish, and the number of students increased considerably. The Christian Brothers, who had a boarding-school for boys in town, were true to their name and offered the Sisters the best of advice. They gave them a list of current good textbooks and the names of reliable suppliers for purchasing household articles.

Toward the end of the month the Sisters were able to get a chaplain too. He was a German priest in exile because of the Kulturkampf and lived near the convent, receiving free board. He said Holy Mass for the Sisters and children, heard confessions, and taught religion and teaching methods to the young Sisters, who were also concentrating on learning French.

There were about fifty people in all at the Alsem-
381

berg house: twenty-four Sisters, who were teachers, homemakers, and novices and then twenty boarders. Only one of them was a German child. There was only one postulant, a Flemish teacher, a maid, a part-time boarder and some women who helped in the laundry. Fortunately, besides the pleasure of two fairly-sized recreational gardens, there was also a vegetable garden of about one and a half acres that stocked their tables. It was a quiet, modest, but lovely spot, and the Sisters were grateful for it.

Despite these good things, however, they were often homesick, and Mother Pauline had the added pain of financial difficulty. For her to be in debt was almost worse than physical distress, and it became a triple cross because actually neither the boarding-school at Alsemberg nor the one at Mont St. Guibert, nor the houses in Bohemia, brought in enough money to pay their own bills.

For Bishop Conrad Martin, though, there was the joy of going to Rome, and they were expecting his return at the end of May or the beginning of June. The trip was a great consolation for him, and the Holy Father had received him most graciously. Mother Pauline was also expecting a visit from her niece, Maria, with her husband at Mont St. Guibert and tried to coax George and Dina to come with them. That would make her very happy.

Meantime there was still doubt about sending Sisters to New Zealand. Pauline had received permission from Rome to start a novitiate in Australia on the islands nearby, but she wrote to Mother Cecilia who was asking for Sisters that they might just as well stay home to study English and then go to America if something definite was not decided.

By July the students in the Flemish parish village school had increased to sixty-nine, but they were so eager and cheerful that it was a pleasure to teach them. The number of boarders at Mont St. Guibert also grew, with the prospect of more to come because the girls were very pleased with the school.

Now was the time for the investing and profession of first vows of the young American Sisters in Pennsylvania, and Mother Pauline was visualizing it. The very thought of it filled her with energy and joy. Yes, those eight German Sisters who were bound to sail for America on August 4 must receive as much enthusiasm and grace as possible too.

So she brought them to Mont St. Guibert, where after special preparation, they pronounced their perpetual vows. Some other Sisters followed them, making temporary vows. Everything was most solemn and beautiful—the decorated chapel, the ceremony, the homily, the singing—an inspiring happening etched unforgettably on their hearts. The day was spent in peaceful silence and prayer, closing with Benediction of the Blessed Sacrament. Then came the happy celebration of the whole community in the evening with song and refreshments and recreation.

The next day Pauline took the eight Sisters to see the house at Alsemberg so they could tell the Sisters in America about it. On Wednesday they returned to Mont St. Guibert and rested a day. On Friday she accompanied them to Rotterdam and there lovingly guided them onto the ship that would take them to America.

It was October when, to her joy, the two Sisters in Oschersleben notified her that they were allowed to stay there and work as visiting nurses in the service of St. Vincent Society, helping the poor. But, knowing the pressure put on the Sisters in the past about their religious habit, she told these two: "If there is any question of putting off your religious habit, say courteously but definitely that the law has no mention of dress, and a lady in Prussia may follow any style she pleases. Since you prefer this modest dress, the authorities can have no objection. Actually, you are wearing the colors of the country, black and white!"

At St. Joseph School in Mont St. Guibert there were now seventy-two people since the increase of boarders, and Pauline wrote to Sister Clara in Paderborn, begging her to ask her father for some plum trees and gooseberry shrubs to plant at St. Joseph's and at Alsemberg. Sister Clara's father had previously given them some trees for the motherhouse, and they had produced many delicious plums. They would be excellent for the Sisters and boarders—tasty and economical. The gooseberry shrubs would serve not only their tables but also decorate the paths at Alsemberg. She fervently hoped he could send those trees and shrubs to Belgium.

Bishop Martin, meanwhile, was far from passively enduring the Kulturkampf as an exiled chaplain. Since his return from Rome, he had been unusually busy writing a pamphlet called "Not Revision But Repeal of the May Laws." It would certainly cause a stir in governmental circles of Germany if and when it reached them. He also wrote another one entitled "Three Years of My Life," telling of his imprisonment, exile, and the reasons for it. It was a report about and to his diocese and was meant to be a

Christmas gift. Mother Pauline eagerly took both manuscripts to be printed and, with the help of the Sisters, managed to distribute them to the Sisters, relatives, and friends in the rest of Europe by carriers and to the houses in North and South America by mail.

Almost as if in knowing retaliation, the Kulturkampf struck the congregation again. Pauline was opening the mail one day in November and sat perfectly still as she held the first letter for some seconds. She drew a long breath and then released it. Mr. Himly had begun a new process of lawsuit against her regarding the property in Paderborn. That man seemed to live for just one thing: to defeat and punish Pauline von Mallinckrodt and her congregation. What a way to close the old year and begin a new one!

Yet, Mother Pauline smiled and her clear eyes shone as she looked across the room at Sister Lioba. Something had suddenly come to her as a pleasant surprise.

"You know, Sister Lioba," she said slowly in a tone that promised she was about to reveal something very good and very unexpected.

"*Before* the Kulturkampf, we had *one* novitiate. *Now* we have *four*—in North America, South America, Bohemia, and Belgium. Before the Kulturkampf, we had a total of twenty-one houses. *Now* we have twelve houses in Europe; twenty-six houses in North America, including a motherhouse, and four houses in South America, including a motherhouse. That gives us—" and she began to puncture the air with her pencil to emphasize each word. "That gives us a total of *forty-two* houses altogether, exactly double of what we had before the Kulturkampf! *That* is the rich, visible blessing of the Lord, dear Sister!"

Sister Lioba clapped her hands and jumped up, grinning delightedly. "Hardly what they wanted, was it, Reverend Mother?"

"Hardly," she agreed. "And in answer to Mr. Jentzsch's demand that I render an account of all the money given me years ago by private citizens for the nursery, I shall respectfully reply that to maintain proper basic principles, I must declare that I am under no obligation whatsoever to render a statement of finances to the authorities and that I have completely and properly utilized the money donated for the little children's nursery school for the designated purpose."

Sister Lioba clapped again and looked at her with admiration.

Pauline caught the look and said quickly, "But I will try to adhere to my old principle, Sister: with all my heart to wish everyone good, to praise the dear Lord in all that He ordains, and always to trust Him with childlike confidence."

The coming of the new year, 1878, seemed to spur her even more to furnish Sister Wunibalda, superior at Mallinckrodt Manor in Paderborn, with sufficient acceptable ammunition for the legal battle so that she could, in turn, provide it for the congregation's attorneys, Predeek, Fischer, and Arents. The ammunition was, of course, all the proper and authorized documents for the purchase and sale of the congregation's property in Paderborn as well as the verdicts of the Supreme Court of Paderborn handed down earlier about it.

Next Mother Pauline turned to the happy matter

of opening new missions in South America. Her joy seemed to give her pen a special swing as she wrote to Mother Gonzaga, the provincial, telling her that both Bishop Martin and she approved of the Sisters' taking new missions at Concepcion, Lebu, Valdivia, and Osorno. In Osorno the Sisters would take charge of a girls' academy. In Valdivia they would manage schools and a hospital. At Lebu a wealthy mine owner, Don Maximiano Errazurus, the brother of a former president of Chile, was the employer of 800 families. He had built a church, convent, and hospital and was paying for the travel and salaries of four Sisters and a priest through the bishop. There the Sisters would teach a school for the poor and manage the hospital. At Concepcion the Sisters would have charge of a large Refuge House started by Dona Modesta Vidal, who was said to be a stigmatist, and her friend, Dona Felipa Ossa, a millionaire. Ten Sisters would be needed. The convent and the church were new and would be the property of the Sisters. Should they leave, these would go to the bishop.

Mother Pauline gladly agreed to send fourteen more Sisters to Chile, ten for Concepcion and four for Lebu, possibly accompanied by two priests. Chile had said it would pay the passage for sixteen persons. Mother Gonzaga would have to furnish Sisters for Valdivia and Osorno. The fourteen Sisters would need special preparation both interiorly and exteriorly for their long trip and new life in South America. So Pauline thought it best to send them in September. But, as was her custom always in dealing with superiors about decisions regarding their houses, she frequently asked *their* opinions after expressing her own and was usually willing to follow them. So she waited for Mother Gonzaga's answer.

Another opinion expressed just at this time she found it very difficult to follow, and it took all her love for God and His will to do so. It was the opinion of Bishop Conrad Martin regarding the mission in New Zealand. Though he had previously been in favor of it, he now thought it was too great a risk because of the present state of affairs. There just weren't enough Sisters. To Mother Pauline, his judgment was an expression of God's will, and so, though it cost her a struggle, she accepted it and gave up the idea of the mission in New Zealand.

Her respect for the opinions of others was not, however, just for those in authority—the bishop and the Sister superiors. No, to her the individual Sisters and their views were very important, and to them she listened as well, especially when about to make assignments.

"It does not depend on the superior alone to make decisions about the Sisters," she said, "but also upon the *Sisters themselves what they might like* and upon our properly filling the various fields of activity . . ."

Before she knew it, carnival time, the prelude to Lent, was upon them, and Thecla, Hermann's widow, came with Anna to Mont St. Guibert for a visit. Because of carnival, there were celebrations with a presentation in German and French by the girls. Even though they were long, the bishop attended both to please the students.

With the beginning of March came the beginning of much suffering for Pauline. It was arthritis, and it was able to slow her as nothing else could. At first she had to stay in bed, and Sister Lioba had to write her letters for her. What became even more painful than the arthritis itself, though, was the fact that it kept her from going personally to the superior at Mühlhausen, who was enduring real agony in an unfortunate situation. This Sister begged to be transferred, but for the protection of her own good name and that of another person, Pauline firmly but lovingly encouraged her to share the cross with her Lord in this Lent, to forgive everyone, and to remain there calmly. Surely Sister had not promised to remain loyal to her Lord only in joy. Surely she intended to stay with Him also in sorrow, to show fortitude, the core of love.

Long after she was up and about, though, Pauline's hands remained arthritic and were so bad that Sister Agnes had to help her dress. She had to wear cotton covered by flannel bandages on both hands for months, but that did not keep her from writing even though her penmanship was worse than usual. One finger in particular gave more trouble than all the others and required that she wear a poultice on it.

In spring Mother Pauline, with Sister Lioba, travelled on business for several weeks to the houses the Sisters still had in Germany and then to those in Bohemia. They stopped at Boeddeken, too, visiting and consulting with George and Dina and also at Paderborn, cheering the Sisters there with their presence and enjoying some relaxation at Alfred's home for a while.

They were back home in Mont St. Guibert in early June, and Mother Pauline was looking forward to the investing of nine young ladies on June 25. Bishop Conrad Martin conducted the ceremony with genuine pleasure, and it was a special lift for the hearts of the Sisters to see the promise of the nine white veils.

Among the new novices was Sister Leonie Straatman, who had entered the community at Mont St. Guibert. She had come from the orphan home in Germany where she had gone with her little brother after her mother's death. She found Mother Pauline very loving to her because of this, and the fact that her brother's name was Hermann also seemed to touch a special spot in Pauline's heart.

As their training in the novitiate progressed day by day under the direction of Sister Regina, Sister Leonie and the other novices became more and more fond of her. Mother Pauline, however, had other ideas and was planning to send her to America in late September. When the novices heard that, they were really disturbed, especially Sister Leonie and another novice.

Together they discussed it and decided that if Mother Pauline knew how much Sister Regina meant to them and their spiritual development, she would let her stay and send someone else to America. Mother Pauline was very loving. They were sure she would understand. But—they would have to speak to her.

Pauline looked up from her desk as the two novices entered.

"Yes, dear Sisters," she smiled, "there is something you want to tell me?"

"Yes, Reverend Mother," they both murmured.

They looked at each other, and then Sister Leonie plunged.

"Reverend Mother, all the novices love Sister Regina very much, and we heard that—"

"I am sending her to America in September?"

"Yes, Reverend Mother—"

"That is true, dear Sisters." Pauline looked kindly at the two fresh young faces in the very white bonnets and veils. "I know it will be a tremendous sacrifice for you, but I also know that you will make it generously."

Sister Leonie wet her lips and touched the arm of the other novice, signalling for her help.

"Please, Reverend Mother," said Sister Leonie pleadingly.

"We came to ask you please not to send Sister Regina," chimed in the other one.

"We need her so much for our training. Perhaps someone else, Reverend Mother?" finished Sister Leonie.

They were not prepared for what happened.

Suddenly Mother Pauline was on her feet, towering over them, her eyes flashing, her face stern. Never before had they seen her like that. They stood immovable, staring.

"How can you ask such a thing? You would dare to prevent the work of God and of the Church?" she thundered, heavily stressing and breaking off each word solemnly in a voice that seemed to come from the bottom of her being.

For an instant the three of them stood in tense silence. Then the two novices managed to speak.

"Please pardon us, Reverend Mother," whispered Sister Leonie as she looked down, flushing.

"We are sorry, Reverend Mother," whispered the other, also ashamed.

Pauline's eyes were serene again, and there was even a slight smile on her lips. But they did not see either. They only heard her voice, and it was once more calm and kind.

"I know very well how much our affections can sometimes mislead us and get in our way to the Lord. But, my dear little Sisters, when it is a question of His will and furthering His work, there is nothing, absolutely nothing that we should not be willing to give Him. He is never outdone in generosity. Our Sisters, your Sisters in America need Sister Regina very much. You wouldn't refuse that wonderful training to them, would you?"

"No, no," came the muffled reply, and their heads were moving from side to side.

Mother Pauline raised the two faces framed in the white hearts and smiled at them.

"See, everything is fine, and all is forgiven. Go now, and pray for Sister Regina and for me." She embraced them both and turned them to the door.

"Thank you, Reverend Mother," they said and left quietly.

Sister Leonie never forgot the incident, and her admiration for Mother Pauline grew more and more as she had the opportunity to observe her during those days in Belgium. She noticed how Pauline insisted on receiving no preferential treatment with a private room that would have required much trouble to arrange because of lack of space. She slept in the dormitory with the others, taking extra care to be quiet when she came home from her frequent travels, extremely tired.

Another detail that struck her was Pauline's poor, coarse shoes. Knowing that Pauline had once been a wealthy lady, Sister Leonie saw those shoes as a very particular sign of her desire to share the poverty of Jesus and of needy people. But what impressed her most was Pauline's kindness in making it possible for Sister Leonie's brother, Hermann, to visit her once more and say goodbye when his sister was to leave for America. Sister Leonie did go to the United States and spent many active years there, carrying always in her heart the beautiful memory of her foundress.

In July Mother Pauline went to Paderborn to serve as a witness at the request of Himly, their opponent, and others in the lawsuit involving the former property of the congregation. She wondered about the other lawsuits. If each of the six cases Himly was holding against the Sisters was to go through the three stages, the suits would be going on for a long, long time.

When she was not in court, or deeply engaged in prayer, or travelling on business, she was making a strong effort to obtain the inheritances owed to a number of the Sisters at this time. The community needed money badly to pay its debts. The amount of tuition coming in from the few places where the Sisters could teach or earn a salary was not sufficient to support all the Sisters still in Europe and also pay for the expenses of travel to the Americas or helping those over there.

But Mother Pauline's trust in God's continuing providence was greater than her distress at having debts. That trust buoyed her up, and the added joy of seeing three more postulants receive their habits from the hands of Bishop Martin in late August lifted her spirits enough to keep hoping for the rest of the money needed to buy the tickets to Chile for twelve Sisters.

Somehow she was able to get it, and on September 7, Pauline and Sister Chrysostoma took them to port of Bordeaux, where they boarded the ship bound for Chile. With them was a priest from Russian Poland who spoke ten languages and was glad to serve in South America. He was forty-five years old and had spent four years in Rome and four in Brussels. The Sisters were sure of having their spiritual needs filled in Chile.

About two weeks later she said goodbye to seven more Sisters at Rotterdam where the boat for the United States was waiting. Gently, very gently, Sister Regina, one of the seven, took Mother Pauline's bandaged left hand and held it carefully, without any pressure.

"Dear Reverend Mother," she said softly and lovingly, looking at the bandaged right hand resting in a sling. "Please take care of yourself. I hope and pray that your hands will get better, especially that right one. I'll be thinking of you," she said, blinking back tears.

Pauline shrugged and smiled. "I must learn to be patient with a little suffering. I have many intentions, you know. My dear Sisters in America are one of them."

Sister Regina's eyebrows went up. "A little suffering? I don't know about that, Reverend Mother. First the incision to relieve the supposed bone inflammation and now a real tendon inflammation are not so little, I think, especially on your hands which you use so much." There was so much more she wanted to say. But time was getting short, so she gave up trying to put everything into words.

"Goodbye, dear Reverend Mother," she murmured, and she leaned forward to let Pauline's left arm encircle her.

"Goodbye, dear Sister, and God be with you," said Mother Pauline lovingly, patting her reassuringly. Then it was farewell to each of the other Sisters, and the waving until they could not see each other any more.

Hardly had the good news of their arrival in America come to Belgium when Pauline heard of the death of one of their most capable Sisters in New Orleans. Yellow fever was prevalent there, and she, with the other Sisters, wondered how many more would be lost to it.

In November, Mother Pauline herself wrote to Mother Gonzaga, Mother Mathilde, and her four assistants in Germany in spite of her bandaged hands. This was so important and so exciting that she had to do it! She had talked it over with Bishop Martin, and he agreed that it was time and it was feasible to hold the first General Chapter of the congregation. So she was inviting them to come to Mont St. Guibert for the chapter which would start June 1, 1879. Mother Gonzaga and Mother Mathilde were each to bring one representative of the Sisters in South America and North America respectively. Later she wrote to Germany with the same news, telling the Sisters that they were to meet between Easter and Pentecost to elect two representatives to the chapter. The bishop of the diocese of Mecheln, Belgium had appointed Bishop Martin to preside over the chapter in his place. Pauline was looking forward to the chapter especially because it would mean the election of someone by the Sisters for the position of superior-general which she was presently holding.

Meanwhile life at St. Joseph School in Mont St. Guibert was progressing fairly well, and the secret of the identity of the chaplain there was being very well guarded. Even the students from Paderborn, who had guessed who he was, kept strict silence about him, telling neither family nor friends.

Other priests of the area were puzzled and wondered about him, especially the dean of priests at Mecheln. The chaplain of St. Joseph School spoke French with a very heavy German accent, showed himself very devoted to God, but mixed with no other priests and never involved himself in parish affairs.

"Don't worry about it," the dean was told when he inquired from the cardinal about the chaplain. "This priest is of the diocese of Paderborn. He is properly authorized and is acting entirely according to his duty."

Reassured, the dean invited him to a meeting of priests at his home. The strange priest came, talked quietly with one or two others, and took the place given him at table.

After the meal, when dessert was served, the dean arose and made the customary toast to the Church and the Pope. The glasses were hardly lowered when he turned directly to the new guest and said: "Rest assured that we are all of one heart with the persecuted German Church, and since you are, they say, of the diocese of Paderborn, if you one day have the honor to meet Bishop Martin, that hero of faith, tell him of the total admiration and sympathy of the priests here."

He lifted his glass again, and so did the others.

The chaplain from St. Joseph School stood up. His face was noticeably paler, and there were tears in his eyes. His voice was gruff with emotion.

"You will never know what your words have meant. I can assure you that Bishop Martin will be as touched by them as I was, and I thank you in his name."

One day, however, the secret did leak out. A coach came rolling down the very steep principal street of hilly Mont St. Guibert, going faster with every foot of its descent. There was a great clatter and skidding of hooves and screeching of wheels as the driver tried to slow it. But with the great pull, the wheels turned too suddenly, balance was lost, and the coach overturned in front of the monument to the soldiers. It banged to the ground, and a trunk meant for St. Joseph School fell out. As it hit the cobblestone street, the force of the impact jolted the lid open.

A few townspeople were near and curiously gathered around it, picking up some things that were scattered. Among them was an envelope addressed to "Monsignor Martin" at Mont St. Guibert. This meant *Bishop* Martin, and it did not take the group long to realize that the chaplain was indeed the well-known bishop of Paderborn, victim of the May Laws, confessor of the faith, exiled by Bismarck with a price on his head.

The pastor of the town immediately took charge of the situation and explained the seriousness of it. He warned of the danger to the bishop and begged the people for loyal silence.

Nothing more was necessary. The letter was put back in the trunk, the lid was closed and locked, and all was delivered to St. Joseph School. The people went home with lips sealed, and Bishop Martin was allowed to continue his hidden life of exile in peace.

Chapter XXIV

"Well," sighed Mother Pauline to Sister Lioba, her secretary, "number 158,516 wasn't the lucky number, Sister Juliana says."

"You mean that was our number for the lottery, Reverend Mother?" said Sister Lioba.

"Yes, and I was hoping so much that we would win. We need the money very badly. Well, God knows best, and we will continue to praise Him in all He does. He will still take care of us. Of that I am positively sure."

Pauline put her bandaged hand to her forehead, supporting it with her elbow on the desk as she sat with her back to the papers laid out there.

"I wonder if Himly will go so far as to bring that new lawsuit against us here to Belgium. That would be very painful indeed. It's bad enough that he is digging up something that is thirty years old, without bringing it to a foreign country." She paused, her wrapped fingers still spread across her forehead.

"Good Father Adami would be outraged if he knew that thirty years after his death and the death of his lawyer, the government would be suing us for the money he left us in his will for the blind children," she continued.

"What kind of man is this Himly?" muttered Sister Lioba almost to herself.

"Very zealous for what he believes in, I'll say that, Sister. So I am willing to forgive him—but it is hard."

Mother Pauline dropped her hand and swung around to the desk again. There was no time for lamenting. She had too much to do.

The first general chapter of the congregation was only five months away, and there were preparations for it to be made. Documents also had to be copied and sent to their lawyers for fighting the various lawsuits being brought against the Sisters. It seemed that the Kulturkampf was raging with new vigor.

Not many days later, on February 20, 1879, Bishop Conrad Martin blessed new habits and presented them to the seven young ladies who stood eagerly before him. As always, his heart and Mother Pauline's were filled with joy by this ceremony and seemed to increase as they looked at the glowing faces of the new novices. It never crossed the mind of anyone there that day that this would be the last investing ceremony Bishop Martin would conduct.

However, another joy Mother Pauline had been eagerly awaiting was crushed in the bud when she received word from Mother Gonzaga that she and her companion would not be able to attend the general chapter. They had both looked forward so much to seeing each other again! But the bishop of Concepción, Chile, would not give permission for Mother

Gonzaga to leave because war had broken out between Peru and Bolivia, and Chile threatened to be involved also. He did not want the provincial away at such a time.

Of all the times that she had found it hard to submit to God's will expressed through authority, this was the hardest for Mother Pauline. She wrote immediately to Mother Gonzaga, telling her of her sorrow. At the same time she shared with her the great fear she had that they might very possibly lose the motherhouse and St. Joseph House in Paderborn. The government was suing them for selling those houses to George and would not acknowledge his ownership.

Mother Pauline left for Paderborn and stayed there for the proceedings of the suits until March 20. By March 26 the verdicts were so bad that George appealed the cases to the higher courts of Berlin. Meanwhile in Paderborn, Pauline consulted her old physician friend, Dr. Haggeney, who had often taken care of the Sisters, about her hands. They were arthritic, he said, and no incisions would help the inflammation.

With the beginning of May, Mother Pauline and Sister Lioba travelled again to Paderborn for the regional chapter of the German Sisters before the general chapter. When that was over, Mother Pauline tried very hard to clear her mind of all other thoughts except the Lord since she and Sister Lioba would now take part in a retreat that was about to begin.

It was hardly over when she was welcoming Mother Mathilde and Sister Philomena from America in huge embraces and standing back to take a good look at both of them. Oh, how good it was to see them! Soon she was seating them and urging them to eat and drink, and asking so many questions all at one time that they were scarcely able to do anything.

After the excitement of their arrival had subsided, the two visitors had the chance to see the changes in the motherhouse, now "Mallinckrodt Manor," and to just look at the empty St. Joseph House across the street. Several times there was a lull when they could chat with Mother Pauline, telling her everything they possibly could about the Sisters and convents in North America. She sat there, listening eagerly, almost hungrily, to all they said as if she could not get enough information about the American missions. Perhaps it was because their news was all positive and joyful, whereas hers was nothing but sad. The very place where they sat, the cradle of the congregation, its property, St. Joseph House, and the orphanage at Höxter, which had been sold to Frau von Metternich, were under the threat of doom by the government. Later Mother Mathilde and Sister Philomena travelled to Berlin with Mother Pauline to confer with the lawyers about the lawsuits.

At last they returned to Mont St. Guibert, and on June 1, the first general chapter opened with Mass in honor of the Holy Spirit on Pentecost Sunday. Besides Bishop Conrad Martin, who presided, there were nine Sisters present: Mother Pauline, the two delegates from North America, two from Europe, Mother Pauline's secretary, the superior of Mont St. Guibert, and two of Mother Pauline's councillors. Sister Anna, her senior councillor, was unable to attend because of illness that confined her to the Blind Asylum in Paderborn.

On the first day of the chapter proceedings, two

Sisters were chosen by the group to be tellers for counting and verifying votes, and another was chosen as secretary of the chapter. Then Mother Pauline gave an account to the delegates of her thirty years in office and of the state of the congregation as she knew it. She praised the unity and religious spirit of the Sisters spread over the world. She begged pardon for her faults and begged also for the election of another to her office. She promised prompt obedience to the new superior-general and thanked the Sisters for their loving obedience to her. The Sisters, listening to her, were deeply moved, and each knew in her heart without hesitation whom she would elect to the office of Reverend Mother.

As the Sisters prepared for the election, Mother Pauline knelt, and in a firm, solemn voice declared that all authority vested in her was now transferred to the delegates qualified to vote and then to the one they would choose to fill her place.

A great hush dropped over the room as the moment of voting arrived. The mere rustle of the paper seemed too loud and bold. Each Sister walked singly to the small table in the center of the room and bent over the paper as she wrote on the ballot. Then she folded it and dropped it into the basket on the table. As the last Sister went back to her place in the semicircle, a surge of relief spread through the group. They relaxed and smiled knowlingly at each other—all except Mother Pauline, who stood quietly praying.

The ballots were counted, opened, announced, and verified by the tellers and then shown to Bishop Martin. The choice was unanimous, except for one vote. All had voted for the same person—Mother

Pauline! They knew that no other Sister was as well qualified to lead the congregation through these difficult times as was their foundress. Bishop Martin rose, smiling and joyful.

"This election has been conducted according to the directions of Holy Mother Church and of your Constitutions, and it is valid," he said loudly. "It is my pleasure to announce that Mother Pauline von Mallinckrodt has been elected your superior general."

There was a burst of applause and happy exclamations as the bishop walked over to Mother Pauline. She was slightly pale, but her blue-green eyes were very bright as the bishop gently shook her hand. The ballots were then burned, and all left the room.

The bell rang loud and long, and everyone in the house went to the chapel where the good news was announced to all. The organ grandly intoned the solemn hymn, *Te Deum*, and enthusiastic voices took it up with joy, filling the chapel with praise and thanks to God for the gift of their Reverend Mother. It was June 5, 1879.

The very next day came the news that set her own heart singing with a praise of God sweeter and purer than any other because it was totally selfless and generous. She managed to thank Him for His wisdom and providence even though the message was that the congregation had lost all five lawsuits at the Court of Appeals. That meant that George was no longer the owner of the motherhouse and St. Joseph House; they now belonged to the government!

She knew what great sorrow the Sisters in Paderborn must have, and she longed to go to them immediately. But they, in turn, knew that the general chapter must be her first concern. They were certain that she shared their pain and worry and would care for them as soon as it was possible.

The chapter members met for the next two weeks, seriously considering various important matters. First came an examination of the Rule and Constitutions. They found that only a single paragraph regarding financial matters had to be changed. It was recorded, and a copy of it with the proceedings of the whole chapter would be sent to Rome. Next, assistants or councillors to the superior general were elected. Following that, reports by the delegates were given regarding the state of the congregation in their respective countries: the Sisters' work, achievements, needs, mode of religious life. Then various Sisters called attention to faults against the Constitutions that sometimes appeared in the Sisters' daily life. All this was carefully considered and recommendations for improvement were made by the chapter members. Then a summary of the whole chapter in the form of a general letter was prepared so that a copy of it could be sent to each house of the congregation. Finally, after all these documents had been signed by each member of the chapter, it was officially closed on June 18, 1879.

About a week later Sister Agnes was in Mother Pauline's office, talking with her. The paper work related to the general chapter was well on its way to completion, and Mother Pauline was now free to do what was very close to her heart: go to Paderborn and deal with the problem of the confiscated motherhouse.

''I am very happy you were elected to be one of

my assistants," said Mother Pauline to Sister Agnes, taking her hand and looking straight into her eyes. "You have already helped me very much, and you are here in Belgium, close at hand."

"I am happy too, Reverend Mother," answered Sister Agnes. "Here, let me help you pack for the trip to Paderborn. I'm sure the Sisters there cannot wait until you come."

Soon Mother Pauline met George and her brother-in-law, Alfred Hüffer, there at Mallinckrodt Manor, and together they tried to find a way for the Sisters to stay there. One bit of good news had filtered through to them and made them glad that they had not given up. Dr. Falk, one of their foremost enemies, had resigned. It had to be a good sign! Perhaps they were on the edge of a new and better age!

A little more encourged, they managed to discuss the case with Himly, his lawyers and theirs being present. Himly finally consented to let George rent the motherhouse from him, the government's representative, and permitted the sick Sisters to remain there with their nurses. He also allowed the children to remain at the orphanage in Höxter with the Sisters, but with a woman appointed by the state as head of the institution. Sixty war orphans would also be added to the group at Höxter by the state, he said in closing.

Mother Pauline nodded in silent agreement. Thank God, thank God, she was saying over and over in her heart. The Sisters and children still had a home, regardless of the circumstances!

Summer was in its full array of beauty and height of warmth when Mother Pauline came back to Mont

St. Guibert at the beginning of July and walked into the main house. She was immensely relieved and glad that so much business had been finished. All that remained now was to give the bishop an account of it.

Bishop Martin was sitting in the sun on the balcony outside his bedroom on the second floor with eyes half-closed. The magnificent gardens below him were full of loveliness, and he was leisurely taking in the sights and sounds and smells of summer. It was so good and so refreshing just to relax and enjoy nature, with no other matter to pressure him! Actually, he was thinking of his dear home in Germany, of his diocese, his people, and daydreaming that he was back there.

He stirred somewhat and readjusted his position in the chair. He felt tired, very, very tired. He was exhausted from the general chapter, he had to admit to himself, even though it had pleased and inspired him tremendously. And then, there was that bothersome old ailment of his that wouldn't let go—a bronchial infection he just couldn't shake off.

But in spite of his fatigue and the heaviness in his chest, Bishop Martin felt—wonderful. A remarkable peace had come over him, deeper and more soothing than any he had ever known before. Inwardly he felt marvelously light and secure and totally undisturbed by anything, even his homesickness. Outwardly, a warm, feathery breeze seemed to be gently massaging his face. Well, the air and the sun would do him good. He would doze here for just a little.

Mother Pauline paused as she came noiselessly into his bedroom and stood looking at him through the open balcony doors. She had knocked, but he had not heard it out there. She had thought as much and so had entered. Now seeing him so still with his back to her, she could not tell whether he was asleep or not.

The bishop truly deserved a good rest, she thought. He had given of himself so extensively to the Sisters during the chapter that he had outdone even his usual generous record of service to them. His homilies every day at Mass and his almost daily talks during the two weeks of the chapter meetings had been extraordinarily beautiful, deep, and practical and had taken much time to prepare and much energy to deliver. He had really made the first general chapter a genuine spiritual renewal for the Sisters, and she was deeply grateful. He had not spared himself in showing a great love for the congregation and a thirst for the holiness of the Sisters, the marks of a true spiritual father. The Sisters must, in turn, take good care of him and obey him.

Mother Pauline hesitated, started to walk to the balcony, then stopped as a thought flashed through her mind. He had not been feeling well with that seeming constant cold he had. By now he must be drained. She would let him alone. Tomorrow was another day, and the report she had to make would not suffer from waiting another few hours. She turned and, without a sound, left the room.

When Mother Pauline finally did tell the bishop what had happened to their property in Germany and the rental made by George, he approved of all. Like her, he was glad the Sisters and children were able to remain in those buildings.

On Friday of the following week, the bishop heard the confessions of all the Sisters, and the next morning, July 12, they all received Holy Communion from his hands, as usual. No one surmised that it was the last Holy Mass Bishop Martin would ever offer. Later that afternoon, he felt very ill and was unable even to spend time in the garden. Hubert, his valet, helped him to bed, and Mother Pauline, greatly worried, begged him to let the doctor visit him.

"*Ach*, Mother Pauline, you are making too much of this, but—all right, if it will satisfy you—I will see the doctor. However—" and he looked at her somewhat sternly—"I want you to go to Rotterdam with the Sisters Tuesday."

"Yes, Your Grace," she murmured, motioning the doctor to enter.

After examining the bishop, the doctor, who was an experienced physician, assured everyone that Monsieur L'Abbé would be well within a few days. He prescribed several days of complete rest, a strict diet, and medicine and promised to return the following Monday.

Everyone, including the bishop, obeyed the doctor's orders to the smallest detail, and on Monday the doctor returned. He found Monsieur L'Abbé much improved and was glad to see the patient sit up for a while to chat with Mother Pauline.

As he left, Mother Pauline followed him to the door downstairs.

"Doctor," she said in a low voice. "I have a favor to ask of you."

"Of course, Reverend Mother, if I can do it."

"Could you possibly make your visit tomorrow to Monsieur L'Abbé in the morning? I want to take our two Sisters who must return to America to Rotterdam tomorrow afternoon. But I do not want to leave unless I know from you whether his condition is good enough."

The doctor saw the deep concern in her kind eyes.

"Most certainly, Reverend Mother," he said with a little bow. "I shall make this my first call tomorrow morning."

That night very few Sisters slept well. Many spent wakeful times praying for the bishop's recovery, and Mother Pauline stayed near his room, ready at the least sign from Hubert to give any help she could.

Next morning the doctor appeared as promised, and Mother Pauline accompanied him to the bishop's room.

"Monsieur L'Abbé at this moment is doing nicely, Reverend Mother," he told her as he closed the door of the patient's room. He had spent considerable time with the bishop in order to evaluate him properly.

"If he continues this way and if no complications develop, he should recover in due time. Yes," he hurried to add as he saw Mother Pauline about to speak, "yes, I am quite sure that you can safely go to Rotterdam, Reverend Mother. I do not foresee any danger."

"Ah, that is good, Doctor," breathed Mother Pauline with a smile. "Then we shall see you tomorrow?"

The doctor assured her he would come, and Sister Angela saw him out. Mother Pauline went quickly to the patient.

"Good morning, Your Grace," she said quietly but cheerfully. "The doctor tells me you are feeling better. I hope it is really true," and she stood looking down at him with questioning eyes.

Bishop Martin coughed a little and took the water Hubert offered him. Then he turned to her.

"Yes, Reverend Mother, it is true. I am feeling better. Much better. And you are not to cancel that trip because of me. I want you to take the Sisters to Rotterdam today. Go now, you must get ready."

"Yes, Your Grace. We will come for your blessing if we may," she said.

"Certainly, certainly," he answered and leaned back on the pillows that propped him.

Mother Pauline went quickly to Mother Mathilde and Sister Philomena.

"The bishop insists that I go with you," she told them, "so I shall do it, of course. But if he should die—if he should die, I will transfer his remains to Paderborn," she said determinedly, looking out in the distance, almost as if she were addressing the world.

"Reverend Mother! You wouldn't" burst out Sister Philomena.

"You cannot take such a risk," objected Mother Mathilde, putting out her hand as if to detain her.

Mother Pauline grasped the hand and playfully patted it.

"Oh, you fearful souls! Who could possibly stand in my way?" she asked, but the two Sisters knew better than to answer. When Mother Pauline's face wore that look and her voice carried that tone, they knew no one could stop her, regardless of who was in her way.

Deciding it was best to see the bishop before his afternoon rest, all three went to his room at noon. With mixed feelings they knelt beside the bed. The

410

bishop blessed them quite solemnly. Each one thanked him and then said goodbye. Later that afternoon they left for Rotterdam and the steamer that would lift anchor the next morning, July 16.

Very early that day Mother Pauline attended Mass and received Holy Communion. It was a day of special memory—the feast of Our Lady of Mount Carmel, the day when, thirteen years ago, she had pronounced her final vows and Bishop Martin had received them. She wondered how he was, and she prayed fervently for him on her way to the steamer, which was soon to leave. She did not want to miss the Sisters who had boarded already the evening before.

She found them without any trouble and embraced them one last time. Except for mutual sending of love and greetings to Sisters at home and the final goodbyes, they spoke little. But there was much in their hearts. Would they see each other again—and Bishop Martin?

Mother Pauline waved until she could no longer see the boat and then set out for the station to wait for the first train leaving for Brussels.

Meantime, things did not go well in Mont St. Guibert. The night of the Sisters' departure for Rotterdam, the bishop had very little rest. When the doctor came the next day, Wednesday, he found nothing definitely alarming, yet he was uneasy. Then, as he stayed on for two hours, watching the patient closely, he began to give him more medicine and apply a chest plaster, for the bishop was in very much pain. Bronchitis had set in, the doctor admitted.

He returned again in the afternoon and stayed

411

with the bishop several hours. At last, the worried Sisters begged him to stay all night to give some relief to the very sick Monsieur L'Abbé, and he gladly agreed. As he sat by the bed with the hours dragging by, time, for him, became slowly-forming beads of perspiration that trickled more and more down the patient's face. The doctor rose and walked to the Sister watching nearby.

"Sister, we must send for another doctor that I know in Louvain and have him come here. The abbé's illness is progressing rapidly, and there is nothing I can do." He dropped his hands helplessly.

Sister moved as fast and noiselessly as possible and hurried downstairs to see that the telegram was sent. Some time earlier, Sister Lioba had left to meet Mother Pauline at the station and tell her the news.

Word of Monsieur L'Abbé's illness had travelled, and the pastor of the town parish as well as the pastor from nearby Hevillers were quick to respond. Together they came to do whatever they could for their sick fellow-priest. When they arrived in the sick-room, they found Father Stamm, the bishop's secretary, not known to them, already with him. The two newcomers promised him their prayers, blessed him, and left. The doctor followed them to the door downstairs.

"Monsieur le Curé," he said to the pastor of Mont St. Guibert, "I advise that our patient be given the last sacraments." Without waiting for a response, he went quickly up the stairs again. With that, Sister Angela answered the doorbell.

It was the doctor from Louvain. She brought him upstairs immediately, and the local doctor introduced him to Bishop Martin. Sick as he was, the bishop yielded to still another examination and answered all the doctor's questions in fluent French even though it was difficult for him to speak. In a little while the two doctors left the room and stood at the top landing of the stairs, consulting together.

Sister Angela, waiting below, looked up. She saw the doctor from Louvain shake his head sadly.

"You have done all one can do," she heard him say to the other. "There is nothing more I or anyone else can do."

Once more she took her rosary in hand but then hurried to answer the door again. The two visiting priests were still standing to one side, unwilling to go, waiting and watching.

"Oh, Reverend Mother!" she cried, as she opened the door to Sister Lioba and a very tired Mother Pauline. She wanted to say more, but could not trust herself to do so without crying. It was seven o'clock Wednesday evening, and she wanted to bring refreshments for them both, but Mother Pauline's face told her it was out of the question. She took their cloaks and then quietly introduced the two priests to them.

"Reverend Mother," said the pastor of Mont St. Guibert, "the doctor recommends that Monsieur L'Abbé receive the last sacraments. Perhaps you should tell him that."

"Thank you, Monsieur le Curé," she said, nodding.

"Father Stamm is here, too," added Sister Angela. "He is with—he is upstairs in the sick-room."

Swiftly Mother Pauline mounted the stairs and passed the doctors.

413

"He has but a few hours more, Reverend Mother. There is nothing more we can do," the local doctor said softly. "My colleague here from Louvain has confirmed it. I am sorry."

"I am sure both of you have done all you could, Doctor. Thank you, gentlemen," she whispered, and her eyes were very sad.

Gently she opened the door and went in. Silently, with a look, she greeted Father Stamm and faithful Hubert and then knelt at the other side of the bishop's bed.

"Your Grace," she said distinctly, bending close to his ear, "the doctor thinks it advisable for you to receive the last sacraments—now." There was just the hint of a catch in her voice.

The bishop's eyes opened and slowly focussed on her face.

"Ah yes, yes,' came his answer, throaty, wheezing, labored, but with a spurt of energy. He reached out a hand to where his priest-secretary was standing on the other side of the bed. "Let Father Stamm— give them—to me," he said with real effort.

Immediately Mother Pauline and Hubert left the room, and while Bishop Martin made his last confession to Father Stamm, they prepared for Communion and Last Anointing. Hubert was to get the special candle and beautiful crucifix blessed by the Pope with the indulgence for a happy death given personally by him to Bishop Martin on his last visit to Rome. Mother Pauline called some Sisters to accompany Father Stamm with lighted candles from the chapel when he would carry the Blessed Sacrament and the holy oils to their dying bishop. She told all the other Sisters to follow in procession up to the patient's door.

Soon Father Stamm looked out, and Mother Pauline, with Hubert, went in quickly. Once more she knelt by the bedside and drew out her Office from her worn travelling basket. Opening to a certain page, she began to pray in a clear voice:

"By Thy agony, O Jesus, and Thy death struggle . . . ."

Instantly the bishop's eyes opened wide. He seemed to be listening intently.

" . . .in union with and in veneration of Thy three hours' agony on the cross, I offer Thee my last agony and the pains of my death."

A wonderful smile lit his whole face. Those were his very own words! It was a prayer he had spoken once spontaneously while preaching in his cathedral to his beloved people. He could still see them all before him. How dear to him were the memories of all the hours spent there with them! And Mother Pauline must have written down that prayer the very same day. Then—her voice, continuing on, called him back to the present.

"Place Thy cross, Thy passion, and death between me and Thy judgment . . .Holy Mary, show me a mother's heart!"

"Amen!" said Bishop Martin loudly.

By now it was eight o'clock, and Father Stamm hurried to get the Blessed Sacrament. The bishop prayed silently in preparation while Mother Pauline prayed and watched. In a few minutes four Sisters with lighted candles entered the room and knelt as Father Stamm devoutly carried the Eucharistic Jesus to the bishop. With more longing than ever, Bishop Martin received His Lord, and a solemn hush fell on everyone—in the room and outside, down the stairs. Each person there felt keenly aware that here was a meeting of heaven and earth that no one wanted to disturb.

At last Father Stamm arose, took the holy oils and began to anoint the bishop. With great respect and affection he said the prayers of remission and forgiveness as he traced the cross in blessed oil on the dying prelate's eyelids, ears, mouth, hands, and feet. Mother Pauline gladly assisted him, receiving the used cotton balls and re-covering the patient's feet. The bishop lay very quiet and docile, eagerly taking in every word and movement with great devotion and joy. Many eyes were filled with tears, but there was not a sound.

Gradually most of the Sisters retired to their rooms or the chapel, and the two pastors and the doctors went home. Mother Pauline, Father Stamm, and Hubert, and a few Sisters kept vigil. Close to eleven o'clock, Mother Pauline noticed the change in the bishop's face. Father Stamm immediately began reciting the prayers for the dying. He held the indulgenced crucifix to the bishop's lips and then put it in his right hand, holding it with him. Mother Pauline took the burning death candle from Hubert and placed it in his left hand, supporting it with hers.

Very feebly Bishop Martin moved the crucifix upward, and Father Stamm realized his intention. Lovingly he helped the bishop's hand trace the cross in the air over the bowed heads near the bed, and as he brought it down, the candle in the other hand flickered strongly as if a last profession of faith. Then the bishop's face dropped to the side, and he was gone. Bishop Martin's exile was over! He was free, truly free! He was home. It was our Lady's feast, July 16, 1879.

Everyone prayed in silence for a while. Then Mother Pauline wiped her eyes and rose, patting the kneeling Hubert gently in sympathy. She nodded to Father Stamm. She knew that he and Hubert would carefully prepare the bishop's body for burial. But she had to hurry! She had a plan, and there wasn't much time.

Word of the bishop's death spread quickly through the house, and Mother Pauline sent for Sister Hildegardis, the superior of the convent.

"My sympathy, dear Reverend Mother," she said, offering her hand.

"Yes, thank you, dear Sister. There is no need for anyone to stay up any longer now. Have the Sisters retire and get some sleep. Tomorrow please make everything fitting to the dignity of our beloved bishop when his body is laid in state. Spare nothing. As you know, I have much to do tomorrow, so I shall not be home. I must still have a meeting tonight. Please call Sister Chrysostoma."

As Sister Hildegardis hurried away, Sister Agnes, still a little breathless, joined Mother Pauline.

"Come, Sister Agnes," said Mother Pauline, striding ahead with her long masculine step, "we have much to do."

Just then Sister Chrysostoma appeared behind Sister Agnes and hurried to catch up with her. Before long, the two of them were seated with Reverend Mother in her office. It was midnight, but Mother Pauline was bristling with energy, her earlier fatigue completely gone.

"Now," she said to the other two, bending toward them, her voice full of challenge and controlled excitement, "this is what we must do tomorrow—" and they planned and prepared for several hours.

The next morning all three knelt at the couch downstairs in the room where the bishop's body had been laid. It was clothed with beautiful and valuable vestments presented by the Countess von Ansembourg and was surrounded by large, graceful green ferns, a cross, and candles. There was no sign of his rank as bishop. Mother Pauline looked at the peaceful face. He could not bless her and her project here, but she knew he would do so very definitely from heaven. So after a brief prayer for him and to him, she and her companions bravely set out on their errands.

After arriving in Brussels, they agreed on a meeting place, and then went their separate ways. Sister Agnes went to purchase the double casket and other things needed to transfer the bishop's body via railroad. Mother Pauline and Sister Chrysostoma went on to Malines to see Cardinal Dechamps and tell him of her plan.

The cardinal had known Bishop Martin from Vatican Council I, having worked closely with him there. He had learned to love and respect him and was sorry to hear of his death. He listened to Mother Pauline first with interest, then with surprise and admiration at her loving loyalty to the bishop and, most of all, at her daring. For, according to the mind of German government officials, Bishop Conrad Martin was a fugitive and a traitor to his country. Also, since the motherhouse of Mother Pauline's congregation and its entire property had been taken by the government, burying someone considered to be an outlaw on this property would be a great risk and could bring serious consequences.

Pauline was fully aware of all that, yet she was not afraid. She was absolutely sure that God would see her through, but she would have to work through the necessary human channels.

"Your Eminence," she said humbly after she had outlined her plan, "I am asking for your permission, your blessing, and your help in this matter—please." She stopped, waiting hopefully.

"Reverend Mother Pauline, what you propose to do is very courageous and commendable, and I most certainly give you my approval and blessing. As for help—" he opened a drawer and took out a business card and hastily wrote a note on his official stationery.

"Go to see this gentleman immediately, Reverend Mother," he advised as he handed both of them to her. "Here is a note of recommendation and introduction from me. He is a trustworthy lawyer and will make the necessary documents for you and also direct you to the other authorities you will have to see."

He rose and came toward the two Sisters who knelt for his blessing. With real feeling the cardinal made the holy sign over them and placed a hand on each one's head.

"God go with you," he said huskily and then stooped to help them to their feet.

The rest of the day was spent going from office to office obtaining necessary documents and passes. The lawyer recommended by the cardinal was very obliging. After drawing up the papers, he directed the Sisters to the Belgian Foreign Office, the Office of the Interior, and the German Consulate. From all these they would have to obtain approval and passes to accompany the body of a priest back to his native Germany. But with the presentation of the papers he had given them, they should have no trouble.

He was right. All the officials made out the travel permits, the Belgian and German seals for the coffin were issued, all as ordinary affairs, and the two Sisters were finally on their way. Later they met Sister Agnes, who was having the two coffins delivered, and all travelled home to Mont St. Guibert.

That evening the pastor and his assistant again visited the Sisters, expressing sympathy for the loss of their chaplain. The Sisters knew it was time now to tell them his true identity and that his body would be taken home. The two priests were shocked to learn who he really was. The assistant had been the bishop's confessor during his stay in Belgium, and he was quite shaken.

"If only I had known he was the bishop of Paderborn!" he said vehemently. He understood now the sad little smile of the bishop when he had told him once to replace his shabby cassock with another one.

He turned and looked at the pastor. Both had the same thought. They had not been able to give him due honor in life, but they would do so now in death. The entire village would be invited to his Requiem Mass, and there would be a fitting procession to the train.

But not everything was ready yet. Mother Pauline called Sister Wunibalda and told her to take the very next train she could get to Paderborn. Once there, she was to have the burial crypt in the lower level of St. Conrad's Chapel prepared for the bishop's body.

Then she was to notify Father Meyer, the head of the Paderborn cathedral, of the bishop's death and ask him to conduct the burial service for him very secretly in St. Conrad's Chapel. Everything, in fact, was to be done very secretly, and Mother Pauline counted on Sister Wunibalda's prudence.

On Friday, the next day, the bishop's body was placed in the oak coffin, and this, in turn, was placed in a leaden one. Then it was carried to the chapel of the convent-school, where the clergy of the area celebrated a solemn high Mass attended by the Sisters, boarders, and townspeople. Meantime, Sister Wunibalda left for the train station.

In the afternoon the double casket was carried to an elegantly-prepared hearse that would take it to the train station. The procession that followed was unusual for that little town. Four priests in full vestments, Father Stamm in civilian clothes, Hubert, the bishop's valet, several gentlemen, the Sisters, and all the boarders escorted the body from the house. The older girls wore black dresses and white veils while the younger ones were dressed fully in white.

For the transfer of a body by train, Belgian law required that it be placed in a special car, that it be accompanied by responsible persons, and that its arrival be telegraphed ahead to all stations on the way.

Mother Pauline was careful, of course, to send the telegram, which was in French. The name she gave was *Professeur Martin* since the bishop had been a professor of theology. It was customary in Europe to refer to priests who were professors simply by that title.

As she finished the message, she waited for the

clerk to finish writing it and tell her the charge. She took for granted that he had taken down all her words correctly. She paid him, thanked him, and left.

But if Mother Pauline had seen what he tele-graphed, she would have been surprised and possi-bly even amused. Somehow the clerk did not hear the whole word, *professeur*, but only the last syllable. In French this would sound like the word *soeur* which means *sister*. As a result, Mother Pauline's telegram read that Sister Martin's body was being transferred to Paderborn for burial. Transferring the body of a nun was nothing to excite any official at any station and would be considered quite uneventful.

Was that mistake providential? Was it God's little joke on Bismarck?

The spacious funeral car of the Belgian train, draped in black, was open and waiting as the proces-sion came to the station. It had two compartments. In one of them, the coffin was placed on a slab, and on that were a crucifix and two fixed candles. In the other, Mother Pauline and Sister Chrysostoma took their seats, both praying silently. Before long, the train pulled out.

Meanwhile, Sister Wunibalda arrived in Pader-born Saturday morning and immediately went to see Father Meyer. She told him of Bishop Martin's death and that Reverend Mother was bringing his body to Paderborn by train. Would he perform the services for the bishop at St. Conrad's Chapel? It would all have to be done with great caution and secrecy.

The good priest was filled with such a mixture of surprise and sorrow and joy all at one time that at first he could hardly manage a sensible sentence.

After a moment, he assured her that he would be there. Several hours later he received a telegram from Mother Pauline asking him to be at the station at one o'clock that afternoon.

The train stopped with a screech at the boundary between Belgium and Germany, and there was some delay. Soon the two Sisters heard the sharp clack of military boot heels outside the compartments. Mother Pauline's pulse began beating faster, but her heart was clinging trustfully to the Lord. Sister Chrysostoma began squeezing her rosary beads so hard that her knuckles went white.

The German officers entered their car, glanced at the coffin and seal, checked their passes in silence, and moved on. There was no further incident.

At one o'clock the train pulled into Paderborn, and Sister Wunibalda was there to meet Mother Pauline and Sister Chrysostoma. Father Meyer stood at a distance so as not to attract notice. As the Sisters moved away toward home, the coffin was placed by trainmen onto a special wagon and driven to the motherhouse. There the driver was directed to take it to St. Joseph Chapel.

In a little while Father Meyer arrived, and Mother Pauline explained that the crypt was not yet ready. But at five o'clock the word came, and the workingmen carried the coffin to the crypt. Softly but solemnly Father Meyer said the graveside prayers for his heroic bishop with only Mother Pauline, Sister Chrysostoma, Sister Wunibalda, and the workers present. Then all watched as the vault was cemented shut by two masons.

The men left, the candles were extinguished, and the three Sisters went up the stairs with Father.

Mother Pauline closed the gates and locked the chapel door. She turned, and facing the others, put her hands together and heaved a tremendous sigh.

It was done! Thanks and praise to God, it was done, her whole body was saying. At last their dear bishop was back in his beloved diocese as he had so long wished—at rest—in spite of Bismarck and his Kulturkampf.

But for her there could be no rest yet. Now that the dangerous task had been accomplished, Pauline knew that she must inform the current church authorities about the bishop. Without delay she hurried to find the vicar general, who was at Bad Meinberg, and later the auxiliary bishop of Paderborn and told them both the whole story. Naturally, they were at first shocked, sad, and then glad.

However, this news was too good, too wonderful to be repressed. The auxiliary bishop and vicar general called a meeting of the priests who composed the cathedral chapter, and they officially notified the government in Berlin of Bishop Martin's death and of preparations being made to give him public honorary burial in the cathedral of Paderborn. Father Meyer was busy, too. On Monday he informed the editors of several newspapers of the event, and soon the news had spread to all the people. Meantime, the brave lady who had caused all this stir took the early train with her companion back to Belgium Monday morning.

On Tuesday the doorbell of the motherhouse in Paderborn began ringing constantly, and the Sister at the door was overwhelmed by the endless inquiries of people about the bishop. Although other Sisters were sent to the entrance to help her, the crowds and questions increased so much that Sister Wunibalda travelled to Mont St. Guibert to get Mother Pauline's instructions in the matter. She returned to Paderborn the same day with Sister Appolinaris.

Reaction from Berlin was just as swift. The Honorable von Puttkammer, who had succeeded Dr. Falk as Minister of Public Worship and Instruction, sent word immediately to Paderborn that permission was granted to hold a public funeral for Bishop Martin at the cathedral. After all, he knew he could hardly send a dead body back into exile, and there was nothing to lose by allowing the funeral.

The dean of the cathedral notified the Sisters at the motherhouse of Berlin's answer, and on Wednesday, Mother Pauline received a telegram from Sister Wunibalda, asking her to come for the funeral. That same evening Sister Chrysostoma and Mother Pauline boarded the train again for Paderborn, arriving the next morning.

Once more Mother Pauline went down to the crypt in St. Conrad's Chapel. There, with her brother, George, and two priests from the cathedral chapter, she watched the masons who had sealed the grave five days earlier, reopen it. The body was identified and officially recognized as that of Bishop Conrad Martin, and then the coffin was carried to the chapel of the motherhouse where the Sisters were busily preparing for a service.

Dark green branches decorated the chapel and softened the brilliance of the many candles. Black streamers hung from the pillars. The coffin was placed in the middle aisle, and at its foot were the signs of the rank of bishop. However, the chapel's door to the outside was still locked while a large crowd kept gathering in the street near the chapel. Conflicting rumors were going around: "The bishop is here!" "No, he is dead, and they say his body is in the Sisters' chapel."

It was already ten o'clock at night, but no one could persuade the people to go home. Finally, when some began to climb the wall and demand to be admitted, George advised the Sisters to open the chapel door. Eagerly the crowds began to stream in and prayerfully file past the casket of their exiled bishop. Some of the men volunteered their services to keep order, and the procession of the bishop's flock paying him their respects lasted all night.

The visitors were not only from Paderborn, however. They were coming from far and near—from Eichsfelda, Bishop Martin's home town, from Saxony, and other places in his widespread diocese. But the people of Paderborn would not be outdone. All agreed that, even though there would be no banners or flags in the funeral procession, not a single adult of the town would remain at home when their heroic bishop was laid to rest.

The next day was July 25, 1879, the feast of St. James, and part of the eight-day celebration of the feast of St. Liborius, who was the patron of the diocese. The streets and plaza near the cathedral were jammed with crowds as the solemn procession brought the bishop's body from the Sisters' chapel to the cathedral. Never before had Paderborn seen such a triumphant funeral! Three hundred twenty-five priests in full vestments followed by thousands of faithful people accompanied the body of Bishop Conrad Martin to the cathedral as the choir of high school students alternated singing with the choir of the cathedral. Both aristocrats and nobodies walked side by side in their tribute to this man of God.

Sister Hildegardis and Sister Angela, who had served the bishop while he stayed in Belgium, had left Mont St. Guibert on Thursday and were now with Mother Pauline, Sister Chrysostoma, Sister Wunibalda, and some other Sisters somewhere in the cathedral, offering the Eucharistic sacrifice for the one who had been their spiritual father and guide, their teacher, their friend, their chaplain.

Actually, it was Pauline who had made all this possible. Yet, as she knelt there, so many and such different feelings flooded her that she no longer remembered the daring and the danger. She was conscious only of an enormous fluid rainbow of emotions flowing in and over her. There was dark loss and grief and worry, but there was also bright hope and trust and joy—and triumph. Yes, that was it—triumph! Gratitude and triumph! How great and magnificent God is, and how wonderful His Church! As she heard the mighty music from hundreds of singing voices that boomed against the high vaulted ceilings of the cathedral, praising God and begging His mercy, she thrilled with pride and enthusiasm in being part of it.

Because of the huge crowd, many could not get into the church for the Requiem Mass. But they were content to stand outside, unable to hear or follow the ceremonies. Later they were permitted to pass the main altar below which the bishop was buried until a special side chapel could be built for him as a memorial.

Little by little, after the closing prayers for Bishop Martin, the great church emptied and grew quiet.

Mother Pauline and the Sisters came out the huge cathedral door, and suddenly Mother Pauline felt very tired. George, who had been waiting there with Dina for her, came over to her.

"George—and Dina," she said and put out her hand.

"Come home with us, Pauline," he said. "Come to Boeddeken for a few days. You need a rest."

"Yes," added Dina. "Bishop Martin would say so, I'm sure, Pauline. Come."

Mother Pauline turned to the Sisters. They were nodding hard.

"Go, dear Reverend Mother," urged Sister Anna.

"Yes, Reverend Mother, please go," seconded Sister Agnes. "We will all take the time to catch our breath, too," she added laughingly.

Mother Pauline smiled back, then turned toward George's carriage. The Sisters were greatly relieved. They would send her things to Boeddeken.

Chapter XXV

"There is something *very* important on Reverend Mother's mind lately," remarked Sister Agnes, flicking the dust from her habit as she and Sister Hildegardis walked toward the community room one evening in August after Mother Pauline had returned from Boeddeken.

"Yes, she is spending more and more hours than ever in the chapel. Sometimes she is kneeling there before the tabernacle as late as ten o'clock at night," answered Sister Hildegardis. "I must admit I am concerned about her. Oh, not because she prays so much," she added hastily, turning to face Sister Agnes, "but because I can see that she is not as strong as she used to be and yet she seems to be driving herself more and more."

"Well, I know that, for one thing, she is concerned about the money we owe for lawyers' fees and court fees in those lawsuits and the bills for the travel of six more Sisters to South America and the ten to North America," said Sister Agnes.

"True. But you know, Sister Agnes, she has had money worries for the past thirty years—since she founded the congregation. So they should not be the cause of any unusual strain," Sister Hildegardis reasoned.

"She misses Bishop Martin very much, especially since Mr. Martin, the bishop's brother, and Hubert and Mr. Fischer, the lawyer, came and packed all the bishop's belongings while she was gone," Sister Agnes went on. "It's only a month since he died."

They were both in the recreation room by now and were sitting together, leisurely doing some needlework.

"Mr. Martin did leave a money gift and souvenirs of the bishop for the house and for individual Sisters, but I think that somehow Reverend Mother feels abruptly cut off and impersonally treated—although she has never said a single word about it," Sister Hildegardis explained.

"That's possible, but Reverend Mother would never pray so long over anything like that," objected Sister Agnes. "And as for a chaplain and retreat master, we were able to get one temporarily from the Redemptorist Fathers through Countess Robiano. So I doubt that she would be greatly concerned about that."

"That reminds me!" Sister Hidegardis jumped up and laid down her sewing. "Father Witmann will be coming tomorrow to start the retreat, and so will the Sisters from Alsemberg. I had better check on their rooms. Excuse me, Sister Agnes," she said, and hurried away.

The retreat did begin promptly the next day, August 18, and proved to be a wonderful spiritual experience for the Sisters of Mont St. Guibert, of Alsemberg, and the eight postulants who made it. Father Witmann closed the retreat on August 28 with the ceremony of blessing and presenting the eight postulants with their holy habits, rosaries, and new names. It was then that the Sisters most missed Bishop Martin, but they felt sure that he was in heaven, obtaining special graces for them and the new novices.

The next day, with the retreat over, Mother Pauline did not keep her assistants in suspense any longer. She knew that they surmised she was considering something special. So she called Sister Agnes, Sister Augustine, Sister Hildegardis, and Sister Lioba to her office and told them what she had been praying over so much.

"Dear Sisters," she said with a big smile, "as you know, I will be sending eight more Sisters to America in September. Then, later, probably in October, I myself will go to visit every single mission where our Sisters are in North and South America one more time!"

One more time! The words made the Sisters' hearts turn cold. Reverend Mother was already sixty-two, and her health was not at all good. Her own words, "one more time," showed that she herself knew she could never stand another trip of ten months and more than 15,000 miles over ocean and foreign lands! In the last six years she had travelled back and forth in Europe more than 105 times either because of lawsuits or finding housing for the Sisters living or leaving in exile. She had already gone once to North America. She was worn out. They were sure

431

they would lose her—their most precious human possession. This time they *must* do something to stop her.

They did. Each of them, sometimes two at a time, objected strongly. They tried to reason with her, giving every reason they could think of for dropping the idea completely.

She listened, looking from one to the other, and then, smiling again in her wonderful way, shook her head.

"Dear Sisters," she said most kindly, "you shall not have elected me as your Mother in vain. I am not only the Mother of the Sisters in Europe, but also the Mother of our dear Sisters in North and South America. I must look to their needs and welfare too."

After all, she had, by this time, sent about 200 Sisters to the Americas, and there were also new Sisters and new missions she had never seen. Besides, if things worsened in Germany, she had to have a good overview of conditions in America for future planning.

Sister Agnes gave a deep sigh and sat back in frustration, her eyes closed. Sister Augustine, Sister Hildegardis, and Sister Lioba looked at each other hopelessly, with keen disappointment and worry. They were all silent and sad. They could not prevent what to them was tragedy.

Mother Pauline felt their sorrow.

"Sisters," she said lovingly, "will you be satisfied that I make the journey if I write to my brother, George, and he consents to my plan?"

The four looked again at each other for a moment, reading a common thought in each face. George would never agree to that trip, they were sure. He would side with them.

Relieved, they all nodded.

"Yes, Reverend Mother," said Sister Agnes, with the others nodding. "If George says it's all right, we will be satisfied." And they left, content at last and confident of winning.

Mother Pauline wrote to George at once, and he did not keep her waiting. He congratulated her on her courageous decision and said that the congregation would receive untold blessings from this trip of hers. She was delighted and hurried to read his letter to the Sisters. Keenly she watched their faces as she read the last word.

There was silence for a few moments. Finally, from the group came a muffled voice.

"There is only one thing left for us to do now, Reverend Mother," said Sister Agnes in a flat tone. "We must put you and the journey into the almighty hands of God and hope for the best."

Soon after, Mother Pauline informed Sister Anna and Sister Wunibalda in Paderborn of her plan with instructions to tell all the Sisters in Germany about it. Then she left for Alsemberg on September 7 to tell the Sisters there. Everywhere, the reaction was the same: hearts heavy with sadness and concern. Of course, the Sisters were glad that those overseas would have the great joy of seeing and hearing her again, but what would be the price? Certainly it was not the money that worried them.

The next day Pauline left for Malines to get the permission and blessing of Cardinal Dechamps for the journey. He was her bishop now, and he granted her both very readily. Then she began to make preparations for the journey.

But first she must help the eight young Sisters destined for North America. On September 22 she and Sister Lioba took them, some from Alsemberg and some from Mont St. Guibert, to Paderborn where she had business to transact.

All this while, her sharp intuition and keen observation of people and events in Europe were being shaped by her unsinkable hope and joy. She had an unspoken conviction that things would soon turn for the better. No doubt she knew that the new pope, Leo XIII, had sent a letter to Emperor Wilhelm I, telling him of his hopes for a good relationship with the emperor in the near future. No doubt she knew, too, that Bismarck had taken a new political bearing by dismissing Dr. Falk and cutting back the laws of the Kulturkampf. Oh, there was hope; yes, there was hope.

So she had written to Mr. Hafner, a friend of the congregation in Sigmaringen, asking that he rent the convent, if possible, to someone who would be willing to vacate it in the event that the Kulturkampf would end and the Sisters could return. They would have to wait, she said, for the election of new members in the Lower House and for the transactions between Rome and Berlin to take place regarding property of the Church and of religious orders taken by the government. But, until then, the house should be maintained and used. Incidentally, she would very much like to have him take Sr. Chrysostoma to see the "King of the Bees" in that area so he could give her information for the Sisters on constructing bee hives and caring for them.

Before leaving for the long trip overseas, Mother Pauline wanted to see and speak to all the Sisters of the Paderborn houses. On September 25 they assembled in the motherhouse chapel, and she told them of her plans: to leave at the beginning of October, arrive in Chile in November, visit all the missions there, then leave for North America in February. She would then visit all the missions there and return home in September, 1880. Perhaps by that time conditions in Germany would be settled so that she could return to Paderborn and live at the motherhouse, preparing for her last journey to heaven.

Then she asked the Sisters for their prayers and appointed Sister Anna as her substitute during her absence. The atmosphere was heavy with emotion, and the Sisters were silent with sorrow.

As always, she wanted to cheer them.

"Dear Sisters," she said, turning and raising her arms in a constant uplifting motion, "trust in the good God! His divine providence will never, never fail us. I will carry you with me. You will be always in my heart and in my prayers! Come, smile again!" And she gestured toward their lips, smiling her own contagious smile.

The next day she took the eight young Sisters to Rotterdam and brought them aboard the *Schiedam* which would sail the following morning for America. Lovingly she cared for their every need, little and big, and encouraged them as she told each one goodbye, saying she would see them soon again in America.

Now both Belgian houses had again to get ready for a long journey, for Sister Remigia and Sister Thais of Alsemberg were to go with Mother Pauline to South America where they would stay, and Sister Chrysostoma of Mont St. Guibert would be her travelling companion for the entire trip. Everyone could see that Sister Chrysostoma was a natural choice. She was in excellent health and spoke English and French very well. She would be of great help to Reverend Mother.

Very early on October 1, all the Sisters attended Mass and received Holy Communion, asking for a safe journey for the travellers and for strength to say farewell. At 7:30, after breakfast, they lined up in the hallway leading to the chapel where Reverend Mother and her companions would pass. A little distance away Father Witmann waited, too. He esteemed Mother Pauline very much and wanted to show it.

Soon she appeared, the three other Sisters following. With great love and self-giving she bade each one goodbye, knelt to receive Father Witmann's blessing, and then left for the station. There were many tears but also many smiles, good wishes, handclasps, and embraces. Several carriages were in front, and the group of Sisters gathered on the front steps of the imposing building to wave. They watched as the luggage was piled onto a wagon and Sisters Lioba, Hildegardis, Maria, Agnes, and Augustine climbed into the second carriage to accompany the travellers to the train.

The ride was only twenty minutes, and once there, the five Sisters were allowed to stay only a few minutes more. But no one could or would trust herself to speak. All that each could do was to gently clasp Reverend Mother's hand once more in silence as the tears came. But Mother Pauline stood there, receiving them and looking at them with such love and such strength that she seemed transfigured to the Sisters' admiring eyes. Then it was time to go.

That same day the travellers arrived at Bordeaux and three days later, October 4, they boarded the small steamer, *Potosí*, which left the port punctually, according to schedule, for the five-week voyage. Mother Pauline was very glad to learn that there were two Irish Carmelite Fathers from Dublin among the passengers. She knew that now there would be the chance to attend Holy Mass daily during the trip. They introduced themselves and were very pleased when Mother Pauline told them she had everything they needed for celebrating the Eucharist. The captain gladly allowed them the use of the second class smoking room for saying Mass at a very early hour.

By today's standards, the *Potosí* was quite small and had none of our modern conveniences. Travelling on it for any length of time meant real hardship. Mother Pauline's constant arthritis and other ailments were bad enough, but the small, tightly closed cabin was torture for her. So she spent most of the time on deck and even took her meals there.

Before long, she won the esteem of the whole crew. She was dignified but warm and friendly. She was outgoing without being bold, and her wholesome womanliness drew out all their Spanish gallantly, from the captain to the youngest steward. All competed with each other to serve her in some way.

At Lisbon, Portugal, the ship took on many emigrants who were poor. Because there was no more room on the steamer, they were crowded into the steerage. At Mother Pauline's request to let them assemble in a better place on Sunday, the captain allowed them to use the large second class dining-room for Holy Mass, and she was happy to see the great number that came.

Many times those poor people down in the steerage needed help, and although Mother Pauline would gladly have gone, illness prevented her. Sister Chrysostoma, however, would quickly comfort her by offering to go to them immediately, and she did. When she returned, she often found Mother Pauline, though exhausted and miserable from seasickness, awed by the vastness of the sky and sea, praying aloud. Even at night in her little cabin, when the rough tossing of the ship, the nausea, her arthritic pain, and the suffocating heat made it impossible for her to sleep, Sister Chrysostoma could hear her whispering God's praises.

"My God, how great You are, and how good!" she would say over and over. She was so taken up with desire for her Beloved that she forgot even her discomfort. It was only the thought of receiving Him next morning in Holy Communion that helped her survive the night because of the tormenting thirst caused by her violent seasickness. In order not to break the fast from food and drink before Communion, which at that time, began at midnight, she would take a small piece of ice at ten P.M. and then nothing more until after Mass the next day.

One day, as Sister Chrysostoma and the two other Sisters returned to the deck after their meal, they saw that Mother Pauline had a visitor. Silhouetted against the sky and railing of the ship were the seated figures of the nun and a little girl, perhaps six years old. When the child had first seen the tall, black-robed lady, standing with her back to her, she gave a half-smothered cry of fear and surprise that made Pauline turn around. But then she had sat down and smiled at the little wanderer, and the two

438

were now eyeing each other. Where had the child come from? wondered the Sisters. How had she gotten up here?

They watched from a short distance as Mother Pauline gently put out her hand toward the little one. The child quickly pulled back, but her large black eyes were still fixed on Mother Pauline's. Slowly, gradually, she began to come closer, until finally, she shyly put her hand in the one stretched out to her. Mother Pauline took the hand in both of hers, then drew the bony little body to her lovingly. Not a word was spoken, but their communication was eloquent.

Lovingly Mother Pauline patted the tangled black hair, smoothed and adjusted the ragged dress. She looked into that small, serious, wondering face and knew only too well what the child wanted. She began to look around, and so did the little girl. Instinctively, they sensed there was food somewhere.

Mother Pauline rose, turned, and looked toward the Sisters. Yes, they had brought her a tray. She motioned vigorously to come and smiled, very pleased.

"Come, Sisters, come!" she called, turning the child toward them. The wondering eyes grew bigger as they saw some more ladies in long black gowns with white hats and bows.

"I have a little friend who is very hungry," said Mother Pauline, as she took the tray from Sister Thais. She drew the thin child to the chair beside her and sat down again. There was only a bowl of good broth and some bread, for that was all Pauline had wanted or could retain. First she took the white bread and buttered it. Smiling, she handed it to the child, who, still very serious, scarcely took her eyes from

Pauline's face.

Cautiously the little one raised it to her mouth and bit. Slowly she chewed, and then, as the good taste filled her mouth and stomach, broke into a smile while her small white teeth went quickly to work on the bread.

Mother Pauline was not sure the girl could handle the soup. She put the tray on the child's lap and then gave her the broth, spoon by spoon. It smelled good, and the hungry little girl was not wary any more. She sipped the soup from the spoon without losing a drop, and before long, she reached to take the spoon herself.

Mother Pauline looked from the child to the Sisters. She was delighted.

"Reverend Mother," said Sister Chrysostoma. "I'll get another tray," and she turned to go.

"No, no, Sister," exclaimed Mother Pauline, putting out her hand. "No, I couldn't eat anything anyway," she said, wrinkling her nose and patting her stomach. "It's better if I do not eat. But this little one—" she paused as she saw the soup and bread gone without a trace, "this little one really needs it. And she shall have it. Every day, if she wants. Bring an apple next time, too, Sister."

"She must be from the people down in the steerage section. But I wonder how she found her way up here—and unnoticed," said Sister Remigia.

"It doesn't matter," answered Mother Pauline. "I'm glad to have her company—and I think she likes our food," she added, laughing. "I shall tell the captain about it and get his approval."

It was almost as if the child understood. She was looking up at Pauline now, and grinning. The lady in black was kind. She would come back. And she did. Every day at noon Mother Pauline shared her lunch with her little friend, speaking German to her with great love and friendliness. It did not matter that the child knew no German. She knew from her voice that this lady loved her, and she was relishing the love even more than the food, which she devoured.

By October 22, they had reached Rio de Janeiro, a Brazilian port that Mother Pauline called "magnificent!" They left their "colossal steamer," as she termed it, in a small boat that took them ashore for sightseeing. On their return, they were able to watch the cargo being loaded and unloaded and saw before them almost literally, a mountain of beautiful oranges, 76,000 of them!

Five days later, the ship arrived in the harbor of Montevideo, Uruguay, where the two Carmelite priests, after celebrating the Eucharist, left the boat. Mother Pauline and her companions were sorry to see them go and prayed fervently that God would not leave them without Mass and Communion for the rest of the long trip. Just as the boat was about to set sail, the chief deck officer met Mother Pauline as she came out of her cabin. He was followed by two Jesuit priests and a Jesuit Brother. Smiling, the officer told her that they were Spanish Jesuits, who could speak French, and that they, like the Sisters, were on their way to Concepción. Mother Pauline beamed, welcomed the Jesuits in French, and thanked the officer heartily. God was good! Once again, He had provided that they would have Holy Mass and Communion.

The last day of October dawned, and that night, they had reached Puenta Arena in Patagonia, Chile.

There they stopped for a bit and then set sail again while it was still night. Mother Pauline was in a festive mood because she was looking forward to the next day, November 1, the feast of All Saints—a glorious feast and one of her favorites. It was one of the most beautiful times of the year in this region, for this was their springtime, unmatched in its loveliness and sunny southern sky.

Mother Pauline drank in all the fresh air and vibrant sunshine and gorgeous sky, but for some time every day in November, she left the deck and withdrew to her cabin. There, holding her blessed crucifix, she made the Way of the Cross—her favorite devotion from childhood on—for the Holy Souls in Purgatory. She had also made it a custom to close each day by singing the litany of Our Lady with the Sisters, concluding with a hymn in her honor.

The feast of St. Charles, November 4, was the anniversary of her first vows, and she had looked forward to celebrating it especially at Holy Mass and Communion. But there was no thought of it. Very bad weather was coming, and no one was allowed on deck. They were sailing through the raging waters of the Straits of Magellan, where the Pacific and Atlantic Oceans met in violent conflict. As they passed through to the Chilean side, called "Land of Desolation," a lashing hail storm hit the ship, and the sailors tied down everything possible.

The night was miserable. About eleven o'clock, Mother Pauline was thrown from her narrow bed against the sharp edge of a table. The impact was so strong and so painful, it was as if she had been stabbed with a knife. For at least a year she felt the effects of that fall. She arose the next morning with difficulty and could not stay even on the small sofa without help.

The storm whipped and tossed wildly for several days until November 6. Then came a perfect southern wind that carried the ship northwest toward the City of Ancud, perched on the Island of Chloe which overlooked all the other tiny islands.

However, the passengers, including the Jesuit Fathers, left the steamer at Coronel, and Mother Pauline and the Sisters looked excitedly for Mother Gonzaga. When no one appeared, the Sisters asked the captain's advice. He referred them to the travel agent.

"Take the steamer, *Santa Rosa*, which is about to leave, to the port of Talcahuano and from there take the train to Concepción," said the agent.

The captain gladly supplied a small boat and an officer to take them to the *Santa Rosa*, which is owned by the same company as the *Potosí*. A second small boat followed, bringing their pieces of luggage. On board the ship, they met two gentlemen who knew their Sisters, and these men took excellent care of them. The Sisters had an admirable reputation in Chile, and the visitors were sharing in it. At the customs office, they did not have to open any bags, but they missed the train to Concepción and had to wait at a hotel for the next one.

Meanwhile, one of the Jesuit Fathers, called the Visitator, had gone ahead to Concepción by wagon and horse. There he sent a Brother to the Sisters in Concepción to tell them of Mother Pauline's arrival in fifteen minutes at the train station.

The Brother returned, laughing and shaking his head. "They wouldn't believe me. They said it was impossible."

Then, Father Visitator went to the Sisters himself, telling them that it was true. He himself had travelled with Mother Pauline and three other Sisters. In a few minutes Sister Eleanore and a Spanish Sister were hurrying to the train station accompanied by a Brother who had been sent to care for the luggage.

What a meeting took place when the train pulled in! All were still breathless as they got into the two carriages provided by the Jesuits and drove to Concepción where the priests were awaiting them. From there they were taken to the convent of the Sisters. Excitement and joy reached their highest peak, and Mother Pauline met not only the dear Sisters she had sent across the ocean, but also the sweet Spanish girls who had entered her congregation and were now young professed Sisters or novices or postulants. She found the native Chileans very charming indeed. It was there that Sister Remigia and Sister Thais stayed for the time being in their first Chilean mission.

Mother Gonzaga was on visitation in Ancud, Mother Pauline was told. So they telegraphed to Sister Laurentia, her first assistant, who was in Santiago with two other Sisters, arranging for an orphanage there. Sister Laurentia came some time later, accompanied by Dona Modesta Vidal, the benefactress who had founded their house in Concepción, and was most eager to meet Reverend Mother. Then they took Mother Pauline and Sister Chrysostoma in a small steamer that cruised along the coast past Lebu, where the Sisters were working among the Indians.

The Jesuits had sent a messenger to tell those Sisters that Mother Pauline was coming, so they came to meet her. Pauline was intensely disappointed that her steamer could not enter the port. Instead the Sisters got into a very tiny boat and rowed to her, risking their lives in the very stormy sea. They spent an hour and a half on board with their foundress, stepped gaily back into the little boat and then were lost to sight behind a towering wave. Some minutes later they could be seen again, wet but happily waving limp handkerchiefs.

In Coral the boat stopped long enough to let the travellers board another small steamer that sailed up the river to Valdivia. There was danger in transferring from one small steamer to another in these badly equipped ports because of the enormous waves, but Mother Pauline ignored it. Her love was stronger than dangerous waters. It was impossible to notify the Sisters at Valdivia of the visit, so they were beside themselves with joy and surprise when Mother Pauline and Sister Chrysostoma stood at their convent door!

Quickly the Sisters gave the visitors a tour of their hospital and then took them back to their steamer. The next day they arrived at Ancud. There, too, it had not been possible to let the Sisters know in advance about Mother Pauline's arrival, so the travellers hoped and waited for some way as they came down the ramp from the boat.

Meantime, Mother Gonzaga, who was visiting the Sisters in Ancud, was deep in her thanksgiving after Holy Communion in the Sisters' chapel early that morning of November 19, 1879. Suddenly she felt a tug on her long mantle. She turned her head sharply and looked into the expressive, excited face of a little deaf-mute boy, who was especially well-treated by the Sisters. He was signing frantically, trying to tell her that some Sisters were at the harbor and that one of them was very tall.

Now Mother Gonzaga had received no word of any kind from Europe that any Sisters were coming to South America. So she shook her head at the youngster and motioned that he should go and let her pray in peace.

In a few minutes, several students came to her and whispered, "Reverend Mother from Paderborn has come!"

Again Mother Gonzaga turned, her starched coif brushing the face of the girl nearest her. "That's impossible!" she said almost out loud. "You are mistaken, girls." Then as they stood there, firm and sure—"Did you yourselves see her?"

"Yes, yes," they answered together. "There are three Sisters there at the harbor!"

Astonished and hardly believing, Mother Gonzaga hurried from the chapel and beckoned to Sister Auguste to go with her.

"They tell me that three Sisters are supposed to have come here on a steamer. I guess we shall have to go and investigate the matter."

Just as they were leaving the convent, the little deaf-mute boy came running to them, waving something in his hand. He was making happy sounds and when he reached them, he thrust a thick black book into Mother Gonzaga's hands. She stared at it for a moment and then let out a delighted cry. It was Mother Pauline's prayerbook, her Office! She was truly here!

Mother Gonzaga patted the boy's head affectionately, picked up her skirts a little, and began almost to run, Sister Auguste trailing her. They must hurry to the harbor!

But they had not gone more than a hundred steps when they stopped dead. Mother Pauline, Sister Chrysostoma, and Sister Laurentia were coming toward them. Mother Pauline put out her arms, and Mother Gonzaga rushed into them. There were cries of joy and happy tears, and veils and bonnets were crushed in mutual embraces. Who would have thought that the one most important to them would be there, in person, with them, at the end of the world, in its most remote part—today?

Immediately Mother Pauline asked whether it would be possible to receive Holy Communion. Fortunately, Holy Mass was still being celebrated, and the Sisters quickly took the travellers to the church. The time for Holy Communion could not come too soon for Pauline, and in a short while she welcomed her Lord with a love and devotion so sincere and all-absorbing that it moved everyone near her. She had often fasted many long hours since, for years, she had had to travel very much and would keep the Eucharistic fast from food and water from midnight till any hour of the day when she could reach a church and receive Communion.

While she was praying in thanksgiving, Mother Gonzaga and the Sisters hurried to prepare the convent and her room for her reception. As she left the chapel, all the Sisters, the Chilean novices and postulants greeted her, and, although she could not speak Spanish, her sweet, kind ways told them what they needed to know. At the same time, she was easily able to read their faces and movements. The word that Reverend Mother had arrived spread quickly through Ancud, and many people, including the bishop and priests, benefactors and leading citizens wanted to meet her.

In Chile the month of Mary is from November 8 to December 8, ending in her great feast of the Immaculate Conception. Since it was springtime, lovely flowers decorated her altar and the Sisters held a devotion to our Lady every evening, which Mother Pauline faithfully attended.

She visited the public hospital in Ancud, too, which the Sisters staffed, stopping to hear the patients, giving money to the poor ones and encouraging and praising all those who worked there.

At the motherhouse she met the novices and postulants and the eighty day students who attended the school conducted by the Sisters for the public. Later Mother Pauline gave the Sisters a most beautiful talk on charity and humility, little guessing that the whole time she spoke, they were seeing in her the living example of her own words.

As soon as Reverend Mother had arrived at Ancud, word was sent to Sister Innocentia, the superior at Puerto Montt, that she should come to Ancud by returning steamer to greet her. The news brought joy to everyone there, and Sister Innocentia did come. She stayed at Ancud for two weeks while her Sisters at Puerto Montt prepared for Mother Pauline's visit there.

At the end of the two weeks, Mother Pauline said goodbye to all at Ancud after Holy Mass. "Let us try to become saints," she said, words that were on her lips and in her letters more and more as time went on. It was December 5 when she and her companion, Sister Chrysostoma, with Mother Gonzaga, boarded the steamer that took them to Puerto Montt in seven hours.

Here was a port town with scattered buildings, surrounded by virgin forests. Before the Sisters had come, a godless anti-German group of people had taken over the building meant to be the hospital. So the young superior, Sister Innocentia, with only a strong trust in St. Joseph, had worked tirelessly with her Sisters to find shelter and beds for the poor sick. Then she had managed to find a shed in which to teach and house some homeless orphans. Later, the German colonists had built a school, a church, and a convent. Many families were presently sending their daughters as boarders to the Sisters at Ancud for schooling. Now, when they saw the Reverend Mother, the people were asking for a school for their boys.

Mother Pauline was pleased and full of admiration for the complex of one-story buildings with adjoining courtyards. The buildings could not be higher than one story because of frequent earthquakes. There were well-arranged hospital rooms and at the other end, school rooms. Close by was the beautiful landscape bordering the sea where trade ships and passenger steamers came and went.

Often here, too, the Sisters invited poor Indian girls of marriageable age to spend several weeks with them. During that time the Sisters instructed them and prepared them for confession, Communion, Confirmation and Matrimony. The course was ended with the celebration of their marriages which were performed in the convent church.

"Do you try to make this occasion as beautiful and memorable as possible for these poor people?" asked Mother Pauline of the Sisters.

"Oh yes, Reverend Mother," answered Sister Innocentia. "We give them a big basket of nourishing food for their trip home," she added.

"Dear Sister, that is really not enough," she said, smiling.

"No, Reverend Mother? What else should we give them?" asked Sister Innocentia wonderingly.

"Let me show you," said Mother Pauline. "Do you give them breakfast after the wedding? Please show me where," as Sister Innocentia nodded. She followed the young superior to the guest dining-room.

"Ah, yes. It is nice," she commented as she looked around the white walls and plain table and chairs.

"Now, there should be a tablecloth here on the table and a bouquet of simple wild flowers with an ordinary but large enough cake, dear Sister. That would do for several couples, as I know you have several couples married at a time. You know, dear Sister, you must make their wedding day as beautiful and unforgettable as possible!" And she looked fondly at her own ring.

One day not long after, she asked the Sisters to have a sturdy horse brought to her. They looked at her in surprise, but she only smiled and repeated her request politely.

"You told me that the only way to get to Valdivia is by horseback, and I really want to try to go to see

450

our Sisters there as well as everywhere else. I *used* to be a good rider." She shrugged a little. "But now I don't know, and there is only one way to find out."

"Reverend Mother!" protested Sister Innocentia. "Please! You haven't been feeling very well—I mean, you should rest. The Sisters in Valdivia will understand."

"Dear Sister Innocentia," said Mother Pauline quietly, patting her hand, "don't worry. I may be old, but I'm not entirely senseless. Just let me try. If I can't do it, I promise, I won't insist."

"Very well, Reverend Mother," sighed Sister Innocentia, and she called on Don Franzisco Schwerter, the father of two of the Sisters, who owned good horses. The Sisters learned to ride on his horses, and after some time he came, leading toward them a very gentle horse, named Castinie.

Mother Pauline smiled, went to the horse, and spoke to her lovingly, stroking her nose and mane. Though Pauline's words were German, the horse understood. She heard the tones of affection in that voice, regardless of the language, and she responded by shaking her head and neighing.

The others were amused and started to help Mother Pauline mount the horse. But many years of no riding made it very difficult for her to reach the stirrup and swing up. That did not stop her. Finally, with the help of a little stepladder and many strong hands, she managed to get into the sidesaddle and grasp the reins. But the tremendous exertion was too much. Her head began to spin and they feared vertigo would seize her and make her quite sick. She had to dismount.

She tried again the next day and the next, but

451

each time it was the same. At last she had to give up the idea of going herself to see her dear Sisters at Valdivia. They would have to arrange something else.

Before most people realized it, Christmas had come. It was unusually beautiful and very different there in Chile. Both Mother Pauline and Sister Chrysostoma marvelled to find roses and lilies around the crib. For them the sounds of Christmas carols in Spanish, mingling with the rich fragrance of those spring flowers made a strange but pleasing combination. The Christ Child was lovelier than ever amid the brilliant colors, and Mother Pauline had more fun than the children watching them dismantle the Christmas tree of its goodies.

On the eve of the feast of the Three Kings, January 5, 1880, Mother Pauline and her companion left in the evening for the steamer which took them, after seven hours, to Ancud. Then they were taken by sloop to the mainland where they made a farewell visit to the archbishop and, after that, to the convent. The Sisters were greatly surprised and keenly disappointed all at one time, first on seeing Mother Pauline and then hearing that she had to leave again for the steamer after two hours. This time the sloop took them to the harbor of Coral, which is two hours' distance by boat from Valdivia, the place Mother Pauline had wanted so much to reach by horse. Informed of her coming by a rider, the Sisters from Valdivia came to meet their Mother, but were very upset to hear that she could be with them only two hours. She had to leave that same evening to continue her trip.

The two Sisters who had come expected to take

her back with them, and so the three who were waiting for her at home were bitterly disappointed when she did not come. Sister Christine cried inconsolably when the two sad Sisters came back and announced that their Mother had to go on because she still had thirty houses in the United States to visit.

The next morning she and Sister Chrysostoma arrived at the mining-town of Lebu, a Catholic community in the middle of a still pagan province. There the Sisters conducted a small hospital and two schools, one with fifty boys and another with eighty girls. However, they, too, could spend only two hours with Mother Pauline and stood with tears on the shore, where swift, foaming waves continually dashed against the many rocks.

As the travellers stepped into a smaller steamer needed to take them farther out to their larger steamer, which could not navigate the dangerous, shallower waters along the town's shore, two of the Sisters of Lebu begged to go along on the small steamer up to the bigger ship. They wanted to have more time with Reverend Mother. The crew agreed, but the water was so wild that the two new Sister passengers had to lie on the floor and hold tightly to something immovable to that they would not be thrown back and forth or out of the vessel. The wind and waves were roaring so loud that no one could be heard, and the Sisters could not speak a word to Mother Pauline. They could only hang on for dear life and say a sad goodbye when the boat reached the bigger steamer.

The stormy eight-hour voyage took them at last to Lota. The following evening they passed Coronel and arrived at Talcahuano, the harbor of Concepción. They boarded the train at Talcahuano, and in twenty minutes, were finally in Concepción, extremely tired and worn out, but happy that the South American trip was completed.

When they arrived at Concepción, the Sisters were halfway through their annual retreat of eight days. They had expected Reverend Mother, but on hearing nothing and having no arrival, they had begun their retreat. By the fourth day, they were seriously meditating on the place of eternal punishment when the guests came.

"We found them deep in hell when we arrived," wrote Mother Pauline humorously in a letter to Germany, "and then, in our honor, retreat was suspended in order to welcome us and have a two-hour recreation with us."

She and Sister Chrysostoma decided to take advantage of the chance for spiritual refreshment and joined the Sisters for the four last days of the retreat. At its close, Mother Pauline told them that she had decided to go back alone to Lebu and spend a week with those very sad Sisters there. That announcement caused real alarm, and everyone tried to change her mind about that trip. They reminded her of the danger of the trip, of its hardships, of her inability to speak Spanish. It was no use. She loved those pioneer Sisters and felt as bad as they did that she had not been able to stay with them. Nothing like hardship would stand in her way.

So on January 16, 1880, she left for Talcahuano and from there for Lebu to spend a week in that little mission. She also made several changes while there to lighten the Sisters' burdens.

Happy that she had brought joy to the Sisters in Lebu, Mother Pauline returned to Concepción and stayed for a week. There the Sisters had an academy for young girls, staffed a public school for girls and a home and training center for wayward girls. Then she had visits from important people, like several ladies of high rank and the bishop, who asked that the Sisters open a boarding-school for girls.

From Concepción Mother Pauline and her companion went to Santiago, the capital of Chile, where the Sisters conducted two institutions. But first Pauline went to nearby Chillan, where she visited an old childhood friend, Caroline de Lommessen, who was a Religious of the Sacred Heart like her sister, Anna. They had many, many things to tell each other, and the afternoon passed too fast.

It was a hot day, and by six o'clock that evening, the two travellers were back in Santiago's train station, red, perspired, and covered with dust.

What was their great surprise to see, not only two Sisters to welcome them, but also a crowd of fashionable ladies with fine carriages, among whom was the German ambassador with his young wife. Mother Pauline and Sister Chrysostoma tried to dodge the crowd, but the other carriages escorted theirs to the convent, whose doors stood wide open in welcome.

All the Sisters came forward to greet Mother Pauline and then led her into the church. There the director of the Sisters' home for orphaned boys, Father Jara, greeted her and gave her a blessing. She was escorted through waiting lines of orphans and Sisters to the sanctuary as little girls tossed flowers before her and an orchestra of thirty musicians played appropriate music.

She and her companion were given special seats, and Father Jara delivered an enthusiastic sermon, praising the courage and love of Mother Pauline in braving the difficulties of a second ocean trip to visit all her daughters in North and South America.

After the church celebration, Mother Pauline was taken to the convent parlor to meet the ambassador and ladies. Finally, when all had gone, she was able to greet the Sisters and have supper with them.

The visitors stayed in Santiago for two weeks. During that time, Mother Pauline suffered much from the intense heat, which was usual during January and February. She experienced also the poor living conditions of the buildings for the orphans and the Sisters. Because of the war between Chile and Peru, there were many war orphans. At the request of the bishop, the Sisters took care of these children, and the government paid an annual fee for them. Because there was room for only 120 children, other orphans had to be turned away for the war orphans.

But the buildings were unfinished, and the furnishings were poor because the ladies who had begun the orphanage earlier had neither time nor money to provide for everything when the orphanage was turned over to the care of war orphans only. There were no ceilings in the rooms, and dirt fell frequently from the roof onto everyone in the rooms. The windows were very small, giving little light and air.

While she was there, a new bishop was installed on February 11, and Mother Pauline found, in talking with him, that she did not agree with him on numerous things. Some of these were written in a contract regarding the buildings and other matters. He wanted her to sign this contract in the name of the congregation. Although she was a very energetic woman and never lost time in a project, Mother Pauline was not hasty in signing anything. So she thought about it and prayed and finally signed. There were things she did not like or want, but because she highly respected church authority, she yielded. She knew from experience that, in time, things at first bitter often turn sweet.

Four months had now passed since she had arrived in Chile. It was time to leave this remarkable land and move on. Mother Pauline gave the Sisters a final conference as she had in all the other houses.

"Let your soul be ever directed to God in pure love, which seeks nothing apart from the fulfillment of His will. Foster a tender intimacy with our Eucharistic Lord. Accept the purgatory of your daily work and suffering with patience; thus by constant purification you will advance steadily toward heaven," she said, not realizing that she had summed up her own life in those parting words.

"Goodbye, dear Sisters,—till we meet in heaven."

Chapter XXVI

Valparaiso was very much alive when Mother Gonzaga and Sister Laurentia arrived there with Mother Pauline and Sister Chrysostoma, and the Sisters, with their own schedule of activities, fit right into its busy flow of action.

"We will go directly to the convent of the Sisters of Providence, Reverend Mother," said Mother Gonzaga, "and after some rest, we shall do a little shopping, get your tickets for the trip to the United States, and make the arrangements for our new mission here in Valparaiso. Would that be satisfactory, Reverend Mother?"

She looked at Mother Pauline with grave concern, still recalling the shocking words that Reverend Mother had said to her days earlier when she had begged her to stay in Chile for a year—"Dear Sister, I cannot. I shall not live much longer."

Against Mother Gonzaga's will the tears began again to rise at the thought, choking her voice and blurring her eyes. She fought for composure.

To her relief, Mother Pauline nodded pleasantly, and soon they were being welcomed by the Sisters of Providence who conducted a hospital for wounded soldiers there. They showed the four travellers their places in a large, airy dormitory and did everything possible to make them, and especially Mother Pauline, comfortable and at home.

It wasn't long before the guests were ready to go again, and they all spent the afternoon taking care of business, returning to the convent very tired. Mother Pauline was extremely fatigued and retired rather early. But she was hardly in bed when terribly painful spasms seized her, and her Sisters did not know what to do.

Mother Gonzaga wanted to call some of the Sisters of Providence who were nurses, but Mother Pauline forbade her.

"They need their sleep badly," she said. "Under no conditions must you wake them."

Frequently the intense pain wrung groans from her, but each time she prayed, offering the suffering as reparation for sin. This went on for a long time, the Sisters watching helplessly, until at last the spasms lessened and ceased, and all could go to sleep.

The next day, the day before sailing, they arose early, went to Mass and Communion, and paid some visits of courtesy. In the afternoon, their trunks and baggage were transferred to the steamer, and at three o'clock, Pauline and her companion boarded the ship, *Lima*, with Mother Gonzaga and Sister Laurentia as visitors until the boat would leave. Some Sisters of Providence came, too, kindly bringing coffee and ice and other things to ward off seasickness. At last it was time to go.

Mother Pauline and Mother Gonzaga said mutual thanks with deep emotion.

"God bless you! God bless each and every dear Sister! God bless Chile!" said Mother Pauline with great emphasis, and she made the Sign of the Cross over the land.

The visitors had to leave, and the passengers crowded to the railing to wave goodbye. On the dock, Mother Gonzaga, Sister Laurentia, and the Providence Sisters stood waving, too, until the ship was out of sight.

"Oh, why did we let her go?" cried Sister Laurentia, looking tearfully into Mother Gonzaga's face.

But there was no answer. They both knew they would never see Mother Pauline again.

For the first few days on the ocean, its name, "Pacific," seemed to be a mockery. It was anything but calm and peaceful and seemed to be like a contrary child, throwing tantrums. Immense waves dashed against the ship as if the ocean was stamping its feet against the boat in a fit of childish fury without reason.

For ten days they sailed through the war zone between Peru and Chile and could get little rest day or night. It was true that the Sisters had what was considered the *Lima's* best cabin on the upper deck. But the first night, the two Sisters were alarmed by loud sounds of continual trampling, roaring, and lowing. The sounds were very close, and they wondered what on earth was next to them.

The next day, Sister Chrysostoma found out that their cabin was directly above the place where ninety cattle were quartered and that it was five feet away from a giant crane that hoisted huge amounts of food and supplies for the Chilean troops onto or off the ship wherever it stopped. That was at least once a day.

She told all this to Mother Pauline and mentioned that there were on board 7000 watermelons alone for the soldiers who fought in the very dry regions of the north. They could expect constant noises and odors of every kind, and they got what they expected.

Passengers who were poor were ordinarily placed in the steerage section, but the cattle now occupied that space. So these people were camped, instead, day and night in the middle of the upper deck, preparing their tea in pots over open fires while both men and women smoked without stopping.

On the fourth day, the ship came into the torrid zone. The ocean became calmer, but the sun was fiercely hot, sending down fiery rays, and the water, in turn, reflected them upward, like a burning mirror, to join the heat that was beating down mercilessly on the boat and its passengers.

The same severe pains that had come over Mother Pauline before the trip, began again and continued. Worst of all, there was nothing that could give her relief. Between the intense pain, the great heat, the rough tossing of the ocean, and the nausea of her seasickness, she was extremely miserable. Added to this was the greatest pain of all, being deprived of Holy Communion, for there was no priest on board and therefore, no Holy Mass. The pain would have been so much more bearable, she knew, had she been able to receive her Lord.

As time went on and with it the unending suffering, she felt sure she was going to die. She would die

461

without a priest. Well, just as the Lord wanted. She put out a hand to Sister Chrysostoma.

"Dear Sister," she whispered, and her face was yellow-white, "if I should die before we reach Panama, let me be buried in the cemetery of Puerto Montt." She stopped and turned her head away, clenching her teeth with pain. Then once more she faced Sister Chrysostoma, taking a deep breath.

"But if I die between Panama and New York," she murmured, "please take my body to Mother Mathilde in Wilkes Barre." She pressed her lips together tightly to suppress a groan.

Sister Chrysostoma took her hand in both of hers and could only nod her head as tears ran down her face. Mother Pauline mustn't die! She mustn't die! A sob escaped her, and Mother Pauline tried to sit up.

"Shhhh, child," she whispered again, putting her finger to Sister's mouth. "Promise me."

"I promise," Sister Chrysostoma said brokenly as she knelt by Reverend Mother's side, but she was terrified with fear. Mother Pauline knew it and squeezed Sister's trembling hands.

Silently Pauline placed the whole congregation in God's hands—the Sisters facing an uncertain future in Europe, the Sisters in the two Americas. He had given them; He would care for them. She wanted very, very much to see Mother Mathilde and the Sisters in the United States. But if He did not want it, so be it. If He wanted to call her now—wasn't that what she had looked forward to for so, so many years? She closed her eyes and prayed softly.

"Father, keep them whom You have given me. Heavenly Mother, extend your mantle to embrace them all!" Then she seemed to sleep, and her breathing reassured Sister Chrysostoma.

Gradually the boat entered the danger area—the war zone. Carefully the captain maneuvered the ship and, little by little, brought it to a stop side by side with two Chilean warships and a hospital ship bearing over a thousand wounded soldiers.

By this time Mother Pauline was feeling much better and had been sitting on deck. Like all the other passengers, she looked with great pity at the burned-out village of Passagna before them and at the ruined barracks of the army that lined the steep hills on the shore. The hospital ship had come only an hour before, fresh from the battle front near Arica.

Suddenly there was a commotion on deck, and the captain with several navy officers, approached Mother Pauline.

"Reverend Mother," said the captain respectfully, lifting his cap. "These officers are from the hospital ship. They have a request to make of you." He turned to the two uniformed men.

"Reverend Mother," said the first officer, bowing and taking off his cap, "we know you are servants of God and of His people. We have many, many wounded men on our ship." He motioned to it. "We desperately need every person we can get to nurse these men. We are hoping that you and your companion here would come to the ship to help them. I promise that you will be protected and well-treated." And once again he bowed, then waited. The second officer bowed too.

Mother Pauline was touched and wished with all her heart that she and Sister Chrysostoma could go and help those poor soldiers who had given so much for their country.

"Sir," she said, sitting up very straight but not trying to rise, "sir, I would be more than happy to grant your request and go to nurse those wounded men. But Sister and I are on an urgent journey to the United States to visit all our houses in that country and assess their needs and strengths. Our time is limited. We really cannot come, much as we should like to."

She watched the faces of the two officers keenly and saw the shadow of disappointment flit across them, controlled though they were.

"But—" she said with great emphasis, "I shall send word to all our houses in Chile, asking them to send some Sisters to you as soon as possible to help with the nursing. Will that do, sir?"

The two serious faces broke into smiles.

"Yes, indeed, Reverend Mother, yes," and they both bowed again and again, holding their caps on their chests. "Thank you very much."

Mother Pauline kept her word. She wrote immediately to Mother Gonzaga, requesting Sisters for that purpose. Several weeks later, she received a letter telling her that some Sisters from every house in Chile had volunteered to care for those wounded soldiers.

On the warships and the shore could be seen many Red Cross workers, doctors, nurses, men, and horses. During the nights there were activities of different kinds—inspections, even shooting. So a blanket of tension seemed to lift from the passenger ship as, after ten days, it sailed out of the war zone and away from the coast of Arica where the sound of cannon thundered over the water. The lapping of the waves, even though rough, seemed gentle and welcome in comparison. The peaceful atmosphere made everyone feel better, especially Mother Pauline, who still had pain at night, but enjoyed pleasant days.

At the boundary line of war operations, the passengers were transferred to another steamer called the *Illo*, which was in the service of a shipping company in England. It, too, carried much freight but much less war equipment and was bound for Panama from Peru.

As it followed its course through the tropical zone, the heat became almost unbearable. Each day new cargo was taken on, and once, during the night, some refugees came aboard. They were the president of Bolivia with his family and staff, fleeing from the hatred of their countrymen.

As Mother Pauline revived, her activity increased, and every evening she was the center of a small group that gathered on the upper deck. The captain also joined them. Because of this contact, she was able to intercede with him for others.

One morning a man in the steerage section was caught stealing, and the captain ordered stern punishment for him. He was shackled by his thieving hand to the mast on the upper deck and made to stand there all day in the burning sun.

By noon, the poor fellow, unable to sit and too exhausted to stand, hung at arm's length from the chain to one side, the cuff of the chain cutting into his wrist. Mother Pauline stood against the railing, supposedly gazing out to sea, but she could not keep from looking at him with pity.

Finally, she walked over to him, and taking her large white handkerchief from her pocket, began to fold it into a soft, narrow band. Carefully she worked the handkerchief in between his wrist and the iron cuff. Slowly the man straightened and touched the sore hand. He looked at her gratefully. That afternoon she was able to persuade the captain to allow him a cool drink of water twice.

On March 12 they crossed the equator into the Northern Hemisphere and headed for Panama. But on arriving in Panama Harbor, Mother Pauline and Sister Chrysostoma were disappointed to learn that the ship they were to take had not yet arrived. The captain kindly permitted them to stay on board. Even though it was winter, the heat was intense, and the mosquitoes were many and pesty. For some reason they let Mother Pauline alone but were attracted to Sister Chrysostoma.

It was decided that on March 16 the captain would escort the Sisters to land where they would take the train across the Isthmus of Panama to Colon and there board the steamer going to New York.

While waiting for the train, Mother Pauline had the chance to talk with a man who was an exile from Russian Poland for twenty-seven years. He was now the most famous engineer in Peru and had built railroads across the Andes, 15,000 feet up. He was much interested in the canal to be built across Panama. She asked about the great difference between the Pacific and the Atlantic Oceans. The engineer confirmed that, saying that the tide of the Pacific was as much as thirty feet high while the Atlantic tide was very low. There would have to be gates and locks to equalize the two oceans at Panama, and they would have to be large enough for big ships. It would take at least eight years to build the canal. Panama was a dangerous harbor.

The train ride cross Panama was truly an unusual experience. Often the trees of the jungle through which they were going were so close to the rails that the train had to literally cut its way through. Every once in a while, teams of black men with knives like swords had to cut down the large weeds and plants that overgrew the tracks. For Sister Chrysostoma, who was a botanist, this was a delight, and she saw many kinds of rare specimens that escaped almost everyone else. The four-hour ride was a magnificent show of primeval forests, Negro villages, vast sugar plantations, and luxuriant vegetation.

By noon they had arrived at Colon on the Atlantic coast. But their ship, they were told, would be two days late in coming, and the city of Colon had no hotel that would meet even the basic needs of a traveller. There was nowhere the Sisters could stay for two days, not even the boat, since the *Illo* could not remain there but had to sail back.

The captain came to their rescue and arranged to have their reservations transferred to the steamer of another line. Mother Pauline was grateful, but she heard that sailing on the Caribbean Sea at the time of the spring solstice was extremely dangerous. "God help us further," she breathed as the ship started across the gulf.

During the next six days they went past poor Jamaica, Cuba, Haiti, the West Indies and on into the Atlantic. They were hoping to celebrate Easter in the United States. By now, they had spent four weeks in the torrid zone, and it was *hot*. But Mother Pauline's arthritic hands were quite well now.

The Negro waiters on the ship fascinated her and she noticed what a contrast their white coats made with their dark skin and how partial they were to the Sisters.

Around March 23, though, trouble began. Violent storms blew up, and one raged for two nights and a day. Instead of the intense heat, they were now experiencing cold and snowfalls. The waves were so high that they covered the ship, even the smokestacks. The noise of the storm was so deafening that they were sure the ship was being wrenched apart, and the travellers felt they would not survive the trip. The storms in the Straits of Magellan had been wild but were mild compared to this.

In her cabin that Monday night, Mother Pauline seriously prepared for death and very fervently made an act of contrition for all her sins. She and Sister Chrysostoma stayed in their cabin like everyone else, and together they prayed all through Tuesday. But the storm grew worse Tuesday night, and they were sure it was the end.

To their surprise, they lived to see Wednesday, and gradually the sea became calmer. By Thursday the passengers were allowed to go up on deck, and they saw the huge funnels of the ship's smokestacks covered with ice and salt from the sea.

On the next day, March 26, Good Friday, after five weary weeks of travel, the steamer finally sailed into New York Harbor. Seven years before, Mother Pauline had seen that same harbor and skyline for the first time and had been an utter stranger there with no one to meet her. But this time, with twenty convents and 208 of her Sisters in the United States, there was a welcoming group at the pier for her and her companion.

Mr. Vehring, a gentleman who had owned a

bookstore in her own town of Paderborn, was wait-ing to greet Mother Pauline, and Father Stumpe from the parish in Melrose, New York, was also there with Sister Sebastiana and Sister Wigberta to take the two travellers back with them.

After they had gone through the customs check, the gentlemen took care of the Sisters' baggage while Mother Pauline sent a telegram to Mother Mathilde at the motherhouse in Wilkes Barre. Then they were on their way home to the convent in Melrose with Father Stumpe and the two other Sisters.

Happy and excited, Mother Mathilde and Sister Philomena went the next day, Holy Saturday, from Wilkes Barre to Melrose to spend Easter with Mother Pauline and Sister Chrysostoma. The Sisters could not help noticing how long Mother Pauline knelt, completely absorbed in prayer, during the service in church and after it .

"Reverend Mother must be completely exhaust-ed after that awful trip," whispered Sister Philomena to Mother Mathilde as they walked home from church. "How can she kneel like that—so long and so still—with her arthritic pain after five weeks of such an ordeal?"

"I don't know," murmured Mother Mathilde in reply. "But one look at her is enough to tell you that we won't have her long. She is ready for heaven, Sister Philomena."

Mother Pauline invited the Sisters from the three houses in New Jersey also to come to Melrose on Easter Monday, and she entertained everyone with stories of her journey to and from South America.

The following day Pauline visited the classrooms of the school in Melrose. The children were at their best, singing their pretty songs and saying their little speeches well for the important visitor. She was very pleased, indeed, and with much grace and love, gave each child a holy picture of Jesus or His Mother Mary or a saint. Later she called on the priests and Brothers of the parish and then spent the rest of the day with the Sisters, who appreciated every minute with her.

On Wednesday Mother Mathilde and Sister Philomena took Mother Pauline and Sister Chrysostoma to Wilkes Barre by train. They left the depot and started for Park Hill. It was evening, and through the dusk came brilliant lights, bursting over the motherhouse in the distance, making gorgeous images in the Susquehanna River that flowed nearby. But those fireworks were only part of the welcome prepared for Reverend Mother.

As they came closer, Mother Pauline stopped, clasped her hands and gave a little gasp of happiness. There it was—the first American motherhouse, standing tall and lovely on the hill! How good it was to see it! It gave real comfort to her heart, which silently felt exiled.

At last they were at the gate, and what a sight it was! All over were signs of celebration. The beautiful American flag was flying, every window in the large house was lit, and two long lines of professed Sisters extended from the gate to the house to welcome their Mother. The love and joy of these Sisters lifted Pauline's weariness away, and she heartily clasped hands on each side as she passed through the ranks to the front door.

There she was met by all the novices and postulants. The sight of their fresh, young, smiling faces moved her deeply. So many of them! Thank God!

The little branch transplanted from the congregation in Europe was growing well in America. It was healthy and strong, and please God, would grow even bigger.

Everyone went first to chapel, and after songs and prayers of joyous thanksgiving, went to the assembly hall. There the children of the boarding school were waiting to welcome Mother Pauline, and after that, the young Sisters presented a short musical program in her honor. Not long after, all went to the dining room for supper.

Mother Pauline's tremendous joy was contagious, and voices were more vibrant than usual that evening at table. Tired though she was, Reverend Mother was so delighted with the motherhouse that she wanted to tour at least part of it before she retired. She was pleased with all she saw, and this was a real joy for Mother Mathilde.

Next morning, she finished inspection of the house and went out to the garden. She had seen the premises around the house earlier when they were wild and uncultivated, so she could really appreciate the great amount of skillful work done by the Sisters here. They had transformed it into the lovely landscape before them now.

As she was enjoying the garden and returning to the house, she and the Sisters saw Father Nagel and the Sisters from Wilkes Barre, leading the children from the parish school in the city, up the hill. They, too, had a program of songs and recitations to welcome Reverend Mother, which they performed with gusto. Mother Pauline won their hearts with her warm, loving sincerity and heartiness and, as usual, gave each child a holy card.

The days passed too quickly for the postulants, novices, and professed Sisters. Many of them had never before seen their foundress, and they were struck by her simple, sincere warmth, her genuine love for all, her unaffected humility. They were almost involuntarily drawn to her, eager to be in the presence of one who was so holy and yet so natural; so very much in love with God and yet so attentive to others. They wanted to know her more and study her.

But it was time to move on. There were still more than twenty widely scattered schools for Mother Pauline to see, and she had set herself the short time of four months to cover hundreds of miles and interview hundreds of people. So on April 16, she was bound for the South. She hoped to escape the terrible summer heat there by going in spring. The first stop on that trip was Harrisburg, Pennsylvania, where she stayed with the Sisters three days.

Her planning, however, did not spare her from heat or thirst or exhaustion. The suffering caused by constant travel in those days was sometimes almost unbearable. But her love was greater, and nothing could stop her from visiting and encouraging her Sisters and those they served. Their love and joy, in return, was compensation enough for her.

Mother Pauline visited in New Orleans and Gretna until May 3, when she left for places farther west. She went by way of St. Louis, where she was to meet with Father Schaefer of St. Nicholas Church and Father Schindel of St. Boniface Church, who wanted Sisters for their parish schools.

She had just returned from one full day's investigation and gathering of all necessary information about the needs and assets of those two parishes and sat down momentarily. Tomorrow she and Sister Chrysostoma would finish their inquiries and come back at noon for final packing. Then they would catch the evening train for Chaska, Minnesota.

"Reverend Mother," said Sister Chrysostoma gently, "is there anything I can get you? You look— tired."

Actually, besides the weariness in Mother Pauline's face, there was a touch of sadness.

For answer, Mother Pauline slightly raised a German newspaper she was holding and tapped it.

"Father Färber gave me this paper and called my attention to this article today. It tells of the funeral of Dina, George's wife! I can hardly believe she is dead, Sister Chrysostoma. George or the Sisters would have written to tell me of her illness and death." Her voice trailed off.

She put the paper down in silence, staring at it for a moment. Dina dead! Poor George. She would have to write to him immediately.

Quickly Sister Chrysostoma tried to think of some answer.

"Perhaps they did write to you about it, Reverend Mother, but it was delayed in the overseas mail. With our moving around the way we do, it could have been sent to another address and now has been forwarded. I'm sure you will hear," she ended assuringly.

It turned out that Sister Chrysostoma was right. The Sisters in Paderborn had written to her the very day of Dina's death and sent the letter to Wilkes Barre, thinking it would reach her soonest that way. It arrived later at another convent.

473

The next afternoon Mother Pauline and her companion took the train from St. Louis and travelled twenty-eight or thirty hours to get to Chaska, Minnesota. They arrived there about twelve-thirty in the afternoon and were very thirsty.

Sister Melania, superior at Chaska, with Sister Brigitta, eagerly greeted the two travellers at the station and quickly guided them toward the convent.

"Dear Sister Melania," said Mother Pauline, "if it is at all possible, I should very much like to receive Holy Communion."

"But Reverend Mother," exclaimed Sister Melania in surprise, "it is already twelve-thirty!"

"Oh, that does not matter," answered Mother Pauline. "I am still fasting. If you would kindly request the pastor, I would appreciate it very much."

The pastor was surprised too, but very much impressed by Mother Pauline's great love for the Eucharist that she would fast so long to receive it. He gave her Holy Communion with great pleasure while his assistant recited the Confiteor and other required prayers. This, of course, was nothing new with Mother Pauline during her travels, but it left a stirring memory with those who witnessed it.

The noonday meal was a gala occasion at the convent that day, and when it was finished, the travellers took a short rest. Then it was on to the school where each teacher conducted an oral examination of her class, and the children had a chance to show their knowledge to the "head Sister."

Once again Mother Pauline and Sister Chrysostoma took the train, this time to Minneapolis. They were met by Sister Cornelia and greeted by the happy Sisters at the convent door. Girls dressed in white also welcomed them with songs and poems. Then the Sisters had Reverend Mother to themselves as they enjoyed their dinner. She toured the classrooms, as usual, and gave each child a small remembrance.

The next day, she went with Sister Chrysostoma and Sister Cornelia to the other Twin City, St. Paul, to pay respects to the bishop of the diocese. After that, Sister Cornelia took the visitors by carriage to see the beautiful Minnehaha Falls and the St. Anthony Falls.

Mother Pauline was consoled by the kindness of the pastor, who celebrated Holy Mass the following morning for Dina. There were several more programs by both children and the Sisters in her honor, that truly pleased her. Friday she spent totally with the Sisters, closing with an enthusiastic talk to them on striving for holiness and practicing real charity.

Her next destination was New Ulm, Minnesota, and since the train left at six o'clock in the morning, everyone had to rise very early. The bell for rising rang at four o'clock that day, and everyone went to chapel to receive Holy Communion. After thanksgiving, all the Sisters gathered to say a sad goodbye to Reverend Mother. They and she knew they would never see her again.

So it was, no matter where she went. She came in all love and humility while the Sisters, the children, the people, the clergy excitedly waited to meet her and outdid themselves to please her. Always there were songs, poems, flowers, programs, examinations, tokens of love and esteem from the school children, and all who were part of the parish. Always Pauline was the smiling, loving Mother, eager to bring the love of God to everyone, completely forgetting her own pain and weariness. People were very precious to her, for in them she saw her beloved Lord.

New Ulm was no exception to the rule, and on May 15, the two travellers were greeted by the pastor, Father Berghold, who met them at St. Peter, a town about forty miles away. He brought them to New Ulm about five o'clock in the afternoon, and the excited children waiting in the classroom for her, rose to the occasion. After her usual tour of all and her final talk to the Sisters, Mother Pauline was ready after six days, to go to Mankato.

There Sister Stephania, superior of the convent in LeMars, Iowa, met the two visitors. They all attended Mass and received Communion in the Jesuit church and then went to the home of Sister Stephania's brother, who lived in Mankato, to wait for the train to Iowa.

Mother Pauline closed her visit in Le Mars on Sunday, the feast of Corpus Christi, (the Body of Christ). After the beautiful procession with the Blessed Sacrament and Benediction, all said goodbye to the two visitors, who left immediately for the train.

The destination this time was Michigan, where Mother Pauline would visit the Sisters in two houses, one at Ionia and one at Westphalia. From there she went to Detroit on June 8 to pay her respect to the bishop and continued on to Rome, New York and then to Albany, where Mother Mathilde and Sister Philomena met her. They discussed plans for the two houses to be opened in St. Louis and after that, all travelled to Newark and Elizabeth, New Jersey to visit the Sisters there.

Mother Pauline next spent two days with the Sisters at New Brunswick and on June 25 arrived in Philadelphia. Examinations were being conducted in the school just then, and she attended them even though she was extremely tired and ill from the great heat. Such fatigue and heat would have stopped an ordinary person, but not Mother Pauline. She moved on determinedly. On July 2, she went to Reading, then to Pottsville and Williamsport, all in Pennsylvania.

Perhaps the most picturesque spot that she visited was the Nippenose Valley where the Sisters had a mission at Bastress. The drive from Williamsport by carriage was through a forest of blooming chestnut trees in the valley that lay at the foot of the Allegheny Mountains. All along the path was blossoming laurel, and the air was fresh and scented by the wild flowers. The sun and breeze played with the trees and plants, that gave cool, refreshing shade. Mother Pauline and Sister Chrysostoma were enchanted by the peacefulness and beauty of the place. It seemed to be raised and set apart from all that was not good and charming.

Suddenly through the woods came a cavalcade of horsemen toward them. They were riding decorated horses and had come to escort the visitors to Bastress. They were the farmers' sons and former pupils of the Sisters, who wanted to honor the newcomers by riding along the sides of the coach. But the path was too narrow, so some rode before it and some behind. Farther up the road, a group of girls in white came to meet them, and Mother Pauline started to alight from the coach. But the superior of Williamsport took her arm. There was more to come.

As they neared the town, they could see many people gathered around the church, and the church bells were pealing joyfully, echoing through the valley. Mother Pauline found everything positively delightful! The church, the school, the convent in this beautiful setting were very inviting. The people were friendly and wholesome, the children, natural and happy. Just to look at the rolling landscape and the mountains looming close, seeming to press against the magnificent sky, gave one a buoyant feeling.

The children were on vacation, but many, who were boarders, had returned for the big welcome to Mother Pauline and her companion. It was easy for the Sisters to persuade her to stay for three days and rest in this relaxing place. They arranged to have their meals outdoors near the colorful flower beds and the garden. In the evenings for their recreation, they sat on the porch, listening to the interesting things Mother Pauline told them about her travels and about their homeland across the sea.

On the last morning, the pastor celebrated Holy Mass in the convent chapel, and a little later, Father Koeper, pastor of Williamsport, came with his elaborate carriage. Mother Pauline served breakfast to both priests, then bade the Sisters goodbye, and got into the carriage. She had spoken beautifully to the Sisters the evening before, telling them to never let the serpent enter their little paradise there in any form whatsoever. Now it was time for Father Koeper to take the visitors to Danville, and they must move quickly because it was hard to leave.

At Danville there were only two Sisters, but Mother Pauline lovingly stayed with them three days. The mission was poor, but the Sisters, the pastor, and children did their best to honor their important guests. In the evenings, Mother Pauline would help Sister Devota carry the food outdoors for supper while Sister Catharina went to ring the Angelus.

The third morning, after Holy Mass, Mother Pauline asked the pastor for his blessing. When breakfast was finished, she blessed each Sister with the Sign of the Cross and said, "Dear Sisters, work hard to become saints!" Then the coach was there, ready to take the travellers to the train. The effect of her leaving was always the same: the Sisters' deep sorrow and their never-to-be-dimmed memory of her and her lovable holiness.

There was a short rest of two days at the mother-house in Wilkes Barre, and then a visit to Dushore, Honesdale, and Mauch Chunk. At Honesdale the Sisters did not get much chance to have Mother Pauline to themselves. The people were eager to meet and speak to her. They came to the convent to visit her and gathered around her after Mass outside the church to talk with her. Pauline was very friendly and kind to all, giving as much time as they needed.

She was especially kind to one man, a cripple, who always came to church in his dog-cart, drawn by a huge Newfoundland dog. This good man had a very special devotion to Mary, the Immaculate Conception, and was delighted when Mother Pauline spent a long time conversing with him in one of the classrooms of the school. He never forgot it. The climax to his joy was her acceptance of a neat case that he had made for her. It held pictures of Jesus and of Mary Immaculate. Mother Pauline was happy that she could help him into his cart, and as they said goodbye, she gently stroked his faithful dog.

At Mauch Chunk, too, everyone was excited. The Sisters had had a very brief chance to greet Reverend Mother when she had first arrived in America in April and her train had passed through there on the way to Wilkes Barre. Now they would have her with them for a while. The visit followed the pattern of all others, but when the time came for parting, they were not sad. They were hoping to see her once more because her train would pass again through Mauch Chunk on the way to New York for her ocean trip home.

And now at last, it was done! The visitation of all the houses in North and South America was completed. She had travelled over 15,500 miles this time in often crude and hard conditions. She had seen and spoken with each Sister of every house privately as she had written in her notebooks. In them she had listed each house of every country and diocese with comments behind them. These notebooks, with her thick Office in German and Latin, she had faithfully carried everywhere in that trusty basket of hers. It had seen many days and many places. It had been with her since she was a young woman attending Mass at Wewelsburg, bringing food and medicine to the poor. She had taken it with her all through the years. It had gone every mile with her and brought comfort to many!

Back at Wilkes Barre in the motherhouse, Mother Pauline found that the retreat for the investing of postulants and the first vows of the second-year novices was about to begin. Fine. She would join them in retreat.

On the morning of August 11, her joy was un-

bounded as she gave twenty postulants, now dressed in their new holy habits and white veils, their Rule
book and white rosary. Mother Mathilde had been a
little concerned whether all these American girls had
the right qualities for perseverance and spoke of it to
Mother Pauline.

But Reverend Mother had no doubts. She voted
to admit all of them to the congregation.

"I myself shall be responsible for this group," she
declared, "and all of them will persevere."

As they crowded around her after the ceremony,
she told them, "I consider this group my very own;
you are all my beloved children for whom I shall care
and pray in a special way."

The entire group did persevere in their vocations.
Thirteen of them lived to celebrate fifty years in religious life and later testified at the process for Pauline's beatification.

On the same morning of that investing, she received the first holy vows of nineteen novices, who
were given the black veil and became junior professed Sisters. For these young Sisters it was a great
privilege to be received by their foundress, and their
joy matched hers.

But she was soon to bring joy of another kind to a
young Sister. On the way home from the church, a
messenger brought word that Sister Demetria was
suffering intensely and would die soon. The Sisters
could scarcely believe it, but it was true. Mother
Pauline hurried to the sick Sister and refused to leave
her for any reason.

Sister Demetria had been very restless, moaning
in pain frequently. Earlier she had asked for a priest,
and finally, at the last fifteen minutes of her life,

Father Schnüttchen came, blessed her, and said the prayers for the dying. Then the young Sister became very calm, and at three o'clock in the afternoon, peacefully passed away with her hand in Mother Pauline's.

It was not just the young Sisters, however, to whom Reverend Mother meant to bring joy. She had a surprise for the older Sisters, too. On August 16, she opened a tertianship or third novitiate at the motherhouse for eight of them during which they would prepare prayerfully for making their perpetual vows. It would last for three months and would be conducted by Sister Barbara, who, like the eight participants, had had to be freed from ordinary duties elsewhere. This was a great grace and joy for the Sisters. They had been forced to wait for this longer than usual because, until now, there had not been enough Sisters to free them from their work for three months. Now a cycle was started, and there would be a tertianship every year, with all the Sisters making final vows in turn!

Although Mother Mathilde and the Sisters all tried to persuade her to stay in America for the winter, Mother Pauline would not yield. She did not have long to live, she said, and she wanted to go home as quickly as possible to see the Sisters in Europe once more. So it was on August 19 that she left many sad hearts behind as she took the train to New York with Sister Chrysostoma, Mother Mathilde, and Sister Philomena. On August 21, the thirty-first anniversary of her founding of the congregation, she boarded the *Donau*, a ship of the Bremen Line. There the Sisters from Melrose, Elizabeth, Newark, New Brunswick, and Philadelphia came with Mother Mathilde and Sister Philomena to see her off.

When the signal was given for all visitors to leave the steamer, she fondly embraced each Sister and kissed her. Then they all stood below on the dock, silently wiping away tears and watching as the moorings of the ship were loosened. As the boat slowly moved away, their eyes were fixed on Mother Pauline, who stood pale and silent, but waved without stopping. Then as the ship passed them, she made the Sign of the Cross over them. They stayed until the flutter of her handkerchief was just a blur on the horizon.

Their Mother was gone, and they would not see her again. But she had succeeded in uniting the congregation of 402 Sisters over three continents, making holy charity its focal point. She had accomplished her mission!

Chapter XXVII

The *Donau* sailed into Bremerhaven on September 2, 1880, and the two Sisters were more than happy to be home again. Mother Pauline had not been seasick at all on the way back, and she had been quietly using the time to form another plan of travel. Actually, she had made up her mind already in America that, once home, she would immediately visit all the Sisters in Europe again. Quickly she sent a letter to Sister Wunibalda in Paderborn, announcing their arrival and asking her to meet them at the station in Paderborn the following afternoon. Reverend Mother wanted to avoid all notice in Paderborn since she was not sure of the attitude of the government toward her yet.

Sister Anna, Sister Wunibalda, and Sister Lioba were there to meet her and joined her and Sister Chrysostoma on the train as far as Salzkotten. From there she wanted to go to Boeddeken to consult with her brother, George, and some of his friends about the advisability of her returning permanently to the motherhouse in Paderborn. She found that George was still away on a trip, and Provincial von Droste met her instead to take her to Boeddeken. Before she left them, Mother Pauline invited the three Sisters to come to Boeddeken the next day so that they could discuss business matters.

The plan worked out very well, and the Sisters had the joy of seeing George and Mother Pauline reunited once more that evening. They left for Paderborn with good news, too. Mother Pauline would be permitted to stay in Paderborn. Sister Anna, who had been Mother Pauline's substitute and was also her secretary and procurator, along with Freiherr von Schorlemer-Alst, a leading member of Parliament, who was visiting George just then, were both able to assure her that relations between the Church and State had improved. Since the Blind Institute had been recognized as a center of public welfare and would not be subject to any unfavorable laws and since Mother Pauline was a permanent member of the board of the Blind Institute, they were sure she could safely reside there. She could go *home*! She could go *home* to Paderborn at last! For a moment, she seemed completely new and young again.

Pauline stayed with George about a week to rest and then sent word to Paderborn that she would come to the motherhouse September 13. There was a great celebration. All the Sisters in the city were invited to tea that evening, and she entertained them with her stories of the Sisters overseas.

But the Sisters were not deceived. In spite of her liveliness and personable charm, they saw the marks of suffering and strain on her face, and, most of all, how she had shrunk. She was no longer so tall and imposing. No, she was stooped, and her firm, manly stride was noticeably slower.

Still, there was no stopping her. She had no more time to rest. She had to visit the Sisters and the children at the Blind Institute. Then she had to go to Herr von Himly to discuss the lawsuit he still insisted on bringing against the Day Nursery she had conducted thirty years before.

It was midnight before she retired, and she was up again at four o'clock the next morning to catch a train with Sister Chrysostoma. They were on their way to Belgium, to Mont St. Guibert for two weeks to plan matters concerning the house there. When they arrived, the announced retreat was in progress, and Reverend Mother would not miss the chance for spiritual renewal. So she joined in the week-long retreat, to the disappointment of the Sisters, who wanted a full week of her company.

A week later she went to Alsemberg to take stock of things there and then returned to Germany. She had found Sister Agnes ill in Mont St. Guibert and recalled both her and Sister Augustine at Alsemberg back to Paderborn.

Her next intended stop was Anrath where the Sisters conducted a hospital, but on the way there, she stopped to visit two old childhood chums of hers, who were both religious now, Sister Anna von Lommessen and Mother Clara Fey. She also visited two priests connected with people in Chile.

The Sisters at Anrath were more than happy with her visit, and from there she intended to go to Gutenberg but, on the way, she took time to see Sister

Meinrada, who was working all alone in the nursery school in Sigmaringen while living quietly with her aged father. That was all the government would permit the congregation to do at Sigmaringen. Only the dear Lord knew what the visit meant to Sister Meinrada.

Three beautiful weeks were spent at the place in Gutenberg with its charming little castle in Lichtenstein. Wisdom told her that this small house and property should become community property, so Mother Pauline travelled to Vienna to make the purchase from Princess Caroline von Lichtenstein, who consented.

She also had the pleasure of seeing her old friend and counsellor, Father Minoux, S.J. at Feldkirch, receiving his spiritual advice in her general confession and his opinion about getting Jesuits for the mission of Puerto Montt in Chile.

At Mühlhausen she was happy to receive the vows of five young Sisters and to witness the clothing of two young ladies in the habit and white veils of novices. With motherly love she accepted the young woman who was just entering the community. This young lady impressed Mother Pauline with her talents in music and language.

There were now only three more places to visit: Weltrus, Oschersleben, and Höxter. Weltrus was close to Mühlhausen, and she was particularly loving to the little community there, who had at the time a very sick superior. Mother Pauline was exceedingly kind and caring to the superior and to the Sisters and made plans to transfer the patient as soon as possible.

Oschersleben was next, where there were just

two Sisters, and then came Höxter, which was one of her favorite places because it was the home for orphans. The Sisters were caring for 102 children that year, and Mother Pauline arrived at a very special time—Christmas!

She had an unusual gift for communicating with children and enjoyed herself immensely with them. She listened with big eyes and great attention as they explained their toys to her, and she, in turn, showed them how to work some of the more complicated ones. She loved to join them as they sang Christmas carols, and when the little ones looked up at her during all the fun, there was no way that they could tell she had a torturing toothache. Only the Sister nurse knew.

By the feast of the Holy Innocents, December 28, 1880, she was back in Paderborn, and announced to the district supervisor that she intended very definitely to live in the Blind Asylum. But he said that, for his part, she could stay in the motherhouse since it was permitted to house sick Sisters there, and her health was not good.

She went to see Himly, too, but she could see that it would take time for the waves of persecution to ebb away. It did not discourage her, however.

"The blessing of the Church is unconquerable, and that is my surest guarantee that the Congregation will flourish again. Let all the demons dance as they please; it will be of no use. God's will is supreme, and I shall continue quietly my task of reconstruction," she wrote to a friend.

The hours of recreation were made very pleasant and interesting by all the stories and incidents she told the German Sisters about their Sisters in North and South America. They never tired of hearing her, and she never grew weary of telling them. But that was not enough.

To her it was extremely important to keep in touch with all those daughters across the seas, and she kept on writing warm, newsy letters to them. In all now, there were twenty-seven houses in the United States, eleven in Chile, and nine in Europe where Sisters of Christian Charity were serving the Lord and His people—a total of forty-seven missions —in the year of our Lord, 1881. In May, she hoped to go to Cologne to open the first *new* mission on German soil.

The severe toothaches that had bothered her of late on her trips and at home continued along with a peculiar exhaustion that she ignored. Then unexpectedly, a message came from Boeddeken. George was ill, and though it did not seem serious, Mother Pauline knew his health was frail and sent Sister Josephine to take charge of nursing him. George had cared for and served the congregation as if it were his own, and it was only right that the Sisters should help him in his hour of need.

But he grew worse, and on March 20, Mother Pauline got an emergency call to hurry to Boeddeken. On Sunday morning he went to confession and received Holy Communion. That evening, the chaplain administered to him the Sacrament of the Sick, anointing him and giving him general absolution.

Mother Pauline stayed by his side, praying with and for him. Tenderly she looked down at him. George was the last of her family, of her dear ones. She had been at the deathbed of each one, and now it was time for George, who had been her support, her adviser, actually her savior through the troubled times. Tears welled up in her eyes.

Although his illness had turned into pneumonia, George was still able to speak. He turned to Pauline and put his feverish hand on hers. There were still some matters he wanted to talk about, and she bent low to catch what he was saying.

After she had answered him and he had finished saying what was on his mind, George sighed and relaxed, sinking more deeply into the bed.

"Pauline," he said, "I'm not afraid. I look forward to seeing the Lord, to heaven—to seeing Dina and Mother and Father—and Bertha and Hermann again! God has been good to me, and I've tried to serve Him, Pauline." He stopped, and she squeezed his hand.

"Pray for me, Pauline," he whispered and closed his eyes. She wiped away one of her warm tears that had fallen on his hand, but her heart was smiling. Good, dear George! What a fine Christian he was. Surely the Lord would be good to him.

It was already late, and the doctor motioned that he was sinking. The rest of the family was called from the short rest they were taking. Slowly, sadly, George's daughter, Maria, her husband, Clemens, her brother, Hermann, Bertha's husband, Alfred, the doctor, the chaplain, Sister Josephine, and Mother Pauline gathered about the bed and knelt.

George opened his eyes, fully conscious, and looked at each one slowly, meaningfully. He could no longer speak, but they knew that he knew them, loved them, and was about to leave them. Then his eyes lit up, his fingers closed tightly over the crucifix after Pauline pressed it to his lips, and there was just one more breath before the end. It was one-thirty Monday morning, March 21.

Like all the Mallinckrodts, George was buried on the family plot at Boeddeken, and the Requiem Mass was said in St. Meinolph's Chapel at the site. He had been much loved not only by his family but by many associates, friends, and tenants of his property. So there was a large group of people to do him honor and attend the simple but solemn funeral.

"I am the last of our family," Pauline told her niece, Maria. "I have outlived my brothers and sister, and now the Lord will call me soon, too," she remarked calmly and almost matter-of-factly.

But, true to her character, she did not sit still waiting for it. She was ready for the call whenever it would come. Meantime, there were people to be cared for.

By March 30 Mother Pauline was given a distinct joy: Himly's power was over! He could harass her and the congregation no longer. His reign ceased with the settling of affairs between government and Church, and Father Drobe was now in charge of the affairs of the Paderborn diocese.

That same day she also wrote an eloquent letter to the German provincial of the Jesuits, begging him to send some Jesuit Fathers to Puerto Montt, Chile to establish a school for boys. Eventually, that was done, and the Jesuit school there became remarkably successful.

Every Monday during Lent, Mother Pauline gave the Sisters a conference, speaking more seriously and with greater emphasis than ever. Her topic was the virtues of community life, and she was extremely practical in what she said. Her hours of prayer seemed to lengthen, and on Holy Thursday, the feast of the Holy Eucharist, she spent hours with the Lord untiringly.

A very big day was coming soon for some of the children of the Blind Institute and some poor children of the city. They were to make their First Holy Communion on the Sunday after Easter, called Low Sunday. Mother Pauline examined the wreaths and decorated candles for the communicants with pleasure, and when she heard that two poor boys, who came every day for a meal for their brothers and sisters and widowed mother, would be in that group, she insisted on giving them their candles herself.

"You and your dear mother must come here tomorrow afternoon for coffee and cake," she told the boys. "We must celebrate Jesus' coming to you. Don't forget!" she said, smiling brightly. The boys shook their heads and giggled happily.

Early next morning she attended Holy Mass at the Blind Institute, her heart full of happiness as she saw the children, sighted and sightless, receive their loving God for the first time. She stayed for the festive breakfast and then gave each child a special little souvenir for the occasion.

That afternoon she spent several very pleasant hours in the motherhouse garden, enjoying the cultivated flower beds and pretty lawn and walking with some Sisters down the path between the linden trees that met in arches above.

The following Monday morning she gave the last conference of the series she had begun in Lent. Since it was now Eastertide, she voiced her wishes for the risen Lord's joy and peace to the Sisters. But especially did she stress practicing overflowing charity, humility, and complete acceptance of God's will, no matter what it might bring.

She spent the rest of the morning in prayer and work and then took the midday meal with the Sisters. Then she met with Sister Lioba on some business matters and later with her assistants, Sister Augustine, Sister Anna, and Sister Agnes.

While they were talking, a severe chill suddenly came over her, and the assistants begged her to end the meeting.

"Reverend Mother, please," said Sister Agnes coaxingly, "go to bed. You really need the warmth when you have such a chill. Come." She took Mother Pauline by the arm, almost lifting her.

But when they got as far as the sofa, Reverend Mother sank down on it, and Sister Agnes could go no farther.

"This is fine, Sister," said Mother Pauline, holding a shawl tightly about her.

"I'll be right back," said Sister Agnes, hurrying away. Very soon she returned carrying a warm drink.

"Here, dear Reverend Mother, this should help to warm you up." As Mother Pauline drank, Sister Agnes put her hand to Pauline's forehead. It was warm—too warm.

"Reverend Mother, you have a fever. You should be in bed," said Sister Agnes emphatically. She took full advantage of her position as Reverend Mother's nurse.

Mother Pauline smiled a little. "Yes, Sister Agnes, but I feel very comfortable here. Please send Sister Lioba to pray the Office with me. I can't do it alone," and she looked at her so winsomely that

Sister Agnes gave in against her better judgment.

Sister Lioba came, but after they had prayed, Mother Pauline herself realized that she ought to go to bed. Her temperature was rising more and more.

She began to feel much worse and asked Sister Agnes to have the priest bring her Holy Communion the next morning since she thought it best that she remain in bed. That night she had very little rest, and violent chest pains began. What was Sister Agnes' surprise to find her up and dressing the next morning at five o'clock!

"Dear Reverend Mother! Oh, no! How can you get up like this when you have such a fever? I thought you wanted Father to bring you Holy Communion here!" exclaimed Sister Agnes.

Mother Pauline fastened her white rosary at her side. "How can I stay in bed when dear Sister Afra will be here at eight o'clock?" she said. Sister Afra was ill and was coming for rest and care at the motherhouse. Mother Pauline wanted to be sure that the sick Sister felt welcome and secure. She must have no doubt whatever that she was loved.

Mother Pauline spent the remaining time until six o'clock in prayer and then insisted on going down to chapel for Holy Mass.

"Please, Reverend Mother, stay here in your room," begged Sister Agnes. But it was no use. So she helped her to the chapel and to the Communion rail. Mother Pauline walked to it and back only with great difficulty and, with Sister Agnes' help, climbed the stairs to her room. Then she collapsed on her bed, fully dressed.

At the same time Sister Constantia was also very ill and close to death, and the priest had been called to be with her. Sister Agnes told Mother Pauline about her.

"Please let me know when Father has come. I want to be there, too," said Mother Pauline. Sister Agnes shook her head hopelessly.

As soon as she heard the priest in the corridor, Mother Pauline got up with great exertion and walked very unsteadily beside him to Sister Constantia's room. Sister Agnes stayed behind them, holding her breath. After Father had given Sister general absolution, Mother Pauline lovingly said goodbye to the dying Sister and, on reaching her own bed, almost fell across it.

"Please, Reverend Mother, get undressed and go to bed," begged Sister Agnes.

"As soon as Sister Afra has come," she answered. "Has her room been warmed up for her and has breakfast been prepared for the other Sisters who are coming?" she asked.

"Yes, Reverend Mother," assured Sister Agnes. "Everything is ready."

When Sister Afra and her companions arrived, Mother Pauline went down to greet them, acting as if everything were normal. She embraced them all, especially Sister Afra, and sat with them a half hour while they ate. Then she took Sister Afra to her room, telling her that Sister Josephine would be there to care for her in every way.

"Is there anything I can do for you or get you, dear Sister?" asked Mother Pauline, holding firmly onto the door knob. Sister Agnes stood guard in the corridor, watching her every move. Finally, Mother Pauline made her way back to her own room, again lying on the bed, fully dressed.

Sister Agnes had meantime consulted the older Sisters, and all of them were seriously worried about Reverend Mother. They agreed that she should have a doctor, but they knew that would not be easy.

"Reverend Mother," said Sister Agnes, as she came close to her bed, "we have called Dr. Haggeney to see Sister Constantia once more, and we beg you, please, to let him take a look at you. You know you have a fever, and we are worried."

"*Ach*, Sister Agnes, very well," murmured Mother Pauline. "Let him come if it will make you feel better." She did not move.

Dr. Haggeney came quickly and soon discovered that her lungs were badly affected.

"Reverend Mother, you are to undress and go to bed immediately for a complete rest—and that is not just for one day. You have pneumonia. I would like you to speak very little and take the medicine I will order for you." He looked at her very seriously, almost sternly.

Now Pauline had never been one to take medicine. So she said sweetly, "But doctor, I am very much afraid of medicine. Medicine is just like grace—it either helps you or harms you."

"Now, Reverend Mother, you know I wouldn't give you anything that could possibly harm you. This medicine will help you. It will break that nasty fever," he said reassuringly. "And I want you to let Sister put this mustard plaster on your chest."

"Yes, doctor," she said meekly. "Thank you," and she nodded to him politely.

That afternoon the fever and chest pains increased. Speaking and even breathing became very difficult for her. Still she asked Sister Lioba to pray

St. Conrad Chapel, Paderborn

the Office with her and after that asked that several letters from America be read to her.

Would she never stop?

Sister Agnes went to her bedside. "Reverend Mother," she said with a desperation that Pauline could not possibly miss, "*please* let those letters go till tomorrow. You simply must rest now."

Reverend Mother nodded, said no more, and just closed her eyes. The doctor came again that evening, and his visit heartened the Sisters somewhat.

Mother Pauline's bedroom was immediately above the chapel and had a window that opened directly into it so that she could easily follow Holy Mass and see the tabernacle from there. She was very grateful for this arrangement, especially now in her illness.

That night, too, was a sleepless one for her, and the nurse, who was resting in the next room, could hear her short, fervent prayers of praise and adoration to the Eucharistic Jesus. Often she asked, "Lord, blot out all my sins." Then again, the nurse even heard "Alleluia!" several times.

Early the next morning, when Sister Agnes came into her room, Mother Pauline said with effort, "Sister, I am very sick. I think it would be best for me to be anointed."

There was something else on her mind at that time, too. At that moment, the priest stopped in her room, and he was just in time.

"Father," she said hoarsely, "would you please dispense me from reciting the Office and our usual prayers—" She broke off, trying to get enough breath to continue. "I find it hard to breathe. I will pray as often as I can." She settled back. It had taken great effort to say that much at once.

"Yes, of course, Reverend Mother," said the priest, "that will please the Lord." Then, as he saw that she was about to speak again, he added, "I will bring you Holy Communion right away."

She smiled and lay back happily. God was good. Father knew what she wanted without her asking. In spite of her high fever and intense thirst, she had not taken any water during the night in her desire to keep the Eucharistic fast customary at that time. She would continue that fast till the very end.

When the doctor came, she asked again for the Last Anointing.

"If you wish to receive the sacrament, you may do so: it will not cause your death," he said very decisively.

Later, Father Meyer came. He heard her confession and then, to her joy, anointed her. Sister Agnes assisted him while seven other Sisters knelt in the room nearby, watching and praying. Mother Pauline was like one transformed. She seemed to be conscious only of the Lord. Her face was striking in its expression of matchless peace, joy, brightness. She remained that way in silent happiness for some time. Finally she said: "Thank you very much, Sister Agnes, for arranging my reception of the Sacrament of the Sick. I am very happy. Now please take Bishop Martin's prayer for a happy death from my basket and say it for me."

Sister Agnes did so immediately, and she smiled gratefully, with real satisfaction.

"Now you are ready for everything, dear Reverend Mother. You have given yourself anew to God for life and death. But you may not give up the hope and the desire to get well again. This is absolutely necessary for your recovery. I am hoping very strongly that the good Lord will not yet take you away from us. We need you too much, dearest Reverend Mother. You may not die yet!" For the first time, the nurse put her face in her hands.

"Our dear Lord needs no one, dear Sister Agnes," she answered softly. "But it is possible that I will recover. All as God wills."

In a little while she called for Sister Wunibalda and Sister Lioba. She asked Sister Wunibalda about debts that were still to be paid and told Sister to take the money she had set aside for Masses to be said for herself and use it to pay their debts. Then she turned to Sister Lioba and asked her to take down some letters.

First, she dictated a farewell to all the Sisters, asking them to pray for her, to keep a good spirit in the congregation, a spirit of loving charity, of humility, of prayer. She was particularly concerned that they show justice in dealing with the students and the servants and that they pay their debts promptly. "Children, I will help you, just as I always cared for you while I was with you here on earth," she told them.

She said a loving farewell to a dear old aunt in Bielefeld and relatives at Boeddeken. She asked Hermann, her nephew, to care for the congregation as his dear father had in the past, to protect it. Last, she dictated a letter to Minister Puttkammer, asking permission to open a kindergarten in Sigmaringen.

At about three o'clock, her brother-in-law, Alfred Hüffer, stopped to inquire about her, and she had him come to her bedside. They spoke of their dear ones and of heaven. Later she asked his advice about her will which she planned to make with Justice Evers at four o'clock.

At last, to Sister Agnes' relief, both gentlemen finished their visits and left.

"Reverend Mother," she said in protest, "this will not do. You must take a rest!"

"But I have accomplished great things today," she managed to get out. Her nurse was much alarmed at her great weakness and sponged her face often, which seemed to help.

"I thank you sincerely," she whispered each time for every small service.

Almost tearfully Sister Agnes told her, "Dear Reverend Mother, do not thank for every little thing. It is so hard for you to speak, and I do it gladly for you." But the thanks continued, even though hardly audible at times.

Although the doctor ordered medicine, meat broth, and gruel to be given her during the night, and although Sister Josephine took the greatest care of her, Mother Pauline had a bad night.

Meantime word had reached the public about her illness, and inquiries were coming in from all sides. The poor waited at the gate, not so much for food as for news of her, praying together for her. Prayers were being offered publicly in the churches.

That day Hermann von Mallinckrodt, her nephew, came to see her and was appalled at her conditon. He insisted that Dr. Weber, near Höxter, be called in for consultation.

"Please, Hermann, no," said Pauline as loud as she could. "Dr. Haggeney is capable and has done all he could." Her face blended away into the whiteness of the bed. Only her eyes stood out, like blue-green burning lights.

"Aunt Pauline, we must. It will not hurt to have another opinion. I will talk to Dr. Haggeney." And he did, standing tall and slim, like his father.

Dr. Haggeney readily agreed. He knew Dr. Weber well, and they were friends.

But Mother Pauline was afraid that Dr. Haggeney might have been offended, so she sent Sister Lioba to explain she had consented only to please her nephew. Her old physician just smiled and sent back the message that he understood and was in perfect agreement.

The following morning they received a telegram bringing Dr. Weber's regrets. He could not come because he himself was ill. Mother Pauline was not sorry.

As the hours passed, she grew more and more silent even when the Sisters were present, but she smiled at them sweetly. Then, in concern, after they had left, she sent a message of apology for not speaking more. Sister Agnes was ordered to apply more mustard plasters, and during the restless night, the patient brought up much phlegm.

By morning her temperature had dropped a little, and the doctor seemed much relieved. He told her she was going to recover.

Mother Pauline was unconvinced. She was even a bit suspicious.

"Sister Agnes," she said directly, "did you post the doctor?"

"Why no, Reverend Mother!" exclaimed the nurse. "Did you think that I asked him to say that just to lift your spirits, dear Reverend Mother?" Sister

Agnes had to smile.

Mother Pauline nodded, smiling a little, too.

"No, I honestly did not see him this morning before he visited you," Sister Agnes, replied, smoothing the coverlet.

At ten o'clock was the funeral of Sister Constantia, and Mother Pauline asked to be told when the procession would pass on the way to the cemetery. She was praying for the deceased Sister when her nephew, Hermann, called again to see her.

This time it was almost impossible for her to speak, so his visit was short. At her request, the priest who conducted Sister Constantia's funeral came to her. She asked for his prayers and his continued kindness to the Sisters in the event of her death.

Her sister-in-law, Thecla, widow of Hermann, came to see Pauline too. For a long time she knelt at her bedside, crying and holding Pauline's hand, which she kissed often. After a while, they talked together briefly, and then Thecla left. Everyone was glad she had had one more chance to speak to Pauline.

As the day wore on, Reverend Mother grew worse, and she asked that the confessor come to her when he came for the Sisters in general that day. She asked too, that the priest bring her Holy Communion once more and that he stay with her at her hour of death.

"I should like very much to be buried silently like Sister Constantia, and please—I believe the Sisters could carry my casket, too, as they did hers."

Tears filled Sister Agnes' eyes. "Yes, Reverend Mother. The Sisters will gladly do as you ask. Now rest."

"And I would be very pleased if just the Sisters attend my funeral, much more than if so many strangers come," she added.

Sister Agnes nodded silently. In her heart there was a great fear. She had noticed that the patient was decidedly worse, and she suspected that the lungs were now paralyzed. She was waiting impatiently for the doctor to make his call.

In due time Dr. Haggeney came and confirmed her fear, sadly admitting there was nothing he could do to save the precious life. He went back to the bedside while Sister Agnes told the Sisters the heartbreaking news.

Sick as she was, Pauline's mind was extremely active, and she sent for Sister Lioba to settle some more business matters. Then she became more quiet.

"Dear Sister Agnes," she whispered to her nurse, "you must get some rest. Let someone else stay with me for a while."

To please her, Sister Agnes went into the next room and begged the older Sisters waiting and praying there to go downstairs. Mother Pauline badly needed more air in order to breathe more easily, and it was too cold to open a window. She promised to tell the Sisters how the patient was doing. No one wanted to leave the house or retire that night.

At one o'clock in the morning, Mother Pauline begged to have her clothing changed. She was very damp and perspired.

"Dear Reverend Mother," pleaded the two nurses, "that is not good. It could cause—your death. Besides, you are too weak."

"There is only one sweat that matters—and that is

the cold sweat of death," she said feebly, but she lay back obediently.

Some time later, however, she begged again for a change of clothing, and the two Sisters could not refuse. But with great, great effort they helped their dying Mother to rise, and with even greater fear and haste, they changed her clothing and Sister Chrysostoma redressed the bed with dry sheets.

Deliberately she was preparing outwardly and inwardly for the great moment—the last moment. She must be ready and fit. Gently and calmly she lay down, holding her rosary in both hands, with the crucifix on her palm.

"Will it soon be time, or must I wait for some time yet?" she whispered to Sister Josephine. There was only one thing more that she wanted—Jesus in Holy Communion.

Sister Agnes thought that it was not yet time, but as she saw the beloved features changing, she called Father Meyer. Mother Pauline wanted first to go to confession.

At two-thirty Father brought her Holy Communion, and no one in the room had ever before seen such devotion as hers. For her there was only one reality in that room, in the world, and He was wrapped in her and she in Him.

Patiently she listened as Father Meyer went on praying prayers of thanksgiving, but she was growing weaker and weaker. Finally, he stopped, and she thanked him.

After some time she asked again for Bishop Martin's prayer for a happy death. "Jesus, be a merciful judge to me," she murmured often.

She moved a hand slightly toward the nurse.

"Greet the Sisters for me," she said, "and tell them that if I have ever grieved any of them, I beg forgiveness of them."

"You have never grieved us, dear Reverend Mother, and we beg your forgiveness, all of us," answered Sister Agnes, tears on her cheeks.

"Please, put the candle on the stove so that I can see it. Please, it would be better if there were two more candles with it. Is there a light in my living-room for the Sisters there?" she asked. She was pleased they were so near.

"O Mary, protect us! St. Joseph, pray for us! May God grant us the grace of perseverance and eternal happiness!" she kept saying. Not even pneumonia or lack of breath could stop Mother Pauline.

At five o'clock it was suggested that Father say Holy Mass which the Sisters could offer for her. That pleased Mother Pauline very much. "Please ask them to pray for the grace of perseverance and a happy death for me," she begged.

Then because it was so early, she wondered about the altar boy. "Has one been called?" she asked. Nothing escaped her mind.

She tried hard to follow the Mass through the little window of her room, asking the nurse about the different parts. Dr. Haggeney had stayed up on the choir loft and stopped to see her after Mass was over.

"Doctor," she said, looking him directly in the eye, "when shall I die? Please don't hesitate to tell me."

"Probably sometime today," he answered in a low voice.

She smiled. "Jesus, be a merciful judge to me!" she said again softly.

Father Meyer had exposed the Blessed Sacrament in the chapel and many of the Sisters were there, praying for her while the older Sisters knelt nearby in her living-room, waiting, weeping, and praying.

At seven o'clock, Alfred, her brother-in-law, came and knelt by her bedside. He had been told by the doctor she would probably not live beyond ten o'clock, and he wanted to be present for her death. Together the two of them had shared the sorrow of Bertha's death, of Hermann's, of George's. Now he wanted to be with her.

Gently he lifted her hand and placed it on his bowed head.

"Pauline," he said brokenly, "bless me and bless my children. Pray for me—for my children. Don't forget us, Pauline. We will be alone now."

Her eyes were very, very bright, and she was much moved. She took several breaths. Keeping her hand on his head, she said slowly, "God bless you, my dear brother, Alfred. God bless each one of your dear children. God bless you all—forever. I will see you again in eternity, Alfred, with Bertha."

He cried, and then rose, taking out his handkerchief. "Thank you, Pauline," he said and turned to go.

"But you will stay here, won't you, dear Alfred?" she said.

"Certainly, Pauline. I shall stay here," he said, backing into the room with the Sisters.

Mother Pauline lay there very calmly, waiting, waiting for Him who was her Love, her Treasure, her All. It was time now. Her turn had come, to go to the place she had longed for since she was seventeen. It was time to go to heaven, to God.

"Jesus, Mary, Joseph, I give you my heart and soul." It seemed that prayer had become more natural to her than breathing.

Sister Agnes noticed that there was no sign of the death agony. Only her features were changing more and more, and the perspiration was greater. Often before she had suffered the agony of death in the dangers of her ocean travel. She was too close to God to fear it now. Sister Agnes pressed the cloth to her forehead, then motioned to bring in the priest.

Then, one by one, the Sisters filed past her bed for one last look at their Mother. She was poised, enrapt, lost in her waiting, in expecting Someone who would fill her complete openness. Though she lay straight, with hands folded over her rosary, her arms seemed to be outstretched, wide open.

She was murmuring indistinctly now, and it mingled with the prayers for the dying. Then she grew silent during the Litany of the Saints.

"All you holy virgins . . ."

"Pray for us" came the Sisters' response. She began gasping.

"All you holy men and women . . ." Two irregular breaths.

Then almost invisibly, Pauline relaxed, inclined her head a little, and went with her Love. There would be no more waiting, for now NOTHING COULD STOP HER.

Inside, second floor of the first Blind Asylum as it is today.
Formerly, twenty tiny cots where in this room for blind children

Living room of the present Boeddeken estate

Epilogue

The day was chilly and overcast in Rome on April 14, 1985, but the crowd of 4000 pilgrims was excited and lively, warmed and brightened by its own joy and happiness. Overhead the bold bells of St. Peter's were clanging, clanging exultantly, deafeningly, endlessly! They seemed to be calling the whole world to witness this glorious event. The air was electric with jubilance! For there, during an outdoor Mass in front of the greatest cathedral of the Christian world, Mother Pauline von Mallinckrodt and Mother Catherine Troiani would publicly be declared Blessèd by Pope John Paul II.

Mother Pauline had died April 30, 1881 and was buried in the crypt of St. Conrad Chapel in Paderborn. She was laid in the very place she had temporarily given the body of Bishop Conrad Martin. Because her Sisters had always been convinced of her holiness, they were able to have the long process of investigation toward her beatification begun on May 1, 1926. It continued on through 1938, 1942, 1958, 1961 as qualified persons studied all her writings, her practice of virtue, and interviewed people who had known her.

Eventually they came to the study of her answers to prayer, particularly to the miracle worked through her intercession for one of her own dear Sisters in 1955. It was their task to see if it was genuine, instant, and lasting. This is the story they heard.

Sister Christophora Ostermann was a young, happy Sister of Christian Charity, who somehow contracted multiple sclerosis. The disease grew so bad that she was taken, legs paralyzed, by ambulance on May 13, 1955 from Paderborn to the Sisters' home for the sick in Wiedenbrück to die. Her case was considered beyond all medical help.

In spite of that, all the Sisters of the German Province and Sister Christophora herself prayed with great confidence to Mother Pauline for recovery. In a few weeks would be Sister Christophora's twenty-ninth birthday. Ah, God willing, He could cure her through Mother Pauline by then.

The day after her arrival there, Sister Christophora tried hard to pick up her New Testament. She needed it to find courage and inspiration. But her sickness made such movement difficult. It took real effort, and she was very weak. By 2:30 she had opened the book but now had to put all her energy into reading because her eyes were badly affected too.

Slowly she made out the place. It was Mark, chapter 11, verses 22-26. "Jesus said to them, 'Put your trust in God.' "

Sister Christophora felt distinctly as if those words had been addressed to *her*. She went on reading.

I solemnly assure you, whoever says to this mountain, "Be lifted up and thrown into the sea" and has no inner doubts but believes that what he says will happen, shall have it done for him. I give you my word, if you are ready to believe that you will receive whatever you ask in prayer, it shall be done to you. When you stand to pray, forgive anyone against whom you have a grievance, so that your heavenly Father may in turn forgive you your faults.

Then Sister prayed, trying to follow the words she had just read.

"Lord, You are the same today as then. Your words were true not for the disciples only but are still so today. Give me the faith I need."

Again she went on reading. Again she prayed.

"Lord, these are Your words. Yes, I believe."

Then fixing her eyes on the words, "Forgive anyone against whom you have a grievance," she forgave everyone from her heart and called on Mother Pauline over and over again.

Mother Pauline's words, "God lets Himself be constrained by prayer," kept ringing in her mind along with two special words of Bishop Baumann, now dead. He had spoken of "reckless faith," and of that she was constantly thinking.

Over and over she repeated, "Yes, I believe!"

Suddenly, she sat up straight. She felt the urge to walk. She *knew* she could walk. She got out of bed, and took about three steps toward the window—all by herself. Then she remembered that she had been told not to get up alone, so she got back into bed, continuing to pray.

She begged our Lady to ask her Son to give this joy to Mother Pauline and to put all in her hands.

"Please, Mother Mary, send a Sister to my room by three o'clock."

At 2:55 there was a light knock on the door, and Sister Julietta opened the door quietly.

"I just wanted to see if there is something I can do for you, Sister Christophora," she said.

To her surprise, the patient said joyfully, "Oh, Sister Julietta, please call the nurse. I want to get up. I know I can get up."

Sister Julietta looked at her with alarm, but said nothing. She left quickly, and in a few minutes, the nurse, Sister Quiriona, was at her bedside. When she heard Sister Christophora's repeated request to get up, she at first thought that the illness had affected the patient's mind. But at last, she gave in.

Sister Christophora was very weak from her long illness, but, with the nurse's help, she walked up and down the room.

Sister Quiriona looked carefully at Sister's legs. There was no more shaking or convulsions, their color was normal, and the paralysis was entirely gone! Sister Christophora was cured!

Soon Sister Belina, the superior, came, and Sister Quiriona showed her what had happened. They both realized something extraordinary had taken place.

Then Sister Christophora went to chapel with the superior and the nurse, and all three thanked God for His goodness and mercy. From there they went to telephone Reverend Mother Mathilde (the second) in Paderborn and tell her the astounding news. Just hearing Sister Christophora herself tell the story over the phone amazed Reverend Mother.

The next day, Sunday, Sister Christophora attended Holy Mass and in the afternoon, Benediction. She did not feel tired or have any pain whatsoever. Today, thirty-one years later, she is still very active in the knitting department at the School for the Blind in Paderborn. Many of the pilgrims who attended the beatification were measured by her for sweaters and

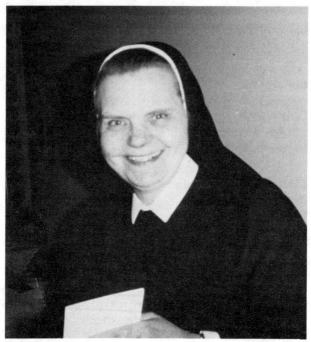

Sister Christophora Ostermann, cured of multiple sclerosis through Mother Pauline

were awed to meet her.

The miracle of her cure has been examined and tested by three separate committees of doctors, theologians, and cardinals. The seven doctors unanimously attested to the genuiness of the cure after carefully examining all the evidence. The theologians and cardinals likewise accepted it. Finally, Pope John Paul II accepted it. He gave her a marvelling smile as she was presented to him in Rome, Yes, Sister Christophora was cured instantly through Mother Pauline's intercession. There can be no doubt that Pauline von Mallinckrodt is in heaven.

So it was that on that overcast, windy April day the impressive procession of priests, bishops, and Holy Father came to the outdoor altar before the doors of St. Peter's to begin Holy Mass.

Solemnly, joyously, the special choir of St. Peter's called the *schola*, with voices in four-part harmony, alternated with the pilgrims in singing the well-known Mass of the Angels.

After the *Kyrie* (Lord, have mercy), Archbishop Degenhardt of Paderborn and Bishop Cella of Frentino each begged Our Holy Father to proclaim Pauline von Mallinckrodt and Catherine Troiana to be Blessed.

Then came an expectant hush in the great piazza. Pope John Paul II rose, holding the special document, and in a solemn voice pronounced them Blessed—in the name of the Father and of the Son and of the Holy Spirit. He also announced their feastdays, naming Pauline's as April 30.

The people burst into cheers and applause, and as they clapped and shouted, the veiling over the huge pictures of Pauline and Catherine, hanging high

512

above the crowd on either side of the cathedral's front balcony, gently rippled upward, revealing the two new holy ones of the Church for all to see! What a thrilling moment!

The Mass continued in a great surge of thanksgiving. A blind girl, symbol of Mother Pauline's special love, read the Epistle written in Braille. Sisters of both congregations of Pauline and Catherine read the intercessory petitions. Children and adults from countries served by both religious orders carried special gifts in procession to the Holy Father at the Offertory to represent the work done by both congregations. He received them all most lovingly. It was a touching and beautiful sight.

The Eucharist grew more solemn and moving as it went on—especially the Consecration. Pope John Paul II, bareheaded, his white hair blown awry by the wind, held Jesus up, turning Him to left, center, right and back—for all to see. Pauline was surely there, adoring with all the saints and angels.

Then long lines of priests processed into the crowd, carrying the Eucharist to even longer lines of happy pilgrims, eager for the Lord. Relatives and Sisters of Pauline and Catherine received Holy Communion from the Holy Father.

Finally, the Pope solemnly intoned his blessing, the organ and choirs boomed "Holy God, we praise Thy name," and the crowd cheered and clapped.

Once again, frail human beings have been proclaimed holy. Two servants of God have let Him bring them to holiness. There is hope, much hope for all of us.

Blessed Pauline has said, "Children, I will help you," and she meant it. Sister Christophora is not the only one she will help. Her love is too great for that. Constant petitions are rising to her, and she is constantly answering.

"All you holy virgins..." (Blessed Pauline, you are certainly one of them), PRAY FOR US!

"All you holy men and women of God..." (Blessed Pauline, you belong to them), PRAY FOR US!

There is a lovely, striking portrait of her that can be carried away as a souvenir—for imitation. It is in 1 Corinthians 13:4-7:

Charity is patient, is kind; charity does not envy, is not pretentious, is not puffed up, is not ambitious, is not self-seeking, is not provoked; thinks no evil, does not rejoice over wickedness, but rejoices with the truth; bears all things, believes all things, hopes all things, endures all things.

Blessed Pauline, show us how to love God and all others!

REFERENCES

Autobiography of Pauline von Mallinckrodt, arranged by Sisters of Christian Charity, Mendham, N.J., 1973.

Burton, Katharine. *Whom Love Impels,* New York, 1952.

Collected Works of Mother Pauline

Chronicles of the Congregation of Sisters of Christian Charity, Vol. II, 1873-1885.

Ernst, Brother, C.S.C. *A Happy Heart,* Notre Dame, Indiana, 1956.

Frenke, Sister Cyrenäa. *In Her Time,* Paderborn, 1974.

Letters of Bernardine von Mallinckrodt to Her Mother, trans. by Sister Gondeberta Remmert, Wilmette, Illinois, 1985.

Letter of Reverend Mother Pierre Koesters, Rome, Dec. 12, 1984.

Meyer, Wendelin, O.F.M. *Pauline von Mallinckrodt,* Münster, 1924.

Multhaupt, Hermann. *Shadow Play: Pauline von Mallinckrodt, Her Life Story in Twenty Short Scenes,* Höxter, 1981.

Mundelein, Archbishop George, Introd. *The Life of Mother Pauline von Mallinckrodt,* Chicago, 1917.

Rosende, Sister M. Ana, S.C.C. *The Spirituality of Pauline Von Mallinckrodt,* Santiago, 1965.

Schmittdiel, Sister Agnes, S.C.C. *Pauline von Mallinckrodt,* (trans. by Sister Mary Angela Blankenburg) Wiedenbrück, 1949.

Schmittdiel, Sister Philomena, S.C.C. *The Virtues of Pauline von Mallinckrodt,* Paderborn, 1881.

Schöpper, Sister Helene, S.C.C. *Pauline von Mallinckrodt, A Strong Woman,* Lippstadt, 1981.

Sisters of Christian Charity. *Enriching Many*, U.S.A., 1942.

Testimony of Witnesses (trans. from German by Sister Mary Gerard Neuhaus), Rome, 1979.